W9-BPS-271

The Dilemma of Accountability in Modern Government

AFFILIATED PUBLISHERS: Macmillan & Company, Limited, London. Also at Bombay, Calcutta, Madras and Melbourne. The Macmillan Company of Canada, Limited, Toronto.

This book was made possible by funds granted by Carnegie Corporation of New York. The statements made and views expressed are solely the responsibility of the contributors.

First published in the United States of America in 1971

Library of Congress Catalog Card Number: 75–144427

Printed in Great Britain

St Martin's Press, Inc., 175 Fifth Ave., New York, N.Y. 10010

Copyright © 1971 by Carnegie Corporation of New York

The Dilemma of Accountability in Modern Government

Independence versus Control

Edited by

Bruce L. R. Smith and D. C. Hague

St Martin's Press
New York

Contents

PART ONE

The Structure of the Problem

PART TWO

The Institutions: Industry, University and Others

Preface

This book is the record of an Anglo-American expedition into terrain that has hitherto for the most part been *terra incognita.* Considering the volume of research by political scientists on the way democratic societies are governed, it would hardly have seemed likely that any significant area of the subject could have remained largely unexplored, and yet that, surprisingly, appears to be the case.

Many years of foundation work have enabled me to become acquainted with the affairs of a considerable number of private, non-profit organisations in the United States and have led to a particular interest in the nature of their varied relationships with government. Introductory essays for two of Carnegie Corporation's annual reports provided an opportunity to sketch out the dimensions of what appeared to be a growing phenomenon in our country – devolution of responsibility by the federal government to private organisations on a contractual basis. It seemed that this process, for all its public benefits, had its limitations as a way of helping to maintain the financial viability of private institutions and that it was producing a new quasi-non-governmental sector about which little was known.

A British reader of one of these essays, David Howell – Member of Parliament, journalist and student of government – first called my attention to the wider significance of this special interest. He pointed out that I was really exploring a new manifestation of the old problem of how independence and accountability can be reconciled in the workings of democratic government. Was not the central question, he asked, really how government could respond to the extraordinary new social and technological challenges of the current age with the necessary speed, flexibility and effectiveness and yet remain fully accountable to the people.

In the United States, I replied, we had, during the post-war era, adopted the device of 'government by contract' on a substantial scale. In the process, we had forged a wide range of new relationships between such federal agencies as the Air Force, Department of Defence, Atomic Energy Commission, National Aeronautics and Space Administration, Department of Health, Education and Welfare, Agency for International Development, Office of Economic Opportunity and various elements of the private sector – industry, the universities, non-profit organisations and others. But what this varied experience added up to we did not know. We had not examined it systematically either in regard to its effects on the two partners or as a new phenomenon in the art of democratic government.

It was David Howell's contention that Britain, although not yet so deeply involved in 'government by contract' as the United States, soon might be and should, therefore, find some insight into the American experience useful. I felt that British interest in the topic would bring a new perspective to bear on it that could be of considerable value to our side. Out of the exchange, which took place in the summer of 1967, grew the establishment of parallel study groups in each country, consisting of academics, civil servants, politicians, industrialists and representatives of non-profit organisations. These groups met together at Ditchley Park in England in March of 1969. The chapters of this book consist principally of papers written for the Ditchley meeting and two substantial introductory pieces by, respectively, Professors Douglas Hague of Manchester University and Bruce Smith of Columbia University, who comment on the Ditchley discussion from the perspective of their national backgrounds.

Those of us from each country who have been most involved in organisation of the project have had somewhat mixed feelings about the question of publication at such an early stage. We are fully aware that this book is an incomplete treatment of a large subject – a tentative venturing into a new field. And yet, knowing that this first statement is to be followed at a later date by a second book based on further bi-national research and discussion, we believe the immense importance of the subject dictates that the results of the initial effort should reach a wider audience in each country now.

All who have participated in the two study groups would, I am sure, wish me to acknowledge here the leadership of our American and British chairmen, Professors Wallace Sayre and

Douglas Hague, the skilful editing which Professors Bruce Smith and Douglas Hague have done in readying the book for publication, and the invaluable assistance given by Mr John Corson and Mr Michael Spicer in planning and administration of the project. Bi-national undertakings often have their difficulties, especially when the subject of discourse is new and one which tends to be bedevilled by transatlantic differences of terminology. Nevertheless, in the course of the project both sides have become conscious of a shared and deeply held commitment to the search for more effective forms of response by democratic governments to the needs of changing societies; and along the path of our discussions we have learned much from each other and made some lasting friendships.

Alan Pifer
President, Carnegie Corporation
of New York

February 1970

List of Participants

Sir Robert Aitken	Deputy Chairman, University Grants Committee
Sir William Armstrong	Head of the Home Civil Service
Mr Bertram M. Beck	Executive Director, Mobilisation for Youth and Henry Street Settlement
The Hon. John Brademas	U.S. House of Representatives
Mr K. A. Bradshaw	Deputy Principal Clerk, House of Commons
Mr William D. Carey	Arthur D. Little, Inc.
Professor Francis S. Chase	University of Texas
Mr D. N. Chester	Warden, Nuffield College, Oxford
Dr Alcon Copisarow	Director and Vice-President, McKinsey & Co. Inc.
Dr John J. Corson	Consultant to the Carnegie Corporation
Sir James Dunnet	Permanent Secretary, Ministry of Defence
Sir Brian Flowers	Director, Science Research Council
Sir Bruce Fraser	Comptroller and Auditor General
Dr Delphis C. Goldberg	Professional Staff Member, Intergovernmental Relations Sub-Committee
The Rt Hon. Jo Grimond	Member of Parliament (Liberal)
Professor D. C. Hague	Manchester Business School
Mr Bertrand M. Harding	Frye Consultants (formerly Acting Director, Office of Economic Opportunity)
Mr David Howell	Member of Parliament (Conservative)
Mr John A. Johnson	Vice-President of the International Division, COMSAT
Professor Nevil Johnson	Nuffield College, Oxford
Professor W. J. M. Mackenzie	University of Glasgow
Mr John Mackintosh	Member of Parliament (Labour)
The Hon. George P. Miller	Chairman, Committee on Science and Astronautics, U.S. House of Representatives

Notes on Contributors

Bertram M. Beck is Executive Director of the Henry Street Settlement and Mobilisation for Youth, Inc., New York City. He has been a lecturer at Smith College and at Hunter College, and has served as Executive Director of the Academy of Certified Social Workers. He received an M.A. in Social Work from the University of Chicago.

Francis S. Chase is Professor Emeritus, the University of Chicago, and resident consultant for the Southwest Educational Development Laboratory and the Research and Development Center for Teacher Education, Austin, Texas. He has served as Dean of the Graduate School of Education, the University of Chicago; Chairman, National Advisory Committee on Educational Laboratories; and Chairman, President's Committee on Public Higher Education in the District of Columbia. His publications include *The High School in a New Era* (coeditor) (1957) and *The National Program of Educational Laboratories* (1968). He received the Ph.D. from the University of Chicago and the L.D. from New York University.

Martin Edmonds lectures in strategic studies in the Department of Politics at the University of Lancaster; he was formerly on the staff of the Government Department at the University of Manchester. His publications include articles in *International Affairs, Europa Archiv* and *A.T.M. Bulletin,* and contributions to *A Nation at War* (ed. R. Higham) and *The Military Technical Revolution* (ed. J. Erickson). His current research is in Defense Analysis and in Civil/Military Relations.

Richard T. Frost is Director of Urban Studies in the Policy Institute of Syracuse University's Research Corporation. He has taught Political Science at Princeton University, Reed College and Syracuse University. He was the national Director of the Office of Economic Opportunity's Upward Bound programme from its inception in the fall of 1965 through the summer of 1967. He received the Ph.D. in Political Science at Syracuse University.

Delphis C. Goldberg has been Professional Staff Member of the Intergovernmental Relations Sub-Committee of the U.S. House of Representatives' Standing Committee on Government Operations for the past thirteen years. He received the Ph.D. in Political Economy and Government from Harvard University.

D. C. Hague is Professor of Managerial Economics at the Manchester Business School. Previously he held the Newton Chambers Chair in Economics at the University of Sheffield and was Visiting Professor in Economics at Duke University, North Carolina. He has also been consultant to the National Economic Development Office. His books include *Managerial Economics* and *Economics of Man-Made Fibres,* and he was part-author of *A Textbook of Economic Theory.*

David Howell is Conservative Member of Parliament for Guildford. He has worked variously in the Treasury (as a non-established civil servant in the Economic Section), on the *Daily Telegraph* (as leader-writer and special correspondent) and in the Central Office of the Conservative Party (as Director of the Conservative Political Centre). He is a trustee of the Federal Trust for Education and Research and Joint Honorary Secretary of the British Council of the European Movement. In 1970 he was appointed Parliamentary Secretary for the Civil Service and a Lord Commissioner of the Treasury.

Nevil Johnson is Professorial Fellow of Nuffield College, Oxford, and Reader in the Comparative Study of Institutions. He was formerly Senior Lecturer in Politics at the University of Warwick. Between 1952 and 1962 he served in the Administrative Civil Service. His publications include *Parliament and Administration: The Estimates Committee 1945–65* (1966); 'Western Germany', in *Specialists and Generalists* (1968); 'Select Committees as Tools of Parliamentary Reform' in *'Parliament in Transition'* (forthcoming); he has also written articles on administrative and political questions in *Public Administration, Parliamentary Affairs* and *Political Studies*.

E. Leslie Normanton is a member of the International Board of Auditors for NATO; in this capacity he has worked with the public services of thirteen countries. He conducts seminars at the Civil Service Centre for Administrative Studies. He is a member of the Editorial Board, *Indian Administrative and Management Review* and author of *The Accountability and Audit of Governments*.

Don K. Price is Dean of the John F. Kennedy School of Government, Harvard University. He has served as Vice-President (for International Programmes) of the Ford Foundation, as Deputy Chairman of the Research and Development Board in the Department of Defense, and on the staff of the Bureau of the Budget and of the First Hoover Commission. He is the author of *Government and Science* (1954), *The Secretary of State* (editor) (1960) and *The Scientific Estate* (1965).

David Z. Robinson is Vice-President for Academic Affairs, New York University. He has served with Baird Associates, Inc., the U.S. Office of Naval Research, and the Office of Science and Technology in the Executive Office of the President. In 1960–1 he was National Lecturer of the Optical Society of America. He received the Ph.D. in Chemical Physics from Harvard University.

J. P. Ruina is Professor of Electrical Engineering, Massachusetts Institute of Technology, a trustee of the Mitre Corporation and a trustee of the General Research Corporation. He has served in the Department of Defence, as President of the Institute for Defence Analyses, and as Vice-President of M.I.T. for Special Laboratories. He received the D.E.E. degree in Electrical Engineering from the Polytechnic Institute of Brooklyn.

Bruce L. R. Smith is Associate Professor of Political Science at Columbia University. He has been a Research Associate in the Social Science Department of the Rand Corporation and has served as consultant to the Office of Science and Technology, the National Science Foundation, and the Center for Urban Education of New York City. He is the author of *The Rand Corporation: Case Study of a Non-Profit Advisory Corporation* (1966). He received the Ph.D. in Government from Harvard University.

Elmer B. Staats is the Comptroller General of the United States, appointed by President Lyndon B. Johnson in 1966 to head the General Accounting Office. He has served as a Brookings Institution Fellow, as both Assistant Director and Deputy Director of the Bureau of the Budget, and as Executive Director of the Operations Co-ordinating Board of the National Security Council. He received the Ph.D. in both Political Science and Economics from the University of Minnesota.

Murray L. Weidenbaum is Assistant Secretary of the Treasury for Economic Policy. He has previously served with the Convair Division of the General Dynamics Corporation, the Boeing Company, the Stanford Research Institute, and as Director of the Economic Research programme of NASA. He has been Chairman of the Department of Economics at Washington University, St Louis, Missouri. His most recent book is *The Modern Public Sector* (1969). He received the Ph.D degree from Princeton University.

Roger Williams lectures in the Department of Government at the University of Manchester. He has been an operational research scientist with the National Coal Board. He has written academic articles on nuclear energy and on British Government; he is currently working on a book on British civil nuclear power.

List of Abbreviations

A.E.A.	Atomic Energy Authority.
A.E.C.	Atomic Energy Commission.
A.G.R.	Advanced Gas-Cooled Reactor.
A.I.D.	Agency for International Development.
A.R.P.A.	Advanced Research Project Agency (Department of Defence).
A.S.P.R.	Armed Services Procurement Regulations.
B.B.C.	British Broadcasting Corporation.
B.O.A.C.	British Overseas Airways Corporation.
B.O.B.	Bureau of the Budget.
C. & A.G.	Comptroller and Auditor General.
C.B.R.	Centre for Business Research, University of Manchester.
C.E.G.B.	Central Electricity Generating Board.
COMSAT	Communications Satellite Corporation.
D/C Organisation	Design and Construction Organisation.
D.C.F.	Discounted Cash Flow technique, for investment decisions.
D.O.D.	Department of Defence.
D.O.T.	Department of Transportation.
E. & A.	Exchange and Audit Department.
F.B.R.	Fast Breeder Reactor.
G.A.O.	General Accounting Office.
H.E.W.	Department of Health, Education and Welfare.
H.T.G.C.R.	High Temperature Gas-Cooled Reactor.
H.U.D.	Department of Housing and Urban Development.

I.C.I.	Imperial Chemical Industries.
I.D.A.	Institute for Defense Analyses.
J.C.A.E.	Joint Committee on Atomic Energy (U.S. Congress).
N.A.S.A.	National Aeronautics and Space Agency.
N.C.B.	National Coal Board.
N.I.H.	National Institute of Health (Department of Health, Education and Welfare).
N.S.F.	National Science Foundation.
O. & M.	Organisation and Methods.
O.E.O.	Office of Economic Opportunity.
O.N.R.	Office of National Research.
O.S.R.D.	Office of Scientific Research and Development (existing during WW II).
P.A.C.	Public Accounts Committee.
P.C.A.	Parliamentary Commissioner for Administration (Ombudsman).
P.P.B.	Planning Programming Budgeting system.
S.G.H.W.R.	Steam Generating Heavy-Water Reactor.
T.V.A.	Tennessee Valley Authority.

PART ONE

The Structure of the Problem

1 Accountability and Independence in the Contract State

Bruce L. R. Smith

The increased complexity of modern government has brought new forms of 'administration by contract' and a wide participation of specialised skills in the processes of policy formation and implementation. Many functions of a traditionally public character, along with a variety of novel programmes, have been contracted out to private organisations. The use of the contract device has frequently rested on the belief that the requisite staff, flexibility of operation and work atmosphere can be more readily obtained via the administrative contract than by creating new independent agencies or by adding to the established executive departments. So extensive is the use of the administrative contract in the United States, and to a lesser extent in Great Britain, that we may perhaps with some verbal licence speak of the modern state as 'the contract state'. This paper is an effort to explore some of the major dimensions of the subject – what do we mean by 'contract'? What, precisely, can be said about the scope, magnitude and policy implications of the widespread delegation of administrative authority to semi-official and private institutions? The discussion should be viewed as a report on work in progress by an Anglo-American Committee, under the sponsorship of the Carnegie Corporation of New York, looking into the problems of accountability and independence in modern government.[1]

1. *'Accountability' and 'Independence': Some Boundaries*

It is not difficult to see how 'accountability' and 'independence' become issues of concern in this context. The private institution must be accountable in several senses; the govern-

3

ment must have the assurance that public funds are spent for the purposes specified and without personal gain to any private individual beyond fair compensation for his services. Appropriate fiscal records must be kept; a 'fair value' must be rendered the contracting government agency; some rules-of-thumb to measure performance are important. And in an overall sense the process of letting contracts must remain firmly in the hands of government officials. The centre of gravity in the making of public policy should, in theory, rest with the formal government and not with the contract apparatus. At the same time, it is widely recognised that some measure of genuine independence is vitally important to effective performance. The contractor cannot perform its task effectively and cannot contribute creatively to the end sought unless it has enough freedom and the right kinds of freedom. There is to some extent an inevitable tension between the values of independence and of accountability, and the contract becomes a device of accommodation. Through the contract, we hope to achieve a satisfactory equilibrium between the conflicting values.

The values of independence and of accountability, however, should not be seen as wholly in opposition. In one sense to satisfy the need for accountability serves to protect independence. For example, if a private institution operated outside of any effective control or direction by the responsible minister or department in a sensitive policy area and began itself to affect policy, the chances are great that political pressures would eventually force the imposition of regulations limiting the institution's autonomy. Similarly, a strong and independent institution with which the government can contract contributes importantly to the goal of accountability. The government can then be confident it will be able to pinpoint responsibility for work performed and establish clear lines of command. In a situation where the contractor is weak, and the lines of authority are blurred, there is greater difficulty in identifying, managing and holding accountable those officials carrying out a complex programme.

The problem can be broadly stated at the start as the need to create the understandings, and institutional arrangements, that will enable the government (in both its legislative and executive branches) to maintain a strong central policy direction over the apparatus of private institutions performing services for the government while giving the private institutions enough independence of operation to produce the maximum incentives for a distinctive and creative contribution to the government. In part the need may be simply to understand and to protect satisfactory working arrangements which have evolved over the past several decades. On the other hand, it may be necessary to develop some new concepts to guide future undertakings as well as to revise those arrangements which appear on close inspection not to have satisfactorily served the public interest in the delegation of authority outside the traditional framework of the government.

2. *The U.S. and the British Experiences*

The British and the American experiences with the delegation of authority by contract present some interesting points of similarity and contrast. In the United States there is considerable concern about the present scale of contract operations and a growing belief that the government lacks effective control over the numerous activities carried on under the contract device. Current fears about the existence of a 'military–industrial complex', for example, are in part attributable to a widespread conviction that military procurement practices give disproportionate influence to industrial contractors in defence policy-making.[2] A vast empire, it is feared, has been created via defence contracting which threatens to usurp the prerogatives of government. In another policy area, opposition to the Office of Economic Opportunity (O.E.O.) and to the war on poverty stems partly from the fear that authority has been contracted out to dubious individuals and groups without a clear specification of the intended purposes, and in consequence federal monies have been put to unforeseen uses which have inflamed the nation's domestic crises.

Many also believe that the contracting practices appropriate to one agency, by a kind of demonstration effect, have been adopted uncritically by other agencies, creating in some cases either an unfortunate emphasis on 'crash' projects, a technological bias in policy formation, or other undesirable consequences.[3] These various concerns have in common the

5

underlying awareness that there has been a 'diffusion of sovereignty'[4] which poses new difficulties in the administration of public affairs. It seems to follow logically, for many American observers, that we need a reassertion of the integrity of the formal institutions of government and a reaffirmation of the centrality of public purposes in the making of policy. Some redressing, in short, is called for in the balance between accountability and independence in the direction of greater accountability, and this is thought to be best achieved by strengthening the central government's position *vis-à-vis* the contractor.[5] Few, however, would wish to see a vast centralised bureaucracy created in the name of accountability.

In Great Britain, the traditional administrative concepts of orderliness, hierarchy and a disciplined chain of command are more strongly rooted both in theory and in practice. Public programmes are supposed to be carried out with a clear delegation of authority and affixing of responsibility at every level, starting with the collective responsibility of the Cabinet for policy[6] and extending to the line administrator's actions. The success or failure of programmes as a whole are to be judged by informed criticism after the fact and ultimately enforced through the electoral process, but the administrative process should not be disrupted by outside intervention before decisions are reached. However, it has become apparent that the traditional doctrine in its pure form is ill-suited to the complexities of modern government. The national needs for specialised skills and services in defence, research, health and other areas have led the British government, in practice, to enter into arrangements with private institutions similar in kind if not in name to the American contract device. There is already a *de facto* breach in the tightly controlled and coherent administrative structures prescribed by theory. It is equally clear that, given the size and complexity of administration today, no minister can be fully cognisant of the activities carried on under his direction.[7] Prior criticism of policy by knowledgeable outsiders, contrary to the traditional doctrine, also appears desirable in some circumstances if irreversible mistakes are to be avoided.

Indeed, many British observers by the end of the 1960s seemed to believe that rigid adherence to the classical notions of a unified civil service acting under strict ministerial responsibility was a chief impediment to effective public accountability. Because of the accompanying secrecy and lack of access to the bureaucracy the citizen had great difficulty in identifying responsibility and in knowing how to influence the actions of government. Making greater use of the contract device thus appeared to be one way to promote accountability by opening up the bureaucracy, widening the arena of policy debate and creating more flexible and responsive administrative units. The interest in the use of the contract intersects with the related concern that British administration is too centralised and to achieve greater efficiency and responsiveness should be substantially decentralised.[8] The impulse in Britain towards greater public accountability in a sense is the reverse of the American. Whereas extreme pluralism in the United States has led to an interest in strengthening the traditional government sector, the British have sought accountability through devices which disperse authority. To be sure there is no unanimity of outlook in Britain any more than in the United States, and a substantial body of opinion still endorses the traditional concepts of public administration. To some British observers the current demands for new services, the pressures for regionalism and the growth of government all underscore the importance of traditional forms of accountability to keep the governing system from breaking apart entirely under the new strains. The subject was, as might be expected, vigorously debated among the British participants at the Ditchley Conference. Sir William Armstrong eloquently expressed a position commanding wide assent when he reviewed the need both to strengthen traditional administration and to invent new ways to serve social needs outside the traditional framework of the civil service.

The differences between the British and the American experiences can perhaps be most easily understood by noting the position of the public sector in the two countries. The public sector, defined narrowly, is relatively larger in Britain with a sizeable fraction of industry nationalised, and with welfare and health programmes dating back at least to the Beveridge Report.[9] The public sector is relatively smaller in the United States than in Britain if one considers a narrow and traditional definition but is relatively larger if one considers the whole of what Alan Pifer has called the 'quasi-non-governmental' sector (i.e. the whole system of tapping private energies for public purposes).[10] Both nations, then, are attempting to achieve a better balance between public and private initiatives in meeting social needs. The British, with a tradition of relying on the public sector, show a willingness to experiment with new forms of mixed public–private organisation, the delegation of authority by contract and other devices to tap a broad range of private skills for public purposes. The defects of the traditional public sector are familiar, and change seems to offer substantial advantages. The Americans, for their part, have experienced the difficulties of managing the modern public sector, and wish to establish a centre of gravity in the system by strengthening the traditional public sector. The nations are at different stages in a developmental cycle. The British, in resorting to the contract as the solution to one type of accountability problem, will likely discover that it creates another accountability problem: *quis custodiet ipsos custodes*?[11] The Americans meanwhile will have begun to absorb the lesson by a partial return to the classical theory and practice of British administration.

Despite the differences between the British and the American experiences, there is a striking similarity in the objectives sought through the contract device and in the new demands on the governing system that have led to administrative experimentation. Both nations have sought a 'mixed' system of public and private initiatives, the avoidance of the evils of centralised bureaucracy, flexibility in the management of novel programmes, the capacity to innovate and to draw on a wide range of skills in society – and, at the same time, to retain a clear central direction in policy and accountability in the conduct of public programmes. In both nations the government has faced rising public expectations for new health, educational, welfare and other services, as well as pressures for making administrative structures more open, accessible and 'closer to the people'. Although it is not likely that the two nations will move towards a 'convergence'[12] in institutional practices, their common goals and their responses to similar kinds of problems provide a fascinating glimpse into the modern governmental process.

3. *The Roots of the Modern Contracting Process*

The contract is not something wholly new to administrative practice. The United States government has used the contract device since the early days of the republic for building roads, canals, dams, delivering the mail, exploring the territories, inspecting steamships and other purposes. An act of Congress of 1860 provided the fundamental law governing the use of contracts for procuring goods and non-personal services until World War II (before 1860 contracts were let as authorised by specific law or sometimes the authority to contract was simply inferred as necessary to achieve purposes established by law).[13] In Britain, where administrative action is less strictly dependent upon statutory sanction, the authority to enter into binding contracts is part of the broad discretionary authority inhering in general administrative powers.[14] The best means to accomplish a goal, as well as the standards of performance required in the civil service, are considered to be matters 'internal' to administration. The British departments have thus been left with wide discretion in the placing of contracts (but some advice on general principles is available from the interdepartmental Contracts Co-ordinating Committee).[15]

What, then, is new or significantly different about the use of contracts which arouses our interest today? The answer appears to lie in a combination of several factors: a greater magnitude in contracting and a shift from the procurement of routine goods and services to esoteric goods and services. In the nineteenth century, and in the twentieth century until World War II, contracts typically tended to be let for goods or services of a familiar character which could be the object of a detailed specification in advance. Open, competitive bidding usually prevailed, with the government awarding the contract to the lowest bidder complying with the advertised requirements for bidding. The government, like other buyers, tended to buy existing goods in existing markets. Moreover, the level of government expenditure on contracting remained small relative to the resources which agencies devoted to their own payrolls and direct operations.[16]

All this began to change dramatically during and after World War II. The magnitude of expenditures on contracts

9

with private institutions rose sharply. New agencies, and new programmes within established agencies, devoted the bulk of their resources to contract activity rather than to direct government operations. As Murray L. Weidenbaum notes, 'Until World War II and for a few years following the end of the war, wage and salary payments to Federal employees continued to be the largest category in the budget. Since then, the biggest item of expenditure has become disbursements under contracts with the private sector for goods and services that business firms and others provide to government agencies.'[17]

In addition, contracts were no longer predominantly let by competitive bidding as in an earlier and simpler day but were now to an increasing extent negotiated between the government agency and the contractor. The Armed Services Procurement Act of 1947 (and the Federal Property and Administrative Services Act of 1949 plus other legislation applying to civilian agencies) authorised exceptions to the traditional practice of open advertisement for bids for various classes of contract activity; and government agencies were quick to use the authority to make negotiated contracts more the rule than the exception.[18] The Defence Department, for example, negotiated 89 per cent of its procurement contracts for fiscal year 1968 as measured in dollar terms and let only 11 per cent by formally advertised competitive bidding.[19] This figure is a rough measure of the shift from the procurement of routine to esoteric goods and services, which changes significantly the nature of the contracting process. The government is no longer merely buying familiar items off the shelf but in many cases is buying something which cannot be precisely specified in advance. Furthermore, the extensive government contracting has changed the structure of parts of the economy, creating new sectors of industry dependent upon government contracts for survival and largely exempt from simple market tests of efficiency.

The greater magnitude in contracting and the shift to the procurement of esoteric goods and services reflect such other trends as: (1) the 'active society'[20] that assumes more and more responsibilities for the health, welfare and good life of its citizens; (2) the increased complexity of policy-making in the scientific age; (3) the need for a whole new range of professional skills to be involved in policy and administration; and (4) the drive for wider popular participation in public affairs and the vague but insistent feeling that ways should be found to make authority less centralised and distant.

As public responsibilities have broadened in the face of rising expectations, it is perhaps natural that government should experiment with a variety of devices, including the contract with private institutions, to increase its capacity to meet the demands for new services, especially where the private sector has strength as a performer or a monopoly of the expertise. One prominent example is in the area of scientific research and complex technical services. The impact of science and technology has greatly stimulated the expansion of government programmes administered on contract both in the United States and in Britain. Because scientists and engineers were not available in sufficient numbers within the government, the emergency period of World War II saw the dramatic use of the administrative contract with academic and industrial laboratories. The pattern persisted into the post-war period; a great many defence and defence-related activities have been performed by industry, universities or special research centres under contract with the government. Government support for the regular activities of the universities on a scale not envisaged before also emerged in the post-war period (in the United States mainly through a system of research contracts and grants for individual projects and in Britain through the University Grants Committee making large institutional grants to universities).[21]

The use of outside performers for research and technical activities has spilled over into other areas of public policy as well. In the United States, for example, the Office of Education supports under contract a score of regional educational laboratories engaged in research and development on curriculum reform and management innovations in local school systems; the Agency for International Development (A.I.D.) contracts with American Universities to provide technical assistance overseas under the foreign aid programme; and the Department of Housing and Urban Development (H.U.D.) seeks through contract arrangements to stimulate technological innovations aimed at the problems of the cities. Beyond the area of research and development – a rather loose term

11

covering a wide variety of activities – there are numerous other uses of the contract of a complex and novel sort. Management, planning and advice, test and evaluation, the supervision of other contractors and the function of fiscal intermediary are only some of those uses helping to bring a new order of complexity into the administration of public affairs. New cadres of skills, generalist as well as specialist, penetrate into the decision process and become accepted participants along with traditional elites such as lawyers and politicians.

Curiously, although the effect of the contracting practices since World War II has been to disperse rather than to centralise power, substantial segments of elite and mass opinion have viewed technology as a driving force behind relentless centralising pressures in 'post-industrial' society. Power is widely seen to be gravitating into the hands of a few technocrats, or in a variation of the theme some implacable logic inherent in the technological process itself dominates the critical decisions and removes government farther and farther from popular control and participation.[22]

In the United States, partly in response to this feeling of estrangement from the powerful institutions of society and partly in response to deep historic tensions concerning the racial issue, a newer form of contracting has evolved which stresses the values of popular participation. It has not been clear whether participation was to be valued for its own sake or for its instrumental value in achieving programme goals, but in the administration of such programmes as Urban Renewal, Model Cities, the Community Action programmes of the Office of Economic Opportunity (O.E.O.), the Elementary and Secondary Education Act, and Mobilisation for Youth, the thrust towards participation-for-its-own-sake clearly became of considerable importance.[23] The government has attempted, in effect, to contract out political power to neighbourhood groups by providing funds and personnel to organise communities at a grass-roots level and by giving the local groups so mobilised a share in framing government programmes. Author Norman Mailer carried the participatory impulse to the ultimate in his campaign for the Democratic mayoralty nomination in New York City with the slogan, All power to the neighbourhoods!'[24] Britain has not yet experienced this newer form of contracting-for-participation

12

born of the strains of the post-industrial society and the nexus of race and poverty. Yet the stirrings of the British nationalities and of youth and the general disenchantment with centralised authority bear certain resemblances to the precipitating American conditions. The participatory contracts are especially interesting because they illustrate in extreme form the tendencies implicit in the 'diffusion of sovereignty': the dispersion of power, the blurring of the lines of authority, the breakdown of the public–private distinction.

A complex set of forces, in brief, has combined to produce something quite different from the older pattern of contracting. Instead of government buying routine goods and services in well-established markets, the net effect of the great post-war expansion in contracting is to produce a vastly more intricate pattern of interactions between public and private institutions, and the penetration of nominally private individuals into the centre of the decision process. Contracting is no longer limited to the logistic periphery of government action but has moved into the main arena of policy-making. Innovative programmes in social welfare, the development of strategic weapons systems, the delivery of health services and other central missions of government are entrusted to private contractors, and there is a natural presumption that the latter in subtle ways share in the making of broad policy. In turn the influence of the government penetrates on an unprecedented scale into the internal life of private organisations. The nature of the contracting process undergoes a transformation: the government lacks clear standards to evaluate performance. The end product sought by the contract cannot be spelled out in detailed specifications and administered by an official who specialises in the mechanics of contract administration. The line which separates legitimate oversight from excessive and self-defeating intrusion into the contractor's internal management is not easy to draw. The problem of enforcing accountability, while not destroying the contractor's independence, is posed in new and subtle ways.

The contributors to this volume are mainly concerned with the problems of the 'new contracting' and other novel delegations of authority to institutions outside the direct framework of the government. The focus is on the issues accompanying the great expansion of the mixed public–private sector since World War II, and especially on the broadening of the contract into an administrative instrument for mobilising private energies on a large scale for public purposes. This is not to say that the 'older' contracting practices, or developments within the traditional public service, are of little interest or significance. The current practices of some government agencies are understandable only when seen as a carry-over from traditional contract administration practices. Common problems exist in the routine and in the more complex contracts, and under certain circumstances what was regarded as routine and 'settled' can become transformed quickly into a controversial political issue. The problem of placing reasonable yet not crippling restraints on discretionary judgement exercised by officials within the bureaucracy remains a central concern of administrative theory and practice, and is directly related to the main themes discussed throughout this book. The boundaries between the familiar and the novel, therefore, should not be too sharply drawn. Nevertheless the great increase in activity has come in the modern public sector: here we find the most difficult, controversial and least understood problems; and also many of the innovative programmes that test society's capacity to keep pace with the rising demands on its governing institutions.

4. *Characteristics and Magnitude of the Contracting Effort in the United States*

What is a contract?

A contract may be defined as an agreement between a government department and a non-governmental institution to purchase a good, perform a service or carry out an assignment, either in general terms or in specific terms, for which the government meets all or part of the money costs.[25] The contract can vary greatly in formality from a simple letter of understanding to a voluminous legal document. It is no less binding for being brief or informal. The contract which provided the legal basis for the MIRV (multiple independently targetable re-entry vehicle) programme, for example, was an exchange of letters between a U.S. Air Force officer and a re-

14

presentative of the defence contracting firm.[26] For almost a year this programme, eventually to cost in excess of $1 billion and to have significant implications for the nation's strategic posture, proceeded with the letter of understanding as legal authorisation for the work being performed by the contractor. Later, in the midst of the Senate debate over the A.B.M. during July 1969, the Air Force formalised the arrangement by completing negotiations on the final contract accord. Senate critics deplored the MIRV contract as a dangerous step-up in the arms race at an inopportune time, but the Air Force defended itself as merely carrying out the details of an agreement entered into the previous year.[27] In some instances with basic research contracts, it is also not unknown for the formal contract to be negotiated after the research has been under way for some time and the results of the project have been fairly well established. With many simple procurement actions, involving small dollar amounts, the contract procedures can be quite informal. But the more typical case is none of these; usually there will be a formal legal document drawn up by contract administrators at or around the time the work begins. The agreement will contain a statement of the work to be performed, provisions on allowable and non-allowable costs, overheads, the use of government facilities and numerous other standard items as well as non-standard items. The elaborateness of the document will depend on the amounts of money involved, the nature of the work, the particular contracting practices of that agency, the amount of interest by high-level officials and other factors.[28]

The terms of the contract have some significance for the problem of accountability, as will be discussed below. But the contract itself is not of decisive importance; the formal contract is merely a step in a process of interaction between agency and contractor.[29] The understandings and interactions that surround the act of signing the contract, and shape the working relationships, are more critical in determining the quality of performance. In all contracts involving complexity and uncertainty (which is true of all the 'new' contracting), trying to prescribe in exact detail every phase of contract operations can become a meaningless ritual.

There are a number of variations to the contract which deserve notice. A 'grant' to a private institution is simply a special kind of contract and is included within the scope of our concern.[30] Frequently time is spent in efforts to spin out fine points of difference between a grant and a contract, but for practical purposes the two can be regarded as the same. Grants can be more restrictive than contracts, or vice versa, depending upon the terms of the agreement; and in each case a product or service is to be delivered to the government whatever slight differences may exist in the manner of reporting.

The 'grant-in-aid' – an agreement involving a financial transfer between different levels of government within the federal system – is, however, generally excluded from consideration here. Both traditional federalism and 'federalism-by-contract'[31] reinforce the role of the federal government as a 'policy formulator' rather than a 'doer', and both illustrate the dilemmas of delegating authority to bodies which develop interests of their own to protect. The two subjects, however, cannot easily be treated within the framework of this essay. Yet it must at least be noted that the pattern of federalism-by-contract does have a bearing on the more traditional devolution of powers to geographically based regional and local governmental units. Sometimes the placing of a contract with a private institution is an alternative to relying on a local unit of government for the same purpose (as, for example, in the Job Corps training programmes administered by industrial firms instead of local government). Or a contract with a private institution can supplement or complement the capacities of local government. Or, as in the Community Action programmes, local government may fear that the federal government is attempting to undermine the traditional pattern of federalism by creating new power relationships with a private constituency. The intersection of federalism-by-contract with traditional federalism presents some extraordinarily complex issues, especially with contracting in those policy areas where state and local governments have traditionally felt themselves to be the principal actors.[32] Defence and space contracting has generally not been marked by the same kinds of sharp conflict with local governing authorities (although even in these areas pressures have mounted to force the federal government to distribute defence and space spending for research and development more equitably across the country).

'Project' and 'institutional' (or 'bloc') grants are sub-categories which refer, in the context of federal research support at institutions of higher learning, to agreements for specific as against broad purposes. Project grants typically (though not always) are of small dollar amounts and support the research of a principal investigator, who controls the funds, while institutional grants are larger in amounts and are controlled by university administrators. (The university in either case nominally receives the funds, but the practical issue is who has *de facto* control.) 'Subcontract' refers to the practice of industrial firms contracting out part of their assignment to other firms. In addition, there are numerous variants used in contracting with industry for research and development – cost-plus-fixed-fee, cost-plus-incentive-fee, fixed-price and the like. In general there has been a trend in recent years towards incentive-type contracts and away from cost-plus contracts.

Subsidies are generally not considered contracts for the purposes of this discussion despite a superficial resemblance. (They involve money payments to private parties for the performance or, in some cases, such as payment to farmers for withdrawing land from production, the non-performance of a task.) In certain circumstances, such as with government subsidies in the private welfare field as Bertram Beck discusses later in the book, a government subsidy can become, in effect, a grant or contract if it carries with it the expectation that certain services will be rendered; the contract then is merely a tacit or informal one.   Excluded as well are tax credits, transfer payments and intragovernmental contracts between different federal agencies (e.g., contracts with the General Services Administration for maintenance services).

Why used?

The reasons, some briefly mentioned above, for resorting to the contract cover a wide spectrum. The common justifications include: promoting innovation in policy and administration;[33] flexibility in the use of talent and human resources;[34] responsiveness to novel and immediate needs where the government finds it simpler and faster to contract than to develop its own competence;[35] getting a service more cheaply than by direct government operation;[36] strengthen-

17

ing the private sector, or private sector organisations, deemed to be important to the public interest;[37] and enhancing certain democratic norms (wide participation in policy formation and avoidance of centralised bureaucracy). There are also collateral objectives sought once the contract device is used, such as protecting small business interests in the placing of subcontracts, guaranteeing equal employment opportunities[38] and furthering state urban development policies.[39]

To what extent have the values sought actually been achieved? This was a matter of lively dispute among the participants at the Ditchley Conference. No clear consensus emerged, but a safe comment seems to be that the record is generally mixed. There have been occasions when the contract device has been an outstanding success, and has enabled modern governments to perform tasks that would otherwise have been beyond the capacity of government. The U.S. manned space effort, the state of military preparedness, the great advances in medical research and the extension of many modern social services all owe much to the contract device. Moreover, certain classes of activity – for example, artistic and cultural programmes – seem exceptionally well suited to contract performance and almost require that the government seek private institutions or individuals. In Britain, the experience with cultural activities has been remarkably similar: such activities as the B.B.C., the British Council and the Arts Council have rarely been placed in ministries.

At other times the use of the contract seems to have had a much more problematic outcome, either creating unforeseen problems, failing to achieve the stated purpose, or merely disguising the failure to deal directly with a refractory issue. Of particular interest is the concern that extensive contracting merely creates the illusion of a Jeffersonian form of limited government and in fact leaves untouched the major problems of big government. Thus in the United States, for example, the federal government still operates with the same civilian work force that it did in 1946 – about two million employees. Since that time there has been a threefold increase in the federal budget; and the states and their subdivisions, which have not resorted to the large-scale use of the contract device, report an increase in total employment from just under four million to over eight million.[40] The increase in federal ex-

18

penditures without a corresponding growth of the federal bureaucracy is largely a function of the extensive post-war federal contracting with private institutions (and grants-in-aid to states and localities). If the aim was to achieve a higher level of government activity without creating a centralised bureaucracy, that aim has been amply fulfilled. It is less evident that other goals, such as flexibility in the use of resources or promoting innovation, have always been achieved. The government finds it equally difficult to close down a contract facility as a direct government installation and in some ways even more difficult because of the greater number of interests involved that can bring political pressure to bear.

Sometimes the control exercised over a contractor exceeds that of a government bureau over its constituent sub-units. One interesting exchange between British and American conferees at Ditchley ended in general agreement that the U.S. government has achieved a greater degree of *de facto* management control over the aerospace industry through the contract device than the British government has achieved by nationalising certain industries. Indeed, a major danger noted with the contract system is the possibility that the same kind of bureaucratic arthritis that afflicts the government will creep out through the administrative contract to the private sector.[41]

Magnitude of use?

The magnitude of use of the contract device in the United States is difficult to define precisely because there is no consistent set of figures free from ambiguities, overlapping categories and definitional confusion. Commentators have usually been forced to make broad general estimates based on data compiled by several different government agencies for somewhat different purposes. The Comptroller General of the United States, Elmer B. Staats, has observed that 'the departments and agencies of the Government are awarding contracts at the current rate of about $50 billion a year to procure property and services for use in their programmes and activities'.[42] Weidenbaum cites the figure of $60 billion for 'Federal Government purchases of goods and services from the private sector each year . . .'.[43]

By returning to the sources used in making the estimates and by sorting out the major idiosyncracies in data compilation, it is possible to gain a somewhat more accurate picture of the magnitude of federal contract activity. The total for fiscal year 1968, as shown in Fig. 1, amounts to $52·9 billion (or approximately 32 per cent of the total federal budget of

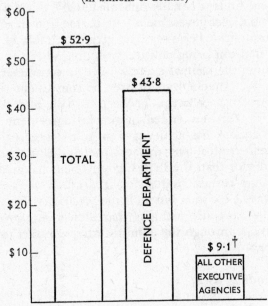

Fig. 1 Federal contracts,* by agency, F.Y. 1968
(in billions of dollars)

* Excludes grants and grants-in-aid.
† The largest civilian agency contractors are as follows:

NASA, $3·4; A.E.C., $2·6; G.S.A., $1·1; Transportation, $0·5; Interior, $0·4; T.V.A., $0·4.

Sources: G.S.A., 'Procurement by civilian Agencies: F.Y. 1968'.
D.O.D., 'Military Prime Contract Awards and Subcontract Payments or Commitments: July 1968–March 1969'.

$172·4 for the fiscal year). The Defence Department is the largest single contracting agency. The contract activity of the non-defence agencies, while still only about one-fifth the dollar level of defence contracting, has nevertheless grown much more rapidly in recent years.

The total for federal contract activity shown in Fig. 1 errs, however, in the direction of underestimation. The G.S.A.

figures for the civilian agencies exclude contracts with educational and other not-for-profit institutions, and both G.S.A. and D.O.D. compilations exclude grants to private institutions. There is no reliable way with present sources to correct for these omissions, but it is probable that the total would increase by at least several billion dollars.

Although grants and grants-in-aid to state and local government are generally beyond the scope of this inquiry, a brief reference to traditional federalism is in order. For one gains a clearer indication of the degree to which the federal government has assumed the role of policy formulator, and has delegated the actual tasks of programme operation, by adding the $18·6 billion spent in fiscal year 1968 on the some 420 separate grants-in-aid programmes to the total of federal contract activity with the private sector. The total then becomes $71·5 billion, or approximately 41 per cent of the federal budget for the fiscal year. When one considers that a large remaining portion of the federal budget goes to fixed transfer payments and interest on the national debt, the sum devoted to programmes involving the delegation of authority either to state and local governments or to the private sector is seen to constitute a very substantial share of the discretionary monies available to policy-makers.[44] The business of giving away money for private institutions and other levels of government to spend under federal guidelines is clearly a major task of the contract state.

The trends are even more clearly seen when one disaggregates the figures and looks in detail at individual agencies. Old-line agencies typically devote the great bulk of their resources to their own payroll and direct operations. For example, the Treasury Department devotes nine-tenths of its budget to wages and salaries aside from interest payments on the national debt; the Post Office spends over three-fourths of its budget on direct employment costs; and the Justice Department budget goes mainly to salary payments for its lawyers, investigators, border patrol agents, prison guards and other employees.[45] In contrast, the newer agencies typify the trend for the federal government to become a policy initiator and goal setter with much of the actual work of government delegated to the private sector or to other levels of government. The payroll of the Department of Health, Education and Welfare represents only 6 per cent of its total budget. The National Aeronautics and Space Administration, established in 1958, spends nine-tenths of its budget on contracts with private institutions, mainly industrial firms, universities and research institutes. NASA employees primarily oversee and review the contractor efforts. The Office of Economic Opportunity, established in 1964, operates primarily through programmes actually conducted by organisations outside the federal government – state and local governments, private industry and special not-for-profit organisations. The Department of Housing and Urban Development, created in 1965, has a relatively small work force which accounts for only about one-tenth of its disbursements. The Department of Transportation, established in 1966, primarily is engaged in the task of making grants-in-aid to the states under federal highway, airport and other programmes. Similarly, the Department of Defence shows a tendency to contract out major portions of its newer activities and programmes as compared to the traditional activities which are still done largely 'in-house' (e.g., in the Navy's own shipyards or in the Army's arsenals).

I have no comparable data for Britain, but to some extent at least similar trends seem in evidence.[46] The portion of expenditures escaping direct Treasury control appears to be increasing, and this is apparently accounted for by rising local government expenditures, the growth of the nationalised sector of the economy and the activities of semi-autonomous boards in health, education, research and other areas. The British participants at Ditchley saw many similarities between the semi-autonomous boards and authorities in Britain and the American contractor institutions. Despite the differences in terminology and formal institutional structure between the two countries, which at times threatened to throw the conference into impenetrable confusion, the functional similarities in the practice of delegating authority to outside bodies began to emerge with greater clarity as the discussion proceeded. Each country sought to achieve certain values of independence by avoiding the normal departmental or ministerial structure. Although the practice had not gone as far in Britain, the British conferees agreed that there was extensive reliance on the devices of delegating authority to outside bodies. This was another case of art imitating life since the actual practice far outstripped the recognition of it in the textbooks on public administration. Professor William Mackenzie noted in his summary remarks at the conference's final session that a careful exploration of the phenomenon of delegated power might substantially revise accepted notions of British administration as centralised and unitary.

In the light of such trends, it is somewhat surprising that commentators, in diagnosing the ills of modern government, continue to deplore the evils of bureaucracy in conventional terms. Peter F. Drucker, declaring that government has grown too big, flabby and overextended, states as 'the main lesson of the last fifty years: government is not a "doer". The purpose of government is to make fundamental decisions ... to govern. This, as we have learned in other institutions, is incompatible with "doing". Any attempt to combine governing with "doing" on a large scale, paralyses the decision-making capacity.'[47] His solution is a policy of 'reprivatisation' – which is 'a systematic policy of using the other, the non-governmental institutions of the society ... for the actual "doing", i.e., for performance, operations, execution'.[48] Congressman John N. Erlenborn states that 'our problem is one of excessive programming and over-management from the standpoint of excessively centralised direction, regulation, and organisational structure.... I believe that we should institute measures to reduce the dominant nature of the Federal Government by creating greater pluralism in other sectors of society.'[49]

In Britain similar arguments have been advanced in the context of the debate on regionalism and the devolution of power. Mr John Mackintosh, M.P., raised the issue for discussion at the Ditchley Conference, proposing for Britain the possible creation of eight or nine large regions with democratic parliaments to take over operational responsibilities from the central government. He also broached the idea of breaking down a large centrally administered programme, say education, into, in the case of England, ten, and in the case of the United States, fifty accountable administrative units, each with an elected board of citizens watching over expenditures. The theory behind the idea being that, since accountability was a mere fiction under the classical administrative theory of the Cabinet being responsible to Parliament for everything happening in the government, the course of wisdom was to create smaller units which could be clearly identified as being responsible for particular policies. The more units that could be thus held accountable, the more accountability there would be. This idea was broadened by Professor Nevil Johnson at the Ditchley Conference into a plea for creating more centres of responsibility in society. So long as the problem was formulated only in terms of the delegating or contracting out of powers from 'the centre', there was a built-in bias against the creation of genuinely independent centres of responsibility and initiative in the society. The problem was, rather, to create a society, perhaps patterned after the smaller Eurpean democracies, whose constitutional arrangements would foster a genuine pluralism.

Whatever one may think of the remedy, the diagnosis, at least for the United States, is faulty. The conditions that Drucker and others describe as the ideal already exist in fact. The federal government, to an astonishing degree, acts in the role of a policy formulator or overseer rather than a doer. If the nation is now in a 'crisis of authority', the fault must be found elsewhere than in the supposition that the federal government has not sufficiently delegated powers to the private sector and to other levels of government.

One suspects that the diagnosis applies only imperfectly in the British case as well. To consider an example: what can be called policy for the development of higher education in Britain is not 'made' at one centre but is the resultant of the actions of the University Grants Committee, various research councils, foundations, industry, the patterns of research support of various ministries, Treasury sensibilities, decisions made within the universities themselves and occasionally the preferences of ministers. More than half of the members of the University Grants Committee are professors from the universities – a case of the affected private interests in an area having a formal role in policy decisions.[50] Although the British governing system is more centralised than that of the United States, the pluralist elements are numerous and the central government is hardly in the position of monopolising all policy initiatives.

Indeed, it is tempting to infer that the arguments of the

24

decentralisers miss the mark badly and that the remedy is not to pluralise power still further but to curb the excesses of pluralism.[51] But such a formulation merely inverts the traditional clichés about the evils of bureaucracy. It is as unhelpful for our purposes to extol the traditional virtues of bureaucracy as to echo the familiar complaints about bureaucratic organisation. We need to break out of the categories of thought that make sharp distinctions between the private sector and the public bureaucracy, and that ascribe unambiguous virtues or vices to either. The reality of the contract state is that there has been an extensive and probably irreversible intermingling of the public and private sectors, and a sharing of functions between individuals who are public officials and those who are nominally private. In both Britain and the United States the broad contours of such a system are clearly discernible, and debates about the principle of the thing in the familiar modes of thought seem beside the point.

At the grand strategic level of policy choice Britain could doubtless still decide on a comprehensive reversal of the practice, perhaps moving in one direction under the Conservatives and in another under Labour, and the same or something similar could happen in the United States. But such an eventuality seems remote; the system in broad outline is likely to remain. The relevant questions then become of the kind: how much and what kinds of private initiative are enough, and under what guidelines from which levels of the formal government hierarchy? What is the appropriate balance to be struck among the values offered by different ways of doing things, granted that in most cases some mixture of public and private energies will be involved? The limited and traditional 'public–private' vocabulary in which we discuss the issues betrays the need to devise a more subtle and discriminating analytical perspective.

Implicit in the calls for 'reprivatisation' is the notion that, by relieving the central government of some burdens, accountability for certain other things at the central level can be made more meaningful. Whether this will prove true depends on the character of the working arrangements between the government and the private sector. It cannot be assumed that the administrative process is composed of separate and distinct functions, such as 'planning', 'broad policy', 'budgeting', 'operations', which can be neatly compartmentalised and assigned to different institutional settings. The details of the administrative process and the higher reaches of policy are a seamless unity. No government agency will delegate all details of programme implementation to outside bodies for the simple reason that effective policy control of the activity would be lost. There will normally be some involvement of the delegating agency in the details of programme execution. The question is how much and what kinds of involvement will assure overall policy control without unnecessarily burdening programme performance or eroding the independence of the performing organisation. Similarly, it seems antiquarian to dispute that outsiders will share in the making of high policy. By engaging in the continuous dialogue of weighing means against ends and ends against means with government officials, the outsiders inevitably take a major part in the appreciative process which shapes the strategic objectives of government. The pertinent question is what the ground rules are under which the outsiders will play the role. To decide whether some delegation of authority can promote greater accountability in government, we need to know more about which arrangements between the public and private sectors have in some sense 'worked', and which have not, and what, indeed, we comprehend under the elusive concept of 'accountability'.

5. Aspects of the Accountability Problem

There are many devices by which a democratic government is held to account for its actions. External and internal audit, scrutiny by mass media, legislative oversight, party responsibility, the electoral process are a few of the common elements of a system of accountability. In the broadest sense accountability is the central objective of democratic government: how can control be exercised over those to whom power is delegated? Democratic theory provides a traditional answer which runs roughly as follows: power emanates from the people and is to be exercised in trust for the people. Within the government each level of executive authority is accountable to the next, running on up to the President or the Cabinet. The executive authority as a whole is accountable to the Congress or Parliament, which is assisted in its surveillance of expenditures by an independent audit agency. Officials are required to submit themselves to periodic elections as a retrospective evaluation of their performances and to receive a new mandate from the people.

The theory appeared to be strained, or at least to require adaptation, as the modern state grew in size and complexity. The emergence of large cadres of civil servants and the dramatic increases in the range of governmental responsibility complicated the traditional formula. With the growth of the contract state in the mid-twentieth century, the constitutional issues reached a new order of complexity and went beyond what could be easily comprehended within the established frame of thought. Citizens in both Britain and the United States, representing important sectors of public opinion, began to doubt that their governing institutions were truly accountable. The feeling of loss of accountability doubtless has played a part in the emergence of what has perhaps been overdramatised as a 'crisis of authority' in the West. There can be little doubt, however, that government today is under severe pressure to provide more and better services, wider participation in its internal workings and increased responsiveness to citizens' demands.

Some of the reasons for the decline of confidence in traditional accountability seem easy enough to understand (even if at times the intensity of the attacks on authority startles the observer of British and American affairs). Government has grown too big and complex for the minister or department head, and still less the chief executive, to know in detail all that happens within the agency or the government on a given programme. Under the circumstances the doctrine of accountability may be seen as a polite fiction. Accountability gets lost in the shuffle somewhere in the middle ranges of the bureaucracy. The citizen's doubt that responsible officials are firmly in charge becomes compounded when extensive contract operations are added to the equation.

The diffusion of sovereignty has occurred to such an extent that many private institutions, such as universities, come under attack for their alleged complicity in policy decisions taken by the government. There is a vague but widely shared assumption that, since private institutions and public purposes are now so intermingled, the major social institutions, or at least those involved in some way in acting as the means to carry out government ends, should be accountable along with public officials. This might be called the doctrine of 'universal accountability'. The chief difficulty with the idea is its lack of discrimination. When everybody is held accountable for everything, no one is effectively accountable for anything. The problem lies in adjusting administrative theory and practice to give practical meaning to the concept of accountability under vastly complex conditions – and this can no more be achieved by the easy assumption that the lines of accountability run in all directions at once than by the idea of the agency head effectively rendering account for matters he does not understand or control. The doctrine of universal-accountability fails because, like the 'chief on top and the expert on tap' notion, it does not pinpoint responsibility clearly enough.

Another pseudo-solution is the doctrine of selective accountability, or the notion that only 'big' matters and the areas where abuses are likely to occur require strict accountability. The trouble with this is that big matters are usually only an accretion of small matters, and that there can be no general agreement on which policy areas are particularly prone to abuse. Accountability for some and not for others would only exacerbate social tensions and make more difficult the restoration of general trust in the fairness of government procedures. The idea of selective accountability is a variant of the old bureaucratic premise – 'watch the other fellow closely but grant me special rules and favoured access to the public treasury'. The need for operative ideas on how to make accountability a reality under modern conditions is urgent, but it must be admitted that there is a remarkable dearth of such ideas despite great dissatisfaction with the present state of affairs and with the older Gladstonian notions of accountability.

The Ditchley Conference sought as a major objective to address this issue. The participants discussed a wide range of administrative relationships and attempted to identify an approach which could prevent abuses of authority without

28

cutting the government off from the use of outside skills or destroying the independence of the private sector. The underlying issues were clarified significantly even though the conference reached no definitive conclusions. One promising formulation was advanced by David Robinson, who viewed the problem as essentially that of achieving the proper balance among three different kinds of accountability, which he termed *fiscal, programme* and *process*.[52]

Fiscal accountability refers to the regularity, in the auditor's sense, of public expenditures. Funds should be spent according to appropriate procedures, in the manner designated by law and by the terms of the contract or agreement, and proper accounting standards should be observed. But this is a minimum standard since the requirement for regularity can be met and the government may still not get 'fair value' for its expenditure.

Programme accountability is addressed to the question of whether the government is actually getting the results it sought through the programme apart from the conformity to standards of propriety in the disbursement of funds. (By this standard, for example, the Upward Bound programme discussed by Frost in this volume would be considered accountable since the programme was successful in minimising college drop-out rates among disadvantaged youth.) Since programme quality cannot be judged easily in many cases, however, a surrogate for programme accountability may be resorted to, which can be termed accountability by process. This refers to the general procedures and method of operation by which a delegated assignment is carried out. In the case of basic research support at universities, for example, the government may require that the investigator devote a certain percentage of time to the project. The assumption here is that if the quality of the effort is difficult to judge directly the substitution of indirect standards will serve as a satisfactory approximation.

A start towards understanding the larger problem, then, could be found in knowing what mixture of these three types of accountability is appropriate for various classes of activity delegated by the government to outside institutions. Finding the right kind of accountability, in turn, was the best guarantee of independence. Robinson was particularly concerned, as were others in both the British and American delegations, that an overemphasis on the rituals and forms of accountability would detract from what is essential – enabling the government to get high standards of performance for its investment.

A related theme was discussed by D. N. Chester and Sir William Armstrong on the British side and by William Carey on the American. They appeared to agree that with innovative programmes, and in general where a high order of creativity and willingness to take risks were called for, a sort of self-denying ordinance was in order about how far the government should go with fiscal and process accountability. To achieve important objectives it would often seem necessary to settle for a broad definition of the purposes sought in a delegation of authority. This view was disputed by other participants, including those most intimately associated with the audit process in government. The United States Comptroller General, Elmer B. Staats, saw great difficulty in disentangling the different threads of accountability. He observed that the General Accounting Office was attempting to move towards the broader conceptions of efficiency audit and cost-effectiveness studies of government programmes, but he continued to discover that failure to achieve broad programme goals and fiscal irregularities were usually closely linked. In any case, the political process seldom afforded the opportunity for a programme to prove itself in broad terms if it failed in narrow regularity terms. The example of some anti-poverty programmes in the United States suggested that misuse of funds could raise such a storm as to endanger the broad purposes and, indeed, the very survival of the programme.

The conferees recognised that accountability operates on many levels within a particularly intricate and criss-crossing pattern of institutional relationships. The various dimensions of the problem include the need for accountability in the supervisory relationships between higher and lower levels of administrative authority within the executive; in the relationships between different branches of government (in the American scene between constitutionally separate executive and legislative branches); in the relationships between central and local levels of government (and also between the central office and field offices within an agency); in the relationships between the government and the private or semi-public institution or body to which authority has been contracted or otherwise delegated; and in the relationships between different levels within the outside institution (and the criss-crossing relations with different levels in the formal government). There is also the need to distinguish accountability in the sense of conformity to standards of professionalism (and to peer judgement) in the case of specialised skill groups with strong extrainstitutional loyalties, and to identify the circumstances in which this form of accountability may be the most appropriate.

It was recognised that a full exploration of the subject would also have to examine in detail the special conditions relating to industrial firms, to universities, to not-for-profit corporations and to nationalised industry, quasi-public boards and authorities, community agencies and the wide variety of other instrumentalities exercising delegated authority or performing services under government support. The conference could not undertake a systematic review of this entire range of issues, nor can I attempt to do so here. Yet in the discussion and in the papers prepared for the conference a number of common and recurring themes can be identified which seem to have broad relevance in both the British and the American context. These themes suggest that, despite the great differences in function, tradition and institutional setting, there are some critical underlying aspects of the accountability problem which deserve attention.

The critical elements include the following: (1) the degree to which the contract instrument or the initial agreement clearly specifies the task to be performed; (2) the managerial competence and quality in the government agency that either contracts out the assignment or regularly interacts with the outside body or institution; (3) the quality of management in the performing institution outside the government; (4) the need to devise special 'yardstick' or quality control measures in the absence of simple market (or other) criteria of performance and the related need to devise graded penalties for non- or mal-performance; and (5) the modern roles of the audit agency and of the legislature.

31

A first lesson to be learned from the experiences of both countries with the transfer of funds to private bodies is that failure to specify the terms of the bargain with some clarity at the beginning almost inevitably leads to trouble. Whether one considers a U.S. poverty grant, the relation between the minister and chairman of the board actually running a nationalised industry, the management of a weapons development programme, there is a requirement to think through the purposes to be achieved and the character of the relationship between the government agency and the non-government institution. Uncomfortable problems left to be sorted out in later working relationships have a way of growing more refractory once commitments have been entered into and divergent expectations have been formalised.

Lack of clarity on central objectives is often combined with efforts to overcontrol in detail. The latter represent a compensation for the troubles partially brought by the initial failure to define purposes and roles. Thus, for example, in the United States the goals of federal programmes of research support at universities have not been clearly specified; they may be variously seen as the purchase of specific research results, aid to science and graduate education in the sciences in general, or to serve as a disguised process of aiding higher education in general. But universities have been burdened by a profusion of detailed requirements for time reporting, overhead allowances and the like, some of which make little real contribution to the goal of accountability. The regional educational laboratories established by H.E.W., lacking a clear definition of their role, have pursued a variety of goals not always to the satisfaction of the parent agency. In Britain the vagueness in the allocation of responsibilities between board and ministry has sometimes led to a form of bureaucratic 'guerrilla warfare' with the ministry sporadically intervening in detailed decision-making. In the United States there is the further difficulty that contract administration in many agencies is the province of a specialised class of officials who may not be central participants in the agency's policy-making process. This may lead to some disjunction between the goals sought by high officials and the day-to-day administration of the contract.

Although the need for a clear definition of purposes and responsibilities is evident, care should be taken not to overstate the importance of this factor. The initial agreement is only one step in a process of interaction, and cannot be made to bear the major burden in the task of achieving effective accountability. Indeed, it will seldom be possible to define in advance exact performance specifications, time schedules or working conditions with many complex types of activities delegated to private institutions. The attempt to control through overly detailed specifications in the initial agreement has usually resulted in failure – whether in the D.O.D.'s 'total package procurement' for weapons systems or the N.S.F.'s 'total effort reporting' for academic scientists. Uncertainty cannot be eliminated by unrealistic standards applied to activities inherently characterised by uncertainty. Standards that are unenforceable are no standards. The need to delegate discretionary judgement to officials within more or less broad standards emerged with the rise of the bureaucratic state and has become even more firmly woven into the fabric of the contract state. It may be doubted whether proposals calling for a return to 'juridical democracy'[53] or administration-by-rule-making[54] can provide a workable solution to the problem of accountability in modern government. The problem of accountability derives from the very fact that executive discretion exists – if rules could be so formalised that officials would merely have to follow the rules mechanically there would be no problem. The initial grants of authority or terms of the agreement accompanying the exchange of funds between donor and recipient should be taken very seriously, with broad purposes defined, operating responsibilities clarified and standards of expected performance spelled out to the extent that this can practicably be done. But the initial understanding usually does not and cannot in itself govern the dynamics of the situation, and for this we must look beyond to the question of management competence.

The use of the administrative contract plainly does not diminish – and may even increase – the need for strong management competence within the government. The managerial competence is vital if the government is to exercise discerning judgement on when, how, with whom, for what purposes and under what safeguards functions will be delegated out or 'hived off' to the private sector. The government must keep a steady and guiding hand on the whole apparatus, or at the extreme the centre of gravity for public policy formation will shift to the institutions that are supposed to be the satellites of the government. More likely, the diffusion of sovereignty may continue until there is no effective centre in the governing system capable of harmonising disparate elements into a whole.

The need for strong management where tasks are contracted out or 'hived off' has been explicitly recognised by the Bell Report in the United States and the Fulton Report in Britain.[55] Neither country, however, appears to have developed fully the capacities that are needed. In Britain, the amateur tradition in administration has meant in practice that some specialised activities, particularly scientific and technological, are not always effectively accountable because of the disparity of expertise between the ministry and semi-autonomous authority.[56] At the same time the dominance of the generalist amateur has had the advantage of preventing the policy initiatives of specialist interests from having direct access to the highest levels of political authority. Proposals are filtered through a process of high-level staff work which is not solely advocacy for new programmes.

In the United States there has been a problem of rather different origins: the generalist tradition in the civil service is weak. There is, in fact, no single civil service but a series of career systems developed in different agencies. Specialised interests in the department-based civil service, in league with congressional allies and interest groups, keep a constant shower of policy initiatives coming to the President. Frequently the government has embarked on large new programmes serving specialised interests without sufficient regard for the effect on policy as a whole. This has advanced

34

accountability in the sense of responsiveness to innovative pressure but has diminished accountability in the sense of enabling the highest levels of political authority to maintain a clear central direction in policy. The President has only a thin layer of White House and Executive Office staff resources to channel the energies of a vast federal bureaucracy and modern public sector.

The right 'mix' of high-level generalist staff, specialist generalists, specialist specialists, technical managers and managers of technical managers, 'in-and-outers' and consultants of various kinds to serve the modern state defies easy analysis. Certainly no simple prescription is possible. But some combination of the qualities of the British and the American career systems might provide a helpful starting point for a reappraisal of the desired qualities of a modern civil service. Specialist competence and generalist outlook, the widespread use of outside talent yet with a permanent core of 'insiders', responsiveness to outside influences plus internal discipline – these are some of the qualities which have to be balanced in a career service equipped to manage the modern public sector. To develop such capacities may require changes in the training for officials, new styles of leadership and organisation, and revisions in traditional theories of administration.

It should be emphasised that the first requisite for effective management of outside institutions to which authority has been delegated is effective management within the government itself. Much of the confusion, the tangled lines of authority and the lack of clearly defined responsibilities which are reflected in the operations of some semi-autonomous bodies are the result of confusion, tangled lines of authority and poorly defined responsibilities within the government, either at the level of the individual department charged with oversight of the delegated activity or more broadly in conflicts among different executive agencies.[57] If the department has no clear policy, or is deeply divided on what it seeks to accomplish through the delegation of a task to a private institution, the conflict will be carried over, and compounded, in the private institution.

The interrelations between government officials and the management officials of the private institution performing a public assignment pose intricate problems. If the government lacks confidence in the private institution's management, the tendency will be strong to intervene obtrusively into what would normally be the prerogatives of private management. Many American observers have felt that this has already occurred to an unfortunate extent – in government relations with the universities,[58] industry[59] and not-for-profit organisations.[60] Some obvious management weaknesses in the private sector, especially in universities, along with the bureaucratic desire to avoid uncertainty and risk as a means of self-protection, have combined to produce this 'over-management' effect. The eventual outcome may be an accretion of rules and regulations limiting the flexibility of the private institution (and perhaps eroding its independence).

Independence cannot, of course, be understood in absolute terms. No organisation working on contract for a government agency or otherwise exercising delegated authority can be totally free from scrutiny of its work, from audit, administrative controls and related constraints that inevitably accompany the performance of a public or semi-public function. Yet there are degrees of independence from customary procedure, funding cycles and administrative routines that are vitally important to effective performance – to accountability in the programme sense. The first and most important requirement is that the private institution have a strong management separate from that of the government agency letting the contract or exercising the oversight, with the ability to hire, fire, schedule work and within some limits determine how the job can best be done. This will usually mean that the staff members should be accountable internally to their management in order to promote the accountability of the institution as a whole to the government. Professional staff members sometimes wish to deal directly with government officials without review from their own supervisors (and, of course, frequent staff contacts at the working level cannot and should not be avoided with many types of activities). Similarly, there are temptations for public officials to circumvent the private institution's management in order to secure directly the services of particular individuals or departments. But such practices tend to undermine orderly working relationships, and to work against the creation of well-managed, resourceful institutions or bodies with which the government can deal on a basis of confidence and respect.

Other important aspects of independence include: (a) independent physical facilities so that there is no confusion of roles between government and private personnel (the mingling of private personnel directly in the agency's administrative chain of command is normally to be avoided) and (b) stability in funding arrangements and insulation from the normal appropriations cycle of government agencies. These factors facilitate the task of management and are usually sought as central goals of management. Physical independence and financial stability, combined with an effective top management, help to produce a general 'climate' of independence and competence which serves the government's interests as well as the interests of the private institution. There are inevitably numerous occasions where a balance has to be struck between the conflicting requirements of independence and of accountability – in such matters as the payment and use of a management fee or indirect cost allowance, the ownership of facilities purchased with government funds, the freedom of contractor employees to speak publicly on sensitive issues relating to their work for the government, the payment of unusual bonuses or perquisites to non-civil-service employees, and the possible presence of public representatives on the governing board of a semi-private entity. Sometimes, as in the American example of Project Upward Bound discussed in this volume, the government may even retain veto rights over the selection of top personnel. The question of where to draw the line between appropriate and inappropriate controls cannot be answered in the abstract; the decisions are difficult matters of judgement in an on-going process of interaction between the government agency and the quasi-governmental body. But some genuine measure of independence, as best protected by competent management, must normally be present if the government is to realise the full benefits of the contract arrangement. The purpose of

37

independence for the contractor is to maximise his motivation and incentive to contribute creatively to the public end sought, and frustrating that intention will mean an unsatisfactory result for the government.

The relationship between top management and the staffs of private organisations (and between the private organisation and the constituencies it serves) has become a controversial issue in some government arrangements with the private sector, especially in the 'participatory' poverty contract programmes in the United States. The federal government has frequently required that such programmes be run in an internally democratic fashion with a high degree of participation by the poor themselves in planning, policy-making and implementation.[61] The emphasis on 'maximum feasible participation' has diffused into different organisational settings, and has complicated the relationship between the government and other private recipients of funds. In American universities, for example, student and faculty groups have at times sought an end to research programmes funded by the defence agencies and used the issue of participation in decision-making as a means to give effect to their aim. What is really the problem in most cases is perhaps not so much the lack of massive participation in all administrative decisions as the need for 'some regular, understood process whereby reappraisal of the competence of administration and the community's confidence in it can be undertaken without waiting for a putsch or rebellion'.[62] It is normally best for management to be held accountable for performance as a whole, which requires that management have the capacity and opportunity to exert vigorous leadership.

The government could, through the power of the purse, force changes regularly in the internal management of programmes funded by public agencies, both as regards relations between management and staff and between the organisation performing the service and the consumers of the service. But such a tactic is a double-edged sword. Whether done in the name of internal democracy, efficiency or popular sovereignty, this could mean an unprecedented intrusion by government into the internal life of private organisations, and also could result, ironically, in a *de facto* shift of real de-

38

cision-making power away from the immediate participants
to a higher level of government.

*Criteria of performance and graded penalties for mal-per-
formance*

A distinctive feature of the modern public sector is that the
government seeks services that frequently cannot be precisely
specified in advance. Appropriate standards of performance
are thus exceedingly difficult to establish. In industrial contracting, for example, the complexity of the assignment often
makes it difficult for the government to standardise the transaction along the lines of a traditional procurement action.
Buying a missile, or new aeroplane, is not like contracting for
a simple known product or commodity as in the days before
the explosion of scientific and technical knowledge. Whole
new industries have grown up with the government as their
sole client and thus normal market tests of performance have
been lacking. Sometimes the principle of 'least cost' is used
implicitly or explicitly in evaluating the performance of defence contractors, but it is evident that this is only a crude
approximation of relevant evaluative standards. Promptness
of delivery, reliability, and something which might be called
'technical inventiveness' are among the relevant criteria that
should be applied in attempting to judge the success of many
kinds of modern defence procurement activities.

The overall rubric of 'value received' for the investment of
public funds has also been invoked as a guiding principle in
evaluating contractor performance. But this concept merely
indicates the primitive state of current thought on the subject; such a notion has no operational meaning. The question
'Has the government got its money's worth?' is unanswerable
unless one can first formulate and answer a number of more
discriminating antecedent questions. We need to know such
things as whether (and to what degree) Contractor A has performed better, for a certain class of activity, than Contractor
B according to some operational definition of the project's
goals. Do both contractors taken together provide the quality
of service that could be provided by an altogether different
type of performer? Does the activity itself contribute as
effectively to the agency's larger purposes as some other activ-

39

ity? A whole series of questions must be posed, often relating to how much? with respect to what end? and compared to what alternative? the criteria sought should not be viewed as the equivalent of production norms for well-understood mechanical tasks; such an orientation would mislead and greatly simplify the problem. There are apt to be few simple formulas, based on objective and easily measurable factors, which are applicable to programme evaluation in the modern public sector.

The search for performance standards should also extend to the government agency itself and its institutional practices, decision-making styles and processes of framing issues. Since simple mechanical guides to decision are seldom available, it is a high art to set up the right interaction of different skills to produce a balanced decision. In this area as well our understanding is relatively undeveloped. Peer judgement, for example, is often used as the proper means to allocate contract and grant funds for scientific purposes and to decide which projects have performed well enough to merit renewed support. For certain kinds of purposes, such as funding relatively small academic basic research projects within an established discipline, this process has worked remarkably well, and in fact may provide the best means for reaching such decisions. (The Office of Naval Research, however, which is one of the most successful U.S. agencies that have been engaged in funding basic research, has never operated on the basis of peer group judgement by a network of advisory panels; it has always preferred to have a strong technical management competence within its own staff so that extensive outside help was unnecessary.) For other purposes, judgement by an advisory panel of scientific peers is much less satisfactory. One cannot rely on the technical peer group when the issue at stake is a large institutional grant, a research project crossing established disciplinary lines, a proposal involving potential conflict between industrial and academic scientists, large facilities having broad implications for a region's economy and numerous other matters. The basis for decision in such cases transcends narrow technical expertise, and involves the judgements offered by the generalist administrator, the politician and the traditional interest group.[63] Peer judgement has been perhaps relied on too

40

much in U.S. science policy, and there has been inadequate exploration of the proper uses and the limitations of the technical advisory panel, but no one has yet invented a more satisfactory way to perform some of the evaluative functions now served by the peer group.

The effort to develop standards of performance ultimately derives its chief significance from the part it plays in the educative process for officials charged with management responsibility. In a sense the question of performance criteria collapses into the broader consideration of good management. What counts most is the process rather than the product; the aim is not the invention of standards to be routinely applied but the exercise of discerning judgement by responsible officials. This seems also to be the lesson from the experience to date with the planning-programming-budget system and its associated analytic techniques. The principal contribution, by attempting to make more systematic and explicit the premises of policy choices, has been to serve as an aid to, not a substitute for, the exercise of executive judgement. No one at the Ditchley Conference, on either the British or American side, seemed much disposed to believe that modern management techniques alone would provide answers to the difficult questions of evaluating contractor performance and achieving effective accountability in modern government. As Wallace S. Sayre has remarked in a different context: 'Management techniques and processes have their costs as well as their benefits. Each new version has a high obsolescence rate, its initial contributions to rationality declining as it becomes the vested interest of its own specialist guardians and/or other groups with preferred access.'[64]

To some degree the government may have to become more of a performer itself in order to develop its managerial capability and to have a truly effective 'yardstick' for evaluating the private sector. But it will be plainly impossible or impractical to duplicate all facilities between the public and private sectors, and the alternative of a Tennessee Valley Authority as a measuring rod to assess the performance of private power companies will not always be available. The complex undertakings, like the 200 billion electron volt (BEV) accelerator, COMSAT and the Public Broadcasting Corporation, can have no competition because of the cost and

41

scale of their operations. The task of devising indices of performance even for such giants as these, though one will seldom emerge with a kind of simple rate-setting formula akin to a traditional utility, nevertheless plays an essential part in the process of good management.

The reverse side of the coin is the need to devise graded penalties which can be applied when performance falls short. A chief difficulty in government–contractor relations, as Mr Bertrand Harding, then Acting Director of the Office of Economic Opportunity, forcefully brought out at the Ditchley Conference, is the absence of 'punishments which fit the crime'. The government often finds itself in the position where the only effective penalty it can invoke is termination of the contract. This may mean cutting off an operation in mid-stream or failing to renew a delegation of authority just at the point when the government wishes to realise the results from its investment. In New York City, for example, the poverty programme has become an established part of city life, and few would consider it feasible to cut off the programme altogether – yet there has been serious maladministration of the programme which demands some kind of remedial action. The problem is not greatly dissimilar with many other types of activities. When the government needs either a complex technological product or a specialised service and has already invested heavily, total and abrupt termination of the arrangement is usually unthinkable – and the threat to withdraw is rightly perceived as empty under the circumstances. However, short of that the government agency may have little leverage over the operation, and may be reduced either to doing nothing or to administering a slap on the wrist. The problem is to invent middle-range penalties which are not so severe that they can never be invoked, yet which carry an impact that cannot be ignored by the performing organisation.

The modern role of the audit agency

The traditional role of the audit agency in Western democracies has been to enforce 'regularity' in the expenditure of public funds, or conformity with accepted administrative and fiscal procedures together with correct accounting and observance of legality in the broadest sense.[65] For several reasons this traditional role has declined in importance. The regular departments of government, first, have developed internal audit procedures and generally have greatly strengthened their financial administration capacities. The minimum requirements of regularity are now largely met by the departments themselves. In addition, the sheer volume of financial transactions in the modern state has made it impossible for the audit agency to check everything; and inevitably the role of external audit has shifted more towards a check of the adequacy and effectiveness of the executive department's internal procedures. The more effectively the audit agency performs in this connection, the more it becomes displaced in a sense to the sidelines of government activity.

In this light it is hardly surprising that the modern role of the audit agency is a matter of dispute and uncertainty. No one doubts that audit, which historically has been so closely tied in with the concept of accountability, will continue to play some part in helping to maintain accountable government. But there is a lack of general agreement over whether the role will be more or less prominent, whether new functions will evolve, and if so whether accountability in the larger sense will be served. Roughly three alternatives seem possible. The audit agency can continue to be primarily connerned with regularity (or in Robinson's terms, 'fiscal accountability') on the theory that an auditor is an auditor is an auditor. The audit agency would make spot checks, perhaps using modern sampling techniques, into agency expenditures, and would continue to review and upgrade the fiscal management capacities of particular departments, ministries or semi-public bodies across the entire spectrum of public activity. Or the audit agency can innovate in its techniques and mission, going beyond regularity into the 'efficiency' audit and evaluating the substance of public programmes. To some degree this has already happened with the office of the Comptroller and Auditor General in Britain and the U.S. General Accounting Office. Both have broadened the focus of their concerns beyond regularity in the narrow sense. Finally, the audit agency can focus its attention on selected areas presumably most in need of scrutiny – nationalised industry, university research, grants to local government, new

43

experimental programmes in welfare, health and education. Under this conception, the audit agency would more or less give up the task of auditing the established government departments to their internal audit units and concentrate instead on the accountability problems of the modern public sector.

A definitive evaluation of these alternatives is impossible here, but a few tentative observations seem in order. It is perhaps misleading to pose the roles as mutually exclusive; the audit agency will probably seek some combination of the three roles. The issue will be where the centre of gravity lies. The difficulties of moving much beyond the traditional concern with regularity seem formidable. Audit agencies tend to have an established 'character' or organisational identity which is difficult to change rapidly or dramatically. One may also wonder, if the role of audit were to evolve more towards programme evaluation or policy analysis, whether the skills, work atmosphere and mores of the agency would be conducive to creative performance of the task. The audit agency itself might need an infusion of outside skills, a contractual relationship with the private sector for specialised advice, in order to make a significant contribution in the review of contract programmes.[66]

A different sort of problem might arise if the audit agency became an influential participant in policy evaluation: an already fragmented policy process would become still more so as further wills have to be concerted, more energies harmonised and additional actors accommodated on an already crowded stage. And to single out the novel and experimental programmes of the modern public sector for special scrutiny might run the danger of burdening the administrative process and stifling the creativity required for successful innovation.[67] Yet it is clear that one cannot realistically expect that contract activities will be insulated from the normal tug and pull of political pressures. As with other programmes, a broad base of confidence in the administration of a contract programme must be created from the start to ensure programme survival, and in this larger context the audit process will inevitably play some part.

There is also the further issue of whether the audit agency should serve primarily as an aid to the legislature or should

44

seek a more independent role. Traditionally in most Western democracies the audit agency has been closely linked to the legislature as an instrument to assist in enforcing the financial accountability of the executive. It is possible to view the function of state audit, however, as going beyond that of only serving as one of the resources available to the legislature in holding the executive accountable. In his paper in this volume, Normanton proposes the creation of a Council on Administrative Efficiency built around the Comptroller's Office which would give the audit agency a more prominent role in its own right in enforcing executive accountability.[68] Although he is careful to specify that the proposed Council would retain close ties with Parliament (and also with the ministries), and would have a reporting rather than a control function, the proposal clearly envisages a larger role for the audit agency as an independent critic of the efficiency of government action at all levels.

The main body envisaged in this proposal, on the one hand, might be so removed from the centres of decision in the government that it would not affect the course of events. If, on the other hand, a guardian class of even broadly trained auditors were to acquire significant power, the ancient question would arise of who guards the guardians. The audit agency, when one considers its general traditions, the backgrounds of the staff commonly recruited and its lack of direct responsiveness to popular control, can hardly be considered the ideal setting to exercise broad judgements about 'efficiency' in government. Basic value premises and fundamental questions of social policy are involved as one moves beyond considerations of efficiency in the narrow sense to efficiency in the large, and issues of the latter sort should remain principally within the province of officials more directly linked to the mechanisms of popular control.

The modern role of the legislature

The legislature, through its review of budgets, investigative powers and ability to capture public attention in dramatising issues, remains a highly important instrumentality for holding the executive accountable. This remains so despite the rise of Ombudsman devices and other administrative innova-

45

tions designed to promote accountability, and despite the general ascendancy of the executive power in the twentieth century. No contemporary legislature has as much power as the American Congress, but all Western legislative bodies in some degree influence the day-to-day workings of government. The contrast between Britain and the United States is again especially instructive for our purposes. Two points are of particular interest: (1) the staff resources of the legislative body, and especially of its standing committees; and (2) the opportunity for prospective as well as retrospective influences on the major policy choices of the executive.

The British Parliament, for a variety of historical and constitutional reasons, does not have a strong committee structure like the U.S. Congress. Yet, as David Howell, M.P., suggests in his contribution to this volume, the recent creation of several new parliamentary committees and the increase in committee activity represent small steps in the direction of the American practice.[69] Although there appear to be definite limits on how far such a development can proceed in the British context, the British participants at the Ditchley Conference generally agreed that some further strengthening of the committee system could proceed without bringing fundamental changes in the constitutional system. (Some participants on the British side felt strongly that the growth of a strong committee system *should* proceed, even at the cost of altering established constitutional practices, in order to open up the bureaucracy and presumably make it more accessible to direct popular pressures.) To make the parliamentary committees more significant, adequate staff resources would have to be available to members individually and to the committees; and the tradition of specialised competence in various policy areas would have to be developed in the working mores of Parliament. The creation of a tradition of specialism combined with the minimum staff competence would bring prospective participation in policy deliberations as alliances of interests developed naturally across ministry and committee lines.

In contrast, the U.S. Congress does not suffer from an overestimation of the capacity of the lay critic. On the contrary, the danger facing the Congress is that specialisation will so dominate its proceedings that concerted attention to the major problems of the time will become impossible. Equally important, Congressmen may become the captives of their own specialised bureaucracies just as their counterparts in the executive branch, the political executives, frequently have become the instruments of the executive bureaucracies which are supposed to serve them.

In most areas of domestic policy, and even certain aspects of defence and foreign policy, the Congress has some role in policy deliberations within the executive branch. Congress usually functions, like the British Parliament, as a retrospective critic of the executive only with respect to some aspects of foreign and national security policy and to some extent with respect to contract activities in general.[70] In certain areas, congressional committees participate so extensively in policy deliberations with the executive that the lines of accountability become difficult to disentangle. Perhaps the most extreme example is the Joint Committee on Atomic Energy which has functioned as a coequal participant in executive decision-making in the field of atomic energy policy.[71] This type of role for a congressional committee is as inimical in its own way to the goal of accountability as the relative absence of committee vitality in the British Parliament. Carrying detailed congressional intervention in the administrative process to this extreme confuses the chain of command, makes it difficult for the executive to develop coherent policy and weakens the unique capacity of the legislative body to introduce a non-expert point of view into the policy process. In a world dominated by experts the legislative body can serve a vital function in giving expression to the consumer's view of government services, the non-expert who knows when the 'shoe pinches' and who can evaluate from a wider perspective the plans drawn up by specialists. That function is compromised when the legislature operates as an auxiliary bureaucracy. Nor can the legislature criticise policy effectively if it shares fully in the making of policy.

The removal of spheres of power from direct legislative review via the act of delegation to outside bodies complicates the legislature's task. The executive authority is able to monopolise information somewhat more easily, escape some constraints applicable to direct government operations, keep policy initiatives disguised and sometimes insulate a new

C

programme from criticism for a time. But in principle the rise of the modern public sector, in the American context at least, does not seem to have drastically altered legislative–executive relations. The legislature has learned to apply the usual leverage: it has begun to insist that the executive have a policy on when and why it will use private institutions; it seeks to evaluate the success in broad terms of the programme involving outside performers; and ultimately it can, just as executive departments can specify the terms of a grant of authority to an outside institution, delimit the conditions under which the executive departments can resort to the delegation of authority.[72] Indeed, some observers believe that certain congressional interests welcome extensive contract activities because these provide an attractive modern form of 'pork barrel' which helps build a constituency in the home district, and because direct access to the level of programme management may sometimes be easier than with programmes directly administered by a regular executive department.[73] However, the Congress generally seems to be engaged in the task of seeking to extend its oversight of the modern public sector by working through the executive departments which sponsor the non-governmental institutions. Such an approach seems more promising than to have the institution directly serving two masters; the lines of accountability should normally run from the private institution to the executive and to the legislature.

The modern legislature does not appear to require any special techniques or resources to cope with the problems of the contract state beyond what is required for a viable legislative role generally: enough staff resources and specialised expertise so that the executive from time to time can be effectively challenged. And the legislature shoud have some prospective, and not merely retrospective, influence in shaping the programmes drawn up by the executive. But the legislature should not be so abundantly endowed with staff resources that legislators become the captives of their own bureaucracies. This is the chief problem which the Ditchley participants from the Congress and from Parliament saw with proposals to form contract advisory institutes or other special staff resources attached to the legislature and designed to assist in the task of holding the executive accountable: such bodies might themselves exercise power without effective accountability.

Carried too far, the desire to participate in executive policy–making would be self-defeating for the legislative body. Accountability is impossible when initial responsibility for decisions is blurred; no one can share fully in the making of policy and still have the detachment to act as critic. The legislator can best serve the end of accountability if his role complements that of his fellow-generalists – the politicians who sit atop the ministries and departments. Both are seeking to inject a viewpoint other than professionalism into the workings of modern government, and while they may not always recognise the fact, they are natural allies whose natural opponents are the bureaucrat experts with a narrower view of reality.

Is there such a thing as a broad social accountability?

A final topic of interest discussed at the Ditchley Conference was the notion that, beyond the formal institutions and procedures of government, one owed a loyalty to 'society' in some larger sense. The notion was never very clearly spelled out, but the thrust of it seemed to involve the feeling that accountability could not be real unless the various parties to an agreement internalised the basic values underlying the political process. Thus, whatever the formal requirements, an activity was accountable if it inspired general confidence and served what were widely regarded as desirable social ends. The underlying values to be observed were both *procedural* and *substantive* in character. Most conferees could feel comfortable with the idea that observing certain 'rules of the game' facilitates the conduct of public business, and that these procedural norms have something to do with the deeper values of the society. But the footing became slippery when the discussion turned to the substantive ends which the political system was supposed to serve. Agreement was forthcoming when the discussion was pitched at a high enough level of abstraction (the-Brotherhood-of-Man-under-the-Fatherhood-of-God, as one unkind critic suggested). The unanimity of view held by all reasonable men had an unfortunate tendency to disintegrate on concrete issues. Nevertheless many Ditchley

49

participants felt that there was at least a partial truth which was worth salvaging in the idea of 'social accountability'.

The argument would run something like the following. All social institutions are (or should be) in some sense accountable to society since they are created, nourished and sustained either by the active or the tacit support of society. They form a kind of social contract with the state which permits them to exist in return for performing socially useful services. The obligation extends beyond what may be narrowly prescribed in the legal articles of incorporation to a share in dealing, as appropriate, with the pressing social problems of the time. Industry, universities, foundations, research institutes, political parties and government agencies should be accountable not merely to their own boards, clientele groups, constituencies and peers but also to 'the people' as a whole. In practical terms, this means that universities should be more 'relevant', industry should recognise its responsibility to help solve social problems, and government agencies should rely less on established interest groups and clienteles in order to contribute more broadly to desired social ends. The Urban Coalition, a loose coalition of liberal–business–labour forces concerned with the problems of the cities in the United States, exemplifies the approach implicit in the notion of social accountability. The Coalition, headed by John Gardner, former Secretary of Health, Welfare and Education, has sought to marshal energies in the private sector on a voluntary basis for an attack on urban ills, especially race and poverty.

The force of the argument is in some measure apparent. The great social problems can be more effectively attacked if the private sector lends its efforts. Private institutions influence many facets of social life, and if they work at cross-purposes to the public sector the effect of government programmes may be diminished or even negated. It is difficult to imagine, for example, how the urban ghetto in the United States, which is the product of actions taken (and not taken) in both the public and private sectors, can be coped with in the absence of a massive effort drawing on a wide range of public and private energies. Indeed, the advantage of the modern public sector over the traditional public sector lies precisely in the fact that society's energies can be mobilised on a broader scale. The government cannot do everything, and it is tempting to think that if only influential leaders of business, labour, education and religion can be persuaded to recognise their responsibilities a vast outpouring of effort will help solve a refractory problem.

The appeal of the idea begins to diminish, however, as one explores further. One problem evident almost at once is a kind of 'invisible hand' assumption: if everybody pursues his conception of the accountability demanded by 'society', the net result will somehow average out to the social good. The pivotal role of the government, in giving some controlling purposes to the whole enterprise, has to re-enter the picture. The experience of the Urban Coalition illustrates the point. After some substantial initial successes the Coalition has been increasingly unable to keep its forces together and voluntary action as an organising principle shows signs of having limited staying power. The energies of the private sector lack focus and tend to dissipate without strong central leadership provided through the political process (and especially a sympathetic President). The root of the problem lies in the logic of 'collective goods'.[74] The farmer has no incentive to withdraw his animals from grazing on the commons because the marginal costs to him are small; every farmer reasons the same way and eventually the commons are destroyed unless collective action establishes a rule binding on all. The individual cannot be expected to bear unreasonable social costs in his own decisions – that is the function of collective action which authoritatively resolves conflict and sets central priorities.

The making of collective choices requires a system which operates in some more or less orderly fashion and is recognised as having general legitimacy. Quite properly, a democratic government does not usually give its bureaucratic officials a free reign to 'do good' in some general fashion or ask that they be directly accountable to 'society'. The bureaucracy is divided into coherent parts to accomplish specific tasks, and bureaucrats are accountable not to everybody but to their administrative superiors. When the government engages the energies of the private sector for certain purposes, it is all the more important that the arrangements sustain confidence in the integrity of the governmental process.

Private institutions have unique strengths and weaknesses, and the government's task in the modern public sector is to be a discriminating user of private talents and resources. Too often the hasty call of public officials for social involvement by private institutions invites confusion, inefficiency and a decline of confidence in government.[75] And if private institutions with a diffuse mandate to share in the exercise of public power on one occasion make a positive contribution, on another occasion, perhaps after they have acquired a taste for power, they may merely pursue their own interests under a cloak of legitimacy.

Behind much of the discontent with the institutions of contemporary society is the belief that only established institutions and organised interests are served at the expense of the poor and the unorganised. Reformers who blame 'the system' as the source of all ills and who call for a return to the virtues of direct democracy, spontaneity and government close to the people follow a well-trod but dangerous path. Their proposals, when adopted, have usually weakened orderly authority and provided an opportunity for the well-organised special interests.[76] Systems, or regularised procedures, should not be seen as obstacles blocking the citizen's access to government, but as necessary means for accomplishing any task, and as safeguards against arbitrariness, abuse of power and a manipulative plebiscitarianism.

All bureaucratic systems, however, seem to suffer from a built-in entrophy, a tendency to run down in efficiency. Goal displacement, or the deflection of initial objectives into such other aims as organisational maintenance, is a familiar phenomenon noted by observers of bureaucratic behaviour. Any system should undergo a constant redefinition as imaginative officials test and stretch its limits and capacities. Perhaps the capacity to innovate, and the willingness to take risks, are so rare in government that they should be nourished wherever found. Certainly the appropriate goal is efficiency in the large rather than efficiency in the small. There is no final answer to the question of when the public official, in the name of social accountability, should disobey his superior, stretch the meaning of a rule, or otherwise depart from his usual norms. The 'inner check' described by John Gaus[77] – the mix of internalised professional and humane values – will

52

ultimately play a large part in the accountability of public officials.

6. *Democratic Responsibility and the Delegation of Authority*

The problem that gave rise to the Ditchley Conference and to this exploratory volume can be broadly stated as the reconciliation of democratic responsibility with the delegation of power. The fact of government is that power, resources and authority are handed over to someone in the expectation that certain services will be rendered. In modern government, the scope of public responsibilities has broadened and new types of performers have emerged to carry out public functions. Where authority is delegated through the nationalisation of industry, formation of government corporations, by creating new independent executive departments, by adding to the established executive departments, by contracting with established institutions in the private sector, by setting up new institutions in the private sector via a contract agreement between the institution and the sponsoring government department, in the form of a mixed public–private enterprise without a sponsoring executive department, or by empowering a special panel or board of experts to decide certain classes of questions – all these involve problems in seeing that those who perform the task are ultimately subject to popular control through the political process. The contributors to this volume explore different dimensions of the subject but each in his own way asks the question: Does the delegation of authority on a wide scale to institutions outside the traditional framework of the government fundamentally alter the nature of the accountability problem?

Douglas Hague reminds us that accountability, in essence, is the price one pays for the benefits of the division of labour and of operating on a large scale.[78] Or similarly: 'the principle of executive accountability is the price which must be paid for the exercise of executive discretion'.[79] All organisations, public and private, old and new, face a problem of control and evaluation that is similar in its essentials. Even the firm operating in the market has no easy way of assessing the

53

contribution of its functional divisions to the firm's overall profits. Thus, under this view, our attention should be directed less towards surface novelties than towards understanding the still unresolved traditional questions of accountability. Others strongly doubt that our current dilemma is an extension of familiar problems or at least believe that the differences in degree are so great as to become differences in kind. An earlier observer put the point succinctly: 'in the contractual system, the problem of discretion in administration, unresolved in the public administration itself, is magnified when power over governmental decisions is turned over to private groups and individuals. . . . By placing the influence over, and sometimes even control of, important decisions one step further away from the public and their elected representatives, the system further exacerbates the problem of discretion.'[80]

A sorting out of the lines of the argument, I believe, would suggest senses in which both views are correct. Undoubtedly there have been instances when effective accountability was lacking in the delegation of authority within the traditional public sector; because an activity is performed by civil service employees in a regular ministry or department hardly guarantees accountability. Sometimes the political executive may control an activity more effectively if it is performed outside the government framework. It is also doubtless the case that many problems of the modern public sector are carryovers from the government's inability to assign responsibilities clearly within its own ranks. When confusion reigns within the formal government structure, that confusion is squared or cubed when passed along to private institutions.

In some senses, the delegation of authority to outside institutions involves the same kinds of considerations as delegating within the government. Within his controlling broad objectives the decision-maker will normally, whether the activity is performed inside or outside the government, seek to give the performer enough freedom to do a creative job;[81] arrange for a manageable assignment that is logically suited to the person or unit selected; delimit the mandate or eliminate any ambiguities in the agreement that might jeopardise his own ultimate authority or power of command;[82] evaluate the effectiveness of the performer at regular intervals; and so

54

on. In other senses, the delegation of authority to private institutions creates problems different from those typically encountered with direct government operations. The exercise of discretionary judgement by individuals who have not usually internalised the norms and values of public service, the financial dependency on government of large sectors of the private economy, the variety and unreliability of accounting and costing procedures in many private institutions, conflicts between proprietary information and the public's right to know, the flow of private persons into the inner councils of government decision-making and the opportunities for creating privileged interest group claimants of an unusual kind on public resources – these are among the numerous matters that appear to pose elements of novelty. Some problems may turn out to be relatively minor, while others may prove refractory. The government, at any rate, faces the danger, to a degree not experienced in a simpler past, of becoming either too powerful or too weak; of extending its reach so far that the concept of 'private' loses all meaning or, conversely, of enfeebling itself through the diffusion of its powers.

Major choices on institutional arrangements are ultimately questions of political theory rather than neutral principles of management. Administrative systems survive, flourish or alter as they serve the larger interests of the politicians – the officials most directly responsive to the wider public. The politicians face unprecedented demands for more and better government services, for change and experimentation, and for new ways to relate the citizen to government. At the same time there is general insistence that government must be controllable and that orderly procedures are particularly necessary in a world of rapid change. Britain and the United States, as relatively stable consensual societies, have enjoyed the rarest of gifts: the capacity to govern with a minimum of coercion. Each nation must learn to satisfy heightened popular expectations – by improving existing institutions and by inventing new ways to serve social needs – within a framework of democratic control if that capacity is to endure.

55

1. The Committee held a conference at Ditchley Park, near Oxford, from 26 March to 29 March 1969 after a period of preliminary exploration on each side. British and American participants are identified in the appendixes at the beginning of the volume. The papers presented here grew out of the working papers prepared for the Ditchley Conference.

2. The 'military–industrial complex' seems to have already earned a place in the pantheon of American villainry, along with such old favourites as 'Wall Street', 'the Trusts' and 'the party bosses'. For a time I attempted to trace the intellectual ancestry of the phrase, from its insertion in President Eisenhower's famous farewell address by speechwriter Malcolm Moos to its absorption in the wider American culture, but gave up the task when the flood of pundits, publicists and commentators using the term overwhelmed the search for fine points of lineage. A recent indictment is Richard J. Barnett, *Economy of Death* (Atheneum, New York, 1969). President Nixon, apparently in an effort to allay some public anxieties, created a 'blue ribbon' commission in the summer of 1969 under insurance executive Gilbert Fitzhugh to study various aspects of defence procurement: see *New York Times*, 1 July 1969, p. 14. The commission is not likely, however, to 'defuse' the issue to any great extent, whatever its findings, because of the heavy representation of defence industry in the commission membership. Congressional interest in government procurement, spurred by reports of cost overruns and influence-peddling in defence contracts, has grown considerably: see *Government Procurement and Contracting*, Hearings before a Sub-Committee of the Committee on Government Operations, U.S. House of Representatives, 91st Congress, 1st Session, 7 parts (Government Printing Office, Washington, D.C., 1969).

3. See Murray L. Weidenbaum, *The Modern Public Sector: New Ways of Doing the Government's Business* (Basic Books, New York, 1969) ch. 3. The New Left fears a 'social–industrial complex' even more ominous than the military–industrial complex if industry became centrally involved under contract arrangements in solving urban problems. See

Michael Harrington, 'The Social–Industrial Complex', in *Towards a Democratic Left* (Penguin Books, Baltimore, 1969), pp. 77–100.

4. This felicitous phrase is borrowed from Don K. Price, *The Scientific Estate* (Belknap Press of Harvard University Press, Cambridge, Mass., 1965).

5. This view is strongly felt in H. L. Nieburg, *In the Name of Science* (Quadrangle Books, Chicago, 1966) ch. x, 'The Contract State', and ch. xii, 'Throwing Away the Yardstick'. From a somewhat different perspective, that of interest representation in the administrative process, Theodore J. Lowi has also expressed concern over the abdication of public functions to private bodies in *The End of Liberalism* (Norton, New York, 1969). Similar concerns over the delegation of power without clear standards are found in a stream of thought expressed by many administrative lawyers, viz., Arthur S. Miller, 'Administration by Contract: A New Concern for the Administrative Lawyer', in *New York University Law Review*, xxxvi (May 1961) 957–90; Henry J. Friendly, *The Federal Administrative Agencies* (Harvard University Press, Cambridge, Mass., 1962); Kenneth C. Davis, *Administrative Law Treatise* (West Publishing, St Paul, Minn., 1958 and 1965 supplement). Among those who dispute the view, believing that government has grown top-heavy and has not delegated enough power, are Peter F. Drucker, *The Age of Discontinuity* (Harper & Row, New York, 1969), Richard C. Corneuille, *Reclaiming the American Dream* (Random House Vintage Books, New York, 1968) (urging the virtues of voluntary action); and Milton Kotler, *Neighborhood Government* (Bobbs–Merrill, New York, 1969) (outlining a scheme for the drastic decentralisation of government power). Eli Ginzberg *et al.*, *The Pluralistic Economy* (McGraw-Hill, New York, 1965), presents empirical data on the growth of the non-profit sector of the economy.

6. For the sake of clarity the reader should note the different usage of the term 'policy' in Britain and in the United States. British usage tends to restrict 'policy' to mean those matters which are personally decided by the minister or by the Cabinet. In American usage the term refers to anything which any actor in the political process chooses to regard as a policy matter. I employ the broader usage, rejecting the notion of a

sharp distinction between ministerial policy and administrative detail.

7. The resignation of Sir Thomas Dugdale in the Crichel Down affair seemed quaintly archaic in the conditions of the late 1960s. David Howell's contribution to this volume, esp. pp. 234–42 below, is a searching discussion of the subject.

8. This view, although perhaps generally more popular with Conservatives than with Labourites, has been best developed in J. P. Mackintosh, *The Devolution of Power* (Penguin Books, London, 1968).

9. Nationalised industry alone comprises about 10·3 per cent of the British Gross National Product (slightly higher when measured on the basis of capital formation). Nationalised industry, central government and local authorities together represent about 25 per cent of the British G.N.P. (from a background paper prepared by Sidney Pollard, 'The Origins and Development of Public Enterprise in Britain', for the Ditchley Conference, p. 10). Nationalised industry or the public corporations are a difficult class of institutions to categorise for our purposes. They are in a sense part of the traditional public sector and also part of the modern public sector; they are self-sustaining and not contractual entities dependent upon continuing appropriations yet they may interact with a counterpart ministry which has some powers of supervision. Perhaps the closest analogue on the American side are the regulated industries and the traditional government corporations (e.g., Tennessee Valley Authority). These institutions – the British public corporations, regulated industries in the United States and the older government corporations – usually are engaged in activities of a commercial character involving a large number of business-type transactions with the public.

10. Alan Pifer, 'The Quasi Nongovernmental Organization', in *Annual Report, 1967* (Carnegie Corporation, New York, 1967). The varying terminology employed by different observers – the 'quasi non-governmental' sector, 'the modern public sector', the 'contract state', the 'independent sector', 'the pluralistic economy', the 'mixed public–private sector' – indicates that research is in its early stages and that the exact boundaries of the subject have not yet been fully defined. Particularly difficult to categorise on the American side are

such entities as the Communications Satellite Corporation (COMSAT), the Public Broadcasting Corporation, the new not-for-profit corporation proposed to take over the functions of the Post Office, and the not-for-profit corporation which will manage New York City's public hospital system. These are not strictly contract entities: they are not dependent upon continuing government appropriations; they do not report to a government department or ministry which exercises overall policy control; they exercise authority directly delegated by statute. Yet they are mixtures of public and private elements, and they pose accountability problems similar to those which accompany extensive contract operations. For further efforts to define the boundaries of the subject, see above, pp. 14–17, and also Douglas Hague's discussion, pp. 70–4. Professor Hague proposes, as one criterion to delimit the focus of our concern, the presence or absence of continuing dependence of the performing organisation upon government appropriations.

11. E. L. Normanton's interesting proposal for a Council on Administrative Efficiency to act as something of a watchdog committee on government efficiency, as outlined below, pp. 337–40, would be likely to encounter this sort of objection. If such a Council became influential, it would need its own watchdog.

12. The notion of 'convergence' in the political systems of different nations as they reach a certain stage of industrial development is effectively rebutted in Samuel P. Huntington and Zbigniew Brzezinski, *Political Power U.S.A./U.S.S.R.* (Viking Press, New York, 1964). See also G. C. Allen, *Economic Fact and Fantasy* (Occasional Paper 14, Institute of Economic Affairs, London, 1969) for a critique of the convergence notion as it has arisen in the context of the debate on J. K. Galbraith's *The New Industrial State* (Houghton Mifflin, Boston, Mass., 1967).

13. On the legal and constitutional basis for contracting, see Clarence H. Danhof, *Government Contracting and Technological Change* (Brookings Institution, Washington, D.C., 1968), esp. pp. 16–69; Miller, in *New York University Law Review*, xxxvi (May 1961); and Don K. Price, *Government and Science* (New York University Press, 1954) ch. 11, 'Federalism By Contract'.

14. British administrators can even enter into a binding contract involving future payments for which funds have not yet been voted by Parliament. E. L. Normanton, *The Accountability and Audit of Governments* (Manchester University Press, 1966), p. 91. On the general position of administration in Britain, see Samuel A. Beer, *Treasury Control* (Clarendon Press, Oxford, 1957) and Fritz Morstein Marx, *The Administrative State* (University of Chicago Press, 1957).

15. Normanton, *The Accountability and Audit of Governments*, p. 92.

16. See above, pp. 21–2.

17. Weidenbaum, *The Modern Public Sector*, p. 11.

18. Danhof, *Government Contracting and Technological Change*, pp. 50–1.

19. *Statement of Elmer B. Staats before the Sub-Committee on Antitrust and Monopoly Legislation, Senate Committee on the Judiciary, on the Effect of D.O.D. Procurement on Competition and Concentration*, p. 4. This figure corresponds to the government-wide norm for negotiated contract awards as against contracts let by formally advertised competitive bidding. Among the civilian agencies, for F.Y. 1968, the percentages of contracting after advertised bidding were as follows: H.E.W. 10·7 per cent; D.O.T. 22·0 per cent; NASA 2·0 per cent; Agriculture 29·2 per cent; O.E.O. 0·00 per cent; and G.S.A. 58·0 per cent. The executive departments often, however, invent new categories in reporting the figures, such as 'competitive negotiation', which attempt to disguise the prominence of negotiated contracts.

20. Amitai Etzioni, *The Active Society* (Free Press, New York, 1968).

21. See the papers by Robinson, Ruina, Goldberg and Hague in this volume.

22. The feeling has become so widespread that there is scarcely a point in reciting sources. Suffice to mention a few of the leading exponents: Arnold Gehlen in Germany, Jacques Ellul in France, Herbert Marcuse in the United States. For a penetrating analysis of the intellectual antecedents of these ideas, see Don K. Price, 'Purists and Politicians', in *Science,* CLXIII (3 Jan 1969) 25–31.

23. See the paper by Beck below, pp. 213–29, and Daniel P. Moynihan, *Maximum Feasible Misunderstanding* (Free

Press, New York, 1969); Kenneth B. Clark, *A Relevant War Against Poverty* (Metropolitan Applied Research Center, New York, 1968); James L. Sundquist, *Politics and Policy* (Brookings Institution, Washington, D.C., 1968) pt IV, and Sundquist (ed.), *On Fighting Poverty* (Basic Books, New York, 1969); Peter Marris and Martin Rein, *Dilemmas of Social Reform: Poverty and Community Action in the U.S.* (Atherton Press, New York, 1967); Hans B. C. Spiegel and Stephen D. Mittenthal, *Neighborhood Power and Control: Urban Planning* (report prepared for H.U.D., School of Architecture, Columbia University, 1968); Stephen Thernstrom, *Poverty, Planning and Politics in the New Boston* (Basic Books, New York, 1969); Herbert Kaufman, 'Administrative Decentralization and Political Power', in *Public Administration Review* (Jan–Feb 1969); and Ralph Kramer, *Participation of the Poor* (Prentice–Hall Inc., Englewood Cliffs, N.J., 1969).

24. A collection of Mailer speeches is in Peter Manso (ed.), *Running Against the Machine* (Doubleday, Garden City, N.Y., 1969). See also Kotler, *Neighbourhood Government*.

25. The Code of Federal Regulations defines a contract as the 'establishment of a binding legal relation basically obligating the seller to furnish personal property or non-personal services (including construction) and the buyer to pay therefor. It includes all types of commitments which obligate the Government to an expenditure of funds and which, except as otherwise authorised, are in writing' (C.F.R., title 41, ch. 1–1.208). There is no accurate way of estimating how many contracts are in existence, but in one sub-class – defence procurement actions – there are several million transactions each year.

26. *New York Times*, 27 June 1969, p. 1.

27. Ibid.

28. An interesting feature of the Project Upward Bound case study in this volume, pp. 169–80, is the reference to Sargent Shriver's practice of personally examining contracts with important policy implications. Shriver, as O.E.O. Director, found the initial grant of authority to the contractor in this case too broad and insisted that precautions be taken to protect the agency's decision-making prerogatives.

29. Danhof, *Government Contracting and Technological Change*, pp. 4–5.

30. As Don K. Price remarks: '... the grant ... differs from the contract only symbolically and in technical detail...': *The Scientific Estate*, pp. 74–5. See also Danhof, *Government Contracting and Technological Change*, p. 4.

31. Price, *Government and Science*, ch. 11.

32. The interests of the states and their localities are not identical, and within some localities the mayors have been more favourably disposed than others towards the new federalism because they wish to use the federal funds to build up constituencies loyal to them which they can use against the bureaucrats and city councils. In general, however, both state and local governments seem to share a suspicion of too much contracting outside the traditional channels of federalism. An alternative strategy on which both states and localities can agree is to press for revenue-sharing schemes that will guarantee them some fixed percentage of federal revenues – a strategy which appeared to pay off when the Nixon Administration in the summer of 1969 announced plans to push for revenue-sharing.

33. E.g., the not-for-profit advisory corporations working for defence agencies. See Bruce L. R. Smith, *The Rand Corporation* (Harvard University Press, Cambridge, Mass., 1966).

34. The Institute for Defence Analyses (IDA), for example, was created to provide scientific talent for the 'in-house' Weapons System Evaluation Group. Private sector skills can be tapped which might not be available for direct government employment. This is the analogue on the American side to the 'escape' theory propounded by Warden D. N. Chester at the Ditchley Conference in explaining the rise of quasi-public bodies in British administration.

35. E.g., Aerospace, Project Upward Bound, A.E.C. contracting with industry for atomic weapons development on the American side; perhaps the Mental Welfare Commission, Parole Board, Marriage Guidance Council on the British side.

36. Normanton, *The Accountability and Audit of Governments*, p. 317, reports, for example, that construction is cheaper by contract. In the United States a series of Budget Bureau circulars designed to instruct the executive departments on when and when not to contract out activities has consistently weighted the cost calculations which the departments were to make strongly in favour of contracting. The

latest Bureau of the Budget circular in the series, Circular A-76 issued on 3 March 1966 has, however, made the cost-comparison factors to be observed by the executive departments less heavily weighted towards the contract approach.

37. For example, the Budget Bureau Bulletin 60–2 issued in September 1959 in the series mentioned in the previous note stated in part: 'It is the general policy of the administration that the Federal Government will not start or carry on commercial-industry activity to provide a service or product for its own use if such a product or service can be procured from private enterprise through ordinary business channels.'

The reasons for resorting to the contract device in the United States are not greatly dissimilar from the reasons why Britain had devolved authority upon quasi-non-governmental institutions, as developed by D. N. Chester at Ditchley and discussed by Professor Hague in his 'The Ditchley Conference: A British View'.

38. Most government contracts contain a clause specifying that the contractor must hire without regard to race, colour, creed and, more recently, sex. Sometimes the use of the contract to promote collateral social and economic objectives can become a subject of intense controversy. Such a circumstance arose in the conflict between Comptroller General Elmer B. Staats and the Labour Department in the fall of 1969 over the so-called Philadelphia Plan designed to place greater emphasis on minority hiring in federal construction contracts. See Paul Delaney, 'Schulz Defends Minority Hiring', in *New York Times*, 7 Aug 1969, p. 23. For a general discussion of the problem of using such contract clauses for the purposes of social control, see Miller, in *New York University Law Review*, XXXVI (May 1961) 958–66.

39. *Preferential Procurement Practices to Further State Urbanization Policies* (Advisory Commission on Intergovernmental Relations, Washington, D.C., 1968).

40. Weidenbaum, *The Modern Public Sector*, pp. 13–14.

41. See the sources cited in nn. 58, 59 and 60 for examples of the subtle (and sometimes not so subtle) ways in which the government may 'overcontrol' the contractor and add regulations that are even more burdensome than with direct government operations.

42. *Staats Statement before the Sub-Committee on Economy*

in Government, Joint Economic Committee, 11 Nov 1968, p. 2.

43. Weidenbaum, *The Modern Public Sector*, pp. v–vi.

44. Of the $172·4 billion federal budget for F.Y. 1968, $44 billion went to fixed transfer payments and $10·8 billion to net interest on the national debt.

45. These and the following figures come from Weidenbaum, *The Modern Public Sector*, pp. 9–10.

46. An inquiry begun under the direction of Professor Mackenzie, the preliminary results of which are briefly summarised by Professor Douglas Hague in the next chapter, has begun to turn up evidence of a surprising number of semi-autonomous bodies of varying degrees of independence from the formal government. See also J. W. Grove, 'Grants-in-Aid in Public Bodies', in *Public Administration*, xxx (winter 1952) 299–314.

47. Drucker, *The Age of Discontinuity*, p. 233.

48. Ibid., p. 234.

49. In Jean Brand and Lowell H. Watts (eds.), *Federalism Today* (Graduate School Press, U.S. Dept of Agriculture, Washington, D.C., 1969), pp. 46–7 and 53.

50. Interest group activity is a salient fact of life in British as in U.S. administration. See, *inter alia*, Samuel H. Beer, 'Representation of Interests in British Government', in *American Political Science Review* (1957) 613–51, and Samuel E. Finer, *Anonymous Empire* (Pall Mall Press, London, 1962).

51. This is the solution of what might be termed the administrative 'purists' or 'traditionalists' on both sides of the Atlantic. Theodore J. Lowi, for example, in his critique of 'interest group liberalism' in *The End of Liberalism* wishes to see interest representation pushed 'a giant step back' from the centre of the policy process so that the role of private interests is diminished in policy and the primacy of public purpose becomes firmly re-established. Lowi's position is essentially an overstatement of a sound view. It is an overstatement because the traditionalist view would pose an artificial separation between government and society – government normally cannot and should not be as insulated from interest group pressures in shaping policy alternatives as this position would urge. Nor is it possible to control the administrative process by strict delegation as closely as this position imagines.

52. See Robinson, 'Government Contracting for Academic

Research: Accountability in the American Experience', below, esp. pp. 108–13.

53. Lowi, *The End of Liberalism*, ch. 10.

54. Administrative law theorists (see the sources cited in n. 5) not infrequently are found among the major proponents of greater reliance upon explicit administrative rule-making. The difficulty with the view is that formal rule-making can comprise only a limited part of the administrative process. The view does as little justice to the difficulties of the administrator's task as the 'strict constructionist' position does to the task of a Supreme Court Justice interpreting the constitution.

55. *Report to the President on Government Contracting for Research and Development* (the Bell Report), reprinted in *Systems Development and Management*, Hearings before a Sub-Committee of the Committee on Government Operations, House of Representatives, 87th Congress, 2nd Session, pt 1, 191–337; and *The Civil Service*, vol. 1: *Report of the Committee 1966–8 under the Chairmanship of Lord Fulton* (Cmnd 3638, H.M.S.O., London, June 1968.

56. See the discussion of this point in the paper by Roger Williams in this volume.

57. Similarly, James W. Fesler, *Area and Administration* (University of Alabama Press, 1949) points out that lack of co-ordination among federal agencies in the field in federal–state relations is often the result of lack of co-ordination at the Washington level.

58. Don K. Price, 'Federal Money and University Research', in *Science*, CLI (21 Jan 1966) 285–90.

59. See the paper by Murray Weidenbaum in this volume and also his *The Modern Public Sector*.

60. Pifer, in *Annual Report, 1967* (Carnegie Corporation), and the papers by Jack Ruina in this volume.

61. The federal efforts to involve the poor in the running of programmes have not always had the desired effects. Kenneth Clark, for example, has argued in *A Relevant War Against Poverty* that the participation of the poor has often meant, in practice, the manipulation of the poor by the 'povertycrats' who run the programmes. On the notion of 'participatory democracy' generally, see Michael Walzer, 'A Day in the Life of a Socialist Citizen: Two Cheers for Participatory Democracy', in *Dissent* (May–June 1968) 243–7.

62. Speech by Kingman Brewster, President of Yale University, reprinted in *New York Times*, 25 Sept 1969, p. 41.

63. See *Biomedical Science and Its Administration – A Study of the National Institutes of Health* (The White House, Washington, D.C., Feb 1965) pp. 191–213; and 'Advisory Councils and N.I.H. Contracts', in the *Report of the Secretary's Advisory Committee on the Management of N.I.H. Research Contracts and Grants, U.S. Dept of Health, Education and Welfare, March 1966*, pp. 9–23 (excerpted in Michael D. Reagan, *The Administration of Public Policy* (Scott, Foresman, Glenview, Ill., 1969) pp. 214–21.

64. Wallace S. Sayre, 'Premises of Public Administration: Past and Emerging', in *Public Administration Review*, XVIII (spring 1958) 105.

65. Normanton, *The Accountability and Audit of Governments*, Harvey C. Mansfield, *The Comptroller General* (Yale University Press, New Haven, Conn., 1939), and Joseph P. Harris, *Congressional Control of Administration* (Anchor Books, Garden City, N.Y., 1965) ch. 6.

66. The General Accounting Office has contracted with private audit firms on occasion when its work load has become excessive. Any extensive use of outside assistance would involve the audit agency in the same kinds of problems as confront the regular executive department when it relies extensively on outside assistance – its capabilities would be enhanced but at the cost of devolving authority to persons or institutions outside its direct management control.

67. The conflict between the G.A.O. and Labour Department over the Philadelphia Plan designed to combat union discrimination against minority group hiring in the construction industry perhaps illustrates the difficulties an innovative programme might face from intensified audit scrutiny.

68. Normanton, 'Public Accountability and Audit: A Reconnaissance', pp. 311–45 below. In certain respects, he appears to view the audit agency as a superior alternative, in achieving effective accountability, to the legislative process. In Normanton's view, strengthening the audit agency is a preferable and more realistic course in the British constitutional context than enlarging the staff and responsibilities of parliamentary committees.

69. Howell, 'Public Accountability: Trends and Parliamen-

tary implications', pp. 238–45. For a critique of the reasons why a substantial departure from traditional practices seems unlikely, see Nevil Johnson, *Parliament and Administration* (Allen & Unwin, London, 1966) and also Professor Johnson's contribution to this volume.

70. The desire to reduce the scope of detailed congressional intervention in the administrative process doubtless has been a tacit motive behind some efforts by executive departments in the United States to delegate authority via the contract to private and quasi-governmental bodies. But the tactic has not always worked or worked for long. Congress has become involved on occasion even in the details of contract negotiation, and when contractor performance falls short on a major issue congressional intervention is likely. See Robert J. Alt, *The T.F.X. Decision: McNamara and the Military* (Little, Brown, Boston, Mass., 1968) and David E. Lilienthal, *T.V.A.: Democracy on the March* (Harper & Brothers, New York, 1953) pp. 125–7 and 168–85.

71. Harold P. Green and Alan Rosenthal, *Government of the Atom: The Integration of Powers* (Atherton Press, New York, 1963) and Harold Orlans, *Contracting for Atoms* (Brookings Institution, Washington, D.C., 1967), ch. VII. For other examples of detailed congressional intervention in the administrative process, see Harris, *Congressional Control of Administration*, ch. 8, 'The Legislative Veto', and the sources cited there, and also Raymond H. Dawson, 'Congressional Innovation and Intervention in Defense Policy: Legislative Authorization of Weapons Systems', in *American Political Science Review*, LVI (March 1963) 42–57.

72. Since in the American context the authority to contract generally requires explicit statutory authorisation, and since the details of administration are in general more subject to statutory regulation than in Britain, this can be a factor of some importance. Theodore Lowi's call for a return to 'juridical democracy' envisages the legislative power asserting itself, not merely over the delegation of authority to bodies outside the framework of the government but over the discretionary power enjoyed by officials within the executive departments as well. The Congress, under this view, would confer only such discretionary authority as would be exercised in strict accord with explicit legislative guidelines. Once

again Lowi overstates the case. This proposal would merely shift the locus of the administrative process without, in practical terms, solving any of the problems attendant upon the exercise of discretionary authority.

73. Vernon Van Dyke, *Pride and Power: The Rationale of the Space Program* (University of Illinois Press, Urbana, Ill., 1964), chs XII and XIII.

74. The notion of a 'collective' or 'public good' (i.e. those goods not usually produced by the workings of the competitive market) is explicated in Mancur Olson, *The Logic of Collective Action* (Harvard University Press, Cambridge, Mass., 1965); Francis M. Bator, *The Question of Government Spending: Public Needs and Private Wants* (Collier Books, New York, 1962); and Garrett Hardin, 'The Tragedy of the Commons', in *Science,* CLXII (1968) 1243. A mathematical proof is in Stephen A. Marglin, 'The Social Rate of Discount and the Optimal Rate of Investment', in *Quarterly Journal of Economics,* LXVII (Feb 1963) 95–111.

75. In New York City there has apparently been a recent increase in the number of private institutions seeking to exercise public functions. A not-for-profit membership corporation on New York's West Side with which I am associated, the Morningside Citizen's Coalition, Inc., encountered difficulties in its incorporation. The Attorney General's Office of New York State was worried about the breadth of our charter in light of the activities of some neighbourhood corporations (e.g. opening up welfare centres in competition with city agencies, running public schools 'for the people', claiming governmental powers by virtue of a conception of neighbourhood sovereignty) and our lawyer was forced to redraft our charter to stress explicitly our educational and research purposes. Sayre and Kaufman have observed, in *Governing New York City* (Norton, New York, 1965), p. 77, 'no careful census of ... non-governmental groups in the city has ever been made, but the number seems to run at least to tens of thousands'. The number and diversity of the city's private groups, many of which already seek to influence various aspects of the governmental process, defy easy efforts to involve 'society' formally in carrying out programmes without bringing vast confusion to the administration of public affairs.

68

76. On the plebiscite as an example of direct democracy in action, see Raymond E. Wolfinger and Fred I. Greenstein, 'The Repeal of Fair Housing in California: An Analysis of Referendum Voting', in *American Political Science Review*, LXII (Sept 1968) 753–69; on the political characteristics of small constituencies, see James Madison, Federalist X and Grant McConnel, *Private Power and American Democracy* (Knopf, New York, 1966), ch. 4; and on government 'close to the people', see Philip Selznick, *T.V.A. and the Grass Roots* (Harper Torchbooks, New York, 1966), James W. Davis, Jr, and Kenneth Dolbeare, *Little Groups of Neighbors* (Markham, Chicago, 1968) and Roscoe Martin, *Grass Roots*, 2nd edn (University of Alabama Press, 1964).

77. John M. Gaus, 'The Responsibility of Public Administration', in Dwight Waldo (ed.), *Ideas and Issues in Public Administration* (McGraw-Hill, New York, 1953), p. 437.

78. Hague, 'Accountability, Independence and Management Science', ch. 16 below.

79. Kingman Brewster speech in *New York Times*, 25 Sept 1969, p. 41.

80. Miller, in *New York University Law Review*, XXXVI (May 1961) 982.

81. The 'accountability of the graveyard' is possible with fear driving persons to perform their assigned tasks, as memorably described in Alexsandr Solzhenitsyn, *The First Circle*, but this is a course as self-defeating as it is injurious to the human spirit.

82. The act of delegating authority creates mutual obligations between superior and subordinate, and makes the superior in a subtle but palpable sense accountable to the subordinate. Yet this close mutual dependence normally does not, and should not, diminish the 'stuff of command' which is the trademark of the artful executive. For a classic experimental study showing that the most permissive management does not necessarily produce superior employee performance, see Nancy C. Morse and Everett Reimer, 'The Experimental Change of a Major Organizational Variable', in *Journal of Abnormal and Social Psychology*, LII ii (March 1956) 120–9.

2 The Ditchley Conference: A British View

D. C. Hague

The initial British interest in arranging a conference on the general problem of accountability and independence sprang from a feeling that the narrower problem of how to combine accountability with independence in the nationalised industries had not yet been solved. Several of us felt that the decision to turn the Post Office into a 'commercial' undertaking made it likely that future British governments, of whatever party, would devolve an increasing range of activities to what Alan Pifer has christened 'quasi-non-governmental' organisations, though it was only late in the conference that Professor Mackenzie reminded us of the term. Indeed, initially, almost the whole British delegation seemed rather taken aback by the concept. However, the issues of accountability and independence in quasi-non-governmental organisations were at once accepted as important ones.

I think it is fair to say that it was only during the Ditchley Conference that most of the British delegation began to realise the scale of the problem we were tackling. At first, we felt some humility in the discussions because we realised that we could not produce examples of contracting to equal the more spectacular parts of the American defence and space programmes. We also realised that the American side had come to Ditchley primarily interested in discussing problems of contracting, not of nationalised industries. Nevertheless, we consoled ourselves by thinking that there was a good deal of contracting in Britain in the defence and aviation fields, not least with Concorde, and that there were lessons still to be learned. We also realised that government departments themselves were contracting out an increasing range of work on economic, social and managerial problems.

As the conference went on, the Americans seemed to put

more emphasis on the activities of quasi-non-governmental organisations, and less on contracting with the private sector. This, I think, made the British side feel finally convinced that the issues being discussed were important ones in both countries and that we could therefore learn a great deal from each other.

We also came to see that if one defined anything which was not actually a government department as a quasi-non-governmental organisation, then there were far more of these organisations in the United Kingdom than most of us had recognised. Under the direction of Professor Mackenzie in Glasgow. Mrs Fanny Mitchell has been drawing up a list of quasi-non-governmental organisations in Britain. It is already clear that there are more than seven hundred of them, and the following list of about sixty gives an impression of the kind of organisation we are dealing with. The classification begins with those organisations that seem to be 'closest' to government and moves on to ones that are progressively less 'close'. However, it must be emphasised that this is only a preliminary classification. Further work is being done in Glasgow by Professor Mackenzie and Mrs Mitchell to see what light a number of alternative classifications throw on the nature of quasi-non-governmental organisations and the way in which they operate.

List of Quasi-Non-Governmental Organisations[1]

Law Commission
Parliamentary Commissioner
Bank of England
Land Commission
Air Transport Licensing Board
Mental Welfare Commission
Parole Board
Countryside Commission
Race Relations Board
Monopolies Commission
Cinematograph Films Council
Water Resources Board
Medical Practices Committee
Regional Hospital Boards

Crofters Commission
Decimal Currency Board
Community Relations Commission
Location of Offices Bureau
Charity Commission
Shipbuilding Industry Board
Forestry Commission
Highlands and Islands Development Board
University Grants Committee
Arts Council
Consumer Council
Scottish Special Housing Association
Cotton Industry Training Board
Industrial Reorganisation Corporation
Covent Garden Market Authority
British Broadcasting Corporation
Independent Television Authority
Sugar Board
Horse Race Totalisator Board
New Towns Commission
Cumberland New Town Development Corporation
Gas Consultative Councils
Domestic Coal Consumer Council
British Council
British Airports Authority
British Overseas Airways Corporation
British Steel Corporation
Central Electricity Generating Board
Gas Council
Electricity Council
Area Gas Boards
Area Electricity Boards
British Railways Board
Regional Railway Boards
National Film Finance Corporation
General Practice Finance Corporation
Health Education Council
White Fish Authority
British Sugar Corporation Ltd.
British Standards Institution
General Nursing Council

Central Midwives Board
Marriage Guidance Council
General Medical Council

At first sight, the problems of classification seem to be almost insuperable, though this is partly because the foregoing list usually gives only one example of each different kind of organisation. The difficulty of classification becomes clearer when one asks why the nationalised industries are seen as 'further' from government than the Regional Hospital Boards, or the Monopolies Commission. The main reason is that the current revenues of nationalised industries come mainly from their trading operations and not directly from government, as with the Regional Hospital Boards and the Monopolies Commission. Perhaps this shows that the source of current revenues has been given too much weight in this initial classification of quasi-non-governmental organisations. If so, this simply emphasises the point that I am trying to make – that classification is not easy and that it is best not to prejudge the work now being done in Glasgow, as we should be if we tried to give more than this preliminary list of organisations, classified in the tentative way.

Another way of getting an impression of the scale on which quasi-non-governmental organisations operate is to consider the amounts of money they receive from the government. All the figures are from the 1969–70 estimates. For grants, the total is £3150 million. Of this, £2800 million is for government departments and local authorities and only £350 million for quasi-non-governmental organisations, though of course this is a substantial sum. Grants-in-aid differ, in that the audit procedure is less detailed and money left over at the end of the financial year does not have to be returned to the Treasury. The total for grants-in-aid in the year 1969–70 is estimated to be £375 million, of which £350 million is for quasi-non-governmental organisations. The figure for spending on research and development is more difficult to work out. The total amount that we have been able to identify in the estimates to be spent on research and development is £250 million. Of this, about £65 million goes to quasi-non-governmental organisations, and a further £25 million to private industry. It is obviously a matter for argument whether this £25 million is to be regarded as expenditure on quasi-non-governmental organisations or not. Finally, there are contracts. These total £400 million and include a further £250 million for research and development. Very little of this money seems to go to quasi-non-governmental organisations in the strict sense. Something like £130 million is spent on research and development work in industry and a further £2½ million on work in universities and research bodies. £75 million is for work under contract carried out with other governments. This includes building the Concorde with France, and guided weapons with Australia. Despite the problems of separating out money going to quasi-non-governmental organisations, if these kinds of amounts go to some seven hundred of them, they are clearly 'big business'.

After the Ditchley Conference, even though it was extremely interesting for those who took part, most of us realised that all we had done was to find the right questions to ask about contracting and about quasi-non-governmental organisations. Alan Pifer described the conference as 'the start of systematic consideration of a new phenomenon in the art of government'. One danger was certainly avoided – that of spending too much time defining terms. I am perpetually fascinated by how much time businessmen in small group discussions, at courses or conferences, will spend in deciding what words mean. Yet business-school teachers discussing the same problems often assume that everyone knows the meanings of all the words used – unless and until difficulties in discussion make the clear definition of some terms necessary. At Ditchley, we followed the latter course. Indeed, towards the end of our meetings, Professor Mackenzie noted that the conference had successfully avoided defining basic terms like 'delegation', 'authority', 'democratic', 'responsibility', 'government', 'public' and 'public interest'.

Since this is a British view of the Ditchley Conference, I shall concentrate on the problem of quasi-non-governmental organisations, because these are what especially concern us in Britain. Obviously, having identified the kind of organisation we mean, the first question to ask is why quasi-non-governmental organisations came into being. Dr Chester suggested four reasons for them. First, the 'buffer' theory saw them as a way of protecting certain activities from political interference.

74

Second, the 'escape' theory saw them as escaping known weaknesses of traditional government departments. Sir William Armstrong enlarged on this, suggesting that the desire was for independence from the financial controls and checks of Parliament and from the rules, regulations and salary scales of the bureaucracy. Third, the 'Corson' theory, following Mr John Corson, wanted to use them to 'put the activity where the talent was', and this might be outside government departments.[2] Against this, however, Alan Pifer suggested that it might prevent one building up, within the government bureaucracy, a group of people with the right abilities. Fourth, the 'participation' or 'pluralistic' theory thought it desirable to spread power. In Nevil Johnson's words, 'the more centres of responsibility the better'.

Professor Mackenzie added a fifth reason for the development of quasi-non-governmental organisations. He pointed out that where a taxi-driver found the main streets too busy, he would use back streets – what were known to taxi-drivers as 'back doubles'. The 'back-double' theory was therefore that if governments, local authorities or other groups found that they could not do things they wanted to do within the existing structure, they would set up new organisations which made it possible to do them. Professor Mackenzie suggested that it might be helpful for academics to work out what kind of structure such 'administrative back doubles' produced. The textbook version of how British central and local government allows for public participation is not very satisfactory.

Finally, the 'too-many-bureaucrats' view, mainly an American one, suggested that if the public thinks a country has too many civil servants, one way of extending government activities without increasing the number of civil servants is to set up quasi-non-governmental organisations whose employees are then not classified as civil servants.

Having defined what was meant by quasi-non-governmental organisations, and having decided why they have been set up in such large numbers, the conference had to decide what it meant by accountability, independence and control. On accountability, the main job of definition was done by Professor Robinson in his paper. He distinguishes three types of accountability. First, there is 'programme' accountability, where those in an organisation are held responsible for the tasks that it performs – the objectives it pursues. Second, there is 'process' accountability, where one is concerned with whether the way the particular programme or task has been carried out is satisfactory. Finally, there is 'fiscal' accountability, where the emphasis is on ensuring that all money has been spent fairly and honestly on the purpose for which it was granted.

During the conference, the concept of 'social' accountability was also developed. This gave rise to a certain amount of difficulty, largely, I think, because we were confusing two things. What some people meant by 'social' accountability was that some organisations would have as part of their objectives – as part of their programmes – the aim of helping a particular part of society. I think we all finally agreed that this was really just a part of programme accountability. However, I think we agreed that there was also accountability *to* society instead of to auditors, governments or other bodies. It seems to me that the term 'social' accountability is therefore best applied to a situation where those responsible for programme, process or fiscal accountability are responsible *to* society. Professor Flowers, for example, pointed out that when the Science Research Council was asked whether its scientific judgements were good, this was a sort of social accountability. The scientific community, as the representatives of the public, was asking whether the judgements made were the right ones.

At the same time, it is important to emphasise that Mr Staats insisted on several occasions that programme, process and fiscal accountability are really three aspects of the same question. For example, it is possible to discover that problems of fiscal accountability have arisen in a particular institution by looking at its programme; that problems of programme accountability have arisen, by looking at fiscal matters and so on. The basic factor is the ability of the person doing the audit. A good auditor concerned with a fiscal audit should be able to identify problems in the programme and the process. If he fails to do so, then he is doing only part of his job. Mr Staats thought it was necessary to look at the process, because a good programme might well fail because of poor administration. Or it might have been a great deal more successful, even than it had been with better administration and controls. Mr Staats thought this was particularly true if the programme was a controversial one politically. Lack of integrity in fiscal or process accountability might then be used to destroy a programme that could otherwise have been very important. I think Mr Staats convinced most of us that accountability, like peace, is indivisible.

The conference found independence a good deal harder to define. One issue was whether independence was an end or a means. As one would expect, the American participants were more willing to see independence from government as valuable in itself, in sustaining the 'free enterprise system'. David Howell wondered whether those who wanted more contracting in the United Kingdom did so in a 'high-minded search for participation' or in a quest for greater managerial efficiency. At Ditchley, the overwhelming majority of participants appeared to see independence as a means to an end. They felt one would get better performance from quasi-nongovernmental organisations if they had greater independence. In the special case of science policy, Brian Flowers suggested that, at least in Britain, government departments would be incompetent in running research laboratories or research organisations directly. With day-to-day control by a government department, the whole objective and morale of such organisations could be very seriously affected. Independence was necessary for this reason.

Perhaps the most explicit comment on independence was by Sir William Armstrong. He thought that one of the facts of life was that a civil service had to work with ordinary human beings, only some of whom were intelligent, objective and hard-working. The search was for a system which got over those disadvantages of the human character which could not be changed, at least in the short run. History seemed to suggest that possible systems could be developed, but that these would always eventually degenerate because people would find ways of getting round them. From time to time it became necessary to replace the system. One could not do without one, because there were not enough intelligent, objective and energetic people to go round examining everything for themselves. One needed a system which would throw things up for general public inspection, so that one could rely on there always being somebody sufficiently intelligent and objective to be able to stop trouble. A system of institutions, and arrangements between institutions, was therefore a necessary evil.

Sir William went on to emphasise that the real advances were going to be made by people with talent. There was no doubt that it was very difficult to build a system which automatically produced creative and innovative people. They were frequently eccentric and difficult, and hated being confined within a system. If one was to provide not only managerial efficiency but also creativity, then a self-denying ordinance was necessary about how far one could go with accountability.

Of course, the essential proposition underlying the whole conference was that independence could not be total. Some degree of control over contractors was necessary. Just as a private contractor who wanted independence for himself would want to ensure that his own employees worked in the way he thought best, so a government delegating activity to a contractor would want to ensure that he performed the task that he was given well.

In fact, the conference spent less time in discussing control than in discussing independence. The title of the conference itself – accountability and independence – implied a tension between a phenomenon (independence) and a process (accountability). The true tension, it seems to me, is between two phenomena – independence and control. It follows that perhaps another reason why so little time was spent on defining control is that independence and control are simply opposites. Greater independence automatically means less control, and vice versa. One could use one term to imply both. One can talk of more independence, and automatically imply less control; or less control, and automatically imply more independence. Whatever the words used, there clearly is a tension here and no one at the conference disputed this.

What the conference did do was to spend a good deal of time discussing what was meant by a 'contract'. In the end, there seemed to be general agreement that there was no clear dividing line between a formal contract and much looser arrangements. Professors Mackenzie and Smith, for example, emphasised that grants and contracts were not to be con-

78

trasted but belonged together on a continuum. Professor Mackenzie thought that, in giving away public money, one did not do so unconditionally – one wanted something for one's money – though it was not clear what the conditions should be. Giving away money was a form of manipulation, not of generosity. The conditions could be very vaguely defined at the extreme representing grants but one moved along the continuum to a contractual situation with a contractual document. He thought that the contractual document could actually turn out to be much looser and more speculative than the conditions implied, in a general way, in making a grant. For Professor Mackenzie this had illuminated why the Social Science Research Council ran into difficulties when it tried to place research contracts rather than give research grants. There was simply no sharp difference. One could make a difference in legal form and enforceability, he supposed, but in each case there was a conditional agreement of some kind.

To simplify the remainder of what I have to say, I shall use the word 'contractor' or 'contract' in the broadest sense to cover *all* situations where authority is delegated to an organisation to carry out an activity. I shall do this whether the delegation is by a formal contract or not. In other words, I shall describe all quasi-non-governmental organisations, as well as all private industry working on government contract, as contractors. Indeed, in this sense, one could describe a ministry as a contractor.

We can now move on beyond definition to matters of substance. Although no one at Ditchley said so explicitly, I think the consensus was that independence should be given in deciding on processes, rather than on programmes. At most, the contractor can expect to be allowed to help to decide on his programme in consultation with those to whom he is accountable. No one at Ditchley supposed that explicit programmes were always drawn up. Yet if this is not done the contractor can never be properly accountable. There is nothing precise for which he can account.

What I think that participants at Ditchley were implicitly saying was that, once the programme has been decided, the maximum amount of independence should be given to the contractor to decide how these objectives can best be

D

achieved. Process accountability will then be concerned with whether the job of carrying out the programme has been done well – in the sense of giving a good balance between costs incurred and results achieved. Fiscal accountability will concentrate on ensuring that the contractor's independence has not been used to spend money improperly, but in imposing as little burden as possible while doing so. Independence is now independence from unnecessarily restrictive rules, regulations and checks – independence from the 'candle-ends' mentality of the traditional accountant or auditor.

If I am right, independence is mainly concerned with the processes used to achieve the aims of the programme, and with ensuring that no unnecessarily bureaucratic rules are imposed to guarantee fiscal accountability. If independence were given to each contractor to determine his own programme this would be more likely than not to lead to inefficiency, or chaos, or both. There may be exceptions to this. Are the universities one?

This leads me to an interesting point which did not come out in the Ditchley discussions, but which I now feel underlay them all. This is that the objectives of any programme of the kind that we are discussing cannot be broader than the objectives of the whole organisation pursuing this programme. If an objective appears in an organisation's programme, then it must be an objective of that organisation. However, while they cannot be broader, the objectives in the programme may be narrower than those of the organisation. An organisation may not be pursuing all its aims in a particular programme. Though simple, I think that this distinction helps to clarify a good deal of what was said at Ditchley.

To return to the main argument, it seems to me that too much interference from outside the contracting organisation in determining programmes will also be undesirable. As the conference proceeded, I became more and more worried that, when it came to the point, participants were more anxious for control over contractors than for their independence. One of the facts emphasised by those in Carnegie Tech. at Pittsburgh, who have developed the behavioural theory of the firm, is that control systems tend to be symmetrical and not asymmetrical, as most people imagine. Control systems ostensibly allow superiors to control subordinates, but in fact allow subordinates to control superiors as well. A subordinate to whom a task has been delegated, or a budget granted, is often able to point to the initial delegation of authority or granting of money and to use this to insist that the superior must not change his mind about how the job is to be done, at any rate during the budget period. At Ditchley, we had the added phenomenon of Parliamentarians and Congressmen who themselves wanted to take part in the formulation of programmes, or even processes. After the government had delegated activities to government departments or quasi-non-governmental organisations, they wanted to help them to decide on their programmes and processes. In fairness, I must add that the British Parliamentarians at Ditchley concentrated on seeking greater control over the programmes of government departments rather than over quasi-non-governmental organisations.

We came to Ditchley to discuss better ways of delegating authority in order to give contractors greater independence. Yet there were moments when we seemed to be advocating the opposite. We seemed to suggest that everyone should have the right to interfere with everyone else in deciding on programmes – if not on processes: that all of us were accountable and wanted to hold others accountable. The fact that a conference convened to discuss how greater independence could be given to contractors was in danger of ending by asking for that independence to be taken away shows just how tricky the problem of balancing accountability against independence really is. I am not saying that all organisations should be completely free to decide on programmes; I have just argued the opposite case. But the number of people involved must be limited. The back-bencher's proclivity to want to interfere in everyone else's business has to be watched. The truth may be that provided processes are completely delegated, there is a lot to be said for involving rather more people, and not fewer, when deciding on programmes. However, this is a difficult problem to which I shall return later.

It seems to me that the papers, especially Professor Robinson's, suggest a number of models through which the problem of accountability can be studied. I think that partial models only can be used at present, partly because this is an early

81

stage in our study of accountability, but partly because the human brain finds it difficult to deal with too many variables at once.

The simplest model would be one with independence and control seen as the two key elements. For any individual contractor, the tension between them would be removed by giving him a contract. This would give him a degree of independence, but at the price of laying down a procedure for making him accountable – subjecting him to audit. The body giving the contract has the control it seeks, while the contractor has an adequate degree of independence.

A second model might explicitly separate out two parallel systems. One would identify the main aspects of the contractor's operations; the other would identify the main elements in the system used to guarantee accountability. Let us suppose, for example, that the contractor is engaged in research or on production. In either case, he will have a programme, a process and a result achieved. This will be the system within which the activity takes place. Alongside this there will be the accountability organisation, which will also have three phases. Here, the aim may be a bigger one – what one might call a super-aim. There will be a super-aim if the accountability process is used to obtain wider improvements, covering production or research by other contractors. The accountability side is then to be seen as either, looked at narrowly, ensuring the accountability of one contractor – making certain that he has completed his work well. Or it may be a more dynamic accountability, leading perhaps to an improvement in a part or all of the whole contracting system.

This immediately leads to the third model. Different aspects of the contractor's activity will be especially important to particular parts of his organisation. For example, those at the top will be more concerned with programmes; those lower down with processes. There will be a similar division in the accountability system. Various parts of the bureaucratic machine for ensuring accountability will be interested in programme, process and fiscal accountability respectively. For example, government departments and the legislature will be particularly concerned with fiscal accountability; the bureaucracies of the university, research institute and government department in process accountability; and

82

the contract, research or programme officer of the body providing funds in programme accountability.

Devising a successful accountability system is not simply a matter of deciding what would be the correct mix between these three types of accountability. One must go on to ask what problems arise in the two organisational structures if emphasis is put on any one of these three kinds of accountability. What kind of institutional arrangement in the contractor's organisation, and in the auditing organisation, gives a satisfactory mix of all three kinds of accountability, in given circumstances? What one wants is no tension, or more realistically a condition of optimal tension. It seems to me that, in many fields, we mislead ourselves into supposing that the best situation is one where there is no tension at all within an organisation. In the world we live in, the much more realistic question is how we can best get an optimal degree of tension. We should note that Professor Mackenzie said during the conference that he favoured the model of optimal tensions, because he felt that 'risk-taking is the nobler course; that conflict is tied up with participation and creativity, whereas mutual harmony, by contrast, seems a soporific idea'.

The final model which seems useful to me is one which represents a different aspect of accountability along each axis of a two-dimensional diagram. Admittedly, the real problem will be multi-dimensional, and cannot therefore be shown on the page of a book. However, some idea of what I mean can be obtained from Fig. 2.

Here, the horizontal axis represents the degree of complexity of the activity. This may range from, say, a repeat order for something simple like a rifle, at the left-hand end, to something quite new and complex, like a spaceship, at the right-hand end. Similarly, the vertical axis indicates the kind of organisational arrangements needed to supervise the contractor. Here, say, a single researcher responsible to a research council might be at the bottom and a complex partnership between the legislature, executive and contractor at the top.

At Ditchley I think we all agreed early in the conference that the important problems for Britain lay in the 'middle range' of both axes. The problems of handling repeat orders of rifles had been dealt with, but Britain was not yet grappling with all the complexities of the space programme. Our organisational arrangements were also not yet very complex. We were mainly concerned with 'middle-range' problems, which were moderately, but not inordinately, complicated. This 'middle range' has been shaded in in a rough way in Fig. 2.

Of course, even this does not complete the picture. One really needs other axes. For example, accepting what Professors Smith and Mackenzie said about contracts and grants merging into each other along a single continuum, one could

Fig. 2

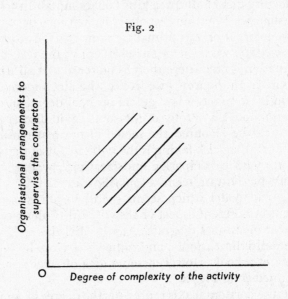

have a third axis which showed the complexity of the contract instrument or of the grant situation. Simple contracts would lie at one end of the third axis, closest to the origin, and complex ones at the other. Similarly, a fourth axis might show the degree of independence given to the contractor, and so on. It would not be realistic to claim that the conference really got to grips with all of these problems, though perhaps to have defined some of the issues precisely was a sufficient achievement in itself.

A major difficulty for all the participants was diagnosed by Professor Mackenzie. He said the conference had demonstrated to him what difficulties undergraduates faced in studying comparative government. At Ditchley we had been deal-

84

ing at a high level of sophistication, and indeed mystification, with the ideas of comparative government. The conference had begun with general concepts, but when the institutions of Britain and America had been placed side by side, this had been a move from the general to the particular. The particular, while extraordinarily rewarding, could never be fitted into a textbook on comparative government. The conference had represented for him, at least, a gain in comprehension, if not in clarity, about the possibilities and the difficulties of comparing institutions.

Even so, some useful progress was made. In particular, three kinds of suggestion were made about how the balance between control and independence in quasi-non-governmental organisations might be improved. David Howell, for example, emphasised the importance of defining the responsibilities of those working at each level in each organisation. He thought this might be done in terms of responsibility for programmes, processes and fiscal regularity. British experience seemed to show that if responsibilities were clearly defined at each level, then two things happened. First, considerably greater independence for contractors was possible. Second, the public or legislature could be told what was going on, and, if something went wrong, who was responsible. Mr Howell thought the case for more delegation of authority in the British public sector was strong. Independence could be established and maintained within a clearly defined pattern of responsibilities, and accountability could actually be increased. Mr Howell did not think that the allocation of responsibility had been clear enough in British nationalised industries. When a problem arose, neither the public nor the legislature was able to find out whose the fault had been. No one knew what the minister had previously told the chairman of the industry to do, or what the chairman had agreed to do. David Howell went on to complain that the relationship between the government and a nationalised industry 'often seems to disappear into the haze of after-lunch discussions between the sponsoring minister and the chairman of the nationalised industry'.

Rightly, I think, David Howell doubted whether the problems of making the nationalised industries accountable would be altered in essence if one denationalised them. He thought that, even if they were denationalised, one would still need to have rules governing the activities of these industries. So, one might well be led back to exactly the problems of account-ability and independence that one had started out to solve. This strikes me as an important point. The real issue at Ditchley was to see how we could achieve a satisfactory bal-ance between accountability and independence in a whole range of organisations. Unless the nationalised industries, or other quasi-non-governmental organisations, are to be pushed back wholly into the private sector, these problems are bound to remain. We shall not alter the essential problems discussed at Ditchley by giving a little more independence to organis-ations that remain neither wholly public nor wholly private. This leads on logically to the question of how to establish criteria by which we can judge the performance of quasi-non-governmental organisations.

I dealt with this problem at some length in my own paper, but would like to note some of the comments made at Ditch-ley by Sir William Armstrong. He thought that anyone pro-viding resources for a quasi-non-governmental organisation had to accept that if one wanted that organisation to develop managerial efficiency, or creativity, or a mixture of them, only very broad goals could be set and process and fiscal accountability could not be looked into too deeply. While this did not mean that fiscal accountability could be aban-doned, Sir William felt that it should not be allowed to con-trol the aims and purposes of particular exercises.

Sir William went on to suggest that the stage currently reached in Britain was that attempts were being made to find criteria, as far as possible non-burdensome ones, by which to judge the performance of public and semi-public bodies of a wide variety. Once these criteria were set, the bodies could then be given independence. However, Sir William did not feel that we had made very much progress in defining these criteria in the United Kingdom. On the whole, he thought it was easier to establish criteria for efficiency in the use of re-sources than in reaching goals and carrying out policies.

This emphasises a point implied in a good deal of what was said, that process accountability is often a good deal easier to arrange than programme accountability. It leaves open the difficult question of how far, once very broad criteria for judging them have been established, quasi-non-governmental organisations can be left to establish their own programmes and whether M.P.s or others should be involved in establishing them.

Sir William said that in making his comments he had tried to indicate the general spirit in which the British civil service was looking for criteria with which to judge quasi-non-governmental organisations. Faced with the bureaucratic syndrome, he thought it was possible to do one of two things: either one could go outside the bureaucracy, or one could try to reform it and improve its efficiency. Britain was, in effect, trying to do both.

The question of how to establish objectives for quasi-non-governmental organisations is linked to the question of how far accountability must be financial accountability. Sir William Armstrong, for example, suggested that accountability was ultimately a financial concept, so that the legislature sought to control the executive by controlling the finance made available to it. While this is true, perhaps we should try to avoid using the phrase 'financial control' so often met with in business – because it is ambiguous. It can mean control *over* finance; or control over an organisation, indirectly, *through* finance. As Sir William's remark implies, we are here concerned with obtaining control over the use of real resources by control over the provision of finance. What matters is to ensure that the real resources that governments and quasi-non-governmental organisations use are used efficiently. Controlling by the supply of finance and by looking at financial criteria is simply one way of doing this.

Financial measures are merely the most general measures of performance that we have, and perhaps we need to consider less general ones too. For example, Sir William Armstrong stressed that, in business, cash accounting had been superseded about a hundred years ago by a system of commercial accounting intended to give a clearer and fairer picture of the state of affairs in the business. This, in turn, was now regarded as insufficient for managerial purposes and various new forms of control and decision accounting – often devised by economists and operational researchers – were being introduced. Sir William noted that government departments were often thought of as being still at the cash accounting stage, and said that in many cases it was true that they were trying to jump to the third stage without passing through the second. I think there was general agreement with these sentiments at Ditchley. The conference certainly took the view that in providing for accountability we had to move beyond traditional accounting criteria to other, perhaps physical, measures of efficiency and performance.

I should like to turn now to what seemed to me to be the other two issues that were most important in the Ditchley Conference. The first of these, quite understandably given the number of M.P.s and Congressmen present, was the role of the legislature and attitudes towards it. This included the important question, touched on earlier, of how far the legislature should be involved in decisions on programmes. The lead here was given by Mr Staats. He thought the congressional discussion of programmes, as opposed to discussions of processes or of fiscal regularity, was a healthy phenomenon, particularly because it encouraged executive agencies to look at programme alternatives. He said there had been much discussion in the United States about the techniques of planning–programming–budgeting (P.P.B.), one feature of which was working out and setting down alternatives. P.P.B. was an instrument used by the executive branch, and the alternatives formulated by the executive were not made available to Congress. However, he could see that it might be possible for alternatives to be formulated by Congress, which could then ask for the appropriate analyses to be carried out by the executive. Mt Staats emphasised that he did not say this to deny Congress more staff, but because this did seem to be one aspect of accountability which could be improved by using the P.P.B. system.

Mr Staats said recent developments showed that the Congress intended the General Accounting Office to review the effectiveness of government programmes, though he repeated that he found it very difficult to separate the different kinds of accountability. The poverty programme, especially, had impressed upon him the difficulty of judging the efficiency of programmes separately from the efficiency of the processes used to carry them out. Mr Staats thought that since Congress held the executive responsible for results, perhaps it should hold the executive responsible for selecting the right alternatives as well. The executive had not always been willing to tell Congress which alternatives had been considered in arriving at a particular recommendation. This was why he did not think that Congress should rely on the P.P.B. system to give it accountability. Congress would have to go behind the programmes submitted in order to discover all the alternatives which had been considered. For example, Mr Staats pointed out that with the American supersonic transport numerous studies had been made by the executive, but only one proposal had been formulated for Congress. It was very difficult for the Congress to go behind such a proposal, because once an executive decision was made federal agencies had a duty to support it. It then had to be left to others outside, perhaps some of those who opposed the project, to try to bring out which information had been considered by the executive.

The American participants at Ditchley seemed to be agreed on the need for Congress to look at programmes, but they were less agreed on what was the best way of doing so. For example, Mr Brademas thought that Congress might itself need to contract out the task of formulating alternatives. Otherwise, it would be at the mercy of the executive on the details of alternatives. Mr Rumsfeld took a similar line, arguing that Congress simply was not given, indeed was even refused, statements of the alternatives considered by the executive, and the studies and analyses lying behind them. Yet the fault did not lie with the executive, but with Congress. Congress had the constitutional power both to insist on seeing the alternatives studied by the executive and to formulate its own alternatives. He thought that by becoming more involved in the decision-making process, Congress would be taking part in a dialogue which could be shared by the public, to whom ultimate accountability was owed. There would then be less chance of an unfavourable public reaction if a particular programme met with difficulties. Mr Rumsfeld thought this applied to the poverty and foreign aid programmes as well as to the allocation of resources to science.

Bruce Smith was not entirely happy about this. He thought that the essence of the unique contribution of Congress was to encourage lay criticism in a world run by experts. Like the executive, Congress could easily become the captive of its experts. The problem of contracting therefore remained that of building lay criticism into the accountability process itself, and not merely on a retrospective basis. At the same time, Congress must avoid blurring the fundamental responsibility of the executive for making critical decisions and running programmes. Professor Smith also pointed out that in Great Britain criticism of government decisions was mostly retro-spective, whereas in the United States the legislature and lay outsiders were both involved in policy formation. The way America used outsiders meant the loss of some elements of accountability, but this was balanced to some extent by a gain in, for example, legitimacy.

This point was taken up by both David Howell and Sir James Dunnett. On fiscal accountability, David Howell thought the problem was that Congress and Parliament needed to make more use of their G.A.O. and Comptroller and Auditor General respectively. The question then would be how far audits undertaken for the legislature should be developed and expanded from random investigations into systematic, regular and comprehensive reviews; from regularity audits perhaps to cost-effectiveness audits. He wondered if such a development was possible at all, given the size of modern government. There were some who argued that this was how to improve public accountability; to take fiscal accountability and build on it, while accepting that Parliaments were incapable of going into government activities in detail and therefore had to rely on outside audit staff to give them reports. This led to another question: How should Parliament receive such reports? A plenary session of Parliament would be incapable of subjecting them to rigorous or sophisticated debate.

However, the main issue raised in this context on the British side was how far the legislature could realistically participate in decision-making. David Howell wondered whether it made sense for a legislature, or its committees, to ask for a full explanation of what went on in various pro-grammes with the idea of pronouncing in detail on them. Perhaps what happens now, in Britain, is the best that can be done. Some improvements have recently been made and the government is now giving Parliament a five-year statement of public expenditure.

Sir James Dunnett wondered how valuable the full details of alternative programmes would be to Congress or Parliament, since they would have been worked through very thoroughly by the executive. In order to comment sensibly on them, it would first be necessary to do a great deal of study. There was then a risk that the legislature would be swamped by detail.

John Mackintosh wondered whether many permanent staff really would be needed in order to explain the Ministry of Defence's working papers fully enough for those members who specialised in defence to offer a reasonably informed commentary on the decisions that had been taken. Such an informal commentary might produce better discussions in the House of Commons, among the defence correspondents of the press, and among the informed and general public on the issues and options open to us in defence.

Sir James's answer was that it depended on the detail in which Parliament wanted to look at such problems. All Parliament might want was the long-term costings made by his department (which raised issues of its own) in order to have a general debate about the broad balance of the programme. Clearly, this did not require a great deal of skilled assistance. To go farther, and have a meaningful debate with the experts on matters of detail, Parliament would need to build up a very substantial staff.

As so often happens in conferences, all this left participants very much where they had been at the beginning. David Howell thought the conference showed that politicians in both countries must be ready to be a good deal more involved than they were traditionally supposed to be in what was usually called 'administration'. He thought that the other feature emerging from the conference, whether politicians liked it or not, was that administrative structures in both the United States and Britain were changing very considerably, and were going to change still more. Politicians had to change too. Even if they had not previously believed in parliamentary reform, they would have to accept that Parliament needed to adapt if it were to maintain its relations – however this was defined – with a changing administration.

Perhaps Nevil Johnson made the most thought-provoking remarks on this issue. He wondered whether the complexity of British and American society was so great that the problem of accountability and independence could not be solved at the central level at all. If Congress or Parliament imagined that they could make broad political accountability effective over the whole area of public and quasi-public activity, they were probably mistaken. His feeling was that the words, and therefore perhaps the ideas, that we used were not radical enough. Perhaps we needed to think in terms of decentralisation, dispersion or devolution, rather than of delegation. Given the scale and complexity of public-sector activity, we had to think in terms of distributing accountability. Nevil Johnson's view was that our thinking would not be right unless we began by getting away altogether from the idea of a centre which delegated, and thought instead of a situation in which there were more centres of responsibility in society, with accountability pushed down to lower levels. In the process, of course, we should make political accountability for certain things at a central level more manageable. Nevil Johnson thought we should accept that small societies, in Europe and elsewhere, had a good deal to teach us. There was a tendency to exaggerate the benefits of economies of scale, as had happened in the argument over local government in Britain.

Nevil Johnson's view that we should perhaps talk of dispersion rather than delegation leads to the final major topic of the conference – participation. It was inevitable that an Anglo-American conference in 1969 should spend a good deal of its time on this issue. We began from a remark made by Mr Harding, who asked whether participation was to be regarded as an objective or as a technique. His own view that it was a technique was shared by Professor Mackenzie. The latter did not think that problems of urban living and urban disorganisation in Glasgow were as bad as they were in New York, but they were bad enough. One of the things which Glasgow had to mobilise was a community organisation with government backing, to put some kind of human order into 'economically and geometrically designed housing estates for the working classes'. The objectives were tolerably clear, and were not likely to be achieved without participation, but Professor Mackenzie would be happier pointing to the objectives and telling the people involved that these could be obtained only with their participation. He supposed he was in favour of participatory democracy, but would prefer it to be instrumental rather than absolute. It is important to record that Mr Harding, while sharing these views, said that in the United States there was a strong body of opinion which saw participation as an objective. He felt that those holding such views perhaps had a higher version than bureaucrats like himself, though he thought of participation as a self-contained, passive, revolutionary procedure.

Not surprisingly, it was the Americans who had most to say about participation. Mr Brademas regarded the Community Action programmes as the 'wave of the future'. The report on them by Mr Staats's office, in spite of some criticisms, indicated that they had been effective in providing many Americans with an opportunity to get into the mainstream of public life, from which they had previously been excluded. All this meant a revolution, or at least an evolution, in ways of making public policy. Unless the United States moved in this direction, Mr Brademas suggested, an effective democracy in a country of 200 million people would simply not be possible. Mr Rumsfeld supported this, suggesting that it was important that there should be communication and dialogue between public and government – itself a form of accountability. Governmental secrecy had to be kept to a minimum. It was not enough for the government to be right, if it treated the British and American people as though their understanding was inferior to its own. In the end, governments would have to be accountable. In Mr Rumsfeld's view, the conference was not really discussing whether governments would be accountable but whether politicians were going to increase the accountability of government at a thoughtful and reasonable rate, or whether it was going to come through violent protest or revolution.

I think that everyone at Ditchley was especially interested in what Mr Harding had to say about participation. Since he was in control of the Office of Economic Opportunity programme, we felt he knew far more about participation than any of us. He thought that there was something very strange abroad in the United States. He and his colleagues were observing and forming part of a fascinating phenomenon. In a way, he said, the middle-class ruling generation was not

93

being completely honest in opening its doors to listen to the people that the poverty programme was serving. He and his colleagues listened to them in great numbers, as they came forward to express in an illiterate, inarticulate and sometimes irrational fashion, their frustration and anger. He and his colleagues listened, as they admitted to each other, with tongue in cheek; but underneath it all something very unusual, perhaps very significant, was taking place. It was not just the case of a condescending middle-class bureaucrat listening to an unmarried mother from Harlem protesting about a reduction in the amount of money spent on a programme she felt strongly about. The point was that underprivileged people were capable, perhaps for the first time, of becoming involved. It was extremely impressive. Where it would lead, or what effect it would have on Congress, he did not know. The same sort of thing was happening in the universities of other countries, but the degree of participation in the United States was unique and portended something very important for the future. It was an exciting and, at times, a rather frightening phenomenon.

Alan Pifer noted that participation had not been a major objective of the contract system in the United States before the poverty programme. There had been other objectives, but the poverty programme had added the participation of previously uninvolved groups. This had certainly given accountability a new dimension, and in a sense there was a conflict between two notions of accountability: to the providers of money and to the new participants. This seemed to Alan Pifer to be the heart of the problem in the poverty programme. Could government money be used to create institutions which, by their very nature and their rules of operation, were going to work under conflicting notions of accountability?

Mr Harding emphasised that one technique being used was for approximately one-third of people on programme boards, and an even greater percentage of employees, to be drawn from the poor. The supply of efficient management to the programme was thus very limited, both in terms of the time it had available and of its quality. This raised very serious problems about improving the programme and about accountability. For example, a project in Chicago had cost

94

$700,000, most of which he felt had been spent rather un-profitably. His organisation had been held accountable to Congress in the most determined fashion. There had been weeks of hearings, with front-page stories castigating not just the project but the whole programme. There had been little concern, at least on the part of those members of Congress who conducted the investigation, with the fact that this had been a social experiment for a purpose. It was true that the project had failed, but much bigger sums were wasted on experiments in the physical sciences. It was asking for trouble to spend so much money, without obvious result, on a social-science project which was politically unpopular both in Chicago and with the senior senator from Arkansas. The problem of accountability was then magnified. On the one hand, it became necessary to deal with groups of people not used to being held accountable; on the other, experiments had to be made in a field where little was known but where answers simply had to be found.

There was a good deal of doubt about the value of par-ticipation in the minds of some of the American participants. For example, Professor Sayre pointed out that the latest ex-periment in participation was the Model Cities programme. Here, 'three simultaneous green lights' were required for action – one at community level; one at City Hall; and one in Washington. Professor Sayre thought this could equally well turn out to be a formula either for consensus or for stalemate. Mr Goldberg was even more unhappy. He hoped that the community action and poverty programmes would not be the 'wave of the future'. While it was true that there was a great need for participatory democracy in the United States, America had too many local governments, and yet not enough local government. The United States had a penchant for creating special districts and for complicating the struc-ture of local government. Alongside the poverty programme, there was a massive social welfare programme, mainly of public assistance. While this had not been outstandingly suc-cessful, and while national standards were needed, a massive amount of money was being spent on public assistance without very much being achieved. The duplication caused by setting up the Community Action and poverty programmes would undercut American local government. Indeed, Mr Goldberg's view was that local government could then be written off in the United States.

Professor Smith was, in some ways, more sceptical than any other American participant. His view was that the poverty-participation element in the programmes was not entirely a felicitous development, because it was based on the implicit assumption that American institutions were inadequate, unrepresentative and unresponsive to the wishes of the American people. This was manifestly not the case. The new developments offered a kind of plebiscitarianism which worked against representative government. It was a politics of frenzy which would work in the long run against the orderly expression and resolution of community conflict through the normal representative processes. Professor Smith thought that these processes were the only form of government possible in the larger society. Thus he came to what he described as 'an autumn pessimism' about the use of the contract. Perhaps the United States had made too much use of contracts and so had reduced the capacity of the regular government machine. If progress were to be made, he thought it would have to come through the activities of traditional government departments. Yet this, too, left him troubled, because here one ran into the tendency of all agencies to decline 'under a sort of incapacitating bureaucratic arthritis'. So, he feared that the United States was condemned to experience 'an endless series of surges of innovation', followed by efforts to try to pick up the pieces after these frenetic periods of activity. Professor Smith came down in the end to the view that in the twentieth century one could not put forward a notion of *insouciance*. Chances had to be taken to cope with the enormous problems that existed. Experiments had to be conducted, even though this might create forces which sought to destroy the system.

While the British could not contribute very much to this debate on participation, David Howell raised a fundamental issue. He wondered whether part of the apparent need for participation in the United Kingdom was a result of inefficient systems for providing accountability. He contended that once we had new budgetary systems, more accountable management and more delegated authority, it would then be desirable to stand back and review the situation. Perhaps the demand which some people detected for even more participation, more regional government, more decentralisation, even for elected regional assemblies, would not be so strong. If Britain managed to make the operation of central government slightly less distorted and slightly more open and visible, then the demand for other forms of participation, while not being eliminated, would at least be diminished.

However, perhaps the most interesting contribution of all on the subject of participation was by Professor Mackenzie. He started from my observation that 'we were all accountable and wanted to hold others accountable'. He felt that this had interesting implications for mutual accountability. Perhaps the suggestion that we were all in turn accountants and accountable was one way of settling the difficult problem of the public and the private, the government and the others, and might even be the key to the word 'democracy'. It supposed a sort of mutuality in the administrative and political systems, and perhaps the revolutionary students had a point, in talking of pluralism and anarchy as possible models of self-government and accountable government. This loosely constructed model, of course, came up against the precisely constructed ideas which could be extracted from the terms 'delegation of 'authority' and 'democratic responsibility'. These were the two lucid and simplified hierarchical models, meaningful both to the academic professor and the man in the street.

One model, delegation of authority, was a system where the governmental boss was 'up there'. This was in everybody's interest, but if he were a good boss he would delegate. The other idea, democratic responsibility, was also acceptable, but it had always been easier for the Americans than for the British to talk in terms of 'we the people'. The phrase too easily reminded British students of the three tailors of Tooley Street, in the nineteenth century, who had signed a manifesto beginning: 'We the people of Great Britain.' 'We the people', of course, meant something different in the United States . . . or did it? But the idea could lead to a philosophical discussion about a recognisable but indefinable something, which was sharply in contrast with the hierarchical system of 'the boss'. Or was it perhaps the hierarchical system turned upside down, with 'we the people' as the boss, and the principle of delegation coming in from the other direction?

These were shrewd, but negotiable, political concepts.

Professor Mackenzie was surely right to treat this subject in this way, and in refusing to share the all-too-common view that everything that present-day students have to say about pluralism is obviously wrong. In commenting on events in Ulster, Mr Callaghan has taken it as axiomatic that anarchy is unacceptable. Fighting in the streets clearly is; but is anarchy of a kind quite so unbearable? Perhaps we all have lessons to learn from the Manchester Business School, which I would see as an example of 'responsible anarchy'. Since, in the Manchester Business School, we take the view that business problems are interdisciplinary, we have steadfastly resisted the idea that we should create the traditional, hierarchical structure of most British universities – with each professor the undisputed custodian of his own subject and department. The problem is that, by eliminating departments, one eliminates what is normally the focal point for the university teacher. For the individual, the solution has been to try to ensure that each member of the staff 'belongs' to some group, perhaps an interdisciplinary group planning a particular course. The hierarchical structure cannot be so easily replaced. It is impossible to prevent a pluralistic structure developing, with individuals taking decisions on their own initiative in a way that the normal university hierarchy would not allow. Yet the organisation survives and works well, though we sometimes wonder how. The answer, I am sure, lies in the fact that, particularly with a new institution, the loyalty of individuals to the organisation is high and their enthusiasm considerable. There must be more overlapping of teaching, and more unnecessary decisions taken, than in a more hierarchical structure. Yet decisions probably get taken more quickly, and the pluralistic structure certainly maintains the enthusiasm of the staff. Perhaps there is more in the idea of a pluralistic or anarchical society than many of us have imagined.

At the same time, I went away from Ditchley unhappy with what David Howell had said about the possibility that the problems of participation might largely fade away once we had a proper system of accountability. David Howell may well be right. Yet my own feeling is that one of the big problems in the twentieth century, certainly in Britain but perhaps throughout the world, is that we somehow have to create a new kind of system. We need national units which are big enough, in some aspects, to give countries the large markets and economies of scale which complex societies require. At the same time, within the nation, we need other units which are small enough to allow people to think and feel that they belong to them. Perhaps we shall somehow have to develop a system in which for the purposes of defence, foreign policy, international trade and so on we belong to a nation or an economic community; for the purposes of everyday living, perhaps we shall have to belong to something much smaller and more easily comprehended.

This introduction gives a very personal view of the Ditchley Conference. No doubt other participants would have emphasised other aspects, or would have mentioned points which I have not considered at all. Nevertheless, I hope that those who have read this introduction will be able to proceed to the rest of the book with a greater understanding of the atmosphere in which the papers which follow were discussed.

Notes

1. For this list, and for the statistics on grants, grants-in-aid and contracts, I am indebted to Mrs Fanny Mitchell.
2. A friend from a developing country has told me of an interesting variant of this. Because that country is short of civil servants, it is impossible for able men to leave the civil service. The result is that none enter. The government therefore contracts out a good deal of work to universities and other quasi-non-governmental organisations. The same men do the work outside the civil service as would have done it within, but they are not classified as civil servants, and cannot therefore be prevented from leaving their jobs!

PART TWO

The Institutions:
Industry, University and Others

3 Government Contracting for Academic Research: Accountability in the American Experience

David Z. Robinson

1. *Introduction*

The growing use of federal research grants and contracts with universities has led to a number of questions about the relationship between the federal government and academic institutions. One major question which has received increasing attention is *accountability*: How is the government to say whether the tax-payer has received adequate return for the funds invested in university research?

Of course, precise accountability in research and development – and indeed in many types of professional activity – is rarely attempted.

Unless the goal of the activity or research is defined very clearly and specifically, success becomes a matter for professional judgement. It is not hard to determine objectively whether a man gets to the moon, or whether a particular instrument meets particular specifications. It is much harder to find a measure of adequacy for legal counsel, for teaching ability, for government administration, for political representation. It is equally hard to define if a scientist or a laboratory has done a 'good job' of basic research.

This general problem of attempting quantitative accountability of the results of mental activity affects all the institutions with which the government contracts for research. Nevertheless, there are differences between universities and other institutions in their relationship to government agencies which have an impact on accountability. For one thing, universities have more prestige than other institutions with which the government contracts. This has definite advantages for the government with regard to its public image. If the Department of Commerce announces that M.I.T. will conduct a million-dollar study on transportation in the Northeast Corridor, few people will ask if the researchers working on it at M.I.T. are capable or if the study is worth while. An announcement that the same study would be undertaken by a government organisation or a commercial research company would be met with more scepticism and more questions. Similarly, when Michigan State University runs a long-term government contract in Vietnam, it lends a certain cachet to United States efforts there, even though the bulk of the people working on the contract have no connection at all with the University at Lansing, Michigan, or its faculty.

University prestige has disadvantages for contracting agencies as well. It is harder for the government to exert control over the operation of university contracts than of those with private industry. A government accountant can be readily cowed by university people, who have independent strength and the self-righteousness that those working in good causes normally have. It is often rather difficult to make professors understand what the government means by accountability. When things go badly, it is easy for a university president, or a group of university presidents, to write the President of the United States or the Secretary of Defence and to obtain a respectful hearing. This kind of access is normally not available to the president of an electronics firm or the director of a government laboratory. As an example of the power of academic prestige, the universities recently forced a change in government accounting policy so that they are reimbursed for the work of faculty members without having to account in detail for faculty time expenditure. Such a policy went against the deeply held beliefs of many accountants.

A second major difference between universities and other institutions lies in their goals. The *institutional* goals of a university are to teach, to perform good research (good in relation to its intrinsic quality, rather than its value to the sponsor) and to do public service. These goals are separate from – and may even conflict with – the goals of a government agency contracting for research. Industry, non-profits and government laboratories, on the other hand, are – in a

104

real sense – more responsive to the government agency that supports them. Now obviously, businesses are interested in making a profit as a primary goal, and that is not the goal of the federal agency buying research. However, usually the business organisation understands the goal of the agency and knows that its performance in responding to this goal will have some effect on its future profits. This difference in approach is one of the major factors affecting accountability in government–university relationships.

A third difference between universities and other performers of research and development is that universities have far less hierarchy. Nominally, funds for research projects are granted to the institution for the use of a faculty member. However, the university in practice allows the faculty member to be an independent director and has little control over his expenditures. If he leaves, his grant would be expected to go with him. Further, universities do not *assign* professors to research projects in the way an employee is assigned in industry. If more than one faculty member is to work on a project, the initiative must usually come from faculty. The university is therefore hampered in what it can do inside the normal structure. When large projects are undertaken, nonfaculty are usually hired to do most of the work.

2. *Accountability: What Are the Contract Goals?*

The major problems involving accountability in government–university contracting come under two headings:

1. Problems arising from differing or unclear ideas as to contract goals.

2. Problems related to confusion about, or differing emphasis on, different kinds of accountability.

Too often neither party to a grant or contract has a clear idea as to the goals of the other. And this vagueness can often hide significant differences between the goals of the donor and those of the recipient.

Jones versus Smith: A hypothetical case study

Professor Jones of the University of South Dakota wants to measure the viscosity of water at high pressure and temperature, in order to improve his understanding of hydrogen bonding. He plans to use three graduate students to help in this work. Professor Smith of the University of Connecticut also wants to measure the viscosity of water for the same reason but in a different temperature range. He plans to use a post-doctoral assistant and one graduate student for the work. Both make proposals to the U.S. Navy and to the National Science Foundation.

Example A: A Navy Development Contract Officer. The Navy, upon receiving the proposals, realises that it needs accurate viscosity data in order to refine the design of a nuclear submarine. In the light of this need, the temperature range proposed by Professor Jones is the appropriate one. The Navy decides to support Jones. If Jones understands the Navy's purpose in offering support, then all is presumably well. If he does not, and he decides to change the temperature range to meet *his* goal of greater understanding, the results might be useless to the agency.

Example B: A Navy Basic Research Contract Officer. Suppose, on the other hand, that, in line with its interest in enlarging basic understanding of material strength, the Navy decides that the most fruitful area of concern is viscosity research. Professors Jones's and Smith's proposals come to a basic research contract officer for review, and he decided that Smith's proposal shows greater understanding of the problems of measuring viscosity accurately. He therefore supports Smith.

In this case the goals of the agency and of Professor Smith are more related. Even though Smith is interested in viscosity only as a tool, there is less likelihood that the pursuit of his research will conflict with the broader goals of the contract monitor. It is still important, however, that Smith understand what the monitor's goals are, so that he won't – say – change his technique from viscosity to thermal conductivity.

Example C: Another Navy Basic Research Contracting Officer. Now let us suppose that the two proposals are received by a Navy contract officer interested in hydrogen bonding. He supports Professor Jones, because he feels that his proposal shows clearer insight into the mechanism of hydrogen bonding.

The goals now are almost identical. Professor Jones can follow where his results lead. He can even decide to change from viscosity measurements to conductivity measurements using the funds which were to be supplied from the Navy contract for viscosity equipment.

In these three examples, while the donor and recipient may have different goals, they are both primarily concerned with *research results*. Navy research officers are – in fact – concerned almost entirely with research results, and they tend to treat the university, non-profit or industry more or less the same for this reason.

The National Science Foundation mission, however, includes not only the support of research but also improvement of science education, development of science manpower and more general distribution of science activity across the nation. These additional goals can lead to different criteria for evaluating research proposals.

Example D: A National Science Foundation Contract Officer. When the two proposals are reviewed by the N.S.F., the N.S.F. chooses to support Professor Jones because he has more graduate students working on the project than does Professor Smith, even though the projects appear to be of equal scientific value.

Professor Jones's research is not restricted, but if he decides to use post-doctoral students to replace graduate students, N.S.F. will be unhappy. When renewal time comes along, N.S.F. might well prefer a proposal from Professor Smith.

Example E: Another National Science Foundation Contract Officer. The Foundation decides to support Professor Jones because he is at the University of South Dakota and not Professor Smith from the University of Connecticut.

Now what if Professor Jones moves to Harvard? Ordinarily a grant transfers along with the professor who moves, but in this case the N.S.F. would probably expect that the grant would stay with the institution if there was anyone who could carry out the work. Jones, of course, will be very unhappy.

When the agency's and the faculty member's goals are

essentially the same (as is often the case with N.S.F. grants for basic research), accountability – in the sense of monitoring for research progress – is seldom an issue. The faculty member's reputation as a scientist depends on his progress in his work. This reputation can be assessed by reading the papers produced under the grant and by review by peers. However, even in basic research projects, if there is a lot of co-ordination needed, as when a piece of equipment is to be flown on a particular research spacecraft at a particular time, then more detailed monitoring is required, because a lot depends on the details of the progress.

The most serious problems of accountability arise – as in Example A – when there is a real conflict between the research goals of the faculty member and those of the contracting agency. These occasions are far more likely to occur when the agency has a very specific interest in the results of the research outlined in the proposal, and has not conveyed this interest to the faculty member.

In summary, the goals of the agency can include: (1) knowing the results of specific experiments (viscosity of water in a temperature range); (2) wishing a certain technique advanced (viscosity measurement); (3) wishing to see the science advanced (understanding of hydrogen bonding); (4) supporting science education through research (graduate education); (5) supporting research in a geographic region (South Dakota v. Connecticut). Usually the faculty member is interested only in goal 3.

3. *Three Kinds of Accountability*

Recent investigations by the General Accounting Office and by some members of Congress have raised up the idea that there has been mismanagement in university research. The complaints involve sloppy accounting practices of institutions, particularly inadequate time and effort reporting, inadequate control of equipment purchases, collection of interest on unexpended grant funds and teaching by people who are only supposed to do research.

Much of the difficulty is due to the difference in the meaning of 'accountability' to people in different parts of the university–government complex.

There are three types of accountability that come to mind. *Programme* accountability has to do with the quality of the work carried on and whether or not it met the goals set for it. *Process* accountability has to do with whether the procedures used to perform the research were adequate, say in terms of the time and effort spent on the work, and whether the experiments were carried out as promised. *Fiscal* accountability has to do with whether the funds were expended as stated and whether items purchased were used for the project, etc. When congressional committees, programme officers and performers mean different things by accountability, troubles can arise.

Programme accountability

The chief desire of the agency at the highest level is to fulfil successfully the goals set out in the project. In the case of research, did the university produce useful results? This is the typical question that the scientific programme officer asks himself. The programme officer and the grant recipient must normally have compatible (if not identical) goals if this question is to be answered in the same way by both parties. Even if the goals are the same, however, difficulties in assessment remain.

In effect, the faculty member is offering to put his best efforts into accomplishing a research task. How can the project officer judge this, particularly if the research result is negative? If the officer is as good a scientist as the recipient, he can personally judge with accuracy whether the effort was adequate, and whether the difficulties that came up were unforeseen. He can also decide that the problem was too difficult in the first place and that the failure itself was interesting.

In practice, even if the research was poorly done, it is rare to find a programme officer that will admit it. For one thing, it means that he (the grantor) made a mistake as well as the grantee. No one likes to admit, even to himself, that he made a mistake. Second, if the grantor were to declare the work inadequate, what kind of penalty could he impose? Should he stop payment for work already completed? I know of no attempt to stop payment to a university for a shoddy job of research, nor, in fact, to stop payment to any other kind of institution. Surely one of the thousands of projects supported by the federal government must have been shoddily done! Once in a great while, a project – usually in industrial applied research – will be cancelled with appropriate penalty clauses paid. As a practical matter, this would seem to be the limit of the government's resource in penalising poor work.

In practice, poor work by an investigator means that there will be no *renewal* of the contract, rather than that the university will not be paid for his work in the past. In practice, also, the difficulty of evaluating work actually done under a contract means that contract monitors and review panels tend to put more emphasis on the quality of the investigator than on the specific research proposal in awarding support.

The best man in the government to apply accountability to scientific research contracts is the scientific programme officer. However, in order to really understand the quality of the work done, the programme officer must be a capable scientist himself or must learn to use good scientific advice. As a practical matter, programme officers lose much of their scientific capability over time, and good contract officers rely on the judgement of advisers from outside the government.

Unless a good scientific officer gets some opportunity for independent judgement, he will not stay in the government. This judgement can be used in deciding programme emphasis to meet agency wide goals.

In summary, programme accountability, which is the type of accountability most meaningful to the agency and the investigator alike, is best obtained when there is good contract officer in the agency supporting the work. Accountability for past performance is usually obtained through renewal (or non-renewal) of future grants.

Process accountability

Given the difficulties of programme accountability, it is often easier and therefore tempting to measure whether the research process was carried out as specified, rather than whether the desired result was obtained.

The distinction between performance and process exists in other types of activity. The result 'A house should be warm

110

when it is $-40°$ outside' becomes translated into a complex building code in which the number of layers of insulation and their composition is specified. Specifications of the process by which a result is to be accomplished inhibit innovation, but are invariably used when the techniques of measuring performance are expensive.

Because research accomplishment is hard to measure in detail, and because successful results do not always occur (unless the result has been obtained before the proposal is written, a not uncommon event), very often both the faculty member and the contract officer will focus on the process. Thus the equipment was purchased, as promised; the faculty member spent full time for a year working on the project, as promised; measurements of viscosity in the temperature range specified were made.

The fact that process accountability is easy has made it attractive in measuring other kinds of mental activity. Many attorneys now charge according to the number of hours spent on the problem, teachers expect to get paid if they meet their classes (not if their students learn), politicians talk about their attendance records (or conceal them).

In general, people like to be judged on performance when their work is successful and to be judged on the process if the work was not successful. The government does not pay extra (except in terms of future contracts) for superb performance, and the university expects it to pay for bad performance if the process was carried out as promised. The university cannot enter into the contract unless it knows that it will be reimbursed for its costs, and so it must concentrate on the process.

Process accountability is therefore a necessary evil, somewhat related to the performance, and relied on by both the institution and the government as a substitute for programme accountability.

Fiscal accountability

Fiscal accountability is related to process accountability but the focus is almost exclusively on the procedures by which funds are accounted for, and on the actual expenditure of funds. Such items as vouchers, time sheets, purchase orders,

E

airline receipts and other minutiae of our advanced civilisation are the playthings of that modern replacement for the Devil, the auditor.

The auditor causes trouble not only to the university but to the programme officer of the agency as well. Discussing the kind of picky details that delight auditors usually annoys both the investigator and the programme officer. 'Where is the receipt for that plane trip you said you took to Washington?' 'When did you sign this undated time card saying that you spent one-third time that month on research?' A man can spend an awful lot of his research time, and a university a lot of its overhead money, dealing with auditors.

The concentration on fiscal accountability by auditors and Congressmen occurs for two reasons. First, it is difficult for non-scientists to judge the value of a basic research programme, and so (in the tradition of the man who, because the light was good, looked under the street lamp for the quarter he had dropped in the alley) they tend to concentrate effort in the things that they do understand, namely money. Second, Congressmen know that the public is more interested in tales of fiscal hanky-panky (or what appears to be hanky-panky) than in discussions of research results.

Thus, you can learn from congressional committees

(*a*) about the company that took a grant with an automatic indirect cost allowance of 15 per cent, and then direct-costed *all* charges, so that it could make a profit from a non-profit grant;

(*b*) about the president of a government-captive non-profit corporation who charged his company for transporting his yacht from Boston to Los Angeles;

(*c*) about the mathematician who collected pay for summer research while vacationing in Greece with his family;

(*d*) about the university that put grant funds into the bank and collected interest until the funds were needed.

Congress gets no real co-operation from the programme part of the governmental agency when it attacks these and other practices. The programme officer is primarily interested in getting the job done, and only cares secondarily about how the money is distributed within the institution. Even if over-payments are made, the recovery of funds usually benefits the Federal Treasury and not the programme of the agency.

From the university administration's point of view, whether a cost is allowable or unallowable is of paramount concern. To the investigator, the arguments between the agency auditors and the institution only cause him time and trouble.

In summary, the programme officer and the investigator are concerned primarily with programme accountability, secondarily with process accountability, and pay little attention to fiscal accountability. The university is concerned with process and fiscal accountability, and secondarily with programme accountability (since the central administration is usually unable to judge the technical worth of a project). Congress and the audit portion of the government agency are concerned primarily with fiscal accountability, secondarily with process accountability, and hardly at all with programme accountability.

Given these differences in viewpoint among the various parties involved in the accountability process, it is easy to see why the practices of one part of the system often make other parts very unhappy.

4. *Some Special Issues Raised in University Research*

There have been a number of special issues raised in discussions of university research which have some relation to accountability.

Grant versus contract

More time has been spent on the issue of grants *v.* contracts than it deserves. A grant *is* a contract. There are no grants that do not have restrictions on the expenditures. It is true, of course, that the recipient prefers to receive something that is called a grant. It makes him feel that he is loved for himself alone and not for what he produces.

It is also true that – historically – contracts were so rigid and involved so much red tape that the grant instrument was invented to give needed flexibility and freedom to the research. In time the conditions under which grants were administered became more onerous, and contract administrators became more flexible. In some ways research contracts looking for results pay less attention to the details of contract administration than do research grants in which the process is important. Thus research grants do not permit more money to be spent on the principal investigator without permission, and they allow fewer transfers between categories than do some research contracts.

In any event, the myth has grown up that a grant is something the recipient wants to do and the government is willing to help him, whereas a contract is something that the government wants done and the university is willing to help out with it. A grant is expected to lose money and a contract to break even; a grant is a gift (conditional to be sure) and a contract is an agreement (flexibly written to be sure). The fact is that in both a grant and a contract, the government is eager to see the work done and the recipient should be eager to do it. The universities are concerned about the flexibility with which *either* a grant or a contract can be administered. From their point of view, the more flexible and permissive the instrument, the easier it is to administer, and probably the better the results. The agency auditor finds that a flexibly written instrument makes his kind of accountability difficult.

'Wholesale' versus 'retail' grants

The bulk of research done at universities and supported by the government is done in the form of individual research projects. This retail support can be contrasted with more wholesale support such as grants to groups of investigators (programme grants), to departments (departmental grants) or to institutions (institutional grants).

Experience in the Defence Department has shown that where management capability exists, long-term programme grants have given great satisfaction. These grants have gone primarily to outstanding places, however.

Accountability on programme grants is much harder than on individual projects. Some of the projects performed under a programme grant will be of low quality. (Half of them, in

114

fact, will be below the average quality of the work done on the grant.) If the programme is more than the sum of its parts, however, then it must be judged on its total effect. If the programme is merely a collection of projects, the projects should have been supported individually for most efficient return.

Ideally, accountability on programme grants requires sophisticated review, at relatively long intervals, using the best advice. Good review does not often happen.

Independence and accountability

The tradition of academic freedom in a university is one in which faculty members (once given tenure) do not expect to be accountable to anyone for the results of their research. This freedom was hard-won and it is precious. When the research involves costs over and above the salary of the faculty member, however, it is up to the professor to make a case for the additional expenditures, and he becomes accountable for these. Thus, in some fields, to do effective work may require some loss of academic freedom.

A physics professor realises that if he wants to do research with a $3 million accelerator, he must make a proposal which will be judged nationally, and he must expect to be accountable for his research. However, despite the necessity for this, he cannot be expected to enjoy giving up some of his freedom in order to get his research done.

A major question facing all universities is how to balance the need for freedom with control over significant expenditures.

A related question is level at which control and decision-making should be exercised. If the purpose of the grant is to advance science, then the competition for funds – and their control – should be national. If the purpose of the money is institutional improvement, then decisions should be made at the level of the institution concerned.

Different grants for different purposes

The American university administrator faces a bewildering variety of grants for different purposes. Some grants are for training, some for research. Although all grants nominally go to the institution, in practice the control of expenditure can lie with a faculty member, a department chairman, a dean or the president. When these grants have different goals, it *is* appropriate that they be controlled differently. If the goal is to improve educational quality across the board, then institutional funds for that purpose are ideal. If training in special fields is desired, it is most efficient to give grants directly to the appropriate part of the institution. If science is to be advanced, individual grants will probably give the best results. Clearly these differences affect what kinds of accountability are possible.

In short in an institution that performs many functions and is supposed to be responsive to the needs of society, one part of that responsiveness may be that it must take and manage grants for many different purposes.

University management

Universities are not hierarchical organisations in America. One does not assign faculty to jobs. But if universities are to do the jobs they are called upon to do, they need management competence and organisational change.

The trend in universities for carrying out their primary function of education is towards democratisation. Faculty and students are calling for more say in the running of the institution that affects their lives. But interminable committee meetings and action by consensus do not get things done. Perhaps when faculty and students understand the difficulties of management, they will call for more rather than less centralisation of authority and responsibility. In any event they may call for more enlightened technical management of government–university relations, if only to have someone else deal with auditors.

In the management of research grants and contracts, a university must balance with sensitivity its responsibility to its own constituent parts, and its responsibility to the public. Secret research, for example, should be done only if absolutely necessary.

5. Conclusion

The American university gets much of its support from the federal government, but this support at present comes for special purposes. For the institution to be accountable to the federal government requires that there by a clearer understanding on the part of professors, university administrators, contract officers, government auditors and Congressmen that there will always be differences in goals, and differences in major concerns among them.

If the understanding exists, and – most important – if the quality of management improves in both the government and the universities, the legitimate need of the university for freedom and of the government for knowledge that its funds are well spent can be reconciled.

4 The University-Managed Laboratory

J. P. Ruina

Universities and Public Service

Universities are regarded as public service institutions with primary responsibilities in teaching and research. Less well understood and defined is the responsibility of universities to render public service beyond their traditional teaching and research functions. This raises a host of issues relating to the definition of what this additional service can and should be, the extent to which limited university resources can encompass broader service without having deleterious effects on teaching and research, the effective interface between the university and the national and local community needs, and the nature and form of accountability for this service.

During World War II universities were called upon to help in the national defence effort and demonstrated their competence to provide services to the government in managing large laboratories of technology. This has remained a major and significant mode for the rendering of public service by some of our larger universities. Now there are new pressures for universities to be involved in meeting national needs in urban matters, environmental control, transportation, etc. As questions arise about these new directions, we should perhaps try to learn from this major piece of recent history of university–government relationships.

Universities by and large have always had liberal policies regarding the time spent by individual faculty and senior administrators in public service activities. These people serve on government advisory committees; they consult for public service and non-profit institutions.

Universities have been willing to form consortia for the purpose of creating and sponsoring special institutions for

118

public service such as the Institute for Defence Analyses, University Corporation for Atmospheric Research, Lunar Scientific Institute, Lowell Institute Co-operative Broadcasting Council, etc.

The university is necessarily deeply involved when it creates and assumes direct management responsibility of a large laboratory of technology for direct government service. Specific examples of such laboratories are the Applied Physics Laboratory of Johns Hopkins University, Lincoln and Instrumentation Laboratories of the Massachusetts Institute of Technology, Livermore and Los Alamos Laboratories of the University of California, and the Jet Propulsion Laboratory of the California Institute of Technology. This category of university-managed off-campus laboratory cannot be defined unambiguously. But for my purpose I want to distinguish these laboratories from both the university-affiliated (but not university-managed) laboratory on the one hand and the essentially on-campus laboratory which is directly and totally in the mainstream of academic activities on the other hand. Cornell Aeronautical Laboratory and Stanford Research Institute for example are university-owned laboratories. But by choice of the owning universities these laboratories are responsible to a separate board of directors and the university affiliation is very much in the background.

Several but not all of the university-managed laboratories are included in a collection of not-for-profit organisations which have been categorised by the government as Federal Contract Research Centres (F.C.R.C.s).

F.C.R.C.s include 'think tanks' like the Institute for Defence Analyses (IDA) and Rand as well as some system engineering organisations like Mitre Corporation and Aerospace Corporation. Although the responsibilities and character of each of the F.C.R.C.s are different, what they seem to have in common is that they are not-for-profit institutions listed by name in the Federal Budget as line items. This usually means that a particular government agency was directly involved in their creation.

For reasons that are not very clear, the F.C.R.C.s funded by the Department of Defence have been the object of special concern by Congress in recent years and as a consequence have had some administrative and financial constraints imposed on them regarding reporting procedures, size, salaries, fees, etc., which do not apply to other D.O.D. contractors. Although the university-managed laboratories have rarely been singled out for criticism, nor has the concern expressed about F.C.R.C.s really been applicable to these laboratories, the same constraints have nevertheless also been applied to them.

The Off-Campus Laboratory

This paper deals with the university-managed off-campus laboratories. These laboratories may or may not be off-campus physically. They may be far away from the campus as Los Alamos is from Berkeley or as close to the campus as the Instrumentation Laboratory is at M.I.T. *Off-campus* is not meant to describe the physical location of the laboratory but rather its relationship to the academic community. In these laboratories the product is primarily dependent on a full-time professional staff for whom teaching and student contact is a secondary responsibility. Faculty and student participation may or may not exist.

The laboratories are not part of the academic structure. They normally report to the university administration through a vice-president and not through an academic officer such as a dean or provost. In contrast to campus activities, they have an internal hierarchical management structure similar to that found in industry and government and consistent with their project responsibilities.

The off-campus laboratories are generally much larger than any campus laboratory. The Instrumentation Laboratory at M.I.T., for example, spends more than $50 million annually, which is as much as all of the on-campus research at M.I.T. combined. The Jet Propulsion Laboratory budget is over $200 million per year.

In every case these laboratories are organised to handle classified work as a matter of routine. Because campus values may prohibit classified work on campus, this is an important factor.

These laboratories were created to serve and receive all their support from federal mission-oriented agencies such as the Department of Defence, the Atomic Energy Commission and the National Aeronautics and Space Administration: the large government consumers of technology. The National Institutes of Health and the National Science Foundation have not been involved in any substantial way. The government continues to share with the university the planning and caring for the welfare of each of these laboratories. This is not generally the case in industrial or on-campus research.

Monetary benefits to the university for maintaining an off-campus laboratory have been greatly misunderstood and frequently exaggerated. In some cases the university receives a fee for managing the laboratories but it is very small. The laboratories do not have independent fiscal resources; they have no endowment and no private money. They depend on the government spigot for day-to-day existence and in this sense they might be considered government captives.

It must be made clear that the funding of these off-campus laboratories is quite a different matter from the issue of government support of universities. The money supporting these laboratories is different in origin and purpose from the money supporting on-campus activities. The amount of money derived from the off-campus laboratory which can be expended for general university welfare in any direct sense is only a very small fraction of the total budgets of the laboratories.

At M.I.T. there is no fee involved. The Lincoln and Instrumentation Laboratories are managed as integral components of the Institute and their contracts are charged on a *pro rata* basis for the indirect expenses of the Institute. The high dollar volume of the laboratories' activities helps to reduce the overhead rates for all Institute activities including campus research and teaching. However, it should be noted here that the overhead cost is based on actual dollar expenditure, audited by the government. It should not be confused with a fee, which, in principle, is free money and legally requires no accounting to the government as to its use. There is, however, a serious problem when a common overhead basis is utilised. Sharp cutbacks in laboratory budgets cannot simultaneously be accompanied by equally sharp decreases in overhead costs. If laboratory budgets are cut, the Institute risks having to assume the excessive overhead costs incurred until a new fiscal equilibrium is attained.

Off-campus laboratories generally originated to meet new and urgent federal needs for which university management was deemed essential. In each case the mix of qualities that any given university had for the purpose was different but it usually included an existing, flexible administrative structure, special technical expertise, demonstrated ability to create and maintain an environment for successful research and development programmes; an ability to recruit and retain top-quality scientists and engineers, and an absence of the profit incentive which was judged incompatible with the purposes of the programme. While an absolute case cannot be made for the view that government, industry or not-for-profits could not have handled this work as well, there is general agreement that the work was in fact handled better in universities than it would otherwise have been.

There is a very high survival rate among these laboratories although only a fraction still concentrate on their original missions. Their programmes continue to have high visibility, their staffs are excellent and their national importance is generally recognised. Each of the laboratories has developed a distinctive character and a keen sense of pride and purpose. It is very natural therefore that each has developed an almost biological will to survive and they have developed the wherewithal to do so.

Variations in the Nature of Accountability

Government sponsorship in science and technology covers the spectrum from basic and applied research to exploratory development and finally to prototype development where equipment is designed for operational use by the government.

The justification for basic research, especially when supported by the mission-oriented agencies, is to broaden the scientific base of the country in technical areas of particular interest to the sponsoring agency, to increase the nation's talent pool in these same technical areas, to raise scientific and technical standards, and to establish meaningful relationships between the sponsoring agency and scientific and technical leaders. The government's interest is in supporting competent people in particular fields of science and technology, at good institutions. Quality is measured by the past success of individuals and institutions, as judged by peers.

Accountability for basic research, judging it in a narrow sense, is strongly polarised. First, there is simple financial accountability. The researcher must justify all expenditures (i.e. travel, equipment) as well as account for the dollars actually spent. Usually, the man who is doing the work – the scientific investigator – has little interest in the administrative process involved here.

The other pole is the researcher's feeling that his real accountability is to his professional peer community. Professors are not likely to look to Washington or even to their universities but rather to their peers throughout the world for judgement of their work. Primary rewards come from success as that group judges it. This is true whether or not there is federal support involved.

What is normal accountability to the management structure and to the sponsor in an industrial setting would be viewed as harassment by the basic researcher in a university setting.

Whereas in basic or undirected research the investigator has relatively wide discretion for what he does and how he does it, in the case of applied or directed research the bounds of discretion are more constrained and relevance to the agency mission is measured more carefully.

Off-campus laboratories engage primarily in exploratory and advanced development. They perform technical analysis; they develop and build advanced components and systems to demonstrate technical feasibility. In this way they add to the storehouse of technology from which the government draws for the design of operational equipment. The technical substance is left to the laboratory but with complete understanding and agreement between the government and the laboratory on the goals, form and costs of all major projects. The government as customer maintains close contact with the laboratory and its staff. Also, accountability to the sponsor for the technical product shifts from the individual scientist or engineer to the laboratory as an institution.

At the end of the scale is engineering development of equipment for operational use. In this case the government is involved in detail at every level of operation. The government writes the specifications. Government people are frequently resident at the laboratory, deeply involved in the details of every step of the development process. Serious questions arise about this kind of effort on a university campus – and here the unique contribution of the university is more questionable.

The Government University Laboratory Triangle

We must recognise that in analysing accountability and responsibility for the university-managed off-campus laboratory we are dealing with three institutional entities – and not two. The triangle includes the laboratory, a powerful nationally known institution in its own right, the university and the government. Accountability and responsibility lines go, in reality, between each of the vertices of the triangle.

In the university–laboratory relationship, the involvement and control which the university administration exercises over the off-campus laboratory is greater than that which a board of trustees might have over a not-for-profit corporation. Boards of trustees, for good and proper reasons, avoid detailed management. University administration on the other hand cannot avoid detailed concern if not outright control of programme choices, personnel policy and fiscal management of the laboratory. The laboratory is accountable to the academic community via the university administration for the appropriateness and quality of its work and the special qualifications it has for doing this work. The laboratory must justify its existence in the value system of the academic community. This is becoming abundantly clear currently and has become a significant factor in shaping these laboratories.

There is generally some flow of staff in both directions between the universities and the laboratories. Permanent faculty appointments are sometimes made from the laboratory staff. Laboratory staff members also teach courses and run seminars on campus on an *ad hoc* basis. Likewise faculty members often join the laboratory staff on a full-time basis for a summer, year, or permanently.

Universities benefit from the expertise that the laboratories bring. The laboratory's programmes can bring a vital-

124

ity to the university's applied science departments and help prevent the technical sterility often encountered without such laboratory resources. They help make available to the university skills and facilities that are not found in academic departments but which are nevertheless fundamental to modern technology. While universities have been in the forefront in basic research, most of the 'action' in technology is in industry, and universities therefore have to make very special efforts to remain involved in the mainstream of technological advance.

Distortion of the academic institution by virtue of the scale of the laboratories has to date been avoided, I believe, because of the implicit acceptance of a 'dual citizenship' with the campus dominant. This is not going to continue to be so readily accepted as major questions arise about campus–laboratory relationships.

Fundamental questions are being raised on campus about how 'public service' is defined and to what extent the university as an institution should be involved in actively influencing government policies and priorities. Formal government determination of national priorities (as measured by budgetary allocations) and judgement in some campus quarters of what should be government priorities are often in conflict. The whole question of community control and campus authority with regard to all university activities, the advisory and consultative roles and the meaning of academic freedom in regard to the large off-campus laboratories – presents a tricky weave of accountability issues. The campus defends its values, which may be in conflict with the laboratories' programme and methods. The laboratories are strong enough entities to permit them to decide that their future lies separate from that of the university. If universities are to continue to manage off-campus laboratories effectively, new modes and new criteria for accountability within the university will have to be developed. The university cannot be oblivious to campus restiveness and concern nor can it subject the laboratories and the government sponsors to the issues of the moment on campus.

From the perspective of the university, its primary justification for managing these laboratories is to provide a public service in line with its special nature. However, the existence of the laboratories forces an intimacy between universities and government which may make for uncomfortable pressures. The university may find itself in the position of feeling that it has to make some compromises with unadulterated intellectual freedom. University officials are under some pressure not to affect adversely the laboratory morale by any criticism of the national programmes on which it works. They are also mindful that the government sponsor might be less than delighted to have government policies publicly criticised by university people who have special knowledge through association with government programmes. These kinds of constraints create a dilemma because, at the same time, the values of the university community – the trustees, alumni, faculty and students – require true intellectual independence and free expression of views.

The university, as a buffer between laboratory and government, can maintain laboratory independence but this may require that the laboratory and the government recognise that the national interest might be best served by permitting and indeed even encouraging the laboratories to be both government contractors and critics. Both the government and the university need *critical faculties*. But within the university structure, balancing these simultaneous obligations and values can be precarious.

The university is not involved in the day-to-day dealings between the laboratory and the government though its presence is sensed by both. Information and the product flow from the laboratory to the government directly.

It is interesting to note that the off-campus laboratories have not suffered accusations in the Congress and in the press of mismanagement or wrongdoing as have some of the 'not-for-profits'. They tend to be run austerely with executive salaries considerably lower than in industry, and without some of the other executive perquisites. Salaries of junior staff are likely to be on the low side of being competitive with industry. University prestige helps provide shelter from unsubstantiated criticism of not-for-profit organisations and, also, helps attract high-level staff despite lower salaries than comparable employment elsewhere. The government seems to have an easier time accepting the operations of the university laboratories than it has accepting the 'not-for-profits'. In general, the laboratory–government relationship is viewed as a constructive one by both parties. The government agencies dealing with these laboratories have a long history of intelligent understanding of the nature of the creatures which the laboratories are. This kind of mutual understanding takes years to develop.

Not discussed in detail here but very significant is the matter of internal accountability. The laboratories, the government and the university each have a structure and a value system which exacts different forms of accountability within its own organisation. Indeed the defence of these internal accountabilities may be a source of conflict in any of these entities relating to any other in the triangle. An example here is the Ballistic Missile Defence System – the government defends it, many neutral university scientists and administrators decry it, the off-campus laboratories may play major roles in its development – also, each of the entities may have a different sense of the need, propriety and desirability of public or private criticism. The laboratory values may justify criticising internally via channels on technical matters, but university faculty and government may choose to operate and express themselves in the public, political arena.

Each of the university laboratories considered here has made valuable contributions to national service. University sponsorship has contributed to their ability to maintain a fair degree of independence. Anyone contemplating new large technological programmes can't help but be favourably impressed by the possibilities of a university-managed laboratory. However, we may be witnessing so much discomfort and unhappiness in the relationships – between the university campus and off-campus laboratory, and between university values and government requirements – that universities and government may shy away from participating in new programmes in this form. It may be decided that the cost of such engagement is higher than the benefits.

Also, with time, the government bureaucratic hand has been getting heavier for the laboratories. There has been a slow but steady increase in bureaucratic, detailed accountability resulting in an erosion of laboratory flexibility and those very qualities which have made university laboratories the valuable resources they are. Productivity in the laboratory environment depends on an assumption of good faith and good performance, the existence of which very detailed accountability seems to deny. Some of the pressure stems from the fear that executive agencies have of congressional and public criticism where transgressions or abuse are given far more weight than success and accomplishment. If strong laboratories are to be maintained, the government executive agencies must live up to their responsibility to be the buffer between Congress, the public and the laboratories.

As national priorities shift and as the realisation grows that imaginative new technology can play a key role in areas different from the traditional concerns of off-campus laboratories, a major flaw becomes evident in the current government–laboratory relationship. These laboratories have had great flexibility in exploring new areas within the current interest of their sponsors. These explorations have been extremely fruitful in technical innovation and have been extremely important in maintaining a creative environment at the laboratories. Unfortunately this flexibility does not apply as the boundaries of the sponsors' interest are crossed. Since the laboratories are 'financial captives', they are severely limited from even beginning to contribute in areas where their skills could be so effectively applied and where their own desire for greater breadth and the interests of the university community would direct them. The problem begs for a new and broadened concept of accountability to the sponsor.

The United States has been unusually successful in inventing new institutional forms and maintaining flexibility in institutional relationships. University-managed laboratories are an example of this success. It would be most unfortunate if the difficult problems confronting university, government and laboratories prevent further utilisation of this institutional arrangement for efforts in new technical directions. The current strains within the university, the erosion of the bond between the government and the university, the frustration of the universities in their attempts to broaden their public service to technical areas where the government does not yet have the funds or administrative machinery for effective programmes are going to make it exceedingly difficult to deliberate and decide on the basis of profound understanding what deserves preserving.

5 The Government-Oriented Corporation

Murray L. Weidenbaum

Introduction

As government agencies, notably those dealing with military and space matters, have come to depend on new systems and equipment of a highly scientific content, they have grown to depend less and less on their own laboratories and arsenals to design and produce the materials they use. Increasingly, the research, development and production of military, atomic energy and space systems are being performed in the private sector via government contracts with large industrial corporations.

Were the governmental purchases similar to those of the private sector, this might not be a noteworthy development. However, so much of these procurement funds is devoted to fairly exotic items for which there are rarely established private markets – missiles, space vehicles, nuclear-powered aircraft carriers, desalinisation systems, atomic energy items and so forth.

As a result, the companies serving this specialised government market develop capabilities different from those required for successful operation in traditional commercial markets. There is a feedback here. As these companies become less effective in competing for private business and more adept at obtaining public contracts, they become heavily dependent on the government customer. Conversely, the Department of Defence maintains little capability to produce the equipment that it needs. Hence, it has come to rely almost entirely on these government-oriented corporations. Both parties – private and public – become 'locked in' to a symbiotic relationship where they depend on each other.

A 'demonstration' effect in other parts of the public sector is now taking place. Civilian government agencies that require on occasion large-scale technological development and production efforts are also turning to the government-oriented corporations. In most cases to date, these are the same corporations as those which dominate the military market, and the products that they produce are similar. The two largest examples are space systems for NASA – an outgrowth of military I.C.B.M. programmes – and the development of a supersonic transport aircraft (S.S.T.) under the sponsorship of the Department of Transportation – an extension of military aircraft developments. Thus far, the government-oriented corporations have not played an important role in domestic welfare programmes. There are growing pressures for changing this situation.

Up to the present time, the two major mechanisms available for decentralising federal activities – the government-oriented corporation and grants to the states and localities – have been utilised in quite different fashions. The government-oriented corporation has been used in national security and related high technology programmes, while grants-in-aid have been used primarily in connection with welfare and other domestic programmes.

The difference in the quality of resources made available for public programmes by the two mechanisms is striking. Compare the income and educational levels of the engineers, scientists and other highly educated, innovative professionals working on missile or space systems with the typical employee of state highway departments or local welfare agencies. Also, compare the concentration of science and technology in national security programmes with their virtual absence from domestic welfare activities. For example, all state agencies combined (excluding colleges and universities) spent a mere $88 million for research and development in 1965 compared to the federal government's R. & D. budget of $16 billion, seven-eighths of which was devoted to military applications, space and atomic energy.[1]

Extending the Use of the Government-Oriented Corporation

In a significant effort at diversification, the major defence contractors in recent years have made numerous attempts to penetrate, as well as to develop, civilian markets within the public sector itself. Although the dollar volumes of these undertakings are still small judged by the scale of military programmes, they do involve government agencies doing business with high-technology private enterprises that were originally attracted to government work by the military establishment.

The present appears to be a period of substantial exploration on the part of both government agencies and business enterprises in assessing the kinds of relationships through which they can successfully do business with each other. It is, hence, early to judge the successes or failures. Four areas seem to stand out as civilian public sector activities where the type of systems analysis and advanced technology possessed by the leading military contractors can usefully be utilised: transportation, water systems, communications systems and regional development.[2]

Improvements in transportation

A current example of innovative transportation work by a government-oriented corporation is the development by Lockheed Aircraft Company of a transportation plan for the Sudan. This work is being undertaken through contracts with the Agency for International Development and the Sudan's Ministry of Finance and Economics. In its systems analysis of Sudan transportation, Lockheed is charged with developing a broad plan for development of all forms of transportation, indicating specific projects and establishing priorities among them.

Within the United States, T.R.W. Inc., is conducting detailed engineering studies of transportation requirements for the Northeast Corridor. The company is evaluating, for the Department of Transportation, alternative modes and travel concepts which can be used in a safe and convenient high-speed ground transportation network.

The systems type of public transportation market in the United States appears to be in an early developmental state. The government funding generally is in terms of hundreds of thousands of dollars, characteristic of exploratory study phases, rather than the contracts in units of tens of millions which are associated with actual production of operational systems.

Development of water systems

Several government-oriented corporations (Aerojet-General, General Dynamics, McDonnell-Douglas and United Aircraft) have been testing to determine whether waste water can be reclaimed through 'reverse osmosis' (filtering out impurities with thin membranes). The General Dynamics Corporation has been working with the sanitation authorities in Los Angeles County and the City of San Diego. Westinghouse Electric Corporation is under contract with the State of Pennsylvania to determine whether techniques used for de-salting water can be employed to purify acid mine drainage, a major source of stream pollution.

As in the case of the public sector opportunities for innovation in transportation, the markets that have developed to date for water systems have been quite limited in terms of effective demand on the part of government agencies both willing and able to award large-scale contracts. Rather, these efforts mainly indicate some of the future potentials for diversification of defence contractors.

Communications systems

Many defence contractors have obtained civilian government contracts in which modern computer technology is drawn upon to improve communication systems, notably in the areas of education, health and justice. For example, Aerojet-General Corporation has been working with the California Department of Education on a computer system for evaluating teacher credentials. Northrop Corporation is under contract with the State of Pennsylvania to develop a criminal justice information system. On a broader scale, Lockheed Aircraft Corporation is designing state-wide information systems for Alaska, California and West Virginia.

It appears that the aerospace and electronics companies have been most successful to date in the new public sector markets involving computer technology and information-handling systems. In many cases, the work concentrated for goes beyond preliminary exploration to the actual installation of operational equipment.

Applying the systems approach to area development

The most far-reaching attempt thus far to apply systems analysis to the economic development of a region is the contract with the government of Greece under which Litton Industries has committed itself not only to analyse and plan the growth of industry in an underdeveloped area, but actually to attract new investment to it. On a much less ambitious level, General Electric Company's centre for advanced studies, TEMPO, is working with the City of Detroit to introduce budgeting techniques learned through its cost-effectiveness work on projects of the Department of Defence.

In view of rising national concern with the complex of racial and poverty problems that are centred in the major urban areas, it is likely that the relatively small undertakings described here will in coming years grow into large-scale government utilisation of private industry. Already, many public and private figures have urged the formation of new forms of government–industry partnerships in order to rebuild in a fundamental way major portions of the central cities of our largest metropolitian areas.

A need for rethinking

It is not hard, thus, to work up considerable enthusiasm for the nation attaining some civilian return on its massive investment in military technology through the type of undertakings described above. However, we now have several decades of experience with the use of the government-oriented corporation in military programmes, and an assessment reveals some serious side-effects. These unintended impacts of the government–industry relationship appear worthy of some analysis, particularly prior to any wholesale utilisation of the government–industry relationship in the civilian public sector.

The following sections of this paper describe the nature of the government-oriented corporation as it has developed in carrying out military and closely related programmes (e.g., exploration of outer space). Some of the generally overlooked effects of the use of this mechanism are examined. The paper ends with suggestions for policy changes which would make private business firms more effective instruments of public policy and maintain their essentially private characteristics.

The Role of the Government-Oriented Corporation

Four-fifths of federal purchase from the private sector consist of goods and services for military programmes. The great bulk of these procurements is not made in circumstances where a great number of firms present sealed bids offering to sell fairly standard commercial stock items at fixed prices. If this idyllic situation were to prevail, it is most unlikely that the phenomenon of the government-oriented corporation would have arisen at all. Rather, the typical federal procurement involves acquiring a highly engineered system designed and produced to the government's own specifications and for which there are no established private markets.

The leading government contractors[3]

An analysis of the composition of the firms supplying these government markets lends important insights into the nature of the government-oriented corporation. Because these high-technology markets are so completely subject to the changing needs of the governmental customer, relationships between buyers and sellers differ from those typical in the commercial sector of the economy. By the selection of contractors, the government can control entry and exit, can greatly affect the growth of the firms involved, and can impose its way of doing business on the companies participating.

The bulk of the contract is let as a result of negotiation with a group of suppliers chosen by the buyers. The governmental buyers normally request proposals from the firms that they consider to be in a position to undertake the magnitude of R. & D. and production required. However keen the competition among the prospective suppliers may become, it will relate primarily to their technological capability and not simply to price. Hence, the nature of the buyers' demands may be far less a direct function of their budgets than of the products or systems available through technological advance. When technology produces space boosters, for example, the federal government begins to develop an effective demand for exploring outer space.

Major portions of the work contracted for are performed by corporations oriented to public requirements rather than market demands. These government-oriented corporations are companies or fairly autonomous divisions of large, diversified corporations whose dominant customers are the defence and space agencies of the federal government. The close, continuing relationship between the government and these corporations is more than regulation by federal agencies or selling in markets where the government is a major determinant of price, as in the case of public utilities, agriculture or mining. Rather, it is the intertwining of the public and private sectors so that it is difficult to identify when specific entrepreneurial or management functions in a given company are being performed primarily by government agents or by private individuals on business payrolls. As will be described subsequently, the contract mechanism provides the basic means for such governmental intervention.

A relatively limited number of companies receive the bulk of the defence and space contract awards. In the fiscal year 1968, the hundred companies obtaining the largest dollar volume of military prime contracts accounted for two-thirds of the Department of Defence total. In the case of NASA, the top hundred companies received nine-tenths of the total contracts awarded during the year.

Who are the government-oriented corporations? An analysis of the size distribution of the top hundred D.O.D. contractors provides another dimension to the structure of government markets. The giants of American industry do not dominate, contrary to much of the writing of the so-called military–industrial complex. Rather, the medium-size corporations receive the largest share of the orders for high technology government products. The twenty-seven corporations with assets of $1 billion or over received only 25 per cent of the D.O.D. contracts in 1965 going to the top hundred contractors. This group includes General Motors, Ford, Standard Oil of New Jersey, R.C.A., Uniroyal, Eastman Kodak, Firestone Tire and Rubber, and International Harvester. In contrast, the thirty companies with assets in the $250–999-million range received 58 per cent of the contracts, a clear majority. Typical firms in this category are the aerospace and electronics manufacturers – Boeing, Hughes Aircraft, Lockheed and North American Rockwell. These certainly are not pygmies among business firms in the United States; neither are they at the very top rung of American industry. As might be expected, relatively small companies did proportionally less well: the thirty-seven companies with assets below $250 million accounted for only 17 per cent of the total.

Another dimension of the structure of this government market relates to the extent of dependence on government work among the major contractors. Again, the data indicate that the firms most heavily dependent on military orders – those primarily oriented to government rather than private markets – are the medium-size companies rather than the giants of American industry. Of the top hundred defence contractors in 1965, for the seven with assets of $5 billion or over, defence contracts equalled less than 10 per cent of their sales in all cases. For those twenty firms with assets in the $1–5 billion range, defence orders equalled less than 25 per cent of sales. In contrast, twenty-one out of the forty-four firms with assets of $100–999 million obtained defence contracts exceeding 25 per cent of their sales; in the case of ten of these firms – Avco, Collins Radio, General Dynamics, L.-T.-V., Lockheed, Martin-Marietta, McDonnell, Newport News Shipbuilding, Northrop and Raytheon – these government orders exceeded half of their sales volume. These are clearly the 'government-oriented corporations'.

Also the majority of the smaller firms, those with assets under $100 million, received defence contracts exceeding 50 per cent of their sales. This experience is hardly typical of the thousands of smaller businesses participating in government markets. Rather, it reflects the nature of the sample, which is limited to firms receiving the largest absolute amounts of defence contracts.

During the past decade, over 80 per cent of the government procurement of high technology products and systems has been made through negotiated rather than sealed-bid purchasing. Clearly, the prices that the government pays for these goods and services are not determined by the interplay of relatively impersonal market forces. Some observers relate the lack of competition and sealed bidding to the concentration of government business within a relatively few firms.

Adverse side effects

The tendency for the military establishment to rely on a fairly limited group of suppliers for the bulk of its needs has resulted in a fairly unique government–industry relationship. In their long-term dealings with these corporations that cater primarily to specialised government markets, federal government agencies such as the Department of Defence and NASA gradually have taken over directly or indirectly many of the decision-making functions which are normally the prerogatives of business management.

A detailed analysis of the largest segment of these government markets, Air Force procurement, recently concluded that 'A new structural relationship has been created in which the Air Force, as a buyer, makes specific management decisions about policy and detailed procedures within aerospace companies that sell defence systems to the Air Force.'[4] This development may well be the most significant long-term impact of governmental procurement expenditures on the private sector of the American economy.

The public assumption of, or active participation in, private business decision-making takes three major forms: influencing the choice of products the firm produces, the source of capital funds that it uses, and its internal operations.[5] It needs to be kept in mind, of course, that this government involvement in private industry arises mainly in the case of the 'government-oriented' corporations which operate primarily in the unique and large-scale nature of military weapon system, space system, atomic energy development and related high technology purchasing by the government. It hardly characterises the procurement of standard conventional items by all government agencies through fixed-price contracts awarded via sealed-bid competition.

By awarding massive contracts for research and development (approximately $10 billion in the fiscal year 1968) the Department of Defence and NASA have come to strongly influence or determine which new products their essentially common group of contractors will design and produce. The governmental customers thus directly finance the R. & D. efforts and assume much of the risk of success or failure. In the commercial economy, in contrast, research and development costs normally are only recovered to the extent that they result in the sale of profitable products. Hence, the decisions to embark upon a product research and development programme are made by the sellers, who bear the risk of not recovering their technological investment.

Of course, government contractors may and do sponsor and fund some of their own R. & D. effort. However, the bulk of their R. & D. is performed under government contract. Much if not most of the remainder is charged as allowable overheads on their government contracts, having met the approval of contract administration officials. In good measure, military and space product design and development is not an intermediate good but an end product which the contractor produces for sale to the government under contract awarded before the R. & D. is undertaken.

A committee of senior government officials, chaired by the then Budget Bureau Director David Bell, reported to the President in 1962 that '... The major initiative and responsibility for promoting and financing research and development have in many important areas been shifted from private enterprise (including academic as well as business institutions) to the Federal Government.' The Bell Committee went on to point out that unlike the present situation where the federal government finances the bulk of the national expenditure for R. & D., prior to World War II most of the nation's research achievements occurred with little federal support.[6]

The government also uses its vast financial resources to supply much of the plant and equipment and working capital used by its major contractors. A survey by the Stanford Research Institute of thirteen of the largest military contractors, covering the years 1957–61, revealed that the cost of government-supplied property exceeded gross company property reported on corporate balance sheets.[7] Moreover, much of the company-owned property was used by the commercially oriented divisions of these companies, rather than by the divisions working on government contracts.

More recently, Department of Defence expenditures for additional plant and equipment to be supplied to its contractors have risen sharply, from $56 million in the fiscal year 1965 to an estimated $330 million in the fiscal year 1967. Historically, the major expansions in government-supplied facilities have occurred during war-time periods. Post-war reductions in such assistance have not been on a scale to offset the expansions during hot war. Hence, the long-term trend has been for large-scale federal supply of fixed capital to these governmentally oriented corporations.

In addition, approximately $8 billion of outstanding 'progress' payments are held by military contractors. Some firms report that such government-supplied funds exceed their total net worth. Military procurements regulations provide specific disincentives for the use of private working capital. As specified in the Armed Services Procurement Regulation, progress payments equal to 80 per cent of the costs incurred in government contracts generally are provided without interest charge to the contractors.[8]

However, should these companies decide to rely on private sources for working capital, their interest payments may not be charged to the contract and hence must come out of their profits. Presumably, this arrangement results in smaller total cost to the government because of the lower interest rates paid by the U.S. Treasury on the funds that it borrows. However, the result also is to increase the extent to which public rather than private capital finances the operations of government contractors. Hence, the financial stake that the government has in the performance of its contractors is increased further.

Perhaps the most pervasive way in which the federal government assumes the management decision-making functions of its systems-type contractors is through the procurement legislation and regulations governing the awarding of these contracts. For example, the Armed Services Procurement Regulation requires military suppliers to accept on a 'take it or leave it' basis many standard clauses in government contracts which give the military contracting and surveillance officers numerous powers over the internal operations of these companies. Since NASA is also governed by the Armed Services Procurement Act, it attempts to follow the A.S.P.R.

These unilaterally determined grants of authority vary from matters of substance to items so minor that they border on the ludicrous. Of course, in many instances these restrictions have been imposed to prevent specific abuses or even in an effort to aid the contractors. One extremely knowledgeable defence official, Graeme C. Bannerman, Assistant Secretary of the Navy (Installations and Logistics), stated that these policy and procedural changes 'are designed not to provide rigidity or to inhibit judgement, but rather to establish a framework within which the widest discretion may be exercised in dealing with each individual transaction'. But then, as Professors George Steiner and William Ryan, commenting on the Bannerman statement, point out:

> It is difficult for us to see how increasing the number of directives which apply to industry, then placing these detailed regulations in the hands of the average contract administrator, will increase the contractor's freedom.[9]

Certainly, governmental policy-makers in the area of military contracting rarely consider the cumulative and long-term impacts on company initiative and entrepreneurship. Viewed as a totality, these restrictions represent a new form of government regulation of industry. This regulation is not accomplished through the traditional independent regulatory commission, subject to the Administrative Procedures Act and similar judicial-type legislation, but rather through the unilateral exercise of the government's monopsonistic market power.

The authority assumed by the governmental 'customer' includes power to review and veto company decisions as to which activities to perform in-house and which to subcontract, which firms to use as subcontractors, which products to buy domestically rather than to import, what internal financial reporting systems to establish, what type of industrial engineering and planning system to utilise, what minimum as well as average wage rates to pay, how much overtime work to authorise and so forth.[10] As Professor Michael Reagan has described, 'When a business firm enters into a contract with the government.... The Quasi-public nature of the contracting firm is given implicit recognition by requirements that the firm conduct itself similarly to a government agency in abiding by policies that bind such an agency.'[11]

My favourite example of the more minor matters covered in the detailed and voluminous military procurement regulations is the prescription that the safety rules followed in the offices and factories of the contractors must be consistent with the latest edition of the Corps of Engineers' safety manual.

This entire philosophy and attitude of close government review of the internal operations of its contractors is so deeply embedded that when statements such as the following one are added to the Armed Services Procurement Regulation they evoke no public or industry reaction:

> Although the Government does not expect to participate in every management decision, it may reserve the right to review the contractor's management efforts....[12]

Cost-plus contracting has shifted much of the risk-bearing from the industrial seller to the governmental buyer. The use of fixed-price contracts by the Department of Defence has increased in recent years. However, a major share of military contracts still is on a cost reimbursement basis. So long as this remains the case, the government determines which items of cost are 'allowable' as charges to the contract, and hence to a large extent this determines or at least strongly influences which activities and which items of expenditure the company can profitably undertake (disallowed costs directly reduce company net profits).

The government–industry relationship is a dynamic one. Numerous changes are made in military procurement regulations in each year. Many of these changes further extend the role of the government in the internal operations of the contractors. The following is a sample of new regulations during the year and a half ending October 1967: In contracts for aircraft tyres, tubes and recapping, the contractor must purchase an amount of rubber from the government's stockpile equal to at least 50 per cent of the value of the contract. The contractor does not actually have to use the rubber from the stockpile in filling the government contract. He can keep it for his commercial work. Similar requirements, somewhat less restrictive in their particulars, must be met by contractors who provide aluminium products, while military contractors must buy all their jewel bearings from the government-owned Turtle Mountain Bearing Plant at Rolla, North Dakota. Of course, if such tie-in contracts were made between two private firms, they would run afoul of the anti-trust laws.

In deciding whether costs of professional and consulting services used by a contractor are an allowable charge to a military contract, the government now decides 'whether the service can be performed more economically by employment rather than by contracting', that is, whether one of its contractors should hire an outside consultant rather than a permanent employee (the government also assumes the authority to review the qualifications of the consultant).

'Help wanted' advertising is no longer an allowable cost if it is in colour. Advertising for employees, if it is to be an allowable cost, must be authorised in advance.[13]

Moreover, the Pentagon recently had reported that it is reviewing 'what actions on the part of the government are necessary to assure that compensation paid to contractor employees performing on government contracts is reasonable'.[14] Also, several congressional committees have shown a growing concern during the past year with the efficiency of defence procurement, the profitability of defence contracts and the controls exercised over federal equipment used by government contractors. Much of the legislative concern appears to be leading to even more detailed regulation of defence contractors. Clearly, the trend for increased governmental involvement in private business decision-making appears to be a long-continuing one.

Analysing the problem from the viewpoint of the individual defence industry executive, Steiner and Ryan reported that when company managers are faced with a large mass of government regulations, they spend time completing forms which ought better to be left to performance. The typical application of government regulations is designed to ensure, on the average, satisfactory performance, or, con-

142

versely, to prevent failures. However, in doing this, the government often inhibits superior performance and innovation on the part of project managers. 'Tightened controls resulted in their performing under their capability.'[15]

Looking at defence companies as a whole, there are numerous specific indications that these government-oriented corporations have displayed little entrepreneurial initiative. The dependence of the shipbuilding companies on government contracts and subsidies is well known. It has resulted in that industry's failure to undertake new product development on its own or otherwise effectively to compete in the open world market. Similarly, the aerospace industry generally has made numerous but only half-hearted efforts to utilise its much vaunted engineering and systems analysis capability to penetrate commercial markets. Their non-aircraft diversification efforts mainly have been limited to the governmental environment with which they are so familiar.

Possible Policy Changes

Recent periods of defence cutbacks gave rise to demands for utilising the supposedly unique research and development and systems management capabilities of military contractors in civilian public sector activities. Indeed, the current concern over the need to respond to the racial problems in the centres of the nation's major cities has resulted in renewed pressures for putting to work the science and intellect of our major high-technology corporations in the fields of education, training, mass urban transportation, urban redevelopment and the reduction of poverty generally. Given a decline in military spending in the near future, such action may also be an effective short-term means of preventing unemployment in defence areas. However, as a matter of long-term public policy, would it be wise for the nation to expand that branch of industry which increasingly develops the characteristics and mentality of a government arsenal? At the least, the possible existence of adverse side-effects should be recognised and taken into account in extending the utilisation of the private corporation in the government's business.

Governmental procurement policies and practices may need to be modified in order to halt the erosion of the basic entrepreneurial character of the films that undertake large-scale developmental programmes for the federal establishment. The plea for 'disengagement' made by defence contractors might be given greater weight, although the public interest would necessitate continuing protection and concern.

One way of reducing the financial dependence of defence companies on the government would be to make interest on working capital an allowable cost on military contracts. Interest on indebtedness is a standard cost of doing business and should be recognised as such. Unlike the period of rapid and uncertain expansion of defence work in the early 1940s, military contracts are now an established feature of American industry. The Treasury no longer needs to serve as banker.

A second way of strengthening the private entrepreneurial character of defence firms is to streamline and reduce the variety and scope of special provisions in procurement legislation and regulations. Let these companies develop their own safety rules to discourage employees from skidding on factory floors. We seem at times to forget why in the first place we prefer to use private enterprise rather than government arsenals to develop and produce most of our weapon systems. It is not because private corporations are better than government agencies at following rules and regulations – at doing it by the numbers. It is precisely for the opposite reason. We hope that private enterprise is more creative, more imaginative and more resourceful.

A third way of reducing the close, continuing relationship between the federal establishment and its major suppliers is to broaden the competitive base. This could be accomplished by encouraging commercially oriented companies to consider military and space work as a possible source of diversification for them. The recommendations concerning interest on working capital and streamlining procurement procedures should help on that score. Also, defence companies could be encouraged to diversify into commercial markets. It may be natural for procurement officials to favour firms whose interests are not 'diluted' by commercial work. However, the diversified company may also be the more efficient one in the long run. Certainly, the diversification of industry both into and out of high technology government markets would reduce the present tendency for a relatively small number of companies to become primarily dependent on federal business.

Another method of broadening the competitive base would be to emphasise production rather than R. & D. as the major point of competition. This could be done by doing more of the design work in federal laboratories and making the designs available to the various private companies who would bid on the production work. Substantial precedents exist for this approach. NASA did the primary development work on the Saturn rocket booster, and subsequently commissioned private industry to produce the boosters. Alternatively, the design and development work could be done in the private sector, with the companies competing for this kind of work not being permitted to bid on production contracts.

At present, much of the military subcontracts go to companies that are prime contractors on other systems. More attention in the award of subcontracts could be paid to small business and other industries not actively participating in the military market as primes. Some thought also could be given to reducing the competitive advantages that accrue to the dominant primes that hold on to government-owned plant and equipment for long periods of time. The free provision of these assets also explains their high profit rates. The simplest approach, of course, would be to curtail the practice of furnishing plant and equipment to long-term government contractors and, instead, to give them greater incentives to make their own capital investments.

Application to civilian public sector activities

Certainly, the detailed day-to-day governmental surveillance of internal company operations which is so characteristic of the weapon and space system markets would appear to be a poor precedent to follow in establishing the relative roles of industry and government in such civil public sector areas as urban rehabilitation, environment pollution control, and training and education.

On the positive side, governmental procurement of goods and services from the private sector might well emphasise the end results desired by governmental decision-makers, rather than the detailed manner in which industry designs and manufactures the final product. In its essence, this is the difference between detailed design specifications prepared by the governmental buyer *v.* clear statements of performance desired by the government. The latter approach, of course, gives maximum opportunity for private initiative and inventiveness to come to bear on the problems of the public sector.

That, of course, is the basic and difficult task of using private enterprise in the performance of public functions without either converting the companies to unimaginative arsenalised operations or letting them obtain windfall profits because of the government's inability to drive hard enough and intelligent enough bargains.

The answer is neither simple nor apparent. In part, however, it does lie in governmental policy-makers and administrators constantly being aware of the need to steer that difficult middle course between governmental arsenalisation of industry, on the one hand, and private interests obtaining high profits unrelated to either the investments they have made or the risks that they have borne, on the other.

Notes

1. U.S. National Science Foundation, *R. & D. Activities in State Government Agencies, Fiscal Years 1964 and 1965* (U.S. Government Printing Office, Washington, D.C., 1967) p.vii and *Federal Funds for Research, Development and Other Scientific Activities, Fiscal Years 1964, 1965 and 1966* (U.S. Government Printing Office, Washington, D.C., 1965) pp. 22–6.
2. Aerospace Industries Association, *Aerospace Technology: Creating Social Progress* (Washington, D.C., 1968).
3. This section is based on M. L. Weidenbaum, 'Competition and Concentration in the Military Market', in *Quarterly Review of Economics and Business* (spring 1968).
4. Edward J. Morrison, 'Defense Systems Management: The

375 Series', in *California Management Review* (summer 1967) 17.

5. This section is based on M. L. Weidenbaum, 'Arms and the American Economy: A Domestic Convergence Hypothesis', in *American Economic Review* (May 1968).

6. David Bell *et al.*, *Report to the President on Government Contracting for Research and Development*, 30 April 1962 (reprinted in U.S. House of Representatives, Committee on Government Operations, *Systems Development and Management* (U.S. Government Printing Office, Washington, D.C., 1962) Pt 1, pp. 202–3.

7. Stanford Research Institute, *The Industry–Government Aerospace Relationship*, xi (Menlo Park, California, 1963) 119.

8. Armed Services Procurement Regulation, section E–503.

9. George Steiner and William G. Ryan, *Industrial Project Management* (Macmillan, New York, 1968) pp. 79–80.

10. Armed Services Procurement Regulation, sections 3–900, 1–800, 1–707, 7–203.8, 6–100, 3–800, 1–1700, 12–601 and 12–102.3.

11. Michael D. Reagan, *The Managed Economy* (Oxford University Press, New York, 1963) p. 193.

12. Armed Services Procurement Regulation, section 3–902.1.

13. Ibid., sections 1–323, 1–327.1, 1–315, 15–205.31 and 15–205.33.

14. Department of Defence, *Defense Industry Bulletin* (Nov 1967) p. 22.

15. Steiner and Ryan, *Industrial Project Management*, p. 145.

Note: portions of this chapter draw upon the author's forthcoming book, *The Modern Public Sector*.

6 Government Contracting in Industry: Some Observations on the Ferranti and Bristol Siddeley Contracts

Martin Edmonds

The disclosure of excessive profits from government contracts with Ferranti Ltd in 1964 and with Bristol Siddeley Engines Ltd in 1965 brought into the open and highlighted a problem which had been of concern to the government and the Public Accounts Committee for a number of years. This was the type and most appropriate form of government contracts with private industry and the accurate estimation of prices. Related to it was the government's parallel concern for quality, innovation, performance, delivery times and, ultimately, accountability. And the problem for concern was becoming more acute; production methods were becoming more complex, lead-times harder to predict and technological uncertainties sometimes impossible to anticipate. Essentially it incorporated two main features: of principal concern was the problem of how to contain costs by stimulating efficiency through incentives. Efficiency in this context involved not only keeping costs down through improved management methods but also balancing costs against time scales, the degree of complexity in the product and quality control. The second feature involved the type and nature of the contract itself, together with the problem of how to correlate the profit return to the contracting company with the government's objective for lower prices through stimulating efficiency.

The Ferranti and Bristol Siddeley contracts were essentially straightforward contracts which, compared with research and development contracts, involved fewer complications and uncertainties. The former was a production contract for an advanced guided missile system following separ-

148

ate contracts that had been placed with Ferranti for development work.[1] In this Ferranti, acting as main contractor, would have already encountered and overcome the majority of uncertainties, particularly technical, encountered in a product of this nature. The Bristol Siddeley contract, which was for the overhaul and maintenance of aero engines, was slightly more involved in that it required the yearly renewal of contracts for each of the engine types in use. As such, it was not one contract but a series of follow-on contracts over a period of time. But in spite of the straightforward nature of the contracts, it was revealed in both cases that the profits accruing to the companies concerned were vastly in excess of the profit level described or implicit in their contracts as 'fair and reasonable'[2] and contained in paragraph 43 of Standard Conditions of Government Contracts for Stores Purchases, September 1962.[3]

Generally speaking, profit percentages on government contracts were considered to be 'fair and reasonable' at between 7 and 9 per cent, though there was provision for this to be higher where there was an element of risk involved.[4] To many this profit level is considered to be totally unrealistic 'if Britain is to maintain a leading position in advanced technology'.[5] As the government is the principal purchaser of advanced technical equipment, some consideration should perhaps be devoted to this argument. In the case of Ferranti, the total profit amounted to £5,772,964, which represented a profit percentage over costs of 82 per cent. Between 1959 and 1963, Bristol Siddeley's contracts brought the company a total of £7,032,000 profit on all their maintenance and overall work for the government, a profit percentage of 74 per cent over costs. On certain contracts, as for example all marks of the Sapphire engine, the profit percentage over the four years was as high as 114 per cent.

Both the Ferranti and the Bristol Siddeley cases were investigated by special committees. Sir John Lang and his Committee reported on the Ferranti contracts (Cmnd 2428); this they followed with a second report (Cmnd 2581) which recommended procedures to be adopted when placing government contracts. The Bristol Siddeley contracts were investigated by a Committee of Inquiry headed by Sir Roy Wilson, which reported to the House of Commons in

February 1968 (*HC* 129). The details of both cases can be found in the two reports, and need not be reiterated here.

What is remarkable in both the cases investigated, despite their immediate differences, is the similarity between them, and the reasons why excessive profits had been derived. This similarity is clearly revealed in the reports of both Committees of Inquiry. but is summarised here to form the basis for an examination of government contracting with private industry in the absence of competitive tendering.[6]

The first similarity has already been noted above, this is the relative straightforwardness in the sense that neither contract incorporated complex incentive-type or unforeseen contingency arrangements and both were negotiated when at least one party had at their disposal comprehensive details of the technical, production, labour and material costs and all possible uncertainties. Uncertainties, as a general term, were minimal in both cases and this was reflected in both contracts. Although the extent of the overestimation of the costs involved in the Ferranti contract has partially been excused because of the technical complexity of a new product, the amount of information technically available at the time of estimating costs and negotiating prices was sufficient to warrant a more realistic contract than that which was eventually agreed. This is particularly so considering that not only had Ferranti done much of the development work but also the prices were negotiated almost four years after production of the missile had begun. The Bristol Siddeley contracts were the follow-on type, and consequently the company had information at their disposal to make more realistic estimates of the work they were doing, and the prices that were being asked. In neither case was the overall complexity of the work or the uncertainties involved a cause of poor estimates of the total costs.

Both contracts, significantly, were fixed-price contracts. This type of contract had for some time been encouraged by the Ministry of Aviation. As far as was feasible, an increasing number of their contracts were of this type.[8] The object in adopting this form of contracting was to encourage efficiency within the contracting firms, and provide an incentive for the contractor to employ new production methods, lower his costs and thereby increase his profit by producing for much less

150

than the agreed price in the contract. There are dangers inherent in this method and these became highlighted in both the Ferranti and Bristol Siddeley cases. It is useless as a method of agreeing a 'fair and reasonable price' unless the price can be related to a clearly defined task. Without this clear definition no accurate or acceptable fixed price can be ascertained. There must also be equality of information between both parties to the contract to enable them to estimate realistic production costs early in the life of the contract.[9]

The procedure for negotiating prices is that estimates of costs are submitted by the contractor on the one hand, and estimates of costs and reasonable profits by the contracting government department on the other. The department estimates are calculated on the basis of labour, materials and bought-out costs, drawn up by technical cost officers, plus estimates of overheads expressed as a percentage of the technical cost officers' estimates and determined by department accountants. In both the Ferranti and Bristol Siddeley cases, the costs submitted by the companies and the totals of the technical cost officers were overestimated. Both cases serve to illustrate the danger inherent in the fixed-price contract, where profits are more easily derived from an overestimation of costs, and therefore the price, than from increased returns accruing to the company as a result of increased efficiency. A second danger must surely be that for further contracts, or follow-on contracts, the company that has reduced costs through efficient management will be penalised in that the negotiated price will be lower because of their previous efficiency, unless recognition and compensation is made of past performance as, for example, in the new contract price.[10]

Thirdly, it was clearly brought out in both reports that the companies concerned withheld information from the Department technical cost officers. This information, in the opinion of the Committees of Inquiry, was a prerequisite if an accurate estimate of costs by the technical cost officers was to have been made. Under the circumstances, it was hardly surprising that the estimates of labour and material costs was inaccurate. Further, the extent to which the total department estimates were out was exaggerated by the existing method of calculating overheads, which was to express them as a percentage of labour costs. If the technical cost officers' estimates were high, so too would be the total estimates for overheads, multiplying the discrepancy sometimes by a factor of five. This was the situation with the Ferranti contract; Bristol Siddeley was slightly different in that the percentage for overheads was not as significant; however, there were in addition extra costs due to double charging.

The issue in both cases centred on two fundamental points: firstly, whether it was the responsibility of the contractor to inform the department that it was receiving excessive profits, and that therefore the negotiated price was unrealistic; and secondly, whether the department in its turn should have free access to the contractor's books when calculating its estimates of labour, material and overhead costs. In the case of follow-on contracts it was a question of whether the department should have access to the past year's records.

Regarding the first point, both Committees of Inquiry confirmed that the companies concerned were all aware that the government was being overcharged. At Bristol Siddeley, despite a merger during the period under review which involved alterations to the structure and organisation within the company, the investigating committee demonstrated that overcharging on government contracts was known at management, executive and board levels.[11] However, they also noted that control and communication within the company left much to be desired. Overcharging was also known at Ferranti's. This must have been especially evident as the Bloodhound contract represented all but a small proportion of the company's total work.[12] Yet this was a consideration that escaped the departmental technical cost officers and accountants as a crude check of their estimates of total costs.

On the second point, both reports noted that the contractors withheld information from department officials. In Standard Conditions of Government Contracts, paragraph 43, there is provision for departmental officials to visit the contractor to 'estimate or ascertain the costs of production of the articles'.[13] It is significant that the department officials concerned interpreted this clause as permitting them only to estimate costs, and not to ascertain them, and for this reason

152

did not insist that they should be given completely free access either to the contractor's factory or to his accounts and records.[14] The estimates of costs worked out in either case by department officials was thus based on inadequate, and sometimes selected, information, plus an element of speculation. In the Public Accounts Committee inquiry into the Ferranti contracts in 1963/4 the department accountants in evidence admitted that they were forced eventually to provide estimates that were 'partly actual, partly estimated'.[15] Even after the excess profits had been disclosed, the Company Chairman still refused to reveal his firm's financial concerns to the Public Accounts Committee. He further argued that in his opinion the department had as much information as had his company when the contracts were negotiated, and that accurate estimating was impossible, anyway, for costs fluctuated considerably at different stages of production and at different times. They tended to increase particularly when the contract neared completion.[16] He omitted, however, to say how this variation in costs over time necessarily affected the total cost on a fixed-price contract, or how this related to the apparent reasons for the overestimation of his contract for the Bloodhound missile. In the case of Bristol Siddeley, vital information about man-hours and piece rates was refused, as were figures for the previous year's operations.[17]

The inescapable fact in both the Ferranti and Bristol Siddeley cases is that the government was grossly overcharged for the work done in the time specified; this is irrespective of the amount of the profits gained by the two companies. In the investigating committee reports, there is implicit in their findings an apportionment of blame for the fact that public money had been spent unnecessarily. There is also an implicit assumption that government contracts are intrinsically and qualitatively different from commercial ones between private companies. How different, and based upon what criteria, is not made explicit; yet this basic consideration appears to be a point of departure between the contractors and the government. Upon these different interpretations possibly depends the extent to which responsibility for the price, the terms of the contract and the delivery dates of the satisfactorily finished product resides with the government department entirely, or is shared between both parties to the contract. For as long, however, as the interpretations of the premise behind government contracts remain implicit, and contracts are drawn up based upon different and conflicting points of view, the problem of accountability for government contracts with private industry will, as the experience of Ferranti and Bristol Siddeley has demonstrated, remain unresolved.

The arguments of the two companies were similar. Both maintained that they were not legally bound to produce their books for examination. To provide such information would certainly disclose the amount of profits accruing to the firm, as well as their systems of budgetary control, accounting procedures and so on. It was the sort of information, in fact, that competitors would find most useful. It is significant to note, however, that both firms were most concerned about having to divulge their profits. They tended to confine their discussion to the issue of whether profits should be seen over a period of time covering a number of contracts, or whether they should be determined singly, contract by contract.[19]

Except as an indication of the extent to which they were overcharged, the department on the other hand were less interested in the total amount of the profits. On a fixed-price contract these are expected to fluctuate as a matter of principle. Their concern was to have that information which would enable them to estimate accurately the price of the finished product, which, anyway, included an agreed profit percentage. They consequently saw the contract negotiations and the calculations of costs differently. They 'hoped and expected' that they would have access to full information.[19] In evidence, however, officials admitted that they felt they had no legal right to it.[20]

The problem thus hinges upon the interpretation which either party gave to Standard Condition 43 concerning the fixing of prices, what constituted a 'fair and reasonable profit', and what mutual assistance should be provided. A complication regarding fixed-price contracts is that subsequent to an agreed price, even when it has been decided upon with equality of information, the performance of the company brings higher profits than previously envisaged through efficient working. This is the principle behind the fixed-price contract; yet these higher profits might well

154

conflict with what was envisaged in the guideline 'fair and reasonable' in Standard Condition 43, and which applied to the original agreement.

The Ferranti and Bristol Siddeley contracts have demonstrated that where fixed-price contracts were concerned, which were non-competitive, it was imperative that equality of information should exist between government and contractor. It has also been argued that this information should be extended to include specialist parliamentary committees, within the limits of genuine security. Perhaps the recent experience of the Select Committee on Science and Technology during their inquiry into military R. & D. may serve as an indication of how little progress has been made in this respect.[21] Publication of costs and profit percentages is standard practice with United States government contracts, and could well be applied in Britain. It has been suggested that such a practice might also serve to promote that efficiency which fixed-price contracts were intended to effect.[22]

It is the aim of government contracts not only to acquire the end product of a given quality and within a given time scale but also to keep prices at a minimum by encouraging and maintaining efficiency within the companies with whom contracts have been placed. It should, however, be noted that these three objectives are not mutually exclusive and, according to the product, differ in their priority. It requires considerable management expertise to balance benefits in one against penalties in others. The use of incentive contracts, giving greater scope to management skills, has been employed to achieve this end. These have principally been the fixed-price and target cost variants. The contracts with Ferranti and Bristol Siddeley have demonstrated not only weaknesses and dangers in this form of contracting but also that the processes depend to a considerable degree upon mutual trust, honesty and co-operation. Such conditions were obviously lacking in these two cases, and other examples can be found.[23] The changes proposed in the Lang Committee Second Report were designed to improve the exchange of information between the government and the private contractor. But if the proposals were to be implemented there could be no guarantee that the additional aim of promoting efficiency would be achieved. The explanation is clear: the incentive for private firms would continue to be to overestimate costs when negotiating fixed-price contracts to act as an insurance against imponderables either encountered during production, or in the accuracy of their own estimating procedures. Nor are firms going to submit estimates on untried, new management and production techniques.

The Ferranti and Bristol Siddeley cases only represent one part of government contracting with industry. To a degree, they are unrepresentative of much government contracting. More complex is contracting for research and development work, where such considerations as accurate estimation of costs, and even equality of information, are relatively meaningless. The record of estimating costs for development work both by government departments and by contractors is worse than that revealed in the Ferranti and Bristol Siddeley cases. The major difference is that estimates discrepancies are not translated into profits to the contractor, but in cost escalation of the total project under development. Yet even where costs have escalated on development contracts beyond the original estimates, there have been instances where information which might have gone some way to account for these increases has been withheld by the contractor.[24] There are many examples of development contracts where the original estimates have been far exceeded: the T.S.R. 2 and the Blue Steel contracts are taken here as representative. In the former case, the original estimate of £80–90 million in 1959 rose to £240–60 million in 1964. Blue Steel estimates rose from £12½ million in 1955 to £60 million in 1960.

It is almot impossible to determine accurately the cost of development of technologically advanced projects. The more the project extends the state of the art, and the more it is technologically uncertain, so the difficulty of even approximately estimating total costs correspondingly increases. This situation has been recognised by the Treasury.[25] In 1961 it was a central concern of the Committee on the Management and Control of Research and Development chaired by Sir Solly Zuckerman, and later, in 1968, of the Second Report of the Select Committee on Science and Technology on Defence Research.[26] Directives to departments have been to keep technical considerations and costs constantly in mind while undertaking project studies and feasibility studies, and in the formulation of operational requirements and specifications. The form of contract favoured for development contracts continues to be the 'incentive' fixed-price or target cost contract in place of the old cost-plus-fixed-fee variety. Target cost contracts are increasingly employed where the project is particularly expensive and technologically complex. The object behind these developments has been to minimise the effect of uncertainties and combat poor cost estimation. But the major problem remains regarding the accuracy of the estimate of costs and consequently the price of the finished product.

Where development contracts are concerned, there has been a discernible tendency to place greater responsibility upon the contractor for estimates of costs, time scales and technological forecasts. In presenting project design proposals, the contractor, whether in competition or not, is now required to submit a detailed breakdown of all costs, technical designs, management controls and time scales for the scrutiny and examination of the contracting department. In addition, the department is also expected to have access to the contractor's accounts, books and records to facilitate this task, and to work out appropriate profit percentages, costs and overheads. Responsibility for subcontractors lies with the main contractor.

An Admiralty Working Party in 1958 undertook an examination of the cost increases over estimates in Navy development contracts. In their findings they recommended a radical change in existing procedures.[27] They argued the case for project managers with financial control over the project. They also made demands for periodic reviews of progress, and a new organisation for control within the contracting firm. Their recommendations were brought into effect in 1962. A similar form of project management was employed in the T.S.R. 2 contract. Arrangements in this instance were provided for a phased and costed technical programme against which the contractors submitted statements of expenditure for comparison at regular intervals. These arrangements were made for each component. In addition, costs were to be regularly examined, revised annually, and expenditure returns checked quarterly. Progress reports were circulated between the Project Director, the Project Management

Board, the Systems Integration Panel, and the Contracts Monitoring Committee.[28]

Even with these systems of cost control and monitoring by both the contractor and the department, the original T.S.R. 2 estimates proved to be totally unrealistic, and costs soared. Explanations offered included the argument that the monitoring of expenditure was 'inhibited by the inadequacy of information made available to them'[29] and that the contractor for engines – Bristol Siddeley – had badly underestimated the costs for engine development, which quadrupled over five years; furthermore, the engine contractor's system of financial control was particularly weak. A similar criticism was made of the Blue Steel contractor's financial control system. Also in this case the original estimates were basically at fault.

The government's record in contracting in the defence field with private industry has been poor. This has generally been the case, in the sense that costs have not been contained or efficiently stimulated irrespective of whether contracts have been for development, production or maintenance. Considerable amounts of public money have been spent, sometimes with no output at the end, as in the case of the £60 million spent on the cancelled T.S.R.2. Estimates of costs have invariably been inaccurate, either because necessary information has been unavailable owing to technological uncertainties and other imponderables, or because it has been deliberately withheld. The government on its part has endeavoured through its position as the only purchaser in several cases to promote or maintain a level of efficiency within those firms with which they have placed a contract. At the same time they have ensured for the contractors a 'fair and reasonable profit; although this has been fixed at a low rate, government departments had tended to err on the side of generosity towards the contractors.[30] To achieve this aim, the government has chosen in the past to use the fixed-price contract wherever possible. Under ideal circumstances, as was pointed out in the Second Lang Committee Report, this type of contract would benefit both parties, but as the system was then being employed, the method of agreeing fixed prices did not always appear to be based on 'reliable estimates of costs which assume efficient production'.[31]

On the basis of this examination of the Ferranti and Bristol

Siddeley contracts, the information presented by the Committees of Inquiry into those contracts, and a brief examination of the T.S.R. 2 and Blue Steel development contracts, one fundamental consideration emerges with respect to government contracting with private industry in the absence of a competitive situation. This is the question of responsibility for accurately estimating costs and keeping to them. The responsibility for beating these estimates where possible through efficient management is a related problem. How to determine responsibility may be expressed in terms of three general propositions. Each carries with it clear implications. The first is that the responsibility for the efficient execution of government contracts should be shared between the government department concerned and the contractor. How the responsibility is shared will be reflected in the contract and the management control system employed. The second proposition is that responsibility should predominantly, or totally, reside with the department. The third is that the contractor should be given a free hand, subject to close auditing.

To some extent the first proposition had already come into effect, though it has taken many forms. As the Plowden Report into the aircraft industry observed in 1965, to reflect the deep involvement of the government in the affairs of the aircraft industry, and to remove the duplication of financial and technical control by the industry and the government, there is a strong case either for nationalisation, which would tend towards the second proposition above, or to have a degree of government shareholding in the industry along the lines of existing arrangements with Shorts Bros & Harland, Belfast, and British Petroleum.[32] Though this second alternative is one which is little tried in Britain, compared to the Continent, it was one to which the Plowden Committee attached considerable weight. Certainly it would constitute a radical step as a method of overcoming the problems existing in government contracting with private industry. Another form of sharing responsibility is that recommended by the Admiralty Working Group referred to above, and exemplified by the elaborate T.S.R. 2 systems of management control. Here major government contracts with private industry carry with them obligations on the part of both contractor and department to establish joint as well as separate systems of

159

monitoring and project management. The lessons apparently learnt from the T.S.R. 2 experience were that such systems were not yet tight enough.[33] On the other hand it has been argued that a further increase in bureaucratic inspection and control would not only remove the dynamism for improvement in production methods and efficiency on the part of the contractor but would also add to the already high degree of duplication.[34] Further, such duplication would be wasteful in time, effort and cost. Perhaps recent experience in the United States would confirm this impression. Lastly, the present system might be continued. But in this event, the spirit of the 'incentive' fixed-price contract, equality of information and honesty in cost estimation must be adhered to by both parties. Further, private industry must seriously endeavour to promote efficiency once the contract has been signed. That alternative methods are being employed indicates that such a voluntary relationship would appear to be impossible, and that the sentiment behind an observation of the Chief Executive of Rolls Royce in 1967 that 'over the past ten years anyone who carried out cost estimation honestly would have lost his job overnight, and he knew it'[35] contains a strong element of truth.

If responsibility for the execution of government contracts was to reside principally with the department concerned, a prerequisite would be a tightening of the Standard Contract Conditions allowing for access to contractors' accounts, production management and operating procedures. This would be necessary to ascertain with a high degree of certainty the prices subsequently to be agreed. The department stands by those estimates, though efficiency in production would theoretically rest with the contractor. But if departmental responsibility were to be meaningful, it should have some say in the organisation and system of production, management and control within the firm if it felt that prices originally estimated were on the basis of production techniques that subsequently proved to be deficient. This point becomes meaningful if the criticisms of Bristol Siddeley's system of communication and control are to be reconsidered in this context.

It is doubtful that industry would welcome such intervention, particularly in firms where government contracts do not represent a large proportion of their total activity. This would include the vast range and number of subcontractors. There is in this type of arrangement the possibility of post-costing, in which prices, costs and profits could be accurately determined. But the procedure would, at the same time, destroy the incentive for production efficiency which is one of the objects of the exercise.

The case for industry to take responsibility for estimates and sticking to them must assume that methods for audit and examination of government contracts are extensive. This would require that costs and profits are accurately recorded and published, as in the United States. The very fact that price targets are known and the performance of management and production is published and can be assessed is considered to be an important incentive. As a *Flight* editorial has succinctly put it,

> The professional engineers on the job know exactly what the targets are, so that cost-control begins on the engineer's drawing board and not in the accountant's ledger. The fact that the engineers and the Civil Servants know that everyone else knows what the targets are is the greatest professional incentive of all.... One published labour-cost figure can be worth a thousand Civil Servants.
> ... This seems the perfect moment for the industry to convert to full public accountability ... the basic presumption must be that books must be open unless a company can prove otherwise not vice versa as now.[36]

The case for this approach to the problem is supported by the argument that the management problems in the technologically advanced industries are 'of a very high order', and that such problems are better resolved by the industry itself, unfettered by bureaucratic interference.[37] Further, costs are closely allied to time, and often bureaucratic considerations cause long delays and stultify management experience and 'risk-taking acumen'. Against this argument is the problem that many companies are non-competitive and that poor performance, however widely broadcast, does not alter the fact that the government should still have to rely upon them at a later date for specific contracts.

Connected with all the problems associated with government contracting, and the proposed alternative methods of overcoming them, is the question of trust, or lack of it, that exists between the contracting parties. The contracts for Bristol Siddeley engines, Ferranti Bloodhound, T.S.R. 2, Blue Steel and Buccaneer all in their ways reflect this point.

If trust cannot be engendered voluntarily, is there a guarantee that it can be improved by systems of enforcement? And if so, will such measures promote efficiency? And even if there is improvement for one reason or another, how, and according to what criteria, can the public still be reasonably assured that it is getting the best price above other considerations?

The British government, in part recognising the problems of contracting with private industry and in part prompted by the disclosure of the Ferranti and Bristol Siddeley profits, formed a working party in 1966 to investigate and make recommendations upon scientific features of public contracting. Participants were government officials and representatives from private industry, including the Confederation of British Industry, and the Society of British Aerospace Contractors.[38] In January 1969 the findings of the committee were reported. Several important and significant aspects of government contracting have been changed.

Arising out of the activities of this working party, a new deal has emerged in which 'fair play contracts replace the law of the jungle, and involve give and take on both sides'.[39] The 'law of the jungle' obviously refers to the past situation, epitomised by Ferranti and Bristol Siddeley, in which there was an absence of mutual trust between the two parties, government access to equality of information was not guaranteed and the interpretation of 'fair and reasonable prices' was far from consistent.

Mr John Diamond, Chief Secretary of the Treasury, hoped that these agreements represented a change in the relations between government and industry. Certainly, the new deal has involved concessions on both sides: the government has agreed to base profit percentages in relation to average earnings of industries over several years, which was one of Ferranti's main arguments, whereas industry has agreed to two main changes over the controversial Standard Conditions on

Government Contracts. The first is that Standard Condition 43 has been revised to ensure no ambiguity regarding equality of information; and, secondly, a new Standard Condition, 48, has been included which makes some provisions for government post-costing. The latter refers to the pricing of follow-on contracts; it allows government departments to check their estimating procedures, and to acquire information freely in the event that a contract should be submitted to the newly constituted Review Board on Government Contracts.

Most important among the new provisions is the establishment of the independent Government Contracts Review Board. It comprises an independent chairman, and has equal membership from government and industry. The Board's functions at present fall into three categories: to receive from either side claims where contracts have incurred excessive profit ($27\frac{1}{2}$ per cent or more) or unconscionable loss (15 per cent or more), to review the new arrangements after three years and to submit an interim report within twelve months on the differences between government and industry on the precise computation of a profit formula.

Incorporated within the terms of reference of the Review Board's third function will be the responsibility to distinguish between development, production and maintenance contracts and to decide the appropriate profit percentages according to these different types of work. In the past, differences in profit levels were related to the degree of 'risk' involved in the contract: the higher the risk, the higher the profit level. Agreement has already been reached on profits and risk which mitigates the argument of the past that profits of production should be higher to enable industry to undertake development, especially on a private-venture basis.

Government contracts between departments and industry can now be referred to the Independent Review Board. The stand, however, that the Board will take regarding excessive profits and losses remains to be seen; it will be interesting to see, for example, what interest they will devote to the efficiency of industry in controlling and executing government contracts and how sympathetic they are with poor management on the one hand, and, on the other, the responsibility for poor contracting and bad price estimates. On the second point, however, it may be that there will be less incentive for government departments to negotiate the best terms 'if it knows it can run to arbitration in the event of trouble'.[40]

Most interesting is the impact that these new arrangements will have upon the types of contracts favoured by industry and government, and the policy of the government to encourage efficiency through contracting procedures. The Lang Committee disapproved of post-costing[41] as this impaired efficiency; Standard Condition 48 now includes it. It has been suggested that the government can claim so much information that this could cause delays and bring about a return to cost-plus contracts which nobody wants, and which do not serve to stimulate efficiency. Further, fixed-price contracts are relatively meaningless if the profits earned through efficiency are reduced after reference to the Review Board, or if government post-costing to 'check their estimates' becomes standard procedure. In the interests of balancing the estimates of government and industry, there may well be a real danger that the incentives of government contracts become eroded, and that the onus of responsibility of the contracting department as buyer to acquire the best conditions possible be shifted to the newly constituted Review Board.

Although the Review Board may be seen as an important step in improving government–industry relations, it is too early to make any assessment of its effect and influence. However, a few preliminary observations may be made in the light of the above discussion. Firstly, there is the question of whether it does in fact represent a change. Immediately, it does not. After Bristol Siddeley and Ferranti, the firms concerned were required to return a considerable proportion of their high profits at the insistence of the government. The Review Board now formulates the process, and, if upheld, permits the claim for repayment to be made by either side. This may save time-consuming and expensive public inquiries, and help to eliminate much acrimonious open discussion. It does not begin, however, to attack the major issues of realistic cost estimates, management efficiency, innovative uncertainties and advances and lengthening lead-times. And it is these considerations, as well as profits that must be incorporated within government contracting.

Secondly, there is the problem of realistic and accurate estimates of costs and prices. The Board appears to be designed to establish where excessive profits and losses have been incurred, and arbitrate accordingly, without apparently recognising that if the original estimates and prices were unrealistic the extent of the profits and losses would be unrealistic also. It seems merely an expedient to make institutional provisions to balance profits and losses to a reasonable gross figure without examining how the gross figures were determined. Post-costing may help to work out the fairest outcome for a bad situation, but it does not go any way towards resolving or ameliorating the problems of government contracting. What is possibly dangerous is that this arrangement, by which the government and industry can arbitrate and come to agreement where contracts have gone astray, may either hide the reasons why the prices and costs were inaccurate in the first place, as concern is directed towards mutual satisfaction in the area in dispute, or take away the pressures and needs to seek improvements in the contracting process itself.

Thirdly, the Review Board does not appear to have any powers to make value judgements upon such issues as a firm's management expertise, contract monitoring procedures, technical and scientific innovative capacity, lead-time overruns, quality and reliability standards, or production capacity, when reviewing contracts. Their terms of reference are confined to an investigation of contracts where large profits and losses have been concerned. They may not, for example, investigate contracts where, but for improved management, a better price might have been negotiated in the first place.

Finally, within their terms of reference, the Review Board does not appear to be able to exercise any degree of independent initiative. They may only arbitrate on contracts submitted to them by either side. They cannot, for example, intervene or participate during contract negotiations. Nor can they recommend the appropriate contract for different types of work. Their influence may possibly be in their brief to report after three years on how the arrangement has worked. If the report is confined to the Board's arbitration work, and does not focus its attention on the broader question of why arbitration should now have become necessary on government contracts in the first place, an opportunity for constructive proposals may be missed. This would be unfortunate considering the information on government contracts that will have been made available over the period under review.

Notes

1. *First Report of the Inquiry into the Pricing of Ministry of Aviation Contracts* (Cmnd 2428, H.M.S.O., London, July 1964) p. 3.
2. Ibid., p. 3. The Ferranti contracts included a clause which reproduced Standard Condition 43, and explicitly stated that fair and reasonable profits would be paid. This was also explicit in the Bristol Siddeley contracts. See *Public Accounts Committee Second Special Report 1966–67 (HC 571)* p. xxii, para. 26.
3. Ibid., app. 111, p. 26. Also *Report of the Committee of Inquiry into Certain Contracts made with Bristol Siddeley Engines Ltd, Report of the Inquiry into the Pricing of Ministry of Aviation Contracts* (Cmnd 2581, Feb. 1965) app. 1, p. 29.
4. *HC* 129, p. 12.
5. R. Maxwell, *Public Sector Purchasing* (a report to the Parliamentary Labour Party Economic Group, Oct. 1967) p. 104. See also Cmnd 2581, pp. 19–22, esp. para. 57.
6. *HC* 129, p. 8, para. 21. On only 6 per cent of Ministry of Aviation contracts was there competitive tendering.
7. *Public Accounts Committee Second Report, Session 1963–4 (HC 22–I)*, 'Guided Weapons Contracts: Ferranti Ltd', p. xxvi.
8. Cmnd 2581, p. 8, para. 16.
9. Ibid., p. 8, para. 16.
10. Ibid., p. 19, para. 53. See also *HC* 129, p. 12, para. 34. A suggested method of encouraging efficiency is to reward past efficiency performance with renewed contracts or higher profit percentages. See 'Report to the President on Government contracting for Research and Development', in *Hearing on Systems Development and Management, House Committee on Government Operations, 87th Congress, 2nd Session, 1962* and reproduced in W. R. Nelson (ed.), *The Politics of Science* (Oxford University Press, 1968) pp. 211 ff.
11. *HC* 129, pp. 30–7.

12. Cmnd 2428, p. 8, para. 26. Also *Public Accounts Committee Second Report, 1963–4 (HC 22–1)* p. xxv.

13. *Standard Conditions of Government Contracts,* Sept. 1962, para. 43, subsection 3(a).

14. Cmnd 2581, p. 10, para. 23.

15. *Public Accounts Comittee Second Report, 1963–4 (HC 22–1)* p. xxiii.

16. Ibid., p. xxvii: 'Their accumulated experience had shown how difficult it was to get even reasonably accurate estimates. . . . In their experience costs rise towards the end of the contract and it is not possible to assess the out-turn till the contract is completed.'

17. *HC* 129, p. 19, para. 46.

18. *Public Accounts Committee Second Special Report (HC* 571, 1966–7) p. xii, para. 26.

19. *Public Accounts Committee Second Report, 1963–4 (HC 22–1)* p. xxv.

20. Ibid.

21. *Second Report from the Select Committee on Science and Technology: Defence Research, 1968/9 (HC 213).*

22. *Flight International,* Editorial: 'The Bristol Siddeley Affair', 6 April 1967.

23. *Public Accounts Committee Second and Fifth Reports (HC* 98–1 and 647–1, 1966–7), 'The pricing of contracts for the Buccaneer'.

24. *Public Accounts Committee Special Report, 1961–2 (HC 23–1),* 'Army Appropriation Account; Development Contracts for Fighting Vehicles', p. lviii.

25. *Public Accounts Committee Special Report,* 1961–2 *(HC 23–1),* 'Treasury Minute on Ministry of Aviation Control of Expenditure on Extramural Research', p. viii.

26. *Report of the Committee on the Management and Control of Research and Development* (Office of the Minister for Science, H.M.S.O., London, 1961) and *Second Report from the Select Committee on Science and Technology: Defence Research, 1968/9 (HC 213).* For a discussion of the problems involved in cost estimating in development contracts, the control of cost escalation, and a distinction between production and development costs, see *Estimates Committee, Seventh Report, 1964–5(HC 358),* 'Electrical and Electronic Equipment for the Services', pp. xi–xvi.

27. *Public Accounts Committee Third Report, 1962–3 (HC* 24–1), 'Navy Appropriations Account', pp. liv-lvi.

28. *Public Accounts Committee Second Report (Part 1) 1966–7 (HC* 98–1), 'Control of Expenditure on the T.S.R. 2 Aircraft', pp. xv–xvi.

29. Ibid., p. xvi.

30. *Public Accounts Committee Special Report,* 1962–3 *(HC* 24–1), 'Treasury Minute on P.A.C. 3rd Report, 1961–2', p. vii: 'The Ministry cannot expect to negotiate contracts under which the contractor is placed at risk of receiving *less* than fair and reasonable remuneration because of the uncertainties in the task or beyond his control.'

31. Cmnd 2581, p. 9, paras 17 and 18.

32. *Report of the Committee of Inquiry into the Aircraft Industry* (Cmnd 2853, Dec. 1965) pp. 83–6, esp. paras 484–90.

33. *Public Accounts Committee Second Report (Part 1) 1966–7 (HC* 98–1), 'Control of Expenditure on the T.S.R. 2 Aircraft', para. 44.

34. Cmnd 2583, p. 83, para. 473.

35. *Flight International,* 2 March 1967, p. 321: 'Management in Aeronautics.'

36. Ibid., editorial, 6 April 1967.

37. Professor Keith Lucas, 'The Industry and its future': lecture at the Royal United Services Institution, 7 Dec 1966.

38. *Flight International,* 9 Jan. 1969, p. 59.

39. Ibid.

40. Ibid.

41. *Second Report of the Inquiry into Placing of Ministry of Aviation Contracts* (Cmnd 2428, H.M.S.O., London, July 1964) pp. 4 and 24.

7 Project Upward Bound: A Case Study

Richard T. Frost

The philosophy behind the War on Poverty stressed the desire to involve private and quasi-public groups in poor areas in the administration of poverty programmes. This was intended, among other purposes, to encourage a wider involvement of organised efforts directed at the less fortunate. Community Action programme grants to local Community Action agencies were a principal means employed by the agency to achieve this end. However, the Office of Economic Opportunity (O.E.O.) used a somewhat different approach in devolving much of the administration of the Upward Bound programme to a private, non-governmental organisation. In the case of Upward Bound, O.E.O. utilised a contract, not a grant, to delegate operating authority. The contractor was a private, non-profit corporation, but not an agency which represented – nor did it purport to represent – a local poverty neighbourhood. O.E.O, contracted out the administration of Upward Bound for many of the same reasons that the more 'conventional' government contracting agencies devolve administrative powers to private corporations through service contracts: to quickly draw together an expert and talented group to administer the programme; to relieve the potential workload burdens from the agency's civil service employees; and to deflect criticism of the government bureaucracy.

The contract between O.E.O. and the Institute for Services to Education (I.S.E.) was a wide delegation of powers. The O.E.O. Director, Sargent Shriver, initially feared that the contract proposal called for too wide a delegation of authority which should be retained by O.E.O. Although the work-plan in the actual contract document did provide for close oversight of the Upward Bound project by the O.E.O. staff, nevertheless the contract remained an example of great devolution of administrative authority. The grant proposals submitted by individual colleges and universities for Upward Bound grants

169

had to be approved by O.E.O., but the agency, in a sense, 'subcontracted' with I.S.E. for the actual surveillance of Upward Bound programmes.

The following narrative discusses the history and nature of the administration of the Upward Bound programme, as I witnessed it as the chief O.E.O. official in charge of overseeing the I.S.E. contract. The story illustrates the advantages of utilising the contract device for the administration of social programmes, as well as the political pitfalls inherent in such a device. Whatever the real motivation behind the congressional critics of the programme, they publicly based their attacks on Upward Bound on the contract device used to administer it. As Albert Quie (R., Minn.) stated his objections to Upward Bound on the floor of the House of Representatives:

Mr Chairman, as I suggested earlier, the relationship of O.E.O. to a private contractor of services, raises several questions which must concern each of us.

First, there is the question of the legality of O.E.O.'s use of contract personnel as a replacement for regular civil service workers. . . .

Second, there is the question of avoidance of personnel ceilings established for the agency.

Third, there is the question of the cost to the Government of performing with contracted services work of a nature normally performed by Government personnel at a far lower cost per hour. . . .

Fourth, there is the question of competitive bidding for any public contract. . . . In short, it appears that the Government, and the American public, have been victimised by O.E.O. acceptance of a grossly underbid proposal.

Mr Quie's points represent the 'traditional' arguments employed to criticise particular government contracts, especially contracts for services as opposed to those for hard-goods. A look at one such contract, Upward Bound, may contribute to a better understanding of why government agencies utilise the contract device to achieve social goals.

When President Johnson signed the Economic Opportunity
Act of 1964, he instructed the new agency, the Office of
Economic Opportunity, to 'wage a total war on poverty in
America', and appointed R. Sargent Shriver, already the full-
time head of the Peace Corps, to administer the new programme. Among some handsome tools available to Shriver for
this purpose was what Representative Adam Powell (D.,
N.Y.) later came to call 'the walking money in Community
Action programme'. The E.O.A. statute provided a formula
whereby 80 per cent of the nearly $1 billion appropriated for
the Community Action programme would be distributed
among the fifty states and their localities, but the remaining
20 per cent, or almost $200 million, could be distributed by
Shriver as he saw fit, within the very general confines of the
legislative mandate.

Shriver decided to establish, with much of his discretionary
monies, what were called 'national emphasis' programmes –
in contrast to the myriad of local anti-poverty efforts which
were conceived locally and sent up for approval through
O.E.O.'s seven regional offices to Washington. His motives
were many, but two factors were paramount. First, as a new
agency reporting directly to the President, O.E.O. had to
gain quick visibility and momentum. Shriver's political success with the Peace Corps and his own background as a salesman – at the Merchandise Mart and as President of Chicago's
School Board – gave him a special drive for political success in
salesman terms. Second, he and his advisers knew that it
would be difficult to create a clear image of the poverty programme, given the great variety of local programmes under
the umbrella phrase 'Community Action'. Without some
more precise identity the programme might have only a
fragile base of political support and prove highly vulnerable
in the event that some projects were embarrassing failures.

The first national emphasis programme was Head Start,
the programme for slum pre-schoolers. It was a political success from the beginning. Four- and five-year-olds don't riot;
they don't use ugly language; they haven't learned to steal;
and they don't sleep with one another. They just come to
school from the slums, whether rural or urban, with a very

small tin cup compared to the big bucket the middle-class youngster brings to the first grade.

Shriver was very excited about the potential of Head Start and ordered a full-steam effort in O.E.O., starting about February of 1965. The agency suffered massive administrative pains in making the effort. Guidelines had to go out to new and clumsy local poverty groups; regional offices, trying to find physical space, people and money, began processing Head Start grants before they even had typewriters on desks. O.E.O. personnel in Washington worked routinely from 9.00 a.m. until midnight, always on Saturdays, and usually on Sundays. So did Shriver – he maintained the same difficult hours in his dual capacity as head of both the Peace Corps and O.E.O.

Yet, by the end of July 1965, O.E.O. had some six to seven hundred thousand American slum children in Head Start classes, half of the local programme run by local school systems and half by private agencies. When the President's wife agreed to have her picture with a child on a poster publicising Head Start, it was apparent that Shriver had an unusual political success in Project Head Start.

But the experience of the agency in mounting this programme was agonising, almost crushing. Everybody had worked too hard; funds to pay the actual operators of Head Start programmes in the localities were delayed, and controversies began to surface over widely divergent salaries among the various programmes and skill groups. Neither O.E.O. headquarters nor its regional offices had prepared themselves adequately to administer operational programmes. Head Start was an instant political success but it was an almost fatal administrative blow to an embryonic agency. O.E.O. learned much from the experience and, as we shall see, subsequently decided to administer Upward Bound very differently.

Head Start for Teenagers

By the spring of 1965, there were about fifty 'pre-college' programmes for 'high-risk' students, all funded by private sources. For example, the Rockefeller Foundation had

awarded a third of a million dollars to each of eight prominent liberal arts colleges to recruit and support Negroes –
preferably males – for these colleges. The Carnegie Foundation had engaged in similar programmes at Oberlin and elsewhere.

The American Council on Education had established a
Committee on the Disadvantaged Student and was beginning
the early phases of a serious effort to alter the historic separation of higher education from the American poor. The U.S.
Office of Education was proposing a 'Talent Search' idea, and
Congresswoman Edith Green of Oregon was planning to in-
sert such a programme in the Higher Education Bill of 1965.

At O.E.O., a young group of staffers in the Research and
Demonstration Section of the Community Action programme
had been talking with Shriver and his top staff about a 'head
start for teenagers' programme, which they hoped might be as
successful as the Head Start programme for pre-schoolers.
Shriver seemed impressed with the idea. As head of Chicago's
School Board he often had talked about the waste of high-
school youngsters standing around the street corners all
summer.

The R. & D. section of O.E.O. proposed that the agency
fund some fifteen teenager programmes in the summer of
1965 as pilot programmes, and after much quarrelling about
an appropriate title for the effort, 'Upward Bound' was
chosen on about 1 July. They also responded warmly to
several locally initiated proposals from the regional offices,
thus giving O.E.O. the chance to say it was responding to
grass-roots ideas, which was clearly the agency's legislative
mandate.

By the middle of the summer, eighteen Upward Bound
programmes were under way, as was a half-hearted effort to
build an evaluation system simultaneously. By August,
Shriver was now pushing hard for a second successful national
emphasis programme, thus energising conversations among
his staff, American Council personnel and higher education
people in the various states.

On 11 September 1965 Shriver appointed me (I was then Vice-President and Professor of Political Science at Reed College, Portland, Oregon) as the National Director of the new Upward Bound programme. That afternoon, in a long conversation with Stanley Salett of the R. & D. staff, Salett proposed that I approve O.E.O.'s tentative plans to maintain a very small Upward Bound staff in O.E.O. but to delegate out to the Institute for Services to Education (I.S.E.) in Pittsburgh most of the administration of the programme. Exactly where this idea had originated is not fully known. Apparently, it was the idea of Salett; Theodore Marchese, a young staffer on the American Council on Education; Sanford Kravitz, then head of O.E.O.'s R. & D. section; and other Community Action officials.

I.S.E.-Pittsburgh was essentially a paper organisation of distinguished educators headed by the president emeritus of Carnegie Tech., John C. Warner. It did have a programme, funded by the Ford Foundation, in the Philippines, but its domestic efforts were in fact only ideas. Its contact with programmes for disadvantaged students came from its overlapping board memberships with the Curriculum Resources Group in Boston, which was a collection of educators from Harvard, M.I.T. and elsewhere, who were trying to develop new curriculum materials for teaching slum teenagers in high schools and colleges. The Curriculum Resources Group had been directly involved in six of O.E.O.'s summer pilot Upward Bound programmes as providers of materials.

Meanwhile, Shriver had allocated $20 million of his discretionary funds for an estimated two hundred Upward Bound programmes to begin in the summer of 1966, including those of the eighteen pilots which had proved successful.

Conversations between Salett, Marchese and I.S.E.-Pittsburgh representatives resulted in the I.S.E. proposal dated 22 September 1965. It went to Shriver for his approval on the twenty-ninth. He was outraged by the extent of the delegation of what he considered were properly O.E.O. functions to a private group. Shriver's objections were made known vigorously to everyone connected with the new programme.

On the same day, the twenty-ninth, Salett called me in Portland and reported Shriver's concerns. I assured the Administrator that four conditions either had been written into the contract or had been agreed to informally with the proposed head of I.S.E.-Washington:

1. That I knew the proposed local head, Dr Robert Christian of Notre Dame, and an important contributor to the C.R.G. work in Boston, and that I trusted him implicitly.
2. That Christian had agreed not to seek out any other contracts for his new agency – thus giving full time and attention to Upward Bound.
3. That Christian had agreed to view his agency as an extension of O.E.O., and himself as the Deputy Director of the programme, doing nothing to which O.E.O. objected.
4. That I.S.E.-Washington would remain as invisible as possible so as to maintain the certainty that it was O.E.O. which was making all the important decisions about Upward Bound and not a contract agency with highly developed influence over the programme.

After several strong complaints about the management fee of $27,000 in the million-dollar contract, Shriver agreed to sign it and did so the same day. So did Emeritus President Warner, who was in Washington for that purpose.

The Contract

The two features which should be noticed about this otherwise standard O.E.O. contract are the work programme against which all future auditors would measure the authorisation of expenditures under the contract, and the second paragraph of part XI, wherein O.E.O. retained full control over the hiring and retention of all of I.S.E.'s professional personnel working on Upward Bound. The work programme had been carefully cleared with all pertinent components of O.E.O., such as its Office of Public Affairs on questions of Upward Bound publicity, and in these clearances, everyone remembered Shriver's concerns about over-delegation.

Ironically, control over I.S.E.'s professional personnel meant that O.E.O. had greater control over the 'Upward

G

Bound staff' than it would have had if the programme were operated 'in-house' with its own civil service people. O.E.O. chose the contract device for Upward Bound for three important reasons, all considered crucial at the time:

1. The administrative agonies surrounding Head Start in the spring and summer of 1965 were on everyone's mind. Nobody wished to relive all that terrible history and all those long work-days if they could be avoided. Exporting those initial problems to a private agency with great flexibility was an obvious solution. O.E.O. chiefs who were involved in Head Start all attest to the crushing burden of endless administrative bottle-necks in launching that programme. With I.S.E. a body of talented administrators could thus be hurriedly assembled without following the confining strictures of civil service hiring practices.

2. O.E.O. and particularly Shriver had a strong sense of the political value of tying in the higher education community, especially the American Council on Education, to the new college-oriented Upward Bound programme. Emeritus President Warner, the Boston Curriculum Resources Group and its ties into Harvard and M.I.T., and the other members of I.S.E.'s board – all these gave Shriver a chance to say that O.E.O. was working very closely with a 'distinguished group of educators' in the administration of its new programme, Upward Bound. In fact, I.S.E. immediately took on Mr Theodore Marchese of ACE as the Deputy Director of I.S.E.-Washington. In short, O.E.O. needed an outside administrative helper and got some 'attachment' to the higher education community as a bonus.

3. The possibility was worrisome that higher education institutions, particularly those with prestige and thus with many choices as to how to employ their energies, might be suspicious of a hyper-political government agency, new and untried, headed by a volatile member of the Kennedy clan. Could it be trusted? What would indirect costs be? How firm could the commitment from the agency be – for one year, two years? If the expectations of slum young people were raised by a college, would this new agency provide the wherewithal to deliver on the promise?

I remember that all of us in the agency who had experience with programmes for the disadvantaged worried much about these questions. Could the new programme be launched successfully in political terms if very few of the one hundred best-known colleges and universities simply did not elect to engage themselves with the new agency? We felt that O.E.O. needed a very real 'buffer' between the colleges and the agency and that the I.S.E. idea was a fruitful way to build that buffer. Thus, in the application process for Upward Bound programmes, colleges 'applied to I.S.E.' in effect, and I.S.E. used the conventional system of academic review panels to develop its recommendations on funding to O.E.O. And the personal contact that a college would have with 'Washington' would be with an academic professional or colleague working for I.S.E.

The advantages that could be gained resemble in some ways those characteristic of the National Science Foundation (N.S.F.) or the United States Office of Education (U.S.O.E.) practices of using fellow-academics to review academic proposals, but there is a distinct difference. O.E.O. was new, and its political thrust and future were volatile. Unlike the U.S.O.E., which had been in existence for one hundred years and had a stable clientele, or N.S.F., with the support of the science community, O.E.O. had a flavour in its early days of an agency whose clientele was strange and difficult to identify – the American poor – and no one quite knew who they were or how to work with them.

Were the Goals of the Contract Idea Achieved?

The first and third goals of the contract idea were largely achieved, but there was much less success with regard to the second. I.S.E. got started quickly, solved its logistic problems quickly, and developed a capability to deal with 250 grant proposals by January 1966. In fact, I spent most of the fall and winter physically at I.S.E. – nine blocks from O.E.O. – because that is where the rugs, good secretaries, parking facilities were, and where the long-distance telephones worked. But more importantly this was where the 'action' was in the Upward Bound programme at that stage in its development. For, indeed, this is where the 'staff' was.

177

The second goal, that of tying in the academic interest groups, was achieved to a much lesser degree. ACE, or A.A.U.P., or A.C.A.C., or the Association of American Colleges, were never really engaged. Very little institutional contact developed between O.E.O.–I.S.E. and these agencies. And when O.E.O. and Upward Bound were attacked by strong Congressional forces in the summer of 1968, hindsight would have created the wish that these agencies had been much more involved. But more on this later.

The third goal was indeed reached, although the casual relationship between the strategy and the result could be doubted. When O.E.O. announced its first fifty Upward Bound grants on 1 April 1966, the list of collegiate participants was impressive, including Harvard, Yale, Princeton, Berkeley, Stanford, Morehouse, Fisk, Howard, UCLA, the University of Minnesota, Swarthmore, Reed and Bowdoin among others.

Epilogue

As is well known, O.E.O. stirred up large political troubles everywhere in the country. Its new programmes competed constantly with established programmes, public and private. The very presence of O.E.O. testified that the established agencies, national, state and local, were not able to reach their own goals. While there was always a playful doubt that the Congress really knew what it passed when it sent the Economic Opportunity Act to the White House in 1964, there was no doubt whatsoever that by 1967 and 1968 they did know and that strong congressional power would soon begin to dismember the agency.

Assaults came from every direction – from mayors who had been bypassed, from governors who had been ignored, from Congressmen who viewed the Community Action machinery in their districts as a potentially competitive political force, and from stable old-line interest groups who had to deal with a new crowd they did not know well and often did not trust. One of these forces was and is the powerful Congresswoman from Oregon, Chairman of the House Special Sub-Committee on Education, Mrs Edith Green. She viewed Upward Bound as an expensive renegade programme, run by a non-educational agency, which competed with programmes in the U.S.O.E. such as 'Talent Search'. Moreover, Upward Bound, by its very presence, seemed to say that the American public school was not adequate for the troubled times. Mrs Green is a former schoolteacher and functionary with the Oregon Education Association.

Mrs Green had tried in 1966 and 1967 to mount an attack on Upward Bound, as she had successfully done with the Job Corps, but she could not then get the House Committee on Education and Labour to go along with her efforts to have Upward Bound legislatively transferred to the U.S.O.E. Finally, in 1968, the full House Committee did propose such a transfer, and during the floor debates in August 1968, the Congresswoman delivered a strong attack on the programme and succeeded in gaining legislation which did transfer Upward Bound to U.S.O.E. as from 1 July 1969. During that attack, she described the relationship of O.E.O. to I.S.E. (by this date called 'Educational Associate, Inc.') as one of apparent collusion between E.A.I. and O.E.O. officials; she also asserted that when I resigned as Director, I promptly went on to the governing board of E.A.I. (not true), and that, in general, O.E.O. had delegated its responsibilities to an obscure contract agency whose origins and practices should be investigated.

A subsequent investigation by the General Accounting Office rated Upward Bound as one of O.E.O.'s most effective programmes. In 'programme accountability' terms, as used in David Robinson's paper, Upward Bound was a distinct success. While the American poor who graduate from high school go to college at the rate of less than 10 per cent, the college-going rate of Upward Bound graduates is currently 82 per cent and their staying power in college is higher than that of the whole college population.

I.S.E. was clearly a captive contract agency, but it seemed entirely happy in this posture. Its professional personnel – and even its janitor – were young academics who wanted to do something about the historic policy of rating American higher educational institutions by the percentage of applicants they *reject*. They had read Michael Harrington, Franz Fanon, James Baldwin, and the literature of protest. Most had visited grimy mining towns in West Virginia or Eastern Kentucky or the oppressive slums of Bedford-Stuyvesant, or New York City's Lower East Side. The captive feature of their existence as a contract agency was entirely agreeable to the E.A.I. staff. And, as expected, when Upward Bound was transferred to U.S.O.E. the contract was terminated. E.A.I. was not upset. They simply looked for the same kind of action elsewhere.

The potential setback to O.E.O. programmes, however, does raise the larger question of the costs that may be incurred in by-passing the formal government and resorting to the expedient of administration-by-contract. The congressional attack on the contract was, of course, only a shadow of the real quarrel, which was to stop O.E.O. from upsetting so many applecarts in American communities. One may suggest that the flurry over the contract was just one more club over O.E.O., which could be used in the larger fight. Yet the intricacies of using the contract device in a highly controversial arena of domestic politics brings added complexity to the traditional problem of accountability in government.

8 Problems of Autonomy and Accountability in Government Contracts for Research and Development in Education

Francis S. Chase

Introduction

In education as in other fields federalism-by-contract in the present decade has expanded rapidly and assumed new forms. The increased reliance on contracting stems both: (1) from the unprecedented range of educational problems and objectives which are now accepted as legitimate federal concerns, and (2) from the complexity of the treatments perceived as appropriate in the light of advancing science and technology. These two factors alone almost preclude any hope that adequate in-government capability for appropriate response can be developed.

In the United States a long-nourished fear of federal control has been an added barrier to direct federal action in education. Grants-in-aid, however, have been an important means of inducing action to meet national needs for education from the eighteenth-century land grants through recent subventions to higher education and to state and local school systems. Until the present decade these grants have been generally small in amount and intended as incentive rather than supportive grants.

The picture began to change in the fifties and assumed a new character in the sixties. A whole new set of arrangements have been added to bring about the changes in education which are seen as essential to the security of the nation and the welfare of its people. Some of these arrangements were contrived to by-pass the traditional educational establishment, which was believed too sluggish to respond promptly to the new demands or to make good use of science and technology for the engineering of change. The new arrangements include contractual relationships between federal agencies and a wide variety of contractors, including industrial and non-profit corporations and community action groups.

Many in government and out become convinced that a union of research and development might be applied to education with results comparable to those achieved in aeronautics, atomic energy and medical science. Others recalled the progress of agriculture brought about largely through the generation of applicable knowledge in the land-grant colleges, the further development of this knowledge in industrial laboratories and agricultural experiment stations, and the transmission of the developed knowledge and new technologies through the agricultural extension services.

The National Science Foundation under its mission for the promotion of science made significant contributions to educational development, beginning in the mid-fifties by lending its prestige and substantial financial support to the national curriculum projects in mathematics and the sciences. The influence of these studies was powerful in two ways: first, by demonstrating the potential for educational reform of focusing a concentration of scholarly and other talents on the design and production of improved instructional systems; and second, by revealing that the existence of superior systems is no guarantee of their effective use.

As the education task force appointed by President Kennedy, and chaired by John W. Gardner, considered how education might be made equal to the demands of what has been called the post-modern age, they were sharply aware of the models furnished by the N.S.F. studies as well as those represented by the linked land-grant college and extension services, the Atomic Energy Commission, the National Institutes of Health and the National Aeronautics and Space Administration. The work of this task force had important effects on the Elementary and Secondary Education Act, which has been heralded as the most revolutionary educational legislation ever adopted by the Congress. Title IV of this Act, through amending the Co-operative Research Act, opened the door to the establishment of the regional educational laboratories as non-profit corporations of a type which

Alan Pifer has called quasi-non-governmental organisations. These laboratories, of which twenty were founded in 1966 and 1967 under contracts negotiated by the Office of Education, joined the previously authorised university research and development centres as parts of the National Programme of Educational Laboratories.

The remainder of this memorandum will draw from the writer's experience with these new educational research and development agencies and will focus on the values of independence and accountability as they are affected by the contract process.

Salient Features of Educational R. & D.

The National Programme of Educational Laboratories, while small in terms of funds committed, affords an instructive example both of factors which dispose a government to contract for services and of difficulties involved in establishing a contract process which will accommodate the values of independence and accountability. Some of the salient characteristics of this programme which need to be kept in mind are the following:

1. The programme at present consists of nine university-based research and development centres, five small research and development operations in early childhood education co-ordinated by a university centre, and twenty regional educational laboratories, each organised as a non-profit corporation with its own board of directors. (Two other university centres established under the Vocational Education Act of 1963 have not been officially designated as parts of the National Programme of Educational Laboratories.)

2. The programme is 'monitored and administered' by the Division of Educational Laboratories, one of five divisions in the Bureau of Research, which is one of several co-ordinate bureaus in the Office of Education, which is administered by a commissioner who is chief education officer of the federal government but subordinate to the Secretary of Health, Education and Welfare.

3. The history of these organisations is brief: the uni-

versity research and development centres were authorised in 1963 under the Co-operative Research Act, and the first two centres were started in 1964, and others as late as 1967; but the laboratories were not authorised until 1965 under title IV of the Elementary and Secondary Education Act and came into existence in 1966 and 1967.

4. The funds committed are modest: the total programme has been operating on an annual budget of approximately $30 million; and no single organisation has yet attained a $3 million level of operation. (The centres receive support from the sponsoring universities, and the laboratories are free to seek additional financial support from sources other than title IV funds; but the contracts with the Bureau of Research probably provide nine-tenths of the total funding of the National Programme.)

5. The programme was not shaped by any carefully worked out plan: both the laboratories and centres were funded as a result of locally developed proposals made in response to open or selective invitations and more or less in accordance with guidelines, which in the case of the laboratories specified little beyond a purpose 'to narrow the gap between educational research and practice', and in the case of the centres an intent 'to bring together interdisciplinary talent and resources to focus on a significant educational problem'.

6. Short-term contracts and funding tied to current appropriations have kept these new organisations on a short leash: contracts with the laboratories are negotiated annually; and, while the centres in some cases have been given five-year extensions, the budgets are still tied to current annual appropriations.

7. There is as yet no general agreement regarding the essential functions of research and development agencies in education or the conditions necessary to successful operation; and this lack of agreement has resulted in unrealistic or conflicting expectations, and been a source of considerable confusion.

The conditions described in the preceding section place serious constraints on freedom of action; and might well have been a prelude to failure. Yet I am persuaded that the centres and laboratories hold great promise for the improvement of education; and a number of them have already developed approaches and instructional systems which are achieving significant success in pilot and field tests, especially with children from sectors of the population for whom traditional schooling has been obviously ill-adapted. With the correction of some of the more serious inhibiting factors, I predict that research and development centres and laboratories will in the years ahead contribute powerfully to sustained and cumulative improvement in education.

Before inquiring into the reasons for this expression of confidence, it may be useful to recall some of the factors which make research and development in education difficult even with the best imaginable provisions for funding and administration.

It is generally conceded that education, while contributing to the advancement of knowledge in other fields, has itself operated from a weak knowledge base and with a heavy reliance on conventional wisdom. It has not only no history of large-scale and systematic research and development; but its ties with the basic sciences have been tenuous and attenuated. In spite of the lethargy now attributed to the schools, education in the United States has a remarkable record of innovation; and a number of these innovations have effected significant transformations in the form and content of learning experiences at all levels. The history of innovation, however, has been highly erratic; and our educational scrap-heap is cluttered with bright ideas only partially developed and with technologies imperfectly adapted to educational use. None of our traditional educational institutions has embraced as a primary function the development and continuous adaptation and refinement of programmes and systems for educational use. Educational personnel for the most part have not been in close touch with those pioneering new concepts and technologies of information processing, systems analysis or systems development.

There are, however, numerous auguries of success. In a remarkably short time the centres and laboratories have provided some convincing demonstrations of the possibility of systematic adaptation of knowledge and technology to educational use. In several cases centres and laboratories are collaborating in managing a set of closely related processes to assess educational needs, fill gaps in the available knowledge, design prototype programmes incorporating relevant knowledge and technology, and proceed from there to the production and successive testing and refinement of instructional and other systems. They are beginning to conceive research and development as a closely integrated system for producing specified changes in educational institutions and processes; and in spite of the confusion regarding functions, strategies of intervention and modes of operation, most of the centres and laboratories in the past two years have achieved a sharper focus, better programme delineation and closer integration of activities.

Although provisions for training research and development personnel for education are obviously inadequate and conditions of employment far from ideal, many of the laboratories and centres have also increased staff capability appreciably within the past two years. Even the more productive organisations, however, are short of many of the specialised abilities relevant to their proclaimed objectives.

Obstacles to Independence and Accountability

Autonomy, at least to the extent of freedom from bureaucratic constraints on staffing, personnel policies and choices among alternative means, is a primary justification for contracting with non-government agencies for the performance of public functions. Undoubtedly, it was and is the intent of Office of Education personnel to assure the independence necessary to creative contributions to educational systems. It has proved difficult, however, to incorporate this intent in the contract process.

Part of the problem is inherent in the nature of education and the current state of knowledge relating to environmental influences on learning, the effects of instructional processes

186

and other factors which condition the effectiveness of educational institutions. Where specifications can be precise as to performance of desired products and where the cost of components and developmental processes can be estimated closely, contracting is relatively simple as contrasted with the situation in educational research and development where the desired products or outcomes often can be specified in only very general terms and the hope of success rests largely on creative imagination linked with rigorous analytical processes. This would argue for increased rather than decreased freedom and for encouragement of venturesomeness, provided adequate assurance can be given of proper accountability for the use of public resources.

The most serious intrusions on the independence essential to creative work arise from the short contract periods and the annual budgeting from congressional appropriations. Related to these are pressures for the adoption of particular processes and more insidious pressures towards instant products. Also related to annual contract negotiations are burdensome requirements for reporting, over-frequent site visits, and other problems of review and evaluation.

Undoubtedly the most important basis for successful research and development is a staff of high capability for the operations involved. Uncertain, short-term and insufficient funding makes employment of qualified persons extremely difficult, especially as there is a critical shortage of persons with the talents, training and experience relevant to educational research and development. Moreover, scientists and other creative workers have a low tolerance for external controls and are not likely to remain in situations where they feel a loss of self-direction.

The present contract process also fails to make adequate provision for the values of accountability. The chief need is to provide a framework within which accountability can operate. It is not guaranteed automatically by incorporation in a university structure or the creation of a governing board. The distribution of authority is so complex that the pinpointing of responsibility is more than usually difficult. Among the parties at the federal level directly and often crucially involved in the decisions which determine basic policies, modes of operation and effects achieved are the Congress through

187

enabling legislation, appropriations and committee influence on federal administrators; the Office of Education as the federal agency of administration, particularly through the officers of the Division of Educational Laboratories and the Bureau of Research; the Department of Health, Education and Welfare and the Bureau of the Budget through their action on Office of Education requests. On the other side in the decision-making processes which are related to the contract process are the governing boards of the laboratories and the university officials and committees to which the centres report; the staffs of the several organisations and the groups with which they interact; and those to be affected by the changes, or lack of changes, produced.

It is recognised that the autonomy requisite to productive research and development can be reconciled with accountability for the use of public funds and other resources only through establishment of orderly and effective processes of review and evaluation. Progress is being made in this direction, but too slowly. Better criteria are needed for evaluating the importance of goals and the adequacy of specifications of objectives, resource inputs and processes. Careful attention is likewise needed to increase the validity of judgements made in assessing factors closely related to goal achievement, especially the quality of leadership, the capability of staff for the operations required, the appropriateness and vigour of the programme-planning processes, the quality of collaborative relationships with other agencies, the provisions for self-evaluation and the character of the provisions for continuing refinement of products – post-installation as well as pre-installation.

Questions to Ponder

How does one explain the considerable success claimed for these operations if the conditions essential to independence and accountability are so poorly met?

A partial answer may be found in the quality of leadership which has been attracted to the more successful laboratories and centres. Several of the directors appear to have mastered the knack of maintaining an important measure of independence under unpropitious circumstances. They are able to communicate to their boards and staffs a feeling of confidence in the future in spite of baffling uncertainties. They constantly behave as if their organisations are entitled to autonomy; and their competence in building the organisations induces others to respect the independence as far as legal requirements permit. They also manifest a patent desire to accept responsibility for productive use of resources and they welcome constructive criticism and evaluation. How long they can maintain these attitudes under existing conditions is another question.

This leads to speculation as to what may be done to improve the contract process. The following questions seem relevant:

1. What can be done to impress upon Congress, the executive branch, the education profession and citizens generally the importance of a really substantial investment in educational research and development? Would either of the following measures help: (*a*) the elevation of the Office of Education to Cabinet status to increase its influence in the councils of government? (*b*) administration of the National Laboratory Programme by a prestigious and highly qualified commission which would receive a hearing at the highest levels of government – rather than by an agency placed low in the government hierarchy.

2. What can be done to move to longer-term contracts?

3. What can be done to train research and development personnel?

4. What can be done to decrease the burdensomeness of the review process and to increase its validity?

5. What can be done to remove unnecessary and detrimental restraints on control of products during the development process?

Perhaps the more effective centres and laboratories will solve most of these problems with the assistance of the Office of Education personnel, if Congress through the measures suggested under question 1 – or otherwise – can be led to provide the additional funding necessary to build on what has been well started.

9 Accountability in Britain's Nuclear Energy Programmes

Roger Williams

This paper examines the problem of accountability for civil nuclear energy development in Britain, with some emphasis also on the kinds of criteria which have influenced the country's commitment and investment in this field. The term 'accountability' can in fact be construed in several ways in this context and a brief description of the nuclear industry in Britain is necessary in order to bring this out.

A public body, the Atomic Energy Authority (A.E.A.), has been responsible both for the development of reactor systems to the point of commercial exploitation and also for the development and manufacture of fuel for power stations based on those systems. The main choice of reactor systems to be developed have seemingly long since been taken. That is, the decisions are past which have since led to the five reactor types – Magnox, Advanced Gas-Cooled Reactor (A.G.R.), Fast Breeder Reactor (F.B.R.), High Temperature Gas-Cooled Reactor (H.T.G.C.R.) and Steam Generating Heavy Water Reactor (S.G.H.W.R.) – and though it may be necessary in the 1970s to decide, for instance, whether or not to develop an alternative breeder system, the earlier richness of choice will certainly not recur. Of course other choices remain to be made in the experimental development of nuclear energy. For example, the extent of further effort on the last four of the above five systems is a continuing question and the level of expenditure on marine nuclear propulsion and on thermonuclear fusion have for some time been subjects for argument. There is also the fact that since 1965 the A.E.A. has been empowered to do work outside the nuclear field, and in this area too decisions will continue to be required.

Britain is presently in her second commercial nuclear power programme. The first, which was revised three times,

190

consisted entirely of Magnox reactor power stations, nine in all, and the second has so far consisted of A.G.R.s. Responsibility for carrying both programmes through has lain chiefly with another public body, the Central Electricity Generating Board (C.E.G.B.), for whom the stations were built and by whom they are operated. (One Magnox station was built, and one A.G.R. station is being built, for the South of Scotland Electricity Board.) The key decisions on commercial programmes are by no means all taken. Apart from decisions on the future of the S.G.H.W.R. and H.T.G.C.R. concepts the timing and nature of an F.B.R. programme will eventually have to be determined.

Britain's nuclear industry has thus consisted essentially of a public monopoly, the A.E.A., on one hand, and a public monopsony, the C.E.G.B., on the other. Sandwiched between have been the consortia, groups of private firms undertaking to construct for the C.E.G.B. commercial power stations based on principles established by the A.E.A. There were once five such consortia and in recent years there have been three but, as is discussed below, the industry is again in the process of regrouping, a process in which the future of the A.E.A. is also involved.

It follows from this short account that the types of accountability to be considered here are, first, the public accountability required of both the A.E.A. and the C.E.G.B., both public corporations but of quite different kinds, and second, the accountability of the consortia and other private firms in respect of such contracts as they have received from the A.E.A. and the C.E.G.B. The criticism which has been directed at the nuclear industry in the last few years has in fact been concerned less with accountability in either of these senses than with the domestic vigour and export performance of the industry – A.E.A., C.E.G.B. and consortia – taken as a whole. However, as is shown in the latter part of the paper, the situation is changing and this prompts consideration of the new meaning accountability will assume with respect to the reorganised industry when this comes fully into being. As to the dimensions of accountability, while the strictly financial aspect is as always very important, the nature of research and development makes inevitable a more general approach to the relationship between effort expended and technical advance achieved, and it is this wider approach which the paper tries to follow.

It is logical to look first at the research side of the nuclear programmes, in effect at the public accountability of the A.E.A. The A.E.A. was created in 1954 from a department of the former Ministry of Supply, the government indicating that while there would be no unnecessary detailed intervention, control over policy would remain more ministerial than was the case with other public corporations. The A.E.A. also differs from other public corporations in that it is financed by parliamentary vote, after the manner of a government department. It reports to the responsible minister, keeps its accounts in a form determined by the Treasury and transmits an annual financial statement to the Comptroller and Auditor General. Since 1954, responsibility for the Authority has fallen in turn to several ministers and since 1964 has lain with the Minister of Technology. In 1967 this minister stated that he did not consider it necessary, right or possible for his ministry to have the facility to evaluate the advice given to him by the A.E.A. In particular, this was because the A.E.A. in its technical assessments could be expected to show the care befitting a public corporation, and because its origin as a department of government meant that it contained within itself the machinery for advising the government. However, the minister stated that individual projects which came up were evaluated by his department to the best of its ability. Noting a dichotomy between the technical and economic aspects of advice, he expressed long-term hopes for a new techno-economic analysis unit which his department was developing. On the matter of the Authority's original choice of reactor systems, he was quite explicit:

> I would be glad to leave it to them because at this stage one would not even have the facts upon which an economic assessment could be made. Their decision ... would be one based entirely upon a scientific assessment ... and here I do not think it would be open to me to have a sensible alternative view unless the expenditure on experimental reactors was so great as really to be beyond the capacity of the country to pay for it.[1]

192

It can be assumed that previous ministers responsible for the A.E.A. have taken a similar line.

The Minister of Power, the minister responsible for the C.E.G.B., stated in 1967 that the policies and advice of the A.E.A. received 'a very powerful check' from the C.E.G.B., since he did not regard the two bodies as having a common interest.[2] He also saw no point in having within his own ministry the capacity to do the same job as that done by the C.E.G.B. This view must be taken to relate to the commercial power programmes. The C.E.G.B. did not really have the expertise to influence the Authority's choice of reactor systems for development, at least until the most recent case, the S.G.H.W.R. When in 1962 the Authority decided to proceed with this system, the C.E.G.B. Chairman, Sir Christopher Hinton (later Lord Hinton), revealed that the Board had different views. Sir Christopher had been a principal architect of Britain's nuclear effort and a member of the Authority until 1958, when he became C.E.G.B. Chairman. Now in early 1965 he stated that the Authority had declined to give the Board the reports of their evaluation of the S.G.H.W.R. and alternative systems. He maintained that 'it is a mistake in policy for a research organisation to launch out into expensive prototype work without taking their main potential user with them'.[3] However, the C.E.G.B. has never seemed likely to be the main potential user of this system, and now that its technical success has been demonstrated its commercial future probably lies elsewhere than with the C.E.G.B.

At the time, the Permanent Secretary to the Ministry of Power was so concerned about this matter that he raised it on his own initiative with the A.E.A. His explanation of the A.E.A.'s response was that 'They [the Authority] are having to pay for it, and in the last resort they had to back their own judgement and do it the way they thought best.'[4] The permanent secretary had still thought that before sanctioning the expenditure, the Treasury should at least be aware of the prospects for the reactor as seen by the Board. These facts emerged in 1963, at which time the main disagreement between the A.E.A. and the C.E.G.B. centred on whether and when the A.G.R. was to be accepted by the C.E.G.B. for the second nuclear power programme. This was finally settled in

1965 and in that year too cross-representation at board level began between the two bodies. Since then the relationship between them seems to have been a very co-operative one. Nevertheless the fact that there were disagreements between the Authority and the Board over the S.G.H.W.R. and the A.G.R. suggests that one must turn to the Authority's actual decisions on reactor development in order to understand properly their great freedom of policy-making and ultimately the degree of their accountability.

Defence requirements formed the original basis of Britain's nuclear plans but the Ministry of Supply's engineers had in mind virtually from the beginning meeting those requirements in ways which would eventually lead on to civil power plants. The fundamental commitment to a gas–graphite line of reactor development was the logical outcome of the initial constraints. Britain in the early post-war years had no supply of enriched uranium so her first reactors had to be fuelled with natural uranium. Of the two moderators about which sufficient information was then available, graphite and heavy water, the latter was ruled out because supplies were uncertain. As to coolants, water was at that time considered risky and water-cooled reactors would have imposed unacceptable siting conditions, so air cooling was chosen. Later, carbon dioxide under pressure was found to be more efficient as a coolant, and thus the Magnox natural uranium, graphite moderated, carbon dioxide-cooled reactor was born.

The A.E.A.'s enthusiasm for the gas–graphite reactor, especially following the world-first of the Calder Hall station, was reflected in its decision to develop the A.G.R., effectively an advanced reactor based on established Magnox technology, as the follow-up to Magnox. The Authority considered that the technical changes occasioned by the shift from Magnox to the A.G.R. were sufficiently major to warrant building a prototype reactor and this became the Windscale A.G.R. Before continuing in this way with the gas–graphite line the A.E.A. had made extensive studies of a range of alternatives, including the light water reactors afterwards to become so successful in the United States.

The A.E.A.'s other main decision in the late fifties on the gas–graphite line was one which made it the chief partner in a European group developing the Dragon H.T.G.C.R., an

194

experimental reactor intended to carry gas–graphite technology beyond the limitations of the A.G.R. It was in the light of this concentration on gas cooling that Sir Christopher Hinton commented in 1961 that, for British needs, 'The cardinal belief of the British reactor creed is that gas cooling is best.'[5]

On the other hand, by 1958 the Authority were persuaded by their feasibility studies that the best immediate alternative to the A.G.R. might well be the heavy water-moderated reactor. By 1960 this idea had evolved into the S.G.H.W.R., and in 1963 the A.E.A. sought and received government authorisation to build a prototype. The S.G.H.W.R. was not, however, an alternative to the A.G.R. when the reactor type for the second nuclear power programme was being considered in 1963–5.

It was believed from the outset in Britain that the thermal reactors, Magnox, A.G.R., etc., would be profitable only if a fast breeder reactor could be constructed to burn the by-product plutonium they produced. Since it was realised that F.B.R.s presented far more difficult technical problems than did thermal reactors, work on them was started even before work on the Calder Hall Magnox reactors. An experimental reactor was constructed and a prototype is currently being built. The present evidence is that this particular type of F.B.R. will have a marked edge, at least at first, over alternatives, and further, Britain may well have a lead in F.B.R. technology.

The Authority have thus invested, to the point of experimental/prototype reactor construction, in five systems. Their report for 1968 contained a formal statement that in appraising development expenditure cost–benefit analysis was used, including discounted cash flow techniques at the 8 per cent discount rate recommended by the Treasury. The Authority had indicated in 1967 that such analyses were attempted, both in assessing the case for development of a reactor system and for continued development of a commercially proven one. Acknowledging that very many assumptions had to be made in such analyses, the Authority stated that 'A programme is only authorised if, over a credible range of assumptions, benefit exceeds cost by a factor judged against the probability of success.'[6] Since these analyses have been the Authority's own they do not affect the main conclusions regarding the Authority's role. These are: First, that the Authority's choices and activities have been almost exclusively decided internally; second, that these internal decision-making processes have mostly determined the content of the nuclear power programmes, together with the configuration of the reactors, down to relatively fine detail; and third, that these things occurred notwithstanding the existence of a policy committee on which the other interested parties, the C.E.G.B. and the consortia, were represented. Finally, if these conclusions have lost any of their force in the last few years they nevertheless summarise the situation which obtained for a long and extremely important time in the development of nuclear energy.

Turning now to the commercial programmes themselves, the second aspect of accountability in the nuclear field appears, namely the public accountability of the C.E.G.B. The significant feature here is how real C.E.G.B. accountability for its nuclear policies was from the outset severely hampered by the existence of overriding government policies. The rationale of the first nuclear programme was outlined in the enthusiastic White Paper which announced it.[7] One of its main objectives was to relieve the coal industry of the 'excessive strains' then being put upon it. Further, the government considered that it had become vital to apply nuclear energy commercially 'with all speed' if the country was to keep its leading industrial position. The electricity authorities and private industry were to obtain 'as quickly as possible' the practical experience needed for a big expansion later. Britain would then be in a position to export her new skills. These intentions were perhaps not too unreasonable, given the assumptions made at the time about the comparative costs of nuclear and conventional generation.

In March 1957 the programme of 1500–2000 Mw by 1965 was for several reasons trebled to 5000–6000 Mw by the same date. The interesting point here is that the Central Electricity Authority, predecessor of the C.E.G.B., was consulted by the government on the first commercial nuclear power programme in 1955 only at short notice, and would have preferred a smaller programme than that adopted in the 1957 expansion. The economics of nuclear power were in fact less favourable in 1957 than they had been in 1955, and this trend continued so that in 1960 the government, under pressure from the C.E.G.B., felt compelled to announce that the nuclear programme would be kept at the lower (5000 Mw) of the two figures projected in 1957, and that it would be stretched, to be completed now in 1968. The justification for the size at which the programme was maintained after 1960 was given by the C.E.G.B. Chairman in 1961. Noting that the programme was probably still too large on technological grounds, Sir Christopher maintained that, since a large industry would be needed in the 1970s, 'One cannot expect to create a large industry by establishing a programme, to destroy that industry by slashing the programme and then to recreate it at one's convenience six or seven years later.'[9]

Unhappy though the economics of the first programme now look, there are none the less mitigating economic points about it which must be borne in mind in a full study. However, it is easy to understand why the Generating Board wished to see A.G.R. economics clearly demonstrated before they were ready to accept it for the second programme. The Board were finally convinced by their own comparative appraisal of the A.G.R. and light water reactors for the Dungeness B site in 1965. The significant feature here is that whereas the electricity authorities were never very happy with the first programme, their commitment to a second one based on the A.G.R. was reached, on their own clear declaration, without political consideration or political pressure.[10] That is, they were satisfied by their own calculations that, for their requirements, the A.G.R. had the edge over its American rivals and the need therefore did not arise for government deliberation on a policy switch which would have involved setting aside British in favour of American technology. The importance of this unequivocal declaration by the C.E.G.B. has, if anything, been enhanced by such criticism as has been levelled against the comparative appraisal they conducted.

This paper has now examined the accountability of the A.E.A. and of the C.E.G.B. for nuclear energy development mainly in terms of the relationships between these bodies and their sponsoring ministries, but it is also relevant to consider here their accountability to Parliament.

The first full parliamentary investigation involving the A.E.A. was conducted by the Estimates Committee in 1958-9, when the Industrial Group of the Authority was examined. The Committee acknowledged its own limitations. For instance, the A.E.A. by that time committed to the A.G.R., was also considering another reactor concept, which later became the S.G.H.W.R., but the Committee felt itself incompetent to judge whether resources could in fact be spared to develop this extra system.[11] The Committee's report mostly commended the Authority, but it has been suggested that the great pains taken by the Authority to assist the Committee partly ensured this.[12]

The A.E.A. falls outside the province of the Nationalised Industries Committee and this Committee dealt with the Authority only peripherally in looking at the electricity industry in 1962-3. Although it has been observed that the Committee 'exhibited considerable ability' in tackling difficult technical and financial matters, the nature of its inquiry rather encouraged it to view problems through the eyes of the C.E.G.B.[13] The Committee seemed to reveal areas of disagreement between the A.E.A. and the C.E.G.B. and one of its conclusions was that 'the evidence which has been recited suggests defects in the existing structure and organisation which may mean that money is not being spent to the best advantage'.[14]

The period 1962-4 was rather a difficult one for the nuclear industry and the investigation made by the Nationalised Industries Committee was one of only two occasions when Parliament heard at some length about the issues involved, the other being a House of Lords debate.[15] Two opposition M.P.s, later members of the Labour government, argued at this time that Parliament was not really helping to create the atmosphere in which decisions would be taken, much less influencing them.[16]

The Public Accounts Committee, using the reports prepared for it by the Comptroller and Auditor General, has each year investigated the Authority's accounts, which of course it could not have done had the Authority been a 'normal' public corporation like the C.E.G.B. Confining itself as usual to the financial side of nuclear energy, and so avoiding the technical arguments for particular policies, it

198

has in this field as in others usually offered valuable and searching criticism. Its analyses have, again as usual, been retrospective so that while its recommendations may lead to, say, changes in contract procedures, the particular cases and instances it examines have normally ceased to be of current concern before they come to the Committee. As an instructive example of its approach an instance which occurred in 1963 is worth mention. The Authority had originally hoped that the fuel for the A.G.R. could be canned in beryllium because of its good nuclear and heat properties. Because they were also aware of its very great disadvantages, stainless steel cans were developed in parallel, and in the event stainless steel proved the better choice. In due course the Comptroller's report, austere as ever, noted that the A.E.A. had spent some £9·7 million on the A.G.R., with more to be spent, together with some £10 million on 'the development and production of beryllium for canning the A.G.R. fuel elements later found to be unsatisfactory and abandoned in favour of stainless steel'.[17] These facts were juxtaposed with a statement by the Comptroller to the effect that he understood the electricity boards were not committed to the adoption of the A.G.R. The A.E.A. chairman had subsequently to answer some difficult questions from the Committee, particularly as to why the metal was put into production before being proved, but the Committee considered the authorisation of reactor prototypes such as the A.G.R. to be a matter of government policy and consequently felt constrained simply to note the absence of a commitment by the electricity boards.[18] Other examples of the P.A.C.'s work are given below in the discussion of the accountability of private firms to the A.E.A.

In 1967 the new Science Committee conducted the fullest review yet of the nuclear industry and brought in several strong recommendations. Three of these require a short treatment here.

On the subject of responsibility for the A.E.A.'s choice of development projects the Committee concluded that 'neither the Minister of Power nor the Minister of Technology appeared to have any very effective technical check on the activities of the A.E.A. and the consequent allocation of public funds for the Authority's purposes . . . Your Committee are

199

not satisfied that, between them, the two Ministers are adequately equipped to assess the value and significance of what the Authority are doing.' The Committee therefore advocated 'the establishment of a technical assessment unit capable of advising the Government on the merits and prospects of particular projects proposed to be undertaken by the Authority'.[19]

The A.E.A. was shown above to have been almost exclusively responsible for the choice of reactor systems to be developed as well as for their later technical establishment. To take particular examples, the decisions to develop the A.G.R. rather than any other type of reactor and to make beryllium the preferred canning material were both reached within the A.E.A. Yet the former was highly significant both because it meant a move away from the basic philosophy of natural uranium reactors and because, provided development were successful, the A.E.A. was virtually determining the reactor for the second commercial programme. The question is really whether the policy of confining immediate development work to the A.G.R. could profitably have been examined by an independent body of the kind suggested by the Science Committee.[20] Fortunately, the A.G.R. has proved both a technically sound and economically satisfactory reactor. In the beryllium case there was certainly a strong body of opinion both within and without the A.E.A. which held this preference to be ill-advised, and here again one must ask whether there might possibly have been savings if the issue had been properly ventilated at the time. As a third and more recent example, in the controversial reduction of fusion research, while the minister believed that 'the most exhaustive consultations have taken place between all those who could conceivably be concerned', an article in *The Times* began 'It is the almost unanimous view of scientists working in this field that his decision was a serious mistake, based on grossly inadequate advice, but since the majority are employees of a public authority, there appears to be a danger that their case may go by default.'[21] The fact is that the A.E.A. has made, and has had to make, its choices not without proper economic concern but rather long before reliable economic facts can be known. There are therefore some grounds for arguing that independent scientific judgement with a wide professional debate would improve such choices. Independent assessment here would presumably lean to the technical, but the cost–benefit analysis of development expenditure being done by the Authority would perhaps also seem more objective if conducted by an independent unit.

The Minister of Technology in his reply to the Science Committee on this point has noted the difficulty involved in establishing a technical assessment unit:

> The Authority itself is the repository of nearly all the national expertise in the nuclear field. They are a public authority and are expected to prepare their technical and economic assessments with great care. Decisions in the nuclear field have, therefore, in the past been dependent on an assessment of the best possible deployment of national resources and the most favourable return on capital.[22]

The minister has also stated that it would be a prime function of the Atomic Energy Board which he was proposing to set up (see below) to 'co-ordinate all proposals for research and development in the nuclear field' and to advise him on future programmes. The Science Committee have not been able to accept that this arrangement will meet the need they have in mind, since they feel that the new Board, because it is to consist of all the interested parties, will be unable to offer impartial advice.[23]

Probably inevitably, there have been critics of the economic premises of the second nuclear power programme, in particular the National Coal Board (N.C.B.). The reaction of the coal lobby in the United States to the rapid development of nuclear energy there has been a similar phenomenon, the important differences being that in Britain, on the one hand, the N.C.B. can speak with a single voice, and on the other there has been a single centre, the Ministry of Power, to serve as the butt of criticism. It was because of such criticism that the Science Committee, though satisfied itself that electricity generated from nuclear energy was cheaper than that from coal, recommended that 'an examination by an independent outside agency of the purely financial aspects of costing of all methods of energy supply should be put in hand and the report published'.[24]

In the case of the first programme, where ordinary economic criteria took second place, Webb has argued that many of the trends which destroyed the projected parity between nuclear and conventional costs could have been predicted.[25] It is possible, though, of course, far from certain, that an independent body might have managed this. In the future, the introduction of new reactor types will certainly involve complex economic analysis, and other than straightforward economic influences may also be at work. The economics of the second programme have certainly been analysed more vigorously than were those of the first, and the Minister of Power has stated his belief that asking an outside body to make a full study of energy costing would be to impose on it 'a heavy task which would not . . . yield commensurate benefits'.[26]

The Science Committee have not accepted this view either, because they feel that the cost of an independent examination (or examinations) would be 'comparatively insignificant' when judged against the cost of mistakes in energy investment. The Committee also fear that, no matter how thorough reviews of energy costs are, if they are confined to official circles then there may be some doubt about the conclusions reached.[27]

The third of the Science Committee's recommendations originally appeared to be of constitutional significance. It ran:

A study should be made of the possibilities of the establishment, within the framework of the British system of government, of a body similar to the U.S. Joint Congressional Committee on [Atomic Energy] to deal with all aspects of energy policy, and provided with adequate expert staff for the purpose.

The author has argued elsewhere that apart from the shortcomings of the Joint Committee and the fundamental differences between Congress and the House of Commons, 'the Joint Committee would still be an untypical model to imitate', one indeed which Congress itself has shown a marked reluctance to follow.[28] The Science Committee has now in fact clarified its intentions, indicating that what it wants are adequate facilities for a 'much closer continuous scrutiny by

Parliament of all matters relating to energy policy' than it considers the Nationalised Industries Committee has time to provide.[29] The Science Committee itself, displaying uncommon persistence for a select committee, decided in 1969 to conduct a follow-up inquiry to discover just how far the reorganisation of the nuclear industry had been carried. The evidence of its second report[30] suggests once again that the problems of the nuclear industry continue to be such as to make well worth while regular attention by a parliamentary committee and it is encouraging that now at least there is a Committee with the remit, willingness and ability to offer a constructive contribution.

It is worth noting that although there have been several useful debates on nuclear energy in the Lords over the years, there have been few enough in the Commons, and when the Science Committee's first report was eventually debated few other than members of the Science Committee itself were present. More promising was the response of the Minister of Technology during this debate. He thanked the Committee for what he described as 'a document of great value' both in itself and because of the stimulus it had been within the industry, and he expressed himself well pleased that the Committee's report gave the contributors to the debate what amounted to equality of information with him.[31] Taking the Committee's first and second reports together, it definitely appears that in the last two years the A.E.A., the C.E.G.B. and policy-makers generally in the nuclear industry have become more accountable, at any rate in the sense of being more answerable, to Parliament. It must be hoped both that the government will continue to look favourably on the Science Committee so that its existence is not threatened, and also that the Committee, having begun so dynamically, does not run out of steam.

The main problems associated with the accountability of the two public corporations in the nuclear field have now been outlined and it remains only to examine the applicability and ramifications of the accountability concept in respect of work in this field performed for the two corporations by private industry. Taking first the case of research, development and design work done by the consortia for the A.E.A., the striking thing is how little of such work there has really been. The problem of accountability in this relationship has not therefore received much attention. (The same is broadly true of A.E.A. contracts with universities, contracts which the A.E.A. has regarded as being in general 'a little more open in application' than those entered into with industry.) The issue is still well worth pursuing here because in spite of not having lost their independence through receipt of A.E.A. contracts the consortia have more or less completely lacked that independence simply as a result of the A.E.A.'s dominance in R. & D. policy-making on the one hand and its ownership of in-house facilities with which to execute its policies on the other. As early as 1959 the consortia, of which at that time there were five, were agreed that they could play a bigger part than had up to then been asked of them in the long-term development of reactor systems, and one of them argued that this was essential if best use was to be made of the greatly extended laboratories with which they had recently provided themselves. Though satisfied with the terms of such contracts as they had received they all wanted more because, they said, the work was too expensive for them to carry out on their own initiative. They recognised that if more contracts were not forthcoming then the number of consortia would have to be reduced, and it was also pointed out that proper use of the consortia's resources under contract to the A.E.A. would enable the Authority to pursue the development of nuclear energy on a broader front than it could otherwise manage. The Authority for their part expressed their intention at that time of meeting the consortia's requests for more work in both research–development and in design, but they did not believe that the consortia had by then become capable of evolving whole reactor systems under contract, nor did they consider that the country either needed or could afford the series of alternative systems which might have been the outcome of such a policy.[32] Thereafter, while the Authority continued to contract out to industry a small amount of design and development work on components for prototype reactors, and all manufacturing, responsibility for development, design and construction of such prototypes still stayed, as explained above, firmly with them. In 1967 one of the three consortia then remaining suggested that the results of such development work were 'not nearly so readily available to industry' as was the case in the United States, and a second felt that £0·3–0·5 million per annum per consortium might profitably be made available by the A.E.A. for the engineering development and exploitation of the S.G.H.W.R. and H.T.G.C.R. systems.[33] This issue has since been overtaken by the reorganisation of the nuclear industry, which is itself intended to lead to a redistribution of research, development and design responsibilities. This is taken up below.

The Authority's considerable self-sufficiency has naturally not extended over all their commitments and requirements and in 1960 the Public Accounts Committee investigated and criticised contracts which the Authority were forced to enter into with private firms.[34] The first was for a certain chemical needed for defence purposes. I.C.I. were already supplying the Authority with this under an earlier contract but increased quantities were required and since there was no commercial outlet for it the company were reluctant to use their own capital to extend their existing plant. Urgency, the knowledge that there was no alternative source either of the material or of the technical know-how required, and the conviction that they could not produce it more cheaply themselves together drove the Authority to accept what they admitted were 'extremely stiff' terms which left I.C.I. with a 'very high' rate of profit compared to what they could expect to get from ordinary commercial ventures. I.C.I. had also taken the position that the earlier contract had worked out badly for them and that the new contract should reflect this. The new £300,000 plant was to be amortised over five years, the manufacturers receiving an annual minimum profit related in part to the capital expenditure involved so that, no allowance being made for the amortised part of the capital, the rate of profit would rise from 17 per cent in the first year to 45 per cent in the fifth. The opinion of the P.A.C. was 'that the Authority should have discussed with the contractor what his terms would [have been] if the Authority had provided the capital, and that in any similar circumstances ... the Authority should, in consultation with the Treasury, reconsider their practice of not advancing capital to contractors who are in a position to provide it themselves'. (The practice of making capital available to contractors unwilling to invest their own is one that the Authority, like other government departments, has followed when it has been essential.)

The second case examined by the P.A.C. in 1960 was in some ways similar to the first in that the Authority, this time in the light of the enlarged civil programme of 1957, had persuaded their single supplier to expand production of the special graphite needed, and had also had to offer inducements to a second company to make up the outstanding amounts. In the circumstances it had not been possible to negotiate break clauses and with the slowdown in the nuclear programme at the end of the fifties the Authority were faced with surplus supplies. The problems identified by the P.A.C. in this case were first that the A.E.A. could only reduce the graphite surplus by taking less than they had contracted for, thereby probably incurring penalties, and second that the capital which the A.E.A. had provided to allow the two companies respectively to expand and to establish their capacities might actually in the event mainly enable those companies to make profits elsewhere.

These last two cases, while interesting enough in their own right, are of only very marginal significance in the context of Britain's nuclear development effort looked at as a whole. Of somewhat greater significance have been the implications of the final form of accountability which has arisen in the nuclear programmes, that of the consortia to the C.E.G.B. in respect of central stations built under turnkey contract. The consortia complained to the Science Committee in 1967 that C.E.G.B. specifications always called for voluminous detail in tenders and that this was followed by a long process of bringing tender and specification into line. This, it was said, could make the cost of a domestic tender as much as ten times greater than that incurred in tendering overseas. Overseas experience was also said to have shown that the C.E.G.B. could reduce its close control over the execution of contracts, thereby permitting substantial savings both to itself and to the consortia, and yet not end up with a plant of inferior performance.

The C.E.G.B. Chairman strongly defended the Board against this charge on the grounds that tenders to the C.E.G.B. included the latest developments in a continually evolving technology whereas those offered overseas were fully debugged in that they were based on plants already sold to the C.E.G.B. He also believed that the C.E.G.B.'s policy on tenders was justified by the high accountability of its nuclear stations. It would probably be fair to say that most of whatever waste there has been in the tendering procedure in Britain has derived less from the C.E.G.B.'s thoroughness than from the fact that two out of every three tenders ordinarily submitted to it by the three consortia have usually had to be declined. The waste then has been as much a fault of the structure of the industry as of the C.E.G.B.

This paper has dealt with the issue of accountability in Britain's nuclear industry as this industry was organised from 1955 to 1968 but, as was several times noted above, the industry is in the throes of reorganisation. This process has proved, hardly surprisingly, a difficult one to carry through and at the time of writing it seems that it will be some time before the industry begins to settle down in its new form. It is, however, clear that when that does happen then the problems of accountability will arise in a quite new guise, a guise likely to have more in common with American experience in the nuclear field than with past British experience. It is also apparent that the transitional phase is posing serious accountability problems of its own. The nature of these new problems can to a certain extent be deduced by considering the direction in which the nuclear industry is being reorganised.

The three consortia have already been replaced by two new design and construction (D./C.) organisations, the third consortium having in effect found no place in the new arrangement. It was originally projected that the D./C. organisations would take over the A.E.A.'s design teams but so far this has worked out in practice only in the case of the fast reactor team, the members of which have been transferred or seconded to one of the D./C. companies. The A.E.A. has a 20 per cent shareholding in each of these companies and the Industrial Reorganisation Corporation (I.R.C.), which was instrumental in bringing about the new structure, has also taken a temporary shareholding in both. It is intended that the I.R.C. will dispose of its holdings fairly quickly and that the A.E.A.'s will shortly be taken over by a new fuel company. This fuel company is to be created, by legislative provision, from the A.E.A.'s present vigorous fuel business and will, initially at least, be entirely government-owned. The government are proposing in addition to set up an Atomic Energy Board, referred to above as likely to have responsibilities as regards the composition and financing of research and development programmes. This Board, which will have representatives from the A.E.A., the generating boards, the new fuel company and the two new D./C. companies, will also be involved in the co-ordination of export arrangements and in major policy matters.

When the whole rearrangement is complete the A.E.A. will evidently be a quite different body, but it has been clear for some time that the industry needed rationalisation, if only to eliminate duplication, and it has also been apparent that the overall emphasis within it needed to be changed to increase exploitation and to produce a research and development effort predicated by the domestic and export markets. These are indeed two of the objectives the Minister of Technology has indicated that he wishes to see achieved. He also wants maximum technical standardisation consistent with effective design competition, and efficient co-ordination between the design and fuel sides of the nuclear industry.

Against this background the new problems of responsibility, accountability and independence can now be outlined. There are perhaps two major areas of uncertainty. In the first place it is clear that the onus of exploiting nuclear technology is intended to rest in future with private industry to a far greater extent. The industry might therefore be thought to resemble somewhat the American one, were it not for the fact that there is to be a public shareholding in both new companies. This arrangement could easily prove a tricky one to operate. The relationship, for example, between the two public shareholdings could be a complicated one to establish and maintain. That is, how will competition between the two D./C. companies work out when a public body holds shares in both? Another point which is not entirely clear concerns the criteria against which the public shareholdings are to be judged. To what influence do the shares entitle the holding body, and conversely, how much of their independence do the D./C. organisations forfeit as a result? Then again, when the public shareholding is taken over by the proposed fuel company, how will the work programme of this company be determined? If this work is done mostly under contract from the D./C. companies, how much independence will the fuel company as a public body retain? Finally, if and when private interests are allowed to invest in the fuel company, how will this move affect its work, the work of the D./C. companies and the relationship between them and the fuel company? At this stage it is easier by far to pose these questions than to arrive at realistic answers.

The second potentially difficult issue stems from the division of responsibility between the new A.E.A. with its more limited capability and the two D./C. companies with their enhanced capabilities. Ideally there would be a clear boundary somewhere on the spectrum from generic work to commercial development. ('Generic work is that necessary to establish the technical and economic viability of a new reactor system, including work aimed at achieving the performance forecast at the time of the system's adoption. Speculative work on improving the system is included.' A.E.A. definition.) Unfortunately, to quote the Science Committee, '...the existing facilities of the Authority, their involvement in programmes of development already running, their control of fuel development and production – and the need for public financial support – all make for a blurring of this theoretical distinction ... there is no hard and fast line of demarcation between the companies and the Authority. There is, and will continue to be, a substantial "grey area"....'[35] In the words of one of the D./C. companies, 'The main change that has taken place, as a result of the re-organisation of the industry, is that now the design and construction companies ... will have a greater influence on the Authority's generic programme and will determine the detailed objectives of the specific R. & D. programme.' And in the words of the other, 'The initiative [will] be substantially with the industrial groups' even though the Authority will continue to possess certain facilities which the groups 'could not conveniently own ... unless they were transferred at a pretty nominal rate'. Meanwhile the Authority consider that generic work will continue to be their responsibility, though even here they feel that 'it should be possible for us in future to place rather more work under contract with the companies than we have done in the past'.

As regards the relationship between the two D./C. companies, they themselves apparently see no incompatibility, again quoting one of them, 'Between collaboration on basic information and fundamentals and competition on design.' This of course takes for granted equality of access by the two companies to work done at the public expense, something which may not always in future be easy to define. The last word on what is still a rather confused situation may be left with the Science Committee. Again noting that the varied development programmes of the D./C. companies will presumably continue to require financial and material support, the Committee state that 'the public interest demands that there should be a considerable measure of official influence over the way that future development is directed. At present this influence is still wielded by the Authority, who show little signs of a serious withdrawal from the important areas of the nuclear field. This we can hardly criticise in the circumstances.'

The two major problem areas which have been sketched out here do not include all the difficulties which may arise. Others which could be troublesome are, for instance, the problem of royalty payment by the D./C. companies to the A.E.A. in respect of foreign sales, and the new complications for the C.E.G.B. if the work-load of the two new companies turns out to be so low that their survival comes to depend upon the 'Buggins' turn next' principle. In the latter event, of course, the pressures for a single D./C. company would probably become irresistible. The pressures and problems which do materialise will undoubtedly manifest themselves at the level of the Atomic Energy Board. The composition, powers and performance of that Board could therefore be the key to the future of Britain's nuclear industry. It may also prove to be very important that there is now only one sponsoring ministry, the Ministry of Technology, for all the interests in the nuclear industry, including the C.E.G.B.[36] In any case it is apparent that if the reorganisation of the industry does remove one set of problems by putting the industry on a sounder commercial footing, it may well pose simultaneously another set, caused this time by the competing alternatives of independence and accountability. The situation must therefore be closely watched so that the side-effects of the industry's cure do not turn out to be more serious than the original disease.

Notes

1. United Kingdom Nuclear Reactor Programme, *Report from the Select Committee on Science and Technology, 1966–67 (HC 381–XVII, 1967)* paras 970, 986.
2. Ibid., para. 1468.
3. *Report from the Select Committee on Nationalised Industries, 1962–63: The Electricity Supply Industry (HC 236–II)* vol. II: *Minutes of Evidence*, para. 3585.
4. Ibid., para. 3928.
5. Sir Christopher Hinton, 'Nuclear Power', in *Three Banks Review*, LII (Dec. 1961) p. 14.
6. United Kingdom Atomic Energy Authority, *Fourteenth Annual Report and Account, 1967–68* (1968) para. 191.
7. *A Programme of Nuclear Power* (Cmd 9389, 1955).
8. *Report from the Select Committee on Nationalised Industries, 1962–3*, vol. III, app. 39, paras 8, 9.
9. *Three Banks Review*, LII, p. 10.
10. *Verbatim Report of the Press Conference on Tender Assessment of Nuclear Reactors for Dungeness B, Held at Sudbury House 29 July 1965*, p. 3.
11. *Fifth Report from the Select Committee on Estimates, 1958–59: U.K.A.E.A. (Production Group and Development and Engineering Group) (HC 316–I)* p. liii, para. 135.
12. N. Johnson, *Parliament and Administration: The Estimates Committee, 1945–65* (1966) p. 60.
13. D. Coombes, *The Member of Parliament and the Administration: The Case of the Select Committee on the Nationalised Industries* (1966) p. 111.
14. *Report from the Select Committee on Nationalised Industries, 1962–63*, vol. I, para. 404.
15. *Hansard* (Lords), vol. 251, cols 1380–457, 10 July 1963.
16. Austin Albu, 'The Member of Parliament, the Executive and Scientific Policy', in *Minerva*, II i 7, and Richard Crossman, *Hansard* (*Commons*), vol. 689, cols 1019, 1020.
17. *Atomic Energy Authority Accounts, 1961–62: Report from the Comptroller and Auditor General*, para. 11.

18. *Third Report from the Committee of Public Accounts, 1962–63, (HC* 275–1, 1963) pp. 388–90 and lxx–lxxi.

19. *Report from the Select Committee on Science and Technology, 1966–67,* p. xlviii, para. 154.

20. See, for instance, Duncan Burn, *The Political Economy of Nuclear Energy* (I.E.A., 1967).

21. Dr C. J. H. Watson, 'Need for Research in Fusion Reactors', in *The Times,* 25 Oct. 1967.

22. *Third Special Report from the Select Committee on Science and Technology, 1968–69* (1968) p. vii.

23. Ibid., p. ix.

24. *Report from the Select Committee on Science and Technology, 1966–67,* p. xxxiii, para. 98.

25. M. E. Webb, 'Some Aspects of Nuclear Power Economics in the United Kingdom', in *Scottish Journal of Political Economy,* xv i (Feb. 1968).

26. *Third Special Report from the Select Committee on Science and Technology, 1966–67,* p. iv.

27. Ibid., p. v, para. 5.

28. R. Williams, 'The Select Committee on Science and Technology: The First Round', in *Public Administration* (autumn 1968).

29. *Third Special Report from the Select Committee on Science and Technology, 1966–67,* p. v, paras 2 and 3.

30. *Fourth Report from the Select Committee on Science and Technology: The United Kingdom Nuclear Power Industry (HC* 401, 1969).

31. *HC Debates,* no. 125, vol. 765, cols 968–9.

32. For details of the A.E.A.'s and consortia's views, see the evidence to the *Fifth Report from the Select Committee on Estimates, 1958–59.*

33. In evidence to the Science Committee.

34. *Second Report from the Committee of Public Accounts, Session 1959–60 (HC* 250–1) paras 3280–363 and 3580–638.

35. This and the following quotations are taken from the *Fourth Report from the Select Committee on Science and Technology (HC* 401, 1969) cited above.

36. The Ministry of Power was merged with the Ministry of Technology in October 1969.

10 Governmental Contracts with Non-Profit Social Welfare Corporations

Bertram M. Beck

It is becoming increasingly difficult to discharge governmental functions in a creative and responsive manner. Government is looked to to discharge many functions which hitherto-fore were carried out by other social institutions. Rapid growth of population and the increases in the density of population compound the need for public services and result in a complexity of organisation that mitigates against efficient and effective operations.

One way around this dilemma is for government to contract with private corporations which may be able to discharge particular governmental functions on behalf of government in a more expeditious fashion than can the strictly government operation. Much of the recent interest by students of public administration in government by contract focuses on the use of the contract to achieve technological and scientific developments where there is a premium on flexibility and creativity. Little attention has been given to the lessons that might be learned from the traditional use of contracts for the discharge of social welfare purposes and the more recent use of contracts in the United States for the stimulation of indigenous efforts in urban centres to launch and conduct self-help programmes among the poor.

The use of private organisations to carry out public social welfare functions goes far back into the history of American social welfare. Up until the Great Depression the use of public agencies to meet welfare needs was largely limited to the care of residual groups whose nature or geographic location made private social agencies inaccessible. The timid interest of states in the field of widows' pensions shortly after World War I was bitterly resisted by private welfare interests who assumed that public administration would injure the welfare of the recipients, who were viewed as the special concern of private welfare interests. Only massive public need during the Depression led to the reluctant acceptance of the notion that public assistance and income maintenance programmes were a function of the government. Dr Donald Howard comments that 'Private agencies' support for this principle sometimes seems begrudgingly accorded, on grounds that only the taxing power of government is adequate to the task, with little emphasis upon the value of the social justice thus established or upon the consummate importance to democratic society of the entire society's concern for its most disadvantaged members without reference to racial, religious or other factors.'[1]

The flow of public money to private non-profit corporations for health and welfare purposes is such that a study of such expenditures in twenty-three urban centres in 1960 disclosed that 'Payments to private agencies represented 28·5 per cent of all public expenditures for institutional care of dependent children, 8 per cent of all public expenditures for family services and foster home care, 13·4 per cent in the case of institutional care for aged persons, and 100 per cent of the maternity home care provided from public funds.'[2]

Use of public funds for purchase of service in the field of child welfare is particularly prevalent, and most particularly in the eastern states, where there are strongly entrenched voluntary agencies. One study of public financing of voluntary agency foster care demonstrated the wide variations between states. It was reported that in 1957 three states made one-half of their expenditures for foster care through voluntary agencies. Seven states reported that one-fourth, but less than one-half, of their expenditures were made through voluntary agencies. Thirty-one states reported less than a fourth, and four states reported no expenditures. Fifteen states used the lump-sum method of subsidy; however, most of these states, as well as thirty-one additional states, also used some variation of a *per capita* system of payments to voluntary child care agencies.[3]

In instances of lump-sum subsidy, grants or *per capita* payment, it is rare that there is an actual contractual instrument. It is difficult, however, to limit discussion of govern-

214

ment by contract to instances where there is an actual contract, since the key issue seems to be the expectations of the public body, whether embodied in a statement of a grant or in a statute or a letter of understanding or an actual contract. Yet in some instances of public support for private agencies the expectations of government are so vaguely formulated that there is little similarity to contract. The declining practice of giving lump-sum subsidies to particular institutions or agencies provides an example of a use of public funds with very little attention to securing the public interest.

A study of the use of such subsidies in the State of Pennsylvania demonstrates the way in which public funds can be misused when public purposes are sought through the use of private corporations. This study reported on a grant first made to a children's institution in 1857. In 1957 there were twenty-nine children's organisations among 242 health, welfare and education institutions for which the legislature made an appropriation biennially of $60 million. The children's organisations receiving grants were favoured among all such organisations in the state primarily because they had historically been recipients. Budgeting procedures in the state remained untouched for a hundred years. The legislative appropriation committee was not interested in having help from the professional social workers in selecting institutions for subsidy. The researcher came to the conclusion that the subsidy system continues to exist primarily from the momentum of historical precedent. It has seriously hampered the development of public child-care programmes and responsible supervision of voluntary programmes.[4]

Scandals resulting from the use of the lump-sum subsidy have resulted in its diminished use, with the current accent being on purchase of care. The concept of purchase of care actually sets a contractual obligation wherein the public body determines what care is needed for a particular individual and then pays a *per capita* rate to secure it. Although this can readily be justified when the type of care being purchased is unusual and highly specialised, it is more difficult to justify when the type of care being purchased is the customary foster care provisions and the like. Sceptics point out that the flow of public money to private non-profit corporations for purchase of care is another label for supporting sectarian or special interests without sufficient regard to public welfare.

Such sceptics point out that the chief factor in the relationship between the public and voluntary agencies is an economic one. Tax funds for welfare purposes have increased markedly while voluntary contributions have remained relatively static in relation to population increase.[5] If the voluntary agencies are to survive, they must secure public funds. The interest of social organisations in their own survival may well be the most important factor creating the extensive use of voluntary agencies to spend public funds.

Previously pointed out was the assumption by public agencies of responsibilities which prior to the late 1920s were carried by voluntary agencies. Faced with loss of function, many voluntary agencies became supplements of the expanded public services by becoming paid agents for the public authority. The interest of social organisations in perpetuating themselves does not spring from any particularly venal motive, but merely the satisfactions derived by the board of directors and the paid professionals from continuing to discharge what they view as a personal and social responsibility.

The Catholic Church has been an important force in the promotion of public funds being used for the support of private welfare corporations. 'Whereas the Protestant churches have generally encouraged the growth of the public services, the Catholic position has been that government should intervene only when people through their family churches and other voluntary associations are unable to provide welfare programmes; furthermore, that when government must act, it should make use of existing voluntary structures to the greatest possible extent.'[6]

At the same time that such public–private arrangements are advocated, church-related sources resist governmental standard-setting and controls of service purchased by the government because of the fear of domination of church by state.[7]

Up until the early sixties, when the anti-poverty programmes introduced entirely new considerations into the arena, the controversy concerning the use of public funds for the support of voluntary social welfare agencies centred around the degree to which those agencies actually facilitated the discharge of a public responsibility. Critics of the trend held that the power of the sectarian and non-sectarian agencies was such that government did not actually call the tune although it paid the piper. The voluntary agencies, it was held, tend to select the population to be served, leaving unserved those who do not fall within the categories the voluntary agencies deem acceptable. In New York City, for example, for many years there was no public child-welfare programme for dependent and neglected children. Since the Catholic and Jewish child-caring agencies were most powerful and most prevalent, this mitigated against the interests of the black children, who tended to be Protestant. After years of contention, a public child-welfare programme was developed parallel to that operated by voluntary agencies. Because of the religious factor, however, this tended towards the establishment of non-integrated child-welfare facilities. It is still true that delinquent children in New York State who cannot be admitted to any private institution with government subsidy tend to go to public institutions that are less able to care for them than the best private organisations.

Actually, the strength of the government agency in setting demands is largely determined by the power of the voluntary agency. In the field of day care in New York City, where the City department contracts with settlement houses and other neighbourhood organisations, the requirements of the public agency are extremely strict and the sponsoring agency has little flexibility. Moreover, as a token towards a semblance of co-operative effort, the private agencies sponsoring a day care facility are required to contribute 3 per cent of the cost and receive no reimbursement for indirect cost. This is in sharp distinction to governmental relationship to profit-making industry, where a cost-plus basis is customary.

Those who tend to look with favour on the use of public funds for the support of private health and welfare efforts point out that the government never picks up the total cost and so the public receives the service supported in part by public money and in part by voluntary contributions. Moreover, it is held that the quality of service given through the multiplicity of small organisations is greater than can be obtained through the less flexible bureaucratic structure of the public.

217

The involvement of private citizens on boards of directors is also held to be an asset that could not be obtained through the use of advisory committees and the like in the public sector. The religious orientation of the sectarian agencies is viewed by some as an asset, although others, of course, see this as a deficit. In New York State the Social Welfare Law mandates that, whenever practical, a child placed away from his parents be placed in an institution or a family of his own faith. In the instance of abandoned children, and others, where there is no information concerning religion, the child is 'assigned' to one of the three major faiths in rotation. Such practices, which appear to some laymen to be in contravention of the Constitution, have not been prohibited by the courts.

Probably the most pernicious effect of governmental subsidy of voluntary agencies is, like the practice itself, historically determined. Voluntary agencies, of course, resulted from the efforts of the rich to help the poor. Consequently, the boards of those agencies, which usually have a key responsibility for raising money, are composed of the well-to-do. Since most of the public health and welfare services are directed to the poor, this has resulted in a situation whereby public money is funnelled into the hands of upper-class and upper-middle-class people to spend on behalf of less privileged people. This places the consumer of services in a position of dependency quite different from that which would exist if he were receiving services given as a matter of right by a public agency supported by all the tax-payers. It also militates against the direct participation of the consumer in shaping of services and this, again, accentuates a destructive dependency role.

Most social welfare agencies subsidised by government started out as what Alan Pifer terms true voluntary associations. Such organisations, according to Pifer, are characterised by actions taken by private citizens in concert on their own volition, not for profit, and outside the initiative and authority of the government. Such organisations, Pifer states, offer the individual an opportunity for self-expression and provide a means through which he can promote his interest or belief by way of collective action. The true voluntary association enables the ordinary citizen to understand better

218

the processes of democracy by providing him with a means to participate in social processes.

Large infusions of public funds changed these true voluntary associations into what Pifer has characterised as quasi-non-governmental agencies or private service agencies. Of quasi-non-governmental agencies, Pifer states that these are organisations incorporated on a non-profit basis and entirely or almost entirely dependent on government support for their existence. They appear to be voluntary organisations but, in fact, the role of the executive, the board, the staff and the consumer is mainly conditioned by government funds. Pifer distinguishes between non-profit corporations that are established with concurrence of governmental agencies to conduct programmes that are best conducted, in the opinion of some public officials, by quasi-non-governmental organisations; and organisations which began as private agencies that have in recent years increasingly become instrumentalities in carrying out public purposes.

Pifer further defines two sub-classes of quasi-non-governmental agencies. The first recognise their quasi-non-governmental status, whereas the second turn to public support as voluntary support fails and continue to think, act and behave as if they were voluntary agencies in the truer meaning of that phrase. The fact that the voluntary social welfare agencies, which are in truth quasi-non-governmental agencies, insist on behaving like voluntary agencies gives rise to the problems that have been presented.

Those social welfare organisations that fall within Pifer's category of 'private service agency' are largely those blessed with an endowment. The private service agencies are described by Pifer as voluntary organisations that are answerable not to a membership but to themselves – that is, to a paid professional staff and self-perpetuating boards of trustees. They are differentiated from the quasi-non-governmental organisations and from the true voluntary associations by the fact that they are not responsive to a membership and the ultimate responsibility lies not with the government or with a body of members, but with a self-perpetuating board of trustees and the professionals. The voluntary social welfare agency which depends on public funds and is not held accountable by government actually becomes a self-perpetuating group falling within this private service agency category.

Into this rather confused arena, the anti-poverty programme introduced its own form of voluntary association, which was asked to become a quasi-non-governmental agency almost moments after its birth. In other words, it took 125 years for government funds to alter voluntary associations formed to serve the poor into quasi-non-governmental agencies which still tended to behave as if they were voluntary associations. Under the anti-poverty programme, this transformation was to take place instantly. The O.E.O., in its early days, forced the development of these agencies because the Office assumed that the job of attacking poverty 'was simply not being done by public and private agencies, nor it was thought, could it be; they were considered too fragmented in their approach, too set in their ways, and they were also seen as being too middle-class, too white, too paternalistic and too alien to be acceptable to those who were most deeply mired in the "culture of poverty"'. The War on Poverty forced social agencies to deal with the idea that, while they advanced under the banner of 'helping people to help themselves', their net effect was often to create dependency rather than self-sufficiency among exiled people.

To carry out the purposes of the anti-poverty programme, cities were required to designate a Community Action agency. In many instances this was an agency organised outside the usual channels of government and incorporated in the same form as a voluntary social welfare agency. The early regulations of the O.E.O., designed to carry out the injunction that there be maximum feasible participation of the poor in shaping the programme required that one-third of the members of the board of such an agency be poor people, or what were called representatives of the poor. Some cities exceeded this requirement. Later, when the anti-poverty programme got into political trouble, Congress mandated that the boards include representatives of public government and the like.

In addition to the Community Action agency in each city, there was created a multiplicity of new organisations, many of which placed in the driver's seat poor people, or at least people who were closer to the poor than persons affiliated with the traditional social welfare agencies. Funds then flowed primarily from O.E.O. to its regional offices and then to the Community Action agency and ultimately to the so-called delegate agencies, which carried out the programme in the neighbourhoods where poor people lived.

The Community Action agencies fulfilled Pifer's description of the quasi-non-governmental agency actually established with the concurrence of governmental agencies to conduct public-funded programmes. The delegate agencies were often true voluntary associations. Sometimes, they were block clubs and other such groups which abound in certain ghettos. They welcomed the opportunity to finally get some public money to carry forward their purposes just as the traditional social welfare agencies had got such money for years. Once they received their funds through government agencies, however, they became quasi-non-governmental but often adamantly refused to subordinate themselves to the public will. In this sense, they again paralleled their more traditional social welfare sisters, but the genesis of their independence was quite different.

Pifer points out that the quasi-non-governmental agency cannot serve the needs of the individual citizen in the way the true voluntary association can. The quasi-non-governmental agency may serve the needs of individual citizens and often does. 'But in the final test [it] must serve public purposes and, if these do not coincide with the individual purposes, government's interest must prevail.'

The failure to realise the predominance of public purposes among many of the anti-poverty agencies was in part a consequence of O.E.O.'s lack of clarity concerning the crucial injunction that there be maximum feasible participation of the poor. Participation was sometimes seen as an end in itself and, when that view predominated, O.E.O. officials seemed to take a position that the government funds were to be spent for the purpose of gaining maximum participation. Thus, the recipient agency was held accountable for the fact of participation of the poor rather than for the attainment of specific programme goals. The more conservative O.E.O. staff placed a larger emphasis on the attainment of programme goals and saw participation as a means.

To further complicate the situation, the predominant

221

groups of poor in the inner city are black or other minorities victimised by racial discrimination. The anti-poverty programme is viewed as an extension of the Civil Rights Movement. Efforts to hold anti-poverty agencies accountable were often seen as extensions of the habitual pattern of middle-class white people dominating the efforts of the poor and put-upon to shape their own destiny.

Mobilisation For Youth, an anti-poverty organisation on the Lower East Side of New York City, was formed three years before the passage of the Economic Opportunity Act with the interest of many people who were instrumental in drafting the Act and administering it in the early years. Many of the component parts of the Mobilisation programme were written into the Economic Opportunity Act and thus the experience of M.F.Y. is instructive. From the very beginning, although M.F.Y. was organised on the model of the traditional voluntary agency, the board of directors had little to do with securing funds, most of which came from public sources. In its early years M.F.Y. launched a vigorous social action programme which resulted in an all-out attack on the agency. The attack surprised many who failed to realise that M.F.Y. was not, in fact, a voluntary association of people who could seek social change according to their own determination. It was not, in other words, a voluntary association; it was a quasi-non-governmental agency that had to serve public purposes. Not all of the public officials who were the targets of M.F.Y.'s attack went along with the notion that public purposes were served by this vigorous effort to change public institutions.

Anti-poverty organisations created in the image of Mobilisation For Youth continued to make this effort to behave as voluntary associations. This was encouraged by public officials who talked about involvement and maximum participation and never made it clear to the poor people being involved that in a quasi-non-governmental agency public interest would ultimately dominate. It is no wonder that the socially exiled now finding their voice do not always clearly perceive the reality of the fact that those who control the purse in the last analysis control the programme. Not only have these neighbourhood groups been deluded by public officials infatuated with their own dogma but they have also been confused by the example of the true voluntary associations, which did become government instrumentalities without serving the public interest. Reference has already been made to the history of child care, wherein quasi-non-governmental agencies did not allow the public welfare department to call the tune. It also has been noted that this topsy-turvy situation was maintained because of the social and political power of these traditional agencies and their boards. One can but hope that the changing political nature of the cities and the coming to power of new groups at the decision-making table will mean that quasi-non-governmental agencies behave as instrumentalities of government whether they are in the anti-poverty sector or any other portion of the social welfare sector.

As we move towards the extension of government seeking to discharge its welfare functions through contracting with private non-profit corporations, the difference between the voluntary association or the private service agency and the quasi-non-governmental agency needs to be highlighted.

In the quasi-non-governmental organisation, for example, the board of directors does not play a vital role in programme-building and policy-making if government is doing its job. The programme is developed by the staff and government agencies determine what will and will not be funded. The board can, of course, instruct the staff not to apply for a specific programme, but in reality it joins with the staff in the everlasting search for funds. Since the government supplies the funds, it also determines basic policies, and the executive is responsible to the board as well as to the government for executing policies set by the public funding source. It is only when government fails to do its job that the board of a quasi-non-governmental organisation can behave as if it were a board of a true voluntary association or a private service agency.

The nature of the relationship of the board to the staff and the government has important ramifications for the composition of a board of a quasi-non-governmental agency. When such an agency is engaged in giving on-going services, the agency's clients should be in the majority on the board. The balance of the board needs to be composed of persons who are not clients but who have connections that will help the

223

agency survive in times of crisis and who will work with the clients in the cross-class-barrier encounters that are so important in our overly stratified society.

True voluntary associations that have gradually glided into the role of being quasi-non-governmental organisations should be forced to re-examine their board composition. A board that was formed for the purpose of getting voluntary contributions to sustain a service desired by a group of individual citizens is not by any means the most desirable board to administer, for example, day care services in a neighbourhood. If governmental funds are the major source of support for a service, people who use that service should be on the board of the quasi-non-governmental agency. They can then interact with government representatives and make the invaluable contribution that only the consumer of service can make. Mr or Mrs Midtown, sitting on the board of such an agency, is most often a captive of the professional, since Mr and Mrs Midtown lack direct knowledge of neighbourhood needs. Professionals of all types are strongly biased in favour of perpetuation of the professional culture.

The infatuation with standards that deny service since the standards cannot be met has long been manifest in the child-care field. This focus on standards, not service, is a consequence of the fact that child-care consumers seldom have a role in the management of child-care programmes. Examples could be cited from every field of service in which a true voluntary association becomes a quasi-non-governmental organisation without the necessary change in the board's composition. The quasi-non-governmental agency has a legitimate and necessary role to play in today's scene. Even with the basic restriction that government must call the tune, a non-profit corporation has certain freedoms with respect to personnel and programme that cannot exist in the true public agency. With growing interest in decentralisation, it may well be that there should be an increased number of neighbourhood corporations to offer health, welfare and educational services. When government plays its proper role and the myth of absolute neighbourhood control is dispelled, then the neighbourhood corporation as a quasi-non-governmental agency offers a possible middle ground between the evils of overly centralised government and attempting to run a highly industrialised society along the lines of a New England town meeting.

Effective government in a democracy demands the multiplication of true voluntary associations as distinguished from the other organisational forms described. Such associations can and must confront governmental bureaucracy and organise consumers of publicly financed services for the healthy and necessary confrontation between the service purveyor and service consumer. This job of organisation cannot be done by the quasi-non-governmental organisations; this is one of the valuable lessons of the anti-poverty programme. Of course, nothing in the nature of the true voluntary association makes it cause-oriented. It is perfectly possible and proper for a group of private citizens to come together to do good in any way that is not illegal. Most of the purposes such voluntary associations pursue are not harmful and often they are helpful, however limited in their effect. The great need today, however, is for voluntary associations that will facilitate social participation, especially by those who heretofore have been exiled from society.

The role of government is not to be a major source of support for voluntary associations, for this can only contaminate and change them. The most valuable purpose voluntary associations can serve is to monitor government, instruct it, badger it and provide for the individual citizen a vehicle for his autonomy as a human being. The day of the voluntary association is here and now. The great evil with which both rich and poor struggle in our industrialised, centralised society is the subjugation of the individual to corporate or state interests. The voluntary association is the vehicle through which the individual can join with others for the achievement of personal identity.

Examples of true voluntary associations are rare. They exist within neighbourhoods but they lack substantial power and therefore are usually not well known. The problem of the true voluntary association, like so many problems, is fundamentally financial. In time it is found that staff is needed, and then money to employ staff. A hierarchy develops and in time what exists is not a true voluntary association but a private service agency that is controlled by a self-perpetuating board. Private service agencies can pursue the

225

same programmatic goals as the true voluntary association. There is nothing, for example, to prevent a family agency or a settlement house (which can properly be described as being private service agencies) from altering its programmes so as to encourage social participation. In some instances, of course, the self-perpetuating board may prefer to give a specific kind of service rather than facilitate social participation. In other instances, the staff may not be presenting the board with the alternatives, and the board, far removed from the persons who should be served, is not aware that there is an alternative to the day-in-day-out operation of services. To correct limitations inherent in a self-perpetuating board, the private service agency needs interaction with organised groups of consumers.

Examples of the impact of form on function can be observed in two organisations on the Lower East Side of New York City that have a single executive director, the previously mentioned Mobilisation For Youth and Henry Street Settlement. M.F.Y., as noted above, is the original quasi-non-governmental organisation in the anti-poverty field. In recent years its board structure has been changed so that forty per cent of the board is composed of programme participants. M.F.Y. has been successful in gaining a satisfactory interchange and a harmonious working relationship between individuals who have city- and nation-wide affiliations and interests in social welfare and neighbourhood leaders who are interested in neighbourhood welfare.

M.F.Y.'s largest problem is finance, and that problem springs from its inability to obtain any source of funds that would maintain the operating core of the organisation. This problem is endemic in quasi-non-governmental agencies dependent upon governmental contracts for survival. In the last fiscal year, M.F.Y. received more than $4 million in grants from federal and city agencies for the operation of demonstration and research programmes, all of which are time limited. The permanent core of M.F.Y. must be supported from the amount granted as overheads. Since all grants are time limited, there can be no stability within the permanent core. Since the amount granted for overheads is often not sufficient to meet costs, vital links in middle management are missing. This problem can only be solved when the government is willing to support the central core of an organisation like M.F.Y. out of recognition of the value of the quasi-non-governmental agency to society.

Henry Street Settlement, on the other hand, falls within the category of a private service agency. Its board has recently adopted a statement of objectives that sees the facilitation of social participation as a major objective of the settlement.

To counteract some of the dangers inherent in the inbred nature of the private service agency, Henry Street is developing a neighbourhood council that will be parallel to the existing board of directors. Henry Street is one of the rare social agencies that still depend on voluntary contributions as a major source of support.

The neighbourhood council being developed at Henry Street will be looked to by the board of directors to initiate any application for public funds for the conduct of service operations. The neighbourhood council will have a major role in directing such operations and may, if it chooses, incorporate and itself seek to conduct these operations. The neighbourhood council will have voting representatives on the board and the board may seek representation on the council. Henry Street is moving in this direction in preference to merely including programme participants on its board because of the belief that in a private service agency the major functions of the board are fund-raising and the development of policy concerning the expenditures of voluntary contributions the board has raised. Many settlements today are adding selected programme participants to their boards, and this is, of course, one way of giving programme participants a share in policy-making. The notion of a neighbourhood board with voting representatives on the board of directors has the merit of providing consumer representatives with a reference group so that they are in fact representatives. The development of parallel boards also provides an opportunity to give the neighbourhood board control over the expenditure of public funds for service operations within the neighbourhood, while leaving the traditional board with the function of raising and expending voluntary funds.

This formulation might be worth the consideration of certain social agencies that are, in fact, quasi-non-governmental agencies. When, for example, a board of directors raises $100,000 that pays for a core staff responsible for expending $500,000 in public funds, it might be advisable to construct a parallel neighbourhood board that would take responsibility for the expenditure of public funds, with technical guidance from the core staff responsible to the 'midtown' board that raised the $100,000.

At Henry Street, where the neighbourhood council is being evolved, a relationship is also being devised between the private service agency and the true voluntary association whereby the staff of the private service agency offers technical resources to genuine neighbourhood voluntary associations. The private service agencies that depend on voluntary contributions from outside the neighbourhood are in a rare position to do this vital job, since they are not competing with local groups for public funds.

In summary, then, there is a long history in America of government funds flowing by contract or other means to private social welfare agencies for the fulfilment of social welfare purposes. The development was greatly accelerated by the crisis of the Great Depression. Because these voluntary associations which received public funds were never forced to re-examine themselves in the light of this important development, the ends sought by government by contract were often not attained. In other words, the government did not necessarily secure improved services for tax-payers through dispersing public funds prior to private non-profit corporations. The advent of the anti-poverty corporations exacerbated the situation.

At a time when the issue of making public institutions more responsive is critical, the use of government contracts to obtain responsive social institutions is promising. Consumer-dominated quasi-non-governmental organisations may well be able to offer health and welfare services in a more sensitive manner than can the giant public bureaucracy or the more traditional middle- or upper-class-dominated private non-profit agency. To obtain the public good, however, government must exercise its power to set reasonable expectations, measure outcome and fund accordingly. The expectations must be broad enough to secure the maximum in creativity and flexibility from the quasi-non-governmental organisation,

228

but not so broad as to allow private purposes to dominate public purposes.

Notes

1. Donald S. Howard, 'Relationships Between Governmental and Voluntary Social Welfare Agencies', in *Encyclopedia of Social Work*, 15th issue (1965) p. 649.

2. *United Community Funds and Councils of America Summary Report, Expenditures for Community Health and Welfare, 1960, Bulletin No. 221* (New York, 1963).

3. Ruth M. Lerner, *Public Financing of Voluntary Agencies Foster Care* (Child Welfare League of America, New York, 1961).

4. William H. McCullough, 'State Subsidies to Private Child Care Organisations in Pennsylvania' (doctoral dissertation, School of Social Service Administration, University of Chicago, 1959).

5. Thomas Karter, 'Voluntary Agency Expenditures for Health and Welfare from Philanthropic Contributions, 1935–55', in *Social Security Bulletin*, XXI i (1958).

6. Arlene Johnson, 'Public Funds for Voluntary Agencies', in *Proceedings of the National Conference on Social Welfare* (Columbia University Press, 1959) p. 89.

7. Sibley Higginbotham, 'The Financial Support of Church-Related Agencies', in *Viewpoints on Issues in Church Social Welfare* (Four Grounds Studies, no. 10, National Council, Episcopal Church Centre, New York, 1961) pp. 3–6.

PART THREE

The Implications for the Government

11 Public Accountability: Trends and Parliamentary Implications*

David Howell

> We wish to draw special attention here to our proposals . . .
> for accountable management and our recommendation
> that departments should be organised on the basis of
> accountable units. . . . These proposals entail clear delega-
> tion of responsibility and corresponding authority. In
> devising a new pattern for a more purposive association
> with government departments, Parliament and its com-
> mittees will need to give full weight to these changes.
> (*Fulton Committee Report on the Civil Service*, vol. 1,
> para. 281.)

A period of major administrative reform is now in prospect
in Britain. In the search for greater flexibility to cope with
new and more complex tasks, modern government has found
itself impelled to turn to new and more decentralised administrative structures and to depend upon a growing range
of extra-departmental and extra-governmental agencies. The
quotation from the Fulton Committee Report reminds us, if
a reminder is needed, that these changes will have profound
implications for the relationship between the administrative
system and Parliament. This paper seeks to survey the
pattern of administrative change, present and prospective,
and to trace through some of the consequences on the attitudes and procedures which make up the parliamentary
system. It falls into four parts.

The first part looks at some of the trends which have led
both to the substantial delegation of responsibility already in
certain areas of British government and to the call, repeated
in the quotation at the beginning, for an extension of the
principle of delegation.

* The opinions expressed in this paper are not necessarily those of
Her Majesty's Government.

The second part examines the pattern of Parliament's response to date to these changes and the evolution of parliamentary thinking about the future developments that may be required.

The third part tries to look more closely at the practical limitations and at the scope of Parliament's role in the future system of government.

The final section turns to the consequences which these developments may have on the Members of Parliament themselves and on the party political system generally.

1. Delegation of Authority in the Public Sector

The Fulton Committee Report lays stress on the need for a modern management framework for the large scale executive and managerial operations undertaken by government to-day.[1] It rightly points out that to function efficiently governments and departments need a structure in which individual managers and management units have clearly defined responsibilities for which they can be held accountable. It goes on to raise, although not to reach conclusions about,[2] the logical step which follows from this, namely the organisational separation, or 'hiving off', of certain operations altogether from the departmental embrace, and their reorganisation in the form of autonomous boards or agencies of state, with separate budgetary control.

Challenging as this may seem to traditional administration orthodoxy, the principle is far from novel in British government. A large range of the managerial operations undertaken by the state are already carried on within a semi-independent framework – notably the provision of a wide range of services – and goods – to the rest of the economy. The most familiar of these are the generation and distribution of electricity and of gas, provision of telephone and postal services, the operation of road, rail and air transport services for passengers and freight, and the production of steel.

The state also offers, through a considerable number of independent boards and agencies, an immense variety of advisory and research services, programmes for the development of everything from nuclear power to forestry and the arts and even a travel bureau.

It must be recognised, of course, that in most of these cases, and certainly in the case of the major nationalised industries, the independent management status, in as far as it in practice exists, has been achieved more through historical and political accident than as the result of a determined strategy of government structural reform. Moreover, as other papers prepared for the conference show in far greater detail,[3] the 'independent' position of nationalised undertakings has given rise to many complex and disturbing problems. Of these perhaps the most notable and noticed have been the inadequacy of accountability to Parliament and the public on the one hand, and the excessive degree of ministerial interference and control on the other, thus giving these great independent bodies the worst of both worlds, neither management freedom nor positive and constructive public control.

In the light of this it may be asked why the authors of the Fulton Committee Report should be pressing for still further extension of the principle of delegated authority. The answer is that in the first place the Fulton Committee is concerned with something rather different from the nationalised sector of industry. It is not trying to weld discarded pieces of the private sector onto the state, as the pre- and post-war policy-makers were attempting to do.[4] The aim behind Fulton and similar proposals is rather to seek to identify and provide a new structure for the executive and managerial functions that at present fall inside departments – many of them in fact generated by the blurred and anomalous links existing between Whitehall and the nationalised industries.

Once responsibilities have been identified, the argument goes, it becomes possible to allocate their fulfilment to individuals, units and independent agencies which may then be held personally and specifically accountable both to their ministers and to Parliament, for the performance of government in their respective fields.

It is this element of personal accountability for carrying out government programmes which the Fulton authors and other analysts of the management structure of government find missing and it is this which leads reformers on to ideas for reorganising, or even hiving off, many of the executive activities of government departments to separate and accountable management units with clearly defined objectives. Examples would include most major technological programmes and research work, inspection and monitoring functions, management of stores, contracts and accounting work, hospital building, retraining of skilled workers, the operation of major social security programmes and a variety of educational projects, motorway building and so on. In each case budget accounting responsibility would rest with the unit itself. As a number of reformers have pointed out,[5] this would involve a sharp break with the Treasury practice of insisting on the right to control and detailed supervision of spending decisions throughout departments.

The Fulton Committee's main preoccupation in supporting this kind of view is very properly the efficiency of government. But it is worth while listing a number of other important consequences which flow from acceptance of the Fulton view.

First, the identification of aims and the quantification of civil servants' activities allows the more effective exercise of review and choice by the policy-makers. If the objectives are known then it becomes possible both to measure success in achieving them and to question them regularly. To decide in favour of a government programme it is necessary to know what is at present being done, how much it is costing, what results are being achieved, what the alternatives are, how much they would cost in comparison, etc. The process of quantification also helps to identify unnecessary overlap, duplication of responsibilities and consequent waste.

Second, the clear delegation and definition of responsibilities allows real and total costs of a programme to be known, and if necessary publicly known. The process forces those concerned to allocate every cost they incur, right up to a proportion of senior executive salaries, to a specific output or function.[6]

Third, the delegated structure, by forcing the executive to spell out its objectives and apportion them, also gives Parliament and the public a better chance to know what programmes are being undertaken, what their cost is and who is in charge of them, and thus to work positively for the improvement of executive government as well as to exert more systematic control on behalf of the public and the tax-payer.

Now it is precisely this kind of cause and effect sequence that

236

opens the way for the more formalised systems of analysis and decision-taking labelled Planning–Programming–Budgeting Systems. Moreover, despite difficulties into which P.P.B. has run in the United States and in other governments, one undisputed advantage is that it provides more information and control at the top and therefore less opportunity for the growth of publicly unauthorised or non-accountable bureaucratic activity. Yet paradoxically, it is because delegation to autonomous units is seen as a means of removing control from ministers and thus *escaping* the net of public accountability that so many public and political misgivings are felt in Britain about changes of this kind. The irony in this is very striking. Constitutional theory, combined with traditional procedures for ensuring financial regularity, dictate that since the minister is responsible, as much as possible should be placed under his direct departmental control. Even the nationalised industries have not escaped this pressure, and have suffered profoundly through having to submit all their capital investment plans, though not their current operating decisions, to their sponsoring ministry for approval.[7]

In practice, the results have been, as so often, the very opposite of those intended. The minister's nominal responsibility not just for strategic policy but for every executive operation of his department has meant no systematic responsibility at all. Worse still, the fear of involving ministers in having to account for operations of which they can have no first-hand knowledge leads officials to excessive caution and secrecy, to insistence on passing decisions up to levels far higher than their merits warrant and to consequent delay. Thus the practical application of the theory of ministerial responsibility, to the point where delegation of authority is actively opposed, has brought managerial inefficiency without any compensating benefits in the term of greater accountability.

The case for a more delegated structure of government, as argued in the Fulton Committee Report, therefore rests not merely on grounds of efficiency of government. Contrary to many fears expressed, the case can be equally strongly argued that nominal ministerial responsibility must now begin to be replaced in modern government by genuine public accountability – to ministers and Parliament – of those in charge of public programmes for their intentions, actions and results. In short, 'responsibility', ministerial and parliamentary, must and can be made the reality which it is far from being at present.

At the same time, it is the positive aspect of public accountability, the need for a fruitful interconnection between the making of policy and the views and reactions of the public who are its beneficiaries that is beginning to be increasingly stressed. Public programmes, the argument goes, require not just the right management structure. They require, in addition, the right degree of political and public support and constructive criticism. The question is whether Parliament, as a body supposedly representative of the opinion and mood of the public, can provide the forum in which this mixture of support and close scrutiny can be provided, whether the support element should be crudely registered by means of the whipped party majority or whether a more refined procedure can be established both for keeping Parliament informed about the progress and cost of public programmes and for keeping the officials concerned more informed about parliamentary and public views and feelings.

2. Parliament's Response to the Changing Structure of Government

The foregoing section can be expanded in the form of a paradox. It is this: there is general awareness among politicians and the public that the mechanisms of accountability, both through parliamentary surveillance of the financial administration of departments and through the practice of ministerial responsibility, are inadequate. Yet the very developments which could make accountability more of a reality – the delegation of authority from ministers to autonomous agencies and contract organisations – are viewed with considerable suspicion. To many people such a trend appears as an attempt to remove still more activities of government outside the processes of public scrutiny, limited and unsatisfactory though those processes may be.

It is a question of 'poor but mine own'. Experienced parliamentarians look back nostalgically to the resignation of Sir

238

Thomas Dugdale over the Crichel Down case[8] as the ideal example of ministerial responsibility in practice. Simultaneously, they may well concede that for every administrative blunder of this kind uncovered, with the price duly paid by the 'responsible' minister for the actions of subordinates about which he knew nothing, there could be a dozen which remain hidden.

Or the paradox comes out again in parliamentary attitudes to the work of the Public Accounts Committee.[9] The work of the Committee, supported by the services of the Comptroller and Auditor General, is much admired in the House of Commons. The random swoop of the Committee on a particular area of activity, helped on by figures from a watchful Treasury which makes it its business to know about departmental spending in detail, is regarded as parliamentary accountability working at its best. Yet the same admirers know full well that detailed financial control from the Treasury is the enemy of efficiency, that for every activity investigated ten programmes drift on uncosted or even unidentified and that the estimates presented to Parliament, based on traditional administrative categories, provide no systematic guidance whatsoever to the spending of public money. As the Fulton Report puts it, 'Even the work of the Public Accounts Committee has not escaped criticism for inducing a play-safe and negative attitude among civil servants (it has been referred to as a "negative efficiency audit").'[10]

M.P.s find it equally difficult to judge the outcome of further delegation when they draw on their experience from the Select Committee on Nationalised Industries, where, in a sense, a crude system of accountability of personnel holding substantial delegated authority has been operating. The record is not encouraging. The Select Committee lacks staff, and in consequence while its reports are thorough they take a long time to complete. The major industries therefore tend to come under review only once every four or five years. Thus there is no question of regular and systematic reporting.

Moreover, while the Select Committee on Nationalised Industries has perhaps been, of all parliamentary committees, the least hesitant until recently about pursuing matters of policy, it has nevertheless found itself from time to time up against the argument that certain questions are matters of policy (i.e. only for the minister) or matters of internal management.

The recent dispute about the Committee's right to investigate the Bank of England[11] is a further reminder to the sceptical M.P. that the creation of more 'autonomous units' may simply mean the creation of more reserved areas of activity to which entry by Parliament and its committees is either forbidden or only allowed on extremely limited terms.

In sum, the argument that a more flexible structure of central government with greater reliance on non-departmental or independent agencies for the performance of public tasks will allow for better public accountability is one on which the House of Commons will need a great many assurances. First, M.P.s will want to know how more delegation can be reconciled with traditional views of the practice of ministerial responsibility. That is to say, if the convention that only a minister should explain in Parliament and public what his department is doing now goes, there will be demands to know how 'payment' for a mistake of the Crichel Down variety is to be exacted.

Second, they will want to know how the M.P.'s right to question the 'responsible' minister is to be reconciled with a further devolution of responsibility. It will not be enough to argue that Question Time each day is of limited and irregular value as a means of calling the administration to account. Occasionally it proves revealing, and these are occasions that M.P.s will not want to surrender. Nor will it be enough to argue that questions on the day-to-day management of the nationalised industries are already forbidden, since this is a prohibition which is a source of constant frustration to parliamentarians.

Third, there will need to be reassurance that accountability in a devolved structure will typically mean something more than the somewhat intermittent reporting by the senior executives of nationalised industries, along with their protective cocoons of civil servants, to the Select Committee on Nationalised Industries.[12]

Fourth, there will need to be assurance on the adequacy of research staff to back up the work of M.P.s involved in calling the responsible heads of the devolved units to account. The experience here, too, has been far from happy. In particular, note should be made of the remarks of the Clerk of the House on Treasury attitudes to the supply of finance for staff,[13] as well as the clashes between the government and members of the Select Committee on Agriculture and the Estimates Committee, both arising from government reluctance to allow for the hiring of staff.[14]

Fifth, while the shortcomings of parliamentary financial control are accepted, the achievements of the system in the field of financial regularity are valued. If management autonomy is going to close areas of detailed management to public scrutiny, M.P.s will want assurances that equally effective controls on financial regularity can be maintained in some other form. Parliament's traditional methods for checking the regularity of expenditure and the Treasury's detailed interference in departmental spending are two sides of the same coin. Both are directly challenged by the growth of independent agencies. M.P.s will have to decide whether, in exchange for greater opportunities to discuss overall performances, they are prepared to leave checks on the details to internal accounting procedures within the agency or unit concerned.

Sixth, in addition to accountability in the narrow sense of financial regularity, M.P.s have looked with favour on the efforts of the P.A.C., aided by the Comptroller and Auditor General, to carry the process of audit into the field of administrative efficiency, and thus, inevitably, of 'policy' in all the strategic senses. Assurances will be needed here also. A reformist argument might be that, as in the case of financial regularity above, greater public supervision of the formulation of policy by heads of units, and wider parliamentary opportunities to evaluate successful performance in relation to particular programmes would more than replace efficiency auditing. It could even be argued that efficiency auditing should be viewed more as an integral part of a modernised management structure than as part of the role to be played by Parliament in securing accountability. But it is doubtful whether this claim will satisfy misgivings as it stands. Certainly the idea that interviews between parliamentary committees and the managers of state of the future, backed up by expert staffs, will be an adequate substitute for the work of the P.A.C. is unlikely to be readily accepted. It will have to be shown that committees of this type are capable of tough policy-probing activity and this in turn will raise questions of the independence and status of such bodies. Certainly, if the contention that delegation allows greater accountability is to be sustained, far more precise definitions of the role which committees will be enabled to play in the process of the making and implementation of public decisions will be required.

3. Parliament's Future Role in the Process of Public Accountability

For the purposes of discussion two broad schools of thought may be distinguished about the development of parliamentary accountability. (The qualification is important since, as has been suggested above, politicians and the public in many cases recognise the validity of both sides of the argument without necessarily being ready to come to decisions.)

The conservative school of opinion draws on the admittedly discouraging experience of select committees trying to grapple with delegated authority. It is inclined to the view that further pressure for delegation from ministers should be resisted. It holds that the pursuit of ministers in parliamentary debate or at Question Time, while an imperfect method, is as good as any at holding a government to account. It argues further that a less general and more focused and systematic form of accountability to Parliament would be an improper incursion upon executive authority and government policy, which it sees as separable and separate from questions of financial regularity and administrative efficiency, in which Parliament has a proper, although cautious, interest. The basic conservative proposition is that it is the government, not Parliament, which governs. The business of government must not be undermined and the business of Parliament is to discuss and pass legislation or debate broad issues of principle and political policy, not to become involved in a semi-management function.

Much of this is accepted by reformers. The weakness of the present select committee procedure is recognised, as is the importance of allowing the government to get on with its business and the value of major debates in bringing political ministers to account. The hub of the difference lies in the rejection of the view that policy and administration can be separated. The reformers point to the vast range of decisions with a substantial policy content that have to be made, and are made, without the knowledge of the political heads. They point to the tendency of modern management methods to decentralise non-strategic decision-making further, as described in Section 1. The proposition that high officials of government can administer huge public programmes efficiently – or at all – *without* the power to make decisions with a policy content is dismissed as absurd, while the reformers also go further in supporting the points made in Section 1 that efficiency requires much fuller delegation of budgetary authority from the centre as well.

The anxieties of the reformers therefore come down to two main questions: how is the very real and growing 'policy' power of the 'administrative' wing of government to be effectively and systematically checked and scrutinised? And how is Parliament to play a more constructive role in promoting the efficiency of administration and thus safeguarding the expenditure of tax-payers' money?

Two sets of answers emerge. First, there are those concerned with law reform to reassert the rights of individuals in face of a more powerful administration. These embrace both the various proposals for the development of a system of administrative law[15] and the decision to set up a Parliamentary Commissioner for Administration (Ombudsman) with powers to investigate particular cases of mal-administration.[16] This paper does not go into these in further detail. The second set of suggested responses revolve round the idea of extending and reinforcing the parliamentary committee system.

In essence, the search is for two things: (*a*) more systematic methods for reviewing a wider area of government activity; and (*b*) for exerting more effective budgetary control through more direct influence on the many decisions of government below the level of strategic priorities decided in Cabinet. In other words, the inseparability of policy, below the strategic level, from administration, and of financial responsibility from executive authority, must be reflected in the new pattern.

From these broad aims certain principles governing the new pattern can be distilled. First, the attempt to exert public accountability through the random selection of subjects each year by each of the Estimates Sub-Committees from the estimates as presented by the Treasury will have to be replaced. A system of *permanent* committees, permanently concerned with certain broad areas of government, will be required.

Second, the committees will require to know, and a more delegated structure of government must be designed so as to enable them to know, much more precisely than at present who in a department is in charge of which programme and what its budget is. They will therefore require civil servants and other executive officers of government to come and discuss policy with them more freely than in the past.

Third, a consequential pressure arises[17] for a reform of the presentation of accounts so that (*a*) they are presented by the department, unit, or agency concerned and not by the Treasury, (*b*) they are presented in a form which enables the total cost of specific programmes and functions to be publicly identified. In other words, functional costing will have to replace the grouping of costs and therefore estimates to Parliament in vague administrative and institutional categories which give no guidance as to the true cost of programmes and thus no opportunity to hold an intelligent discussion of likely costs and benefits.[18, 19]

Fourth, by placing public responsibility on individuals for programmes, the committees will automatically create a sense of personal commitment and an incentive to maximum management efficiency which does not exist at present. This will vastly reinforce the system of random checks on efficiency maintained through the work of the P.A.C. In addition, it is a matter for debate whether each committee should not have its own arrangements and staff for carrying out efficiency audits within any of the departments within its area of investigation.[20]

Fifth, the committees must be in a better position than Parliament is at present to publicise and to inform the public about their scrutinising work. They might well make more effective use of television and other media than the House of Commons itself. They would thus be helping to bridge the gulf identified by many between Parliament and the public on the one side and the administration on the other.

Finally, committees playing this kind of role would provide a platform as well as an investigatory forum. That is to say, they could be viewed from the administrative side as a means of winning public support and understanding for public programmes – as part of the public decision-making process – rather than purely as a device for exerting parliamentary and public rights to be informed and to call to account.

4. Accountability and the Party System

The development of a network of parliamentary committees on the lines described above raises serious and complex questions for the party system at Westminster. There is first the sheer physical problem of finding the bodies to man the committees. One of the strongest arguments against more committees has been the claim that far too much of an M.P.'s week is already taken on existing legislative committees which have to be somehow filled by the parties.[21] Will it therefore be possible for the parties to fulfil their duties at the committee stages of bills if M.P.s' time is to be heavily committed on the new non-legislative committees? And will this not detract still more from the already thinly attended debates of the whole House five days a week?

If there is an answer to this it would have to lie in the direction of less frequent meetings of the whole House – say, Monday, Tuesday and Thursday – and simplified legislative procedures, although this immediately raises further delicate questions of conflict between Parliament's legislative role and its scrutinising role.

A second problem concerns the position of the chairmen of the new committees and indeed the whole issue of their independence from the government and the party machine supporting it. In the past it has been the practice to appoint chairmen from the governing party – except in the case of the Public Accounts Committee[22] – who can be relied upon to steer their committees well clear of awkward interference in policy. This has not always worked and is plainly bound to work less as the committees take it upon themselves to probe deeper and deeper into the formulation of policy.

Two extreme situations could in theory emerge. Either governments could retain and use fully their power to appoint and dismiss chairmen at will, with the consequence that pliant chairmen would always be appointed and the critical aspect of the committees' work undermined. Or governments would have to surrender their powers of appointment, presumably to the committees themselves, with the consequence that independent power bases would develop and challenge seriously the authority of the executive, as in the American experience, exemplified in particular by the rise of Senator Joe McCarthy.

Is there a middle way between these situations? Clearly, if Governments were to continue to regard all criticism on policy from their parliamentary supporters as a challenge to party authority there could be no outcome short of suppression of the committees at the one extreme, or complete independence with consequent fragmentation of the two-party system at the other. The prospect of creating what Woodrow Wilson once called 'government by Standing Committee chairmen', and of repeating the worst excesses of the labyrinthine congressional committee system would be enough to deter any government from proceeding along this path.

But there is no inherent reason why party bosses should inevitably take the gloomiest view of criticism and vigorous independence in committees. Rather than see the strains in the present system develop further it could be that party leaders would be prepared to run their parties on a looser rein, to appoint committee chairmen for a fixed period, thus surrendering at least some executive power, and to adopt a more tolerant and flexible attitude generally to committee work. As long as it was understood that the committees reported to Parliament and not over the head of Parliament and the public, there is reason to believe that this kind of formula could work.

If this is the kind of compromise which emerges between façade committees on the one hand and 'Joe McCarthy' power bases on the other then there would be important implications for M.P.s themselves. An M.P. entering Parliament today may see himself in one of two roles. Either he aims in due course to become a member of the government and sees Parliament as the route to that position. Or he intends to play a less ambitious role, contributing where he can to the wisdom of his party, supporting it through thick and thin without seeking to lead it. In both cases he acts first and foremost as a party man, and only second as a representative of his constituents and of the people at large.

But under the kind of committee system described above an entirely new situation arises. He now has to decide whether to be a party man with an eye to a job in the Administration or whether he wants to carve out a different career as a public critic on one of the committees. If the latter he may well have to steel himself to disputes with his party leaders, to pursuit of certain issues in public in the certain knowledge that he will embarrass his party colleagues who happen to be in the Administration, and in general to a much more independent role than hitherto. This in turn has important implications in the field of candidate selection and local party attitudes which lie outside the scope of this paper but which should not be ignored.

A final problem concerns the professional staffing of the secretariats which the new committees will need. It has been argued that this need will give birth to new bureaucracies which will thereupon establish tacit alliances with the very bureaucracies which the committees are supposed to investigate. Obviously there is a danger here but, unless the elected Members are unusually inept, it is hard to imagine them being hoodwinked by this kind of development. The danger could grow if legislators allowed their own staffs to grow too large and themselves to become bureaucratised. But staff and secretariats on a modest scale should not be so susceptible to this danger.

At the time of writing the House of Commons is teetering on the brink of a plunge into an expansion of the committee system. It is not at all certain what it wants. No clear decision has been reached on whether the Estimates Sub-Committees should be turned into permanent specialist committees, or whether new committees should be set up on a permanent basis and the Estimates Committee allowed to wither. At the beginning of the 1968–9 Parliament the Estimates Committee was reduced in size on the grounds that the staff might be needed for new specialist committees.[23] But meanwhile the Agriculture Committee was being peremptorily threatened with termination on the grounds that it had only been an experiment which was now completed.[24] And both the Science and Technology Committee and the Agriculture Committee were experiencing continuing difficulties in getting both the powers and the resources they needed to carry out what they conceived to be their duties of investigation.[25] With a further delegation of ministerial authority within the Administration as a *fait accompli*, and the growth of more, and more powerful, independent agencies, it could well be that the cause of these committees, and the case for more committees, will receive far stronger backing from all parts of the House. But for the moment the House, and particularly the more senior sections of both major parties, see as many problems as advantages in a further major expansion of committees in number and scope. This may change, but only very slowly.

Notes

1. See in particular vol. 1, ch. v.
2. Ibid.
3. See paper by D. C. Hague.
4. Pre-war 'nationalisation' measures included the B.B.C., London Transport and the Central Electricity Generating Board.
5. See 'Management by Objectives in the Civil Service', by John Garrets and S. D. Walker, published by the Civil Service Department, for some lucid comment on the conflict between individual managerial accountability and traditional civil service concepts.
6. For some thinking coming from within government on this issue, see *Occasional Paper No. 4 on Output Budgeting*, from the Centre for Administrative Studies and published by the Treasury.
7. The most recent report from the Select Committee on Nationalised Industries is highly critical of this system and proposes the unification of ministerial responsibility for the

long-term policy of nationalised industries in one ministry (*HC* 371).

8. The decision to go back on official undertakings regarding the sale of Crichel Down by the Ministry of Agriculture was taken without the knowledge of the minister. He nevertheless tendered his resignation and it was accepted, 20 July 1954.

9. The Public Accounts Committee conducts its investigations on an after-the-event basis, reporting on situations which have occurred, on average, two years before. The Estimates Committee is divided into four sub-committees which look at the estimates as soon as they are presented to Parliament. Each sub-committee may then tackle one or two subjects or categories of estimates within the ensuing parliamentary year.

10. *Fulton Report,* para. 281.

11. *Report from Select Committee on Nationalised Industries* (*HC* 371).

12. The Select Committee tends to get round to dealing with each industry about once every five years, although there is no predictable pattern.

13. The Clerk of the House, Sir Barnett Cocks, was reported in *The Times* of 7 Nov. 1967 as deploring Treasury attempts to cut down on parliamentary staff.

14. Three new specialist committees have been recently set up – Science and Technology, Agriculture and more recently Education. In autumn 1968 the government announced both the termination of the work of the Agriculture Committee and the reduction in the Estimates Sub-Committees from five to four. In both cases, shortage of staff was among one of the chief reasons given.

15. See, for example, 'Let Right Be Done', by the Society of Conservative Lawyers, C.P.C. 1966.

16. The P.C.A. began work in April 1967. Criticism of the restricted scope of his powers both of investigation and in questions of securing redress has been widespread.

17. The Parliamentary Committee on Procedure has now launched a major study of the methods of presentation of estimates, with a view to their reform.

18. The Report of the Canadian Royal Commission on Government Reorganisation (the Glassco Report) recommended changes along these lines.

19. The Bundestag is to be presented in the coming financial year with functional basis accounts in parallel with institutional basis accounts on the traditional pattern.

20. See p. 241.

21. In the 1967–8 Parliament M.P.s found themselves involved in two or more committee stages of bills simultaneously, so great was the rush of legislation. Anyone who suggested the creation of more committees at that time was greeted with a hoarse laugh.

22. The chairman of the P.A.C. is always drawn from the Opposition.

23. See p. 242. In cutting down the Estimates Committee the government appeared to be playing off its dismayed members against those who wanted more specialist committees.

24. See *Hansard*, 14 Nov. 1968, col. 625.

25. Science and Technology has found tacit resistance but avoided outright conflict. The Agriculture Committee ran into head-on conflict with the executive over a proposed visit to Brussels to investigate E.E.C. farm policy. At one stage they were almost turned back at the aircraft door.

12 Independence and Accountability in Government Support of Academic Science: A Congressional Perspective

Delphis C. Goldberg

The support of science by the federal government has grown tremendously since World War II, but this support has materialised largely unplanned in response to a variety of independent forces and events. Ranking prominently among those influences were the reconversion of the nation's unprecedented war-time mobilisation of science (leading to the creation of the A.E.C., O.N.R., N.S.F., and the transfer of O.S.R.D. medical research contracts to N.I.H.) and the subsequent challenge posed by Sputnik to America's position in space exploration and its supply of highly trained manpower (resulting in the creation of NASA and passage of the National Defence Education Act).

The federal interest in science has been directed mainly to the support of research, including facilities, and secondarily to manpower training. Except for the National Science Foundation (and the Office of Education with respect to non-specialised academic facilities, laboratory and library resources, and graduate fellowships), science is supported through numerous separate agencies not for the purpose of aiding academic institutions but rather as an instrument for accomplishing government missions. In practice, however, many federal agencies have taken a fairly broad view of the areas of science and the kinds of research that are contributory to their missions.

This paper will be directed to an examination of government support of scientific research in academic institutions and draws heavily on the grant experience of the Public Health Service, and more particularly of the latter's principal research arm – N.I.H. It is noteworthy in this connection that P.H.S. has emerged in recent years as the single largest source by far of the federal research funds spent by institutions of higher learning. Other federal agencies providing large amounts of money for academic research, in order of magnitude are the Department of Defence, N.S.F., NASA, A.E.C. and the Department of Agriculture. For basic research alone, P.H.S. provides educational institutions considerably more than N.S.F., the agency primarily responsible for supporting basic research.

Contracts or Grants

It should be said at the outset that any effort to distinguish intrinsically between grants and contracts is a most unpromising endeavour. Both are valid fiscal-legal instruments for establishing the terms and conditions of research support and as such they serve the same purposes. A given agency's use of one rather than the other is principally the result of tradition and attitudes rather than a function of the type of work or institution supported. This is readily apparent from the fact that while N.I.H. and N.S.F. have used the grant route in dealing with educational institutions, A.E.C. and O.N.R. have preferred the use of contracts. Some agencies use both grants and contracts. At times an individual investigator may receive both grants and contracts from two or more federal agencies in support of his work.

Since 1958 all federal agencies having the authority to enter into contracts for basic research at institutions of higher education have been authorised also to use the grant,[1] but some have continued to support such research by contract. Consequently, unless a special meaning is intended for certain kinds of contracts or grants, these terms are really interchangeable.

Concepts of Independence and Accountability

Independence and accountability are relative terms which gain more concrete meaning from the purposes and circumstances of government support, and from the investigator's particular role in the research activity.

Independence of the academic scientist, in the context of government support of the research of an individual, must certainly involve his freedom to propose a project of his own choosing and, once approved, to perform the research without technical interference – but in conformity with the work-plan and all requirements and restrictions that are part of the support agreement. The conduct of research is normally subject to the policies and procedures of the investigator's institution as well as those of the government.

Accountability ordinarily entails periodic reports on the investigator's progress in achieving his research objectives, as well as adherence to the financial and other administrative requirements of the grant. Research progress reports, however, serve principally as agency records for prospective use in connection with grant applications the investigator may file in the future, rather than as an instrument for evaluating his current performance.

Beyond these elements of administrative accountability the investigator is accountable to his profession. This takes the form of judgements by his peers in the course of reviewing research proposals submitted to government agencies, in evaluating his contributions to the scientific literature, and, more generally, in according him recognition in his professional field. This form of accountability, however, must be considered complementary to, not a substitute for, the accountability that is required by federal agencies to assure the proper and prudent expenditure of public funds.

The nature of the scientist's independence is more complicated in large grants for multiple-purpose projects (e.g. programme-project grants or grants for the support of an entire institutional division) and in the performance of directed research. Obviously, in situations like these the independence of even the research director will be restricted to some extent by the desires and needs of his associates or by government specifications. Independence here will necessarily vary with the circumstances, but should mean as a minimum the freedom of the investigator to participate or not participate as he wishes.

From the standpoint of the grantee institution, each school is responsible for verifying that its investigators are in fact performing the research described in the grant instruments and are doing so in conformity with federal and institutional policies. The institution assumes this responsibility by virtue of its endorsement of grant applications, its acceptance of federal funds, and its transmittal of expenditure and progress reports. Each institution also assumes responsibility for seeing that grant funds are used only for their stated purposes.

In addition to the accountability of the investigator and his institution, there is also the concept of political accountability. This involves the responsibility of the government agencies supporting research to follow faithfully the intent of Congress, and to be answerable to the Congress for the programmes they administer. Where agencies operate under very general statutes that permit broad administrative discretion in their implementation, they acquire an added obligation to adopt adequate safeguards to assure equitable and objective programme administration.

Origins and Forms of Support for Academic Science

The first Morrill Act of 1862 is generally regarded as the beginning of the federal government's use of grants-in-aid, as well as the earliest form of federal assistance to higher education. In its traditional meaning, a grant-in-aid may be defined as the payment of funds by one level of government to be expended by another level for a specified purpose, usually on a matching basis and in accordance with prescribed standards and requirements.

The Morrill Act provided aid to the states, through the revenues derived from the sale of land grants, for the establishment and maintenance of colleges devoted to agriculture and mechanical arts. The objectives of the grant were carefully spelled out, conditions were placed on the use of the revenue derived from the sale of granted lands, and annual reports were required.

The Hatch Act of 1887, which authorised the first annual money grant, provided federal funds for the establishment of agricultural experiment stations at the land-grant colleges, thereby linking agricultural education closely with scientific research. The second Morrill Act of 1890, together with later amendments, brought the land-grant institutions continuing sums of money annually for the support of resident instruction.

The passage of the Smith–Lever Act in 1914 marked the beginning of the modern grant period. This programme, providing for co-operative agricultural extension work administered through land-grant colleges, introduced such new features as an apportionment formula, equal state matching of the federal grant and advance federal approval of state plans. Similar conditions were attached to the much larger grant programme for highways established two years later.

In contrast to the categorical formula-type grant which has been the conventional instrument for conveying federal assistance to the states, and in some instances to participants chosen by them, government support of academic science during the past quarter-century has generally been given on a project basis. Project awards permit federal administrators considerably more discretion in the distribution of funds than a programme that allocates money by formula.

Moreover, the enabling legislation for many science programmes gives federal agencies broad discretion for determining not only the method of selecting grantees and the size of awards but also how the available funds are to be divided among university, not-for-profit and industry performers. In some instances, the authorising statutes are silent also with respect to how much of the research should be conducted in government facilities and by non-governmental laboratories, although this as well as other substantive matters may subsequently be decided by the Appropriations Committees of the Congress.

Project versus Institutional Support

The project grant has become the predominant if not the sole method used by federal agencies for supporting university research. Research support has been extended by some agencies in recent years beyond the traditional type of project, involving an investigator working alone or with a few close associates, to include support for broader 'programme-project' and centre-type programmes. Grants for the general support of institutional research activities and for the development of 'centres of excellence', presently used in somewhat differing forms by N.S.F. and N.I.H., represent still another recent development.

With the exception of N.I.H.'s general research support and N.S.F.'s institutional grant programmes, both of which allocate funds by formulas related to the level of participation in regular project grants, these constitute forms of project support. Applications are judged principally on the basis of scientific merit, and no institution or class of institutions is automatically entitled to a grant in accordance with objective criteria. In short, grants to institutions of higher learning for scientific research, and training programmes as well, are usually contingent upon the judgements of federal agencies.

This heavy reliance on the project system is in marked contrast to the earlier method of supporting education and research at land-grant colleges. Although it is widely acknowledged that federal grants to these institutions were an important influence in upgrading the quality of their activities in agriculture, engineering and the natural sciences, there is little sentiment today for distributing research grants by formula in place of the project system. There is sentiment, however, for using supplementary mechanisms to moderate some of the effects of project grants.

Foremost among these effects is the high concentration of both research and training grants in a relatively small number of educational institutions. Another significant effect is the weakening of institutional loyalties and leadership as faculty members look to Washington for their funds. Yet another undesirable consequence is 'the flight from teaching', and particularly the disinclination of senior faculty members to be involved in undergraduate teaching.[2]

There is a growing interest in developing forms of general federal support for higher education as a whole, for particular types or segments of institutions. This interest is motivated partly by the desire to give institutions a larger role in determining the uses of grants, but perhaps even more as a means of achieving a broader geographical distribution of funds and of helping to meet rising educational costs. Such support, if it comes, is likely to be provided through formula grants based on objective criteria in the law governing the entitlement in institutions to awards.

Hearings were held late in the 90th Congress and again in the 91st Congress on bills for institutional science grants introduced by Representative George P. Miller. An amended version of the Miller bill was reported by the House Committee on Science and Astronautics on 15 September 1969, but it has not been approved by the Rules Committee for further House consideration.[3] It is noteworthy also that the American Council on Education has prepared a document analysing five proposed formulas, including that of the earlier Miller bill, for making general support grants.[4]

It has been suggested that packaging narrowly defined research grants into broader forms such as 'programme-project' or institutional grants would provide incentives to institutions for greater fiscal responsibility.[5]

While broader forms or research support might be desirable to accommodate certain kinds of scientific inquiries, or as a means of reducing administrative costs, the N.I.H. experience with programme-project grants is not altogether reassuring.

Peer reviews of a number of N.I.H. programme-projects have shown that these umbrella-type grants are used locally to support poor as well as good research. A common complaint voiced by review panels is that such grants carry some projects that would not be approved on their own merit. It should be noted, however, that programme-project grants are ordinarily controlled in educational institutions by a principal investigator in much the same way as individual research projects. Consequently, there is no special incentive for institutions as such to involve themselves in maintaining quality or in achieving economies.

Regardless of what an agency may call its support mechanism, it is essential to know (1) how the institution is structured for decision-making with respect to broader grants of this kind, and (2) the extent of organised faculty and administrative participation in both scientific and management questions. The degree of discretion permitted under a grant tells us nothing in itself about institutional responsibility.

One consideration in judging the value of programme-project grants is whether or not educational purposes as well as research are to be served. One can justify a lower average quality of research if education is an objective. If this is the case, however, criteria other than research quality should also be used in awarding grants and the ground rules for eligibility should be stated accordingly.

The Uses of Institutional Grants

A critical question relating to relatively unrestricted grants concerns the uses to which they would be put. It is difficult to predict the resulting expenditure patterns with any precision, other than to speculate that they would vary from institution to institution. This, of course, is a reasonable expectation since a primary purpose of institutional support is to give expression to local needs as viewed by the receiver.

Some guidance in this matter is provided by N.I.H.'s experience with the general research support (G.R.S.) grant. The data from this programme are indicative of how institutions already receiving moderate to very large amounts of project money choose to spend supplemental grants.

Of the approximately $43 million spent under the G.R.S. programme in 1966,[6] more than half (53 per cent) was used for personnel and one-quarter went for the purchase of equipment. Consumable supplies took another 10 per cent, and 6 per cent of the total was used to support trainees. The medical schools, which accounted for approximately three-fifths of all G.R.S. funds, followed a similar expenditure pattern. This distribution of G.R.S. expenditures has remained fairly constant over a four-year period.

Viewed somewhat differently, although 43 per cent of the total expenditures was devoted to research projects (including the support of personnel), nearly half of this research money was used in connection with established projects and the rest for new or pilot projects. The medical schools applied somewhat less than a third of their grants directly to research projects, with about half the project money used to supplement established research.

Expenditure data for N.S.F.'s institutional grants programme show a much larger proportion (62 per cent) of the $10·4 million total in 1966 spent for equipment, supplies and central facilities, and only 13 per cent for faculty salaries. However, 14 per cent was reported for research projects, a

258

part of which is believed to have gone also for faculty salaries. Another 6 per cent of total expenditures was used for student stipends. Data are not available to show the full extent to which these grants were used to support projects. N.S.F. believes that the salary expenditures were predominantly for research conducted primarily during the summer months.[7]

If the N.I.H. experience has predictive value, we can expect educational institutions to use additional general but research-oriented grants primarily for faculty salaries and secondarily for equipment and supplies. If the expenditure pattern of N.S.F. grantees were to prevail, most of the money would be used for equipping and supplying the institutions and relatively little for salaries.

These patterns would seem to indicate that established institutions are more interested in strengthening their faculties and acquiring equipment, including such central resources as computers and animal facilities, than in supporting new research projects. This disposition to employ unrestricted funds for strengthening institutional capabilities should have a bearing on the manner in which any future institutional grants are distributed. It also suggests the need for suitable administrative arrangements within each participating institution for allocating its general-purpose grants equitably and productively.

Common Issues in Federalism and 'Federalism by Contract'

The problem of achieving national objectives through broad rather than narrow forms of federal support is not limited to educational institutions. An analogous situation exists in the relation between the federal government and state and local governments, as witnessed by the current debate on revenue-sharing.[9] This device has attracted attention as a means of introducing more flexibility in to the federal aid system and of achieving a better balance between fast-growing local needs and federal resources.

Federal categorical or special-purpose grants have served the valuable role of harnessing co-operative governmental effort in the accomplishment of national legislative objectives. They have enabled the federal government to respond to particular social, economic and cultural needs on a nation-wide scale through the machinery of the states and their political subdivisions.

However, the grant system has become cumbersome, confusing, increasingly inefficient and difficult to manage as new programme categories have been added to existing categories within functional fields like education, health and welfare.[10]

It should be noted in passing that the federal government has increasingly relied on project grants in dealing directly with local government in programmes like urban renewal, public housing and airport development. Although much smaller in their aggregate dollar amount than formula grants, project grants now constitute approximately three-fourths of the more than 400 federal grant-in-aid authorisations in effect today. As in the case of research project grants, these programmes allow the administrators considerable discretion in awarding grants and place a premium on the ability and resources of applicants for developing persuasive proposals.

Both revenue-sharing and bloc or consolidated grant arrangements (the combining of existing categorical grants into larger functional packages) are highly favoured by the governors and state legislative leaders. Revenue-sharing is generally considered attractive by city and county officials only if the proposed formula would by-pass the states in allotting funds directly to local governments, or if the formula earmarks a portion of the grants for local use.

If we view revenue-sharing as a form of general support grant, many of the objections raised against this concept would appear to have relevance for the government–university relationship.

It has been contended that revenue-sharing would be wasteful because the states have not done a good job of managing their own resources; that revenue-sharing would reduce the pressure on the states to make needed fiscal and administrative reforms, thereby perpetuating inefficiency; that the availability of such revenues would cause the states to reduce their own tax efforts; that by further divorcing spending from the responsibility for raising the money, states would be less careful in their expenditure of public funds; and that if revenues are shared without specific provision for local government, the cities that are most in need will not be helped because state legislatures tend to favour the rural and suburban areas.

On the other hand, a different set of objections can be directed at both categorical grants to the states and project grants to educational institutions. These would include the weakening of executive and legislative control at the state and institutional levels over policies and programme priorities; distortion of the receiver's spending patterns by inducing the shift of local funds to aided rather than non-aided activities; and the development of close specialist-to-specialist relationships in aided programmes with the exclusion of the executive in important matters involving policy and administrative control.

These effects can be minimised, of course, by strong executive leadership. But one cannot ignore the plight of the governor or university president who refuses federal funds because of their limitations in today's highly competitive political and academic worlds.

Along with the use of categorical grants to states and project grants to educational institutions (both of which have often served to weaken executive authority), and the by-passing of the states by engaging in direct dealings with local governments, the federal government has developed still another administrative technique – the use of private or quasi-non-governmental organisations to administer co-operative programmes.

This latter development is most striking in the poverty programme, where the Office of Economic Opportunity has made frequent use of private non-profit organisations to administer local Community Action programmes. As of September 1965, 74 per cent of all Community Action agencies were under non-governmental sponsorship.[11] By giving communities the alternative of using either public or private non-profit agencies, the Economic Opportunity Act permitted private sponsorship in those places where cities and counties were uninterested in participating, where limited political boundaries militated against an effective programme, or where an agency broadly representative of diverse social and economic interests in the community might be constituted most effectively under private auspices. But this arrangement

261

also made it possible for the private organisations, armed with public money, to attack the policies and practices of local governments in such areas as welfare, housing and education. Indeed, fighting the 'establishment' became a common occurrence and even an operating philosophy in some agencies.[12]

It should be recognised that the use of non-governmental agencies for administering public programmes, while more prevalent today, is not a new development. The Department of Agriculture, for example, has long used private local organisations in some of its programmes, notably the Agricultural Stabilisation and Conservation Service and the Farmers Home Administration. The A.S.C.S., a programme of price support, production adjustment and conservation encouragement, is administered locally through elected farmers' committees which are financed largely by federal funds and exercise important administrative and quasi-judicial powers. The late Professor Morton Grodzins was highly critical of the Department of Agriculture for establishing 'its own system of local governments'. He accused the department of contributing 'to the low state of rural (especially county) government' by enabling the A.S.C. offices to compete with county government in attracting leaders and skilled personnel, and by depriving the counties of grant programmes that could be used to raise standards of personnel, organisation and performance.[13]

What we are concerned with here are questions of political and financial accountability, as well as the organisational form best suited to producing favourable programme results.

One is tempted to believe that accountability will be greater if grant-supported programmes are performed by public agencies than by private agencies, since such an arrangement has built into it an authoritative basis for additional political accountability. Moreover, state and local governments normally have established financial control systems, while adequate operating policies and management controls are often absent in newly organised private agencies.

In practice, however, accountability is a function of the quality and the maturity of an organisation and its management, rather than of its public or private character. There probably have been as many scandals, proportionately, in the handling of federal grant funds by state agencies as by private non-profit organisations.

The use of private committees or agencies operating outside normal governmental channels to distribute public funds calls to mind Vannevar Bush's proposal for the creation of a National Research Foundation operated by a part-time board of non-governmental scientists appointed by the President. The board would have selected the Foundations' executive director and controlled the distribution of research grants to the universities.[14] In vetoing the Foundation bill, President Truman said in part:

> It would, in effect, vest the determination of vital national policies, the expenditure of large public funds and the administration of important governmental functions in a group of individuals who would be essentially private citizens. The proposed National Science Foundation would be divorced from control by the people to an extent that implies a distinct lack of faith in democratic processes....
>
> The Constitution places upon the President the responsibility for seeing that the laws are faithfully executed. In the administration of this law, however, he would be deprived of effective means for discharging his constitutional responsibility....
>
> There are other compelling reasons why control over the administration of this law should not be vested in the part-time members of the Foundation. The Foundation would make grants of Federal funds to support scientific research. The recipients of these grants would be determined in the discretion of the Foundation. The qualifications prescribed in the bill for members of the Foundation would insure that most of them would be individuals employed by institutions or organisations eligible for the grants. Thus, there is created a conflict of interests which would inevitably give rise to suspicions of favouritism, regardless of the complete integrity of the members of the Foundation.[15]

The statutory advisory councils attached to the ten N.I.H. Institutes and the National Institute of Mental Health have no direct responsibility for administering federal research and training grants, although their affirmative recommendation is required by law before any grant can be awarded. While this arrangement does not vest executive functions *per se* in non-governmental personnel, it came perilously close to doing so under the circumstances that prevailed in the late 1950s and early 1960s. In those affluent years grant applications approved by the study sections (technical review panels also composed of non-governmental consultants) were virtually rubber-stamped by the councils and then, with few exceptions, approved by the Surgeon General for funding. To the extent that public officials set up organisational arrangements and procedures designed to accept and implement the recommendations of non-governmental advisers, it is questionable that government funds are actually subject to executive control.

It is significant that most consultants to N.I.H. and N.I.M.H. are simultaneously investigators whose research is supported by these agencies; many of these scientists appear regularly before committees of the Congress as expert 'citizen witnesses' to advocate larger appropriations for health research.

Prior to World War II there was widespread fear in the academic community that federal support might entail government interference in or even control of university affairs. This fear was largely responsible for the establishment in federal agencies of advisory bodies comprised mainly of university scientists to participate in the grant process. Advisory bodies were conceived also as a protection against bureaucratic action that might lower research standards or inject politics into academic sciences.

The situation today is quite different. Not only is government interference no longer considered a serious threat but the universities themselves have, along with a variety of professional organisations, become actively involved in urging the Congress and the executive agencies to provide greater research support.

The value of the university as a social institution is not called into question by frankly recognising that universities have become an important pressure group. The merit and the priority of academic claims on the public purse should rightly be decided in competition with other public needs through our regular political processes.

Although it is widely accepted that institutions of higher learning have a threefold responsibility – education, research and community service – the relative attention they give to these separate but interrelated activities is greatly influenced by the availability of government funds. Because almost all federal money is awarded for relatively narrow purposes, the institutions which receive a high proportion of their budgets from federal sources will tend to mirror national policies.

Unfortunately, there is no coherent national policy for academic science. The programme-mix at any given moment is the product of many independent forces, aided at times by catalytic events and personalities.

What has occurred on an increasing scale since World War II has been the skewing of institutional activities towards research, under the influence of federal grants. Where training grants have been provided, as in the N.I.H. programmes, the money has been available principally to train specialists for research careers in the biomedical sciences. Federal agency policies have not been directed significantly towards encouraging institutions as such to strengthen their educational capabilities.

This emphasis on research, together with the project system, has had its detrimental effects. It has led to a lessened interest in teaching as well as a marked change in the values of faculty and students alike.

The Committee on Science and Public Policy of the National Academy of Sciences saw the trend away from teaching as stemming from a lack of strong policy within the universities themselves, although it also acknowledged the need for enlightened policies in those federal agencies which award graduate fellowships and research grants.[16]

A similar concern for teaching was recently voiced by John Perry Miller, Dean of the Yale Graduate School. Like Clark Kerr five years earlier, Dean Miller saw project support serving to alienate the investigator from his institution. He said:

The gains to the university, then, have been many: the flowering of research, new facilities, support and concern with graduate education. But at the same time, there has been a diversion of the attention of faculty from teaching to entrepreneurship. In many institutions, the faculty and for that matter, their students, raise more funds per year than the development office and alumni fund.

But more than this, these methods of financing our universities have led to reduced teaching loads, more hands to do the same amount of teaching, less concern with undergraduates, less concern with curriculum and less availability of faculty. The undergraduate curriculum becomes the province of concern of those persons and disciplines that are passed over in the game of grantsmanship.

Dean Miller added:

We ... have been engaged in making the case for increasing support by government to our universities. But our emphasis has been too much upon the magnitude of our needs and too little upon the character of our needs. We cannot afford much more bounty upon the terms on which we have been receiving it.[17]

The Congress has not been disposed to consider the needs of educational institutions in their totality, nor has the executive branch encouraged the Congress to do so. Instead, the approach of both branches has been piecemeal and opportunistic, with primary emphasis on the research objectives of the mission-related agencies and on the need for scientific manpower as viewed by each agency.

Federal aid to higher education is today largely a by-product of programmes for the support of scientific research. The executive branch, which should have adequate planning resources, has not provided notable leadership in developing a unified national programme for higher education, and the Congress as an institution is not well suited to the task of comprehensive planning.

The present centrifugal tendencies are illustrated by the disparate and often competing graduate training programmes that have emerged independently in many federal agencies. While opinions may differ on whether the numerous programmes which provide financial support for graduate and

266

post-graduate science training constitute an excessive federal commitment[18] there is strong evidence of a relatively greater need and justification for government assistance at the undergraduate level.

Moreover, federal support of graduate students has been very unevenly distributed among academic fields. Data for the 1962 fiscal year show federal awards, as a percentage of full-time graduate enrolments in each field, were highest in the biological sciences (41 per cent) and lowest in education (2 per cent), the social sciences (5 per cent) and engineering (8 per cent).[19]

While not directly comparable, a National Academy of Science's survey of the sources of support of doctorate recipients in fiscal year 1967 appears to confirm these findings; it shows federal support highest in the biological sciences and lowest in education and arts and humanities, although relatively high levels of support were also reported in engineering and the social sciences.[20]

What is more revealing, however, is that the proportionately heavy federal investment in the biological sciences has not produced a proportionate increase in Ph.D.s. While the number of earned doctorates has shown an annual increase in all fields in recent years, the increase has been as large in the fields receiving little support (larger in the case of education) as in the biological and other sciences where federal support is concentrated.[21] This relationship suggests that existing federal policies for assisting graduate students may be favouring certain groups over others, rather than serving to attract students to fields of special national importance.

Opportunities for Improving Grant Administration

Federal reliance on project grants for accomplishing agency missions has led over a period of time to the use of these grants partially for non-research purposes. As a consequence, many institutions have become highly dependent on project support to the point where their educational programmes are jeopardised by a reduction in federal research expenditures. Medical schools in particular are feeling the pinch of the federal government's current restrictions on research spending, owing largely to the fact that many of them have pieced together teaching programmes by using very small fractions of the time of a large number of faculty members paid from research grants. It may be argued that education is much too important a matter to be left to the indirect and sometimes suspect nourishment from sponsored research and special-purpose training programmes.

This development raises basic policy questions such as these: Should the strongest institutions receive a disproportionate share of federal support for education as a by-product of the ability of their faculties to attract large research funds? Is it in the national interest that the strongest institutions be further aided in 'cornering the market' of potential science talent, both research and teaching, as a result of the research activities and expensive facilities and equipment acquired with federal funds? And should research grants be used as a form of support for the training of graduate students?

On the government side, the growth of project-type support has become very costly in scientific manpower, much of which is recruited from university faculties. In the process of developing continually growing research support programmes, the science agencies have generally increased their demand for non-governmental consultants and their scientist-administrator staffs as well.[22]

N.I.H. and N.I.M.H., for example, presently employ 2498 persons with doctoral degrees, of whom 503 are wholly or primarily engaged in administering extra-mural grant programmes. Of the 503 doctorates, 203 are M.D.s. N.S.F., which has no research facilities of its own, employs 179 doctorates in the administration of its programmes.

While science agencies would also require highly trained professional staffs for policy development and institutional liaison under formula grants, the size of these staffs could undoubtedly be much smaller.

However, economy in administration is less important a consideration in choosing between methods of support than the relative efficiency of those methods for accomplishing programme objectives and their consistency with other national purposes.

The project grant, like the categorical grant to the states, has been a valuable device for combining federal resources and

268

leadership with local programme performance in dealing with important national problems. But like the categorical grant, the project grant has been overused; the project system has also become cumbersome, increasingly inefficient and destructive in some respects to local institutions.

The adoption of some form of institutional grant for academic science, or for higher education as a whole, is a logical next step for the federal government. It would compensate for the undesirable effects of project grants and assist colleges and universities in meeting rising educational costs. But the size and character of such a programme should be determined in relation to a national science plan and the quality of institutional management. It is essential that a national plan for academic science establish the criteria for making rational choices among science fields and activities.

To be politically feasible as well as equitable, an institutional grant would have to be available on the same terms to all accredited institutions of a specified type (e.g. graduate schools, four-year colleges, medical schools) so that all states and regions would benefit. Congress might require as an eligibility condition that each school establish a qualified committee, consisting of a cross-section of the faculty and top management, to determine the optimum distribution of the grant money.

It is unlikely that institutional grants would support, on the average, as high a quality of research as would be supported by the same amount of money expended through peer review at the national level. The N.I.H. experience with general research support grants suggests that such funds would be extensively used to supplement existing research projects – thereby consuming more money than N.I.H. thought necessary for the performance of those projects. Moreover, peer reviews of the more restricted programme-project grants have shown the tendency of investigators who control these funds in the institutions to use them partly for the funding of research projects which have insufficient merit for national support.

Whether the distribution of federal research money by the institutions themselves would more likely encourage high-risk, innovative research than decisions made at the national level is a debatable point. The established investigator and

269

orthodox ideas would undoubtedly be favoured under either arrangement. There is the possibility, however, that with discretionary funds and appropriate machinery for allocating the money, institutions might be willing to provide modest support for the talented young investigator with unconventional ideas.

In any event, it might be advisable to place a limitation on the proportion of any institutional grant that might be used for research to prevent any substantial undercutting of the more selective method of evaluating projects by central peer review. Such a limitation would give impetus to the use of the grant for broader institutional purposes, including those related more directly to education.

Any sizeable new programme of federal aid for science research and training is likely to arouse congressional interest in the quality of institutional management.

Educational institutions, particularly the schools where federal funds are concentrated, have become 'big business' in their operation of research activities, but few of them have significantly modernised their management practices. Their reluctance to do so is rooted in academic tradition and in the absence of strong external pressures. The resistance to change is probably related in large measure to the fact that insufficient effort has been made to separate those elements that are necessary for academic freedom and intellectual activities from the predominantly administrative aspects of grants.

These two sides of the grant coin are interrelated, of course, with administrative management imposing some constraints on the investigator's freedom of action. The problem on balance is one of devising the administrative requirements that are necessary for achieving the government's objectives in a way that minimises conflict with the degree of personal freedom which may be essential for intellectual work.

Much of the present weakness in institutional management can be attributed to the establishment of the project system as a relationship between the investigator and a government agency, without the chief executive of the institution having been a party to the arrangement.[23]

Even today it is not uncommon for agency staff to authorise (or refuse to authorise) the use of grant money for a particular purpose without advising the institution's financial office of the decision. This makes for an interesting situation when federal auditors find that the grant has been expended in violation of government or institutional policies.

There is little reason to expect the efficient use of grant money unless institutions themselves assume a positive responsibility and are adequately equipped for the role. A meaningful stewardship of federal grants presupposes that an institution has installed some type of formal management system utilising modern accounting and auditing methods, central purchasing, inventory control and other normal business techniques.

In this connection, the Wooldridge Committee's Administration Panel expressed concern that:

> ... effective systems for central purchasing and inventory control seem not to be universally present in the grantee institutions. Each of them, we think, should be expected by N.I.H. to furnish assurance, through a simple inventory system, that any proposed purchase of a major piece of equipment is in response to a need the institution cannot fill except by a new acquisition. N.I.H. should also expect any grantee institution to furnish assurance, through a sufficiently strong central purchasing operation, that its buying is done in an orderly, well-regulated, easily auditable manner.

In the Panel's view, 'certain minimal standards of competence might properly be established by N.I.H, as prerequisites for any institution proposing to become or remain a legal grantee'.[24]

More recently, the H.E.W. Audit Agency found 'a need for improved property records, physical controls, and usage controls and for strengthened internal controls over purchases' in grantee institutions. The agency reported that frequently 'available equipment was not screened before new equipment was purchased, that required H.E.W. approval was not obtained, that purchases were made outside the grant period, and that procurement practices did not provide assurance that needed equipment was obtained at the most reasonable prices'.[25]

Clearly there is a need for institutions to improve their

capability for managing grants, just as there is a need for federal agencies to administer programmes in a way that strengthens, rather than weakens, local responsibility. Further, there is considerable room at the federal level for greater interagency uniformity in the policies, procedures and forms applicable to grants.

Not only is there poor co-ordination of grant policies and procedures among the federal agencies supporting research, but co-ordination is reported to be inadequate even within a single agency like the Public Health Service.[26]

With the federal government now paying a very high proportion of the cost of academic research, public interest in how institutions use this money is likely to increase regardless of whether the government enlarges its commitment.

The Role of Congress

Political accountability is obtained, in the final analysis, through the activities of the Congress in authorising programmes, appropriating funds for their support, and reviewing programme administration.

Over the past quarter-century the federal government has become increasingly involved in a great variety of complex problems and activities, most of which require specialised knowledge for the performance of legislative as well as administrative responsibilities. Because of the volume, variety and specialised nature of legislative work, the Congress must of necessity operate through committees. Moreover, Congressmen are able to devote only limited time to legislative matters, including committee work, owing to the numerous services expected of them by their constituents.

Congress has a constitutional role to legislate, to determine policy independently of the President. Its effective performance of this creative role has varied mainly with social and economic conditions and the urgency for governmental action, the character of presidential leadership, and the adequacy of its own staff resources.

Even in highly technical areas it is the responsibility of the Congress to pass judgement on proposals originating in the executive agencies or elsewhere. In weighing agency pro-

272

posals and alternative policies, the Congress obviously cannot and should not be dependent upon the evidence and analysis furnished by the administrators. A responsible legislative body must have a permanent professional staff capable of gathering and analysing the complete range of policy alternatives applicable to the issues under study. However, this does not mean the committees of Congress must themselves employ large staffs of highly trained scientists.

The primary need is for generalists with superior analytical ability who are capable of locating the best sources of technical information on any problem and of framing the proper questions for sharpening issues and otherwise assisting the committee to make informed decisions. Certain committees may, in addition, find it valuable to have their own highly trained science specialists, as several committees presently do. Committees may also call upon the resources of the Science Policy Research Division in the Library of Congress, which employs specialists in a number of disciplines. In general, the Congress already has access to outstanding scientists both in and out of government as witnesses and consultants, and it could scarcely accomplish more by recruiting productive scientists for full-time employment. Although many committees do need more staffing to take full advantage of available sources of scientific information and advice, this is a matter which could be remedied without new institutional arrangements.

A more serious and growing problem for committees is that of securing disinterested, objective advice from outside government as scientists in the universities and elsewhere in the private sector become more and more dependent upon federal agencies for their support.

With the specialisation of committees has come the disposition of members of Congress to follow committee recommendations when voting on bills that are not politically controversial and do not conflict with a member's strong personal views or those of any substantial segment of his constituency. A committee's recommendations will also tend to carry great weight if members have confidence in its chairman and in his knowledge of the subject.

Congress is by its very nature a pluralistic institution. Within each house of Congress there is a much greater diffusion of authority than one should expect in the executive branch, where the President is unquestionably the chief executive.

The consideration of science legislation is divided in the House and Senate among a number of separate committees in much the same way as the administration of science programmes is distributed among mission-related agencies. In addition, science programmes are subject to congressional scrutiny by different kinds of committees concerned with legislative authorisation, the appropriation of funds and the review of expenditures.

The partial overlapping of responsibilities among committees creates a heavier work-load for the executive agencies, but it also provides some added prospect that agency proposals and operations will be critically reviewed. For example, each standing committee of the House is required to 'exercise continuous watchfulness of the execution by the administrative agencies concerned of any laws, the subject matter of which is within the jurisdiction of such committee'. The Committee on Appropriations is specifically authorised by the House Rules to conduct studies of the organisation and operation of any executive department or agency as it may deem necessary to assist in the determination of matters within its jurisdiction. And the Committee on Government Operations is charged with the 'duty of studying the operation of Government activities at all levels with a view to determining its economy and efficiency'.

Because of the committee structure, opportunities exist for the development of countervailing forces in the Congress on particular matters. The House Rules Committee may temporarily block bills reported favourably by legislative committees, and the Appropriations Committee may recommend less money than the Congress has authorised for a programme – or more than proposed by the President, especially if the authorising legislation sets no limitation on funds. Further, the committees of the House and Senate concerned with foreign relations, or with efficiency and economy in government, may challenge the position of the committees responsible for Defence Department legislation in connection with specific issues of military policy or procurement. At times one committee may assume the role of protector for a government agency and actively seek to enlarge or defend the agency's programmes, while another committee may play the role of critic, forcing that agency to justify its stewardship of public funds.

While the legislative process may appear cumbersome and even frustrating, we should not lose sight of the essential role in accountability performed by the Congress in our system of government. The performance of Congress often looks disorganised not only because the Congress is a pluralistic political body but also because its actions are constantly open to public view. Decision-making in executive agencies is frequently disorderly too, but the public sees only the end result and not the process.

Nevertheless, the Congress does need improved organisation and better staffing. It also needs better methods of reviewing and evaluating the peformance of federal agencies and of grantees in their use of science funds. The annual authorisation and appropriation hearings are not very effective methods for evaluating programmes unless they are preceded by in-depth committee staff work designed to obtain objective information for developing penetrating lines of questioning. Moreover, annual hearings provide too little time for thorough programme review, and they might beneficially be supplemented (or replaced to some extent) by more comprehensive hearings scheduled at less frequent intervals.

Despite these problems, it is safe to say that the government's interest in academic science will continue and in all probability expand in the years ahead. For science has become an integral part of our lives and an important instrument for social progress. As the nation's need and public demand for higher education continue to grow, government will be called upon increasingly to underwrite the costs. We can hope that more planning and less pragmatism will guide our future science policies.

Notes

1. Public Law 85–934.
2. The pros and cons of project grants were well stated by Clark Kerr in these terms:

. , . Scholars seem to prefer dealing with their professional counterparts in Washington rather than with their colleagues and administrators at home. Also the university's internal process of distributing funds would be generally less selective and less flexible than the federal research project approach. Within a university, the tendency is to give each faculty member about the same opportunity and once having given it to keep giving it thereafter; but the project method allows more attention to exceptional merit and has the advantage that all projects may end some time. Additionally, federal agencies are more responsive to particular national needs than the universities would be, given the same amount of money to spend according to their own priority system.

There are, however, clearly detrimental effects. Some faculty members come to use the pressure of their own agency contacts against their university. They may try to force the establishment of a new administrative unit or the assignment of land for their own special building, in defiance of general university policy or priorities. These pressures, of course, should be withstood; they speak well neither of the professor nor of the agency. Also, some faculty members tend to shift their identification and loyalty from their university to the agency in Washington. Their concern with the general welfare of the university is eroded and they become tenants rather than owners, taking their grants with them as they change their institutional lodgings. The university, as Allen Wallis, president of the University of Rochester, has remarked, becomes to an extent a 'hotel'. The agency becomes the new alma mater. The research entrepreneur becomes a euphoric schizophrenic. (*The Uses of the University*, Harvard University Press, 1963.)

3. The purpose of the bill (*HC* 11542) is 'to promote the advancement of science and the education of scientists, engineers and technicians through a national programme of institutional grants to the colleges and universities of the United States' (*House of Representatives Report No. 91–490, 91st Congress, 1st Session*).

4. American Council on Education, Working Papers for the Commission on Federal Relations, *General Federal Support*

276

for Higher Education: An Analysis of Five Formulas (Aug. 1968).

5. This view is expressed by Don K. Price, 'Federal Money and University Research', in *Science*, 21 Jan. 1966, p. 288.

6. This total includes $11 million spent by hospitals, research organisations and other non-educational institutions. It excludes expenditure data from three institutions whose reports were not complete. Information supplied by the Division of Research Facilities and Resources, National Institutes of Health.

7. Information supplied by the National Science Foundation.

8. The term 'Federalism by Contract' was used by Don K. Price to describe an 'improvised form of federalism' that makes use of private institutions for the conduct of federal science programmes. 'This new system of relationships, based on the administrative contract, not only gives support to scientific institutions that yet retain their basic independence, but it also creates new ones that become equally independent' (*Government and Science* (New York University Press, 1954) p. 67).

9. In its simplest terms, revenue-sharing is a system of distributing centrally collected revenues to the states on a per capita basis with few or no conditions attached to their use. Some proposed formulas take into account state tax effort as well as population.

10. The Advisory Commission on Intergovernmental Relations has commented on this situation as follows:

The rapid expansion in number of grants has affected their role in partnership programmes. From the point of view of the grant recipients – State and local governments – the sheer number, variety and complexity of grants make it all but impossible for eligible recipients to be fully aware of what aids are available, which Federal agencies administer them and how they suit particular needs. A major complaint of State and local governments concerns this 'information gap'. One consequence has been that by July 1967, 13 States, 23 cities and one county had established Washington offices to keep track of grant programmes and to conduct active follow-through with Federal agencies in expediting grant applications. Several cities, 300 counties and 46 States (as of July 1967) had established Federal aid co-ordinators.

'Grantsmanship' has become a popular new game in Washington, played most effectively by alert State and local governments. If they do not have Washington offices – or perhaps even if they do – they find many consultants at hand whose business it is to keep informed on available grant programmes and help their clients in applying for them. (*Fiscal Balance in the American Federal System*, vol. 1 (Oct. 1967) p. 151.)

These observations would appear to apply equally to educational institutions in their dealings with federal agencies.

11. Advisory Commission on Intergovernmental Relations, *Intergovernmental Relations in the Poverty Programs* (April 1966) p. 28.

12. Dissatisfaction with some private Community Action agencies led Congress to amend the law in December 1967 to give elected local governments more responsibility for local anti-poverty programmes. The law now requires that a Community Action agency be a state, a political subdivision of a state or a public or non-profit agency or organisation designated by a state or political subdivision (Public Law 90–222, section 210).

An exception is provided where the state or local government is unwilling to designate an agency or where the designated agency fails to submit a plan which meets certain criteria. In this event, the O.E.O. director may fund another public or private agency; if private, one-third of its board members must be public officials.

In recommending these changes, the House Committee on Education and Labour observed that while about 80 per cent of the Community Action agencies are private non-profit, there is little or no correlation between an agency's legal form and the success of its programme. The Committee felt, however, that 'Unless a community's governing structure endorses the community action agency, there is little hope that the agency will be able to realise its vital potential for planning and co-ordination. This will happen only if the community action agency is viewed as an instrument of the community it serves and not as the vehicle for implementing federally established objectives' (*House Report No. 866 to Accompany S. 2388, 90th Congress, 1st Session*, p. 22).

13. Advisory Commission on Intergovernmental Relations, *Intergovernmental Relations in the Poverty Program*, pp. 33–4.

14. Vannevar Bush, *Science, the Endless Frontier, A Report to the President* (1945).

15. The National Science Foundation Act of 1947, veto message of the President, 6 Aug. 1947: *Congressional Record*, app., 15 Aug. 1947, pp. A4442–A4443.

16. *Federal Support of Basic Research in Institutions of Higher Learning* (1964) p. 93.

17. Presidential address at the annual meeting of the Association of Graduate Schools, San Francisco, 21 Oct. 1968.

18. Projections of manpower requirements in the sciences have been severely criticised at times. Saunders MacLane observes that 'enthusiasts for the utility of science occasionally argue for big expansions in the number of young scientists being trained. This approach runs the danger that a mere emphasis on quantity can stifle the quality necessary to true originality and fruitful scientific growth.'

In commenting on the Gilliland Report of the President's Science Advisory Committee, and particularly its proposal for increasing Ph.D.s in mathematics by 300 per cent in ten years, MacLane said:

This recommendation for mathematics is utter nonsense: Ph.D.s in mathematics, currently of good average quality, are turned out rather slowly and 'by hand', in the sense that each Ph.D. thesis is different in style and requires individual direction. The number of professors of mathematics able to direct such theses is limited, and the work of directing too many theses can become a distraction. . . . Moreover, such a recommendation encourages universities without adequate mathematics faculty to establish Ph.D. programmes in mathematics. (Regrettably, this already happens too frequently.) The young students attracted to such schools would receive inadequate training, often in obsolete fields of research; it is a well-established observation that able students so trained are nearly always ruined for further serious scientific work.

(See Saunders MacLane's paper 'Leadership and Quality in Science', in *Basic Research and National Goals* (a report to the Committee on Science and Astronautics, U.S. House of Representatives, by the National Academy of Sciences, March 1965) pp. 197–8.)

Bryce Nelson, writing in a recent issue of *Science* (31 Oct. 1969, pp. 582–4), reported that the Bureau of the Budget thinks the United States is producing more scientists than it can place in suitable scientific jobs.

Speaking mainly of the scientist seeking a career in basic research, Nelson said:

> ... The days of a salary and security 'gravy train' for the scientist of only average abilities seem to be drawing to a close. Unless the tendency to cut back on federal science spending is reversed, it may well be that the scientific profession will be winnowed to those able scientists who are driven primarily by love of their work. Although such a forced sifting would be hard on many of the scientifically mediocre, it seems unlikely that it would drastically reduce the high quality of American science. A brisk winnowing might even help.

19. Unpublished data from a survey by the Intergovernmental Relations Sub-Committee, House of Representatives. These figures relate only to direct federal support and do not include students who receive financial assistance from employment on research projects.

20. National Academy of Sciences, *Summary Report 1967, Doctorate Recipients from United States Universities* (May 1968) table 3.

21. Ibid., fig. 1.

22. A high official of the National Institute of Mental Health has described the role of the scientist-administrator as follows:

> In essence, the scientist-administrator is viewed as an expert in the *process* of Federal grantsmanship as well as in the *content* of the research area for which he has responsibility; his expertise is readily acknowledged and often drawn upon by the grant applicant. If he has only peripheral scientific competence in the general area, the grant

applicant will nonetheless defer to his opinion if for no other reason than that he, the scientist-administrator, is also the person who is knowledgeable about the process of grantmanship.

(Eli A. Rubinstein, 'The Federal Health Scientist-Administrator: An Opportunity for Role Integration', in *American Psychologist*, Aug. 1968.)
23. The need for clear concepts of institutional responsibility was described in a paper by two N.I.H. officials:

... The principal accomplishment of establishment of regulation and promulgation of policy and procedures [in 1962 in response to criticism by the House Intergovernmental Relations Sub-Committee] was to define the respective responsibilities of government agencies and of the universities. The regulations and policies emphasise that the sponsoring *institution* is the party primarily accountable to the government for the proper administration of research projects and grant funds. This emphasis in no way diminishes the scientific and fiscal responsibility of the investigator, nor his key role, but it does define more explicitly the working relationships between the grantor agency and the elements of the academic and scientific communities involved in the federally sponsored research.

Actually, the accountability of the institution (rather than the investigator) was inherent in the terms of the grant agreements from the first. It was administrative practice or usage that modified the concept. The philanthropic or science patron role assumed by the agencies led to direct communication on most matters between investigators and agency staff. University administrators were left without significant roles in the chain of research administration. This situation was tenable twenty years ago when few universities and colleges regarded research administration as an important part of academic administration. The investigator was considered to be a free agent in the light of the contemporary interpretation of academic freedom.

(Karl R. Reinhard and John F. Sherman, 'Administration: Continuing Challenges, Maturing Capabilities', in *Sponsored*

Research in American Universities and Colleges, ed. Stephen
Strickland (American Council on Education) pp. 78–9.)
24. *Biomedical Science and its Administration, A Study of
the National Institutes of Health* (report to the President,
1965) pp. 119–20.
25. U.S. Department of Health, Education and Welfare,
Office of the Comptroller, H.E.W. Audit Agency, *Audit
Observations Concerning Acquisition and Control of Equipment by Universities and Nonprofit Organizations under
H.E.W. Programs* 10 Oct. 1968), letter of transmittal.
26. The House Committee on Governmental Operations reported in this connection:

> The P.H.S. has also permitted unjustifiable variations
> among its bureaus, divisions and institutes in the inter-
> pretation and application of agency policies. There is a
> large degree of independent action by P.H.S. units in
> situations where the uniform implementation of policies is
> both intended and desirable. Some differences are to be
> expected in a large organisation, but others are purely
> arbitrary and result from inadequate central direction and
> supervision.
>   ... The structure of the Public Health Service, and
> especially N.I.H., is so decentralised and its staff so admini-
> stratively independent that often one component does not
> know how another is implementing the same policies.

The report further stated:

> This committee and others have, over the years, attributed
> N.I.H.'s management difficulties largely to a highly per-
> missive attitude that allows the Institutes to go their
> separate ways. Nevertheless, this situation has continued
> basically unchanged to the present. The low esteem of
> administrative management in N.I.H. was epitomised 5
> years ago by the Director's statement that after research pro-
> jects are selected for support all subsequent administrative
> actions are 'essentially trivial'.

(*The Administration of Research Grants in the Public
Health Service* (House Report no. 800, 20 Oct. 1967) pp. 58
and 60.)

282

13 Financial Accountability to Parliament

Nevil Johnson

Financial accountability to Parliament as it has developed in Britain has been very much concerned with what might be called 'certification of expenditures', that is to say with the judgement of past performance. This predominantly *post facto* approach to accountability is perhaps less widely accepted in a number of other countries, notably in the United States, where for obvious reasons the involvement of Congress in decisions about the future levels of expenditure and the content of spending programmes has been far closer than has been that of Parliament in Britain. In addition there has been an earlier and more widespread acceptance in the United States of the idea that accountability procedures can be viewed as tools of management, as yielding information which facilitates corrective action in the field of current programmes and offers criteria by which decisions on future commitments can be shaped. But this switch of emphasis in the notion of financial accountability has hardly yet taken place in Britain, though there are signs both in the executive branch of government and in Parliament that changes may be in the offing. At the present time, therefore, it is necessary to pitch this discussion of accountability in terms of what has so far been accepted doctrine and practice in relation to accountability. To do otherwise would entail the risk of offering speculation instead of a summary of what has actually taken place.

Since the completion of the cycle of financial control under the aegis of Gladstone in the sixties of the last century, the emphasis in Britain has been almost exclusively on procedures which would enable Parliament to exercise a *post facto* check on the manner in which monies had been spent for the purposes approved by (but not proposed by) Parliament. Though it was held fairly soon after the establishment of the modern procedures of audit and accounting that the processes of accountability should yield results which will affect future performance, the accountability which Parliament was justified in claiming must not be confused with any demands Parliament might make to participate in the determination of expenditure, in short in the planning of public spending programmes.[1] In fact the House of Commons has never so far laid serious claim to a share in determining the level and content of expenditure, and even with regard to taxation its role has been chiefly that of a critic (and sometimes, let it be said, an effective critic). But the functions of the House in relation to finance have mirrored the traditional relationship between government and Parliament; the House provides an arena for argument and debate, and in the case of taxation, for counter-proposals. For this reason no special attention will be paid here to the wider problems relating to the treatment of expenditure proposals and taxation on the floor of the House. If the term 'accountability' is introduced in this context, it can only be in the very broad sense of the duty of a government to offer a political justification of its proposals to the House of Commons, and to confirm this by mobilising its supporters in their defence.

Given this way of thinking about the respective roles of government and Parliament in the control of expenditure, it was natural that financial accountability should be seen as something basically outside the area of political argument on the floor of the House of Commons. It has been primarily the concern of select committees, bodies set up to carry out a more or less judicial task of inquiry and to report back to the House. This means that this paper deals mainly with such committees and the administrative organisations which serve them. References to the House of Commons as a whole will be limited to such aspects of the procedures of accountability as have some direct implications for what the House itself does. Of the financial committees the most important is the Public Accounts Committee, which must be considered in conjunction with the Comptroller and Auditor General and the Exchequer and Audit Department. Rather illogically the Estimates Committee must also be treated nowadays as a committee concerned with financial accountability, although strictly speaking its order of reference suggests a species of *a priori* control. The work of the Nationalised Industries

284

Committee comes in part into the area of financial accountability. The new committees of administrative scrutiny deserve a brief mention only in so far as their broad terms of reference would permit them to engage in the *post facto* scrutiny of expenditure: as will be mentioned below, experience of these committees is too short to permit any firm generalisations about the degree of interest in financial control which they have so far shown.

1. *Current Patterns of Financial Accountability*

That a government should be accountable to Parliament for the expenditure of funds voted to it is a commonplace of liberal parliamentary doctrine. As far as the practice of accountability over the past century goes, it is possible to distinguish three aspects, viz. (*a*) the check for regularity or legality; (*b*) the check for economy or the avoidance of waste; (*c*) the check for efficiency or the optimum use of resources.

These aspects of accountability also represent phases of development, which can be linked with changes in political attitudes towards state expenditure: regularity and economy fit in with a Gladstonian view of retrenchment in expenditure, efficiency is a response to the modern willingness to let public expenditure increase. But all three aspects of accountability remain relevant: the transition from one to another does not render the others superfluous. It merely means that the task of maintaining accountability becomes more complex.

Traditionally the Public Accounts Committee has been Parliament's main tool for securing accountability in the first two senses. But it has also for many years now been concerned with efficiency and effective spending. The Estimates Committee and the Nationalised Industries Committee have been mainly interested in economy and efficiency, especially with efficiency in the broad sense of satisfactory administrative arrangements. Other committees of scrutiny are said to have the purpose (among others) of stimulating efficiency in the departments of state. Here again it seems likely that efficiency, in so far as it is a preoccupation of these new committees, will be viewed in terms of sound organisation and procedures. These various committees and such official backing as they have will be considered in the order just indicated.

The Public Accounts Committee, the Comptroller and Auditor General and the Exchequer and Audit Department

The arrangements for accounting to the House of Commons for the expenditure of monies appropriated date from the sixties of the last century: the P.A.C. was set up in 1861 and the C. & A.G. established as head of the Exchequer and Audit Department in 1866.[2] The main functions of the C. & A.G. are defined by statute.[3] His audit is one of accountancy, appropriation and authority. That is to say, in the first place he has to check the regularity and legality of expenditures.

Though the emphasis was from the start on regularity viewed from the accountancy and appropriation standpoint, the influence of the P.A.C., whose servant and mentor the C. & A.G. is, worked in the direction of widening the concept of regularity so that it came to include considerations of prudence, responsibility and economy. The Committee and the C. & A.G. became keen to identify and reprove wasteful spending. Gradually in the course of the present century the notion of economy changed further and came to include a somewhat imprecise concern with the efficient control and management of resources, i.e. not just with spending in the narrow sense but with the organisation and procedures required for efficient spending. As the present Chairman of the P.A.C. remarked recently in a memorandom to the Select Committee on Procedure, 'the Committee's field of interest has extended to the elimination of waste and extravagance, the encouragement of sound practices in estimating, contracting and financial administration generally, and the need to obtain what is usually described as "value for money" '.[4] The initiative in this direction has probably come on balance more from successive Comptrollers General than from the P.A.C., though the latter has certainly encouraged this shift of emphasis.

The C. & A.G.'s preoccupation with efficiency in the management of expenditure appears clearly in his reports to Parliament. In 1966–7 he underlines the attention paid to 'systems of control and accounting'.[5] In a paper to the P.A.C. on the control of university expenditure it is remarked that 'My examination would be directed to investigating on a test basis at selected institutions, their *arrangements* for control of supplies and services, equipment, residential accommodation, research and capital projects (tendering, contracting, programming). This examination would enable me to report to Parliament on *the effectiveness of the financial administration* of public funds by the universities....'[6] This shift to a scrutiny of procedures and methods of control and planning has to a certain extent added a new dimension to the cautious and impartial reports of the C. & A.G. and has opened the way to wider-ranging inquiries by the P.A.C. So far, however, it is a fair generalisation that issues of economy, i.e. savings which could have been made on particular items of expenditure, still bulk largest in the C. & A.G.'s observations. There is still some way to go before the move towards an efficiency audit finds expression in a thorough-going scrutiny of organisation, management procedures and techniques by the C. & A.G.

The P.A.C. receives the annual reports of the C. & A.G. and such special reports as he may make, and in the light of his observations investigates particular points which he has highlighted, taking evidence normally from the permanent secretaries who are also accounting officers of the departments. The influence of P.A.C. inquiries on Whitehall is well known, at any rate as a force making for financial rectitude; so is the close co-operation between the Committee and the Treasury. It is worth underlining the extent to which the P.A.C. relies on the work of the C. & A.G. Its success has owed much to the availability of a firm factual basis on which to work and of advice on the issues of importance calling for further investigation.

The achievements of the Committee are fairly clear. It adds parliamentary authority to the financial discipline exerted by the C. & A.G. and the Treasury on the spending departments; it can scrutinise, publicise and criticise wasteful and excessive expenditure; it makes recommendations both of substance and procedure which are normally heeded (the more so as they usually run parallel to the Treasury's wishes). Summing up, one may say of the P.A.C.'s work:

287

(*a*) It has been a source of pressure in favour of the detailed amendment of financial behaviour, e.g. if a particular grant is criticised as lavishly administered, the department will take care to avoid the criticism in future.

(*b*) It has publicised a number of major 'scandals' unearthed by the C. & A.G., e.g. the Ferranti Co. overpayments and the costing of the British Siddeley aero-engine contracts. Such discoveries exert a political pressure and may lead to substantial revisions of procedure, organisation and even of policy.

(*c*) There is a contribution to an efficiency audit by the P.A.C., but at present this is hard to quantify. Its extent and character remains obscure. Clearly financial procedures are affected by the P.A.C.'s findings. There is less evidence of a sustained influence in terms of organisational change, the introduction of new management techniques, the review of functions or the reassessment of conflicting objectives within the departments. Indeed, as we shall see below, P.A.C. reports do not generally reveal such a broad concern with administration and management as do those of the Estimates Committee and the Nationalised Industries Committee. This partly reflects the strength of traditional concepts of the P.A.C.'s task, partly the sheer practical problem that a small committee of fifteen members does well if it manages to deal thoroughly with all the issues of regularity and economy raised in relation to one set of annual accounts.

The area of financial accountability under discussion is, as already indicated, distinguished from most other forms of government accountability to Parliament by the presence of a specific professional organisation to do the ground-work, namely the Exchequer and Audit Department, headed by the Comptroller and Auditor General.[7] Currently the E. & A. Department employs just over 500 staff. There is no need here to comment on the independent status of the department and its head, except to point out that the authority of the C. & A.G. is attributable in part to his status as an officer of Parliament and to the judicial characteristics of his functions. A concern with regularity and a judicial style of behaviour tend to be natural partners.

The characteristics of the E. & A. staff deserve some

comment. Recruitment is mainly from the executive level of the civil service; professional accountancy qualifications are not required, though many auditors may acquire these in the course of their careers. The status of the department's staff has been fairly modest, reflecting its relatively humble position in the civil service hierarchy. There is, however, no evidence to suggest that this factor has impaired its efficiency as far as the carrying out of a regularity and economy audit goes. Indeed the quality of the C. & A.G.'s reports testifies to the thoroughness, accuracy and acumen of his staff in the discharge of audit functions as traditionally understood. On the other hand there are some grounds for believing that the lack of high prestige and of formal qualifications may nowadays have an inhibiting influence on the Exchequer and Audit Department in the rapid development of efficiency audit techniques and concepts, and in tackling the broader analysis and evaluation of policy which such techniques may call for. Certainly the contrast between the qualities sought by the G.A.O. in the United States and those with which the E. & A. Department is still satisfied is suggestive of different approaches to the demands of the audit function.

As a result of the current scale of public expenditure two developments have taken place which need to be mentioned. First, most government departments have substantial accounting branches which supplement the work of the E. & A. Department. These accounting branches themselves ensure a high level of regularity in financial transactions in the departments and prepare the material on which the appropriation accounts are based. To this extent the E. & A. staff is relieved of much detailed work. This links with the second point, the need to rely on test audit in modern conditions. A complete scrutiny of accounts has long been impossible. Test audit inevitably entails the risk that some mistakes, perhaps serious ones, will slip through the net. This risk would, however, be more acceptable if it were clearer than it is at the moment that the audit process was making a continuous impact upon organisation and upon planning and control procedures. Linking these two points together, one can argue that because the departments themselves have built up accounting units, in principle the E. & A. staff might now be expected to concentrate less on the traditional checks for regularity and economy, and devote more effort to the broader issues of managerial efficiency. Here one comes back to the problem alluded to in the previous paragraph, namely whether the present audit unit has quite the weight and diversity of experience to enable it to develop its role in directions clearly demanded by the needs of effective expenditure and control in present conditions.

In the House of Commons the Public Accounts Committee enjoys high prestige. It attracts a fair proportion of capable and senior Members, some of whom serve for long periods. Attendance for the investigatory sessions of the Committee is good and it is reasonable to assume that the Committee members are on the whole satisfied with what they achieve. It is noteworthy that in the discussions of changes in committee structures and functions since about 1964, few people have pressed for changes in relation to the P.A.C. The Committee makes a continuing impact on civil service behaviour, perhaps still mainly in the direction of maintaining rather old-fashioned concepts of financial management. Occasionally it makes a major impact on ministers, e.g. in the wake of the Ferranti disclosures or in persuading the government to subject university expenditure to the C. & A.G.'s audit. Given the strictly *post facto* nature of most of its inquiries there has been little change of policy with the departments.[8]

The feedback from the P.A.C. to the House of Commons is very modest. The inquiries and reports of the Committee rarely have a direct link, substantive or procedural, with what the House is debating and deciding. One report a year is normally debated. Experience suggests that unless issues of political interest are raised the House does not find P.A.C. reports congenial material for debate (quite apart from the inevitable time-lag). Moreover, the debating of P.A.C. reports must necessarily be something of an academic exercise. The cycle of financial business in the House does not yet make room for the regular consideration of past performance (e.g. in relation to continuing programmes of expenditure) or of the bearing which methods of financial control and planning might have on current estimates. The absence of a specialised legislative committee system also means that there is no possibility of drawing on the material emerging from the scrutiny of expenditure when legislation involving financial programmes is under consideration. Here there is a marked difference between the possibilities open to the House of Commons and those present in the U.S. Congress.

The Estimates Committee: The transformation of 'a priori' *control into a species of financial accountability*

It was to some extent awareness of the fact that P.A.C. control is strictly *post facto* which prompted the setting up of a committee to consider current, not yet approved, estimates. The chequered career of the Estimates Committee from 1912 to 1945 testified to the difficulties involved in developing any means of *a priori* control of spending. For governments the exclusion of policy questions from the order of reference was a *sine qua non*. The remit to consider what economies might be achieved within the limits of the policies proposed forced the Committee to concentrate on trivia. After 1945 it modified its method of working and discovered an approach compatible with its order of reference which allowed it to establish itself as a committee making a useful contribution to the pattern of financial controls exercised by committees on behalf of the House.[9] The post-1945 approach was to pay more attention to administrative structures and methods of work as they relate to selected areas of expenditure and to an assessment of whether 'value for money' was being secured. Thus the Committee's post-war reports have tended to fall into two categories (though often overlapping): reports in which, because of the characteristics of the services provided under the estimate head chosen (e.g. legal aid, industrial training schemes), it is possible to make specific proposals for future financial savings as well as to comment on organisational problems; and those in which the range and scale of expenditure examined compel the Committee to concentrate more or less exclusively on administrative and management questions (e.g. Treasury control of establishments, recruitment to the civil service, the Home Office, etc.).

With the switch of emphasis from the search for specific savings in current estimates to the probing of administrative arrangements and procedures in order to relate these to a judgement of financial efficiency, the Estimates Committee has in important respects become a committee of *post facto* accountability, entitled, however, to ask questions about the implications of past performance for future action. For this reason it is plausible to argue that the work of the Committee now represents an admittedly rather amateur contribution to an efficiency audit of government spending. The bearing which the lack of a professional staff has on this point will be taken up again below.

The impact of Estimates Committee reports on the departments has been patchy. They often lack the precision and relatively narrow but deep factual basis of P.A.C. reports. The political weight of this fairly large committee (until recently forty-three members, then thirty-six and now thirty-three) has been slight too. The trend towards a broad study of organisational problems and of the efficacy of administrative arrangements as related to current tasks and policies meant that reports became more discursive and their recommendations less precise. Disagreement with them became easier and more defensible. The parallel with the style and content of many Royal Commission reports may be drawn: easy to consign to the pigeon-hole.

The Committee's link with the House of Commons has also been loose. Increasingly its work (with the exception of the inquiries into supplementary estimates) has had no connection in time or substance with the estimates currently before the House for approval, and to which theoretically the Committee's inquiries are linked. In more recent years the House has, however, shown some interest in debating reports from the Committee and since 1960 has usually set aside a couple of days per session for this. These debates have generally been quiet affairs, chiefly for the minority of specialists and interested parties closely concerned with the reports under discussion. Nevertheless it is likely that the chances of public debate have added something to the authority of the Committee *vis-à-vis* the departments and persuaded them to treat more seriously the recommendations put forward.

In some respects the work of the Estimates Committee (and, as we shall note below, of the Nationalised Industries Committee too) has acquired some of the characteristics of a wide-ranging efficiency audit. Admittedly the Estimates Committee is in no position to carry out searching analyses of management methods, of techniques of controlling financial

292

outlays against performance of services, of the extent to which quantitative methods of programming and control can be applied, etc. To this extent the term 'efficiency audit' is being used very loosely. It is rather a question of emphasis. The Estimates Committee has interpreted its remit in such a way that it has devoted a lot of attention to administrative problems. It has tended to say, 'Here is an estimate for this or that service: let us see how the department is organised and equipped for the job and how effectively it is coping with it.' This explains the emphasis (clearly visible in the Committee's recommendations in many reports) on organisational adaptation, which is without doubt an important aspect of the issues which have to be raised in the course of an efficiency audit.

Against this background it is worth referring to the problem of staffing the Committee, which so far has been served only by clerks of the House (and the occasional external adviser). The idea of a permanent staff peculiar to the Committee has usually been rejected. It is hard to envisage what experience and qualifications they would need, so diverse and unpredictable is the field covered. The whole conception of a staff employed by and directed by a select committee has also aroused hostility in Whitehall. In addition it is almost certain that many members of this committee (and probably of others too) still share a view of lay control which makes them reluctant to rely too heavily on permanent advisers.

The solution proposed more than once in the past has been to amalgamate or link the Estimates Committee with the Public Accounts Committee so that the C. & A.G. could then serve both Committees. This again has been rejected (e.g. in 1946) on the grounds that the C. & A.G. exercises an essentially impartial, *post facto* control, and that he and his staff would be compromised if brought into the scrutiny of more current arrangements and problems.

It is probable that there is no advantage to be gained from pursuing the proposal for a staff special to this Committee, investigating in a broad and probably ill-defined manner different areas of administrative action in accordance with the interests and preoccupations of members. A more efficient and politically less controversial approach might be to think again in terms of developing the functions of the Exchequer and Audit Department (perhaps in conjunction with the Treasury) so that it would be able to make available the results of a systematic and continuing study of the efficiency of departmental operations, which could then be used by the Estimates Committee or a successor as the basis for part of its work. In this way one comes back to the idea of merging the Public Accounts Committee with the Estimates Committee, with both of them supported by a Comptroller and Auditor General with wider functions than he normally exercises now. This possibility will be looked at again in Section 3.

The Nationalised Industries Committee

Technically this Committee must be counted as one concerned partly with financial accountability, since its order of reference requires it to examine the reports and accounts of the nationalised industries. But the published accounts of the nationalised industries are auditors' accounts which present the formal financial position, but do not purport to yield much information which will permit an analysis of problems relating to economy and efficiency in the management of these industries. In this respect they differ considerably from the C. & A.G.'s reports on the government sector. This means that the Committee hardly has a good basis for thorough financial scrutiny. In addition, like the Estimates Committee, the Nationalised Industries Committee is not backed by a professional staff comparable to the Exchequer and Audit Department, but has to rely on its clerks (plus recently a specialist assessor) and on the information provided by departments and boards.

Given the situation just outlined, it is not surprising that over the ten or more years since its establishment as an effective Committee of Inquiry the Nationalised Industries Committee has concentrated rather less on financial scrutiny than on broader surveys of economic and organisational problems affecting the nationalised industries. The relatively large (and increasing) number of nationalised concerns has meant that the Committee can examine an industry not more often than once in seven or eight years, and it may in future be hard to achieve even this coverage unless the Committee continues to operate as two sub-committees (a recent innovation in its procedure).

Despite these qualifying remarks on the financial scope of the Committee's work, it is reasonable to draw some comparison between its inquiries and those of the Estimates Committee. Like the latter it has emphasised organisational and management questions – how are economic objectives defined and policy decisions taken, what external constraints affect an industry, what is the internal administrative structure like, how are staff resources distributed and employed, according to what criteria are financial resources deployed and in what sense, if any, does an industry seek to achieve optimum use of resources? It is generally agreed that working on these lines the Committee has been able to make a useful contribution to the critical appraisal of the performance and problems of the public sector of industry. Like the Estimates Committee it has made a great deal of information available, has brought some issues more openly into the area of public argument and has exerted some pressure on ministers (albeit highly variable in intensity) to reconsider major policy questions affecting both the targets and structure of certain nationalised concerns. Whether the Committee has made a significant contribution to overcoming the persistent financial problems of some industries (e.g. British Rail) or to clarifying major issues in the future use of resources (e.g. coal) is very doubtful. In this connection the Committee probably lacks the resources for such a thorough analysis of past performance as would give its recommendations real authority in relation to future policy decisions.

It has often been argued that Parliament has insufficient means of ensuring that the public sector of industry remains accountable for its performance.[10] To a large extent this is the consequence of the still prevailing theory of nationalisation, i.e. that the public corporation is a device for ensuring a larger degree of autonomy in relation to Parliament (and in principle to ministers too, though it has not generally worked out like this) than departments of state enjoy. Further it is reasonably clear that the subjection of nationalised concerns to the kind of detailed regularity and economy audit carried out by the C. & A.G., with its subsequent overtones of political censure, would inhibit the management of these industries and thus to some extent conflict with the aim of running them as commercial enterprises. On the other hand it cannot be forgotten that the financing of the public sector of industry is a major item in the overall budgetary planning of the state. It follows that Parliament cannot be expected to be indifferent to the manner in which financial allocations to this sector are employed. Some form of accountability is clearly necessary.

The foregoing remarks offer some clue to how the concept of financial accountability might be developed in relation to the public sector. The work of the Nationalised Industries Committee in recent years has been directed mainly to the clarification of economic objectives and to the scrutiny of organisation and management methods. Its weakness has been attributable mainly to the lack of a sufficiently systematic basis on which to work. This could be remedied if there were arrangements for the continuing efficiency audit of these industries, the results of which could be used by a parliamentary committee in connection with its attempts to isolate significant problems. This is not to suggest that a parliamentary committee would itself carry out a kind of supplementary efficiency audit; rather that it would build on material made available to it, underpinning in this way its conclusions both in relation to the standard of performance of these industries and to outstanding questions requiring policy decisions. The recent report of the Nationalised Industries Committee on ministerial control of the nationalised industries[11] offers some pointers in this direction, though it is unlikely that they will be taken up in the form suggested by the Committee.

New select committees of administrative scrutiny

The aim underlying the establishment of new select committees in the past two or three years was to give Members additional opportunities for taking part in administrative scrutiny, more specialised by area and subject, and broader by being freed from the veto on the discussion of policy issues. Committees for Science and Technology, Agriculture and Education and Science have so far been set up.[12] The broader order of reference of these Committees may encourage them to pay less attention to financial and economic issues: to this extent they will not contribute much to the extension of financial accountability. So far, however, experience of these new devices is too short to permit valid generalisations about the likely pattern of development. The Science and Technology Committee has shown some inclination to emphasise, like the Estimates Committee, questions of value for money, coherence of economic objectives and management methods.[13] The Agriculture Committee has roamed more widely afield, and the same goes emphatically for the Education and Science Committee. The most that can be said at present is that these experiments might conceivably lead to nuclei of specialisation among Members of Parliament which could be harnessed in the pursuit of more effective financial accountability. The possibilities here have, however, to be judged with extreme caution against the background of rather dilettante experimentation which has characterised recent developments in the select committee structure of the House of Commons.

2. *Parliament and Financial Accountability: Some Limiting Factors*

The record of the House of Commons select committees in the field of *post facto* financial accountability is not bad compared with that of many parliaments. The parliamentary systems of many other countries, particularly on the continent of Europe, do not allow the legislatures such an active role in the investigation of administration and in the scrutiny of past performance. This does not mean that there are no sound arrangements for ensuring financial accountability or for checking on efficiency, only that they tend to be found within the state apparatus itself. The results of such control may not be fed into the legislature at all, or if they are, may be neglected by the legislature.[14] In contrast parliamentary intervention in the determination of expenditure, which is non-existent in Britain, may in some other countries be a factor of importance, as is obviously the case in the United States. There is no doubt that the relative emphasis on accounting to Parliament in Britain is a reflection of and compensation for the dominance of the executive in the fixing of public expenditure. These factors have to be borne in mind in any realistic appreciation of financial accountability as it now operates and of possibilities of future development.

When considering the limiting factors in relation to developing financial accountability procedures in new directions, it is worth beginning with parliamentary resources. Members who are at all interested in these problems probably fall into three groups:

(i) A radical minority who would like to see a shift away from *post facto* accountability to some sort of *a priori* intervention in relation to the level and composition of spending programmes. Generally this approach has been regarded as an unprofitable one to pursue within the framework of politics and government in Britain.

(ii) A fairly substantial group of Members, many with experience of select committees, who believe that the current arrangements are a reasonably adequate way of ensuring as much accountability for the use of financial resources as Parliament can expect to claim. This group would accept the subsidiary role of the House of Commons committees, but would emphasise the value to the House and the departments (as well as to nationalised industry) of inquiry and challenge by lay Members of Parliament, operating in a non-party context. This is broadly the traditional view, and tends to be shared with variations of emphasis by ministers and civil servants.

(iii) A minority (to some extent mainly composed of younger Members) who stress analogies between many operations of government and private business, and who are, therefore, anxious to see the development of efficiency audit concepts. They would like to see Parliament backing such a development and making use of it to strengthen accountability to Parliament. This group overlaps with the first one, some Members being anxious to use new methods of financial management only for the control of programmes already in train, others being keen to involve House of Commons committees in determining the level and composition of programmes.

298

The British political environment, including the strong habits of the House of Commons itself, suggests that the second view is likely to remain the most influential in relation to future trends in the pattern of financial accountability. It is to be expected that select committees will continue to exercise their financial and administrative controls by what may be called 'discursive inquiry', hoping in this way both to inform the public and to stimulate the executive branch to self-criticism. At the same time it is reasonable to hope that the third approach, which found vigorous expression in the recent report of the Procedure Committee on the Scrutiny of Public Expenditure and Administration and is reflected too in the earlier Treasury Green Paper on *Public Expenditure: A New Presentation*, may gradually gain support, leading to some switch in emphasis and method in the select committees themselves. This possibility does, however, depend very much on the manner in which the executive instruments for ensuring accountability are developed in order to provide more comprehensive tools of efficiency audit. Those in this third group in the House of Commons need to remember that Members themselves are not in a position to operate as substitutes for effective audit arrangements in the public services: at best they can hope to add an additional dimension of political awareness and insight to the results of inquiries already carried out by professionals. Further, it is important to avoid the risk of overestimating the analogies between business and government: to do so is naïve, and may indeed suggest greater managerial autonomy for the public services and less accountability to Parliament.[15]

Inescapably the kind of financial accountability which can be achieved must depend to some extent on what Members want and are capable of doing. Britain has a highly professional political class, but the professionalism of the politician is that of a generalist and all-rounder whose specialism is the judgement of political relevance. The British political system has not produced a high proportion of Members of Parliament whose knowledge and inclinations fit them for the specialised work involved in checking on the efficiency of public expenditure. Moreover, evidence from the past twenty years suggests that many of those who played a major part in the work of the three main committees concerned with forms of financial control were Members with outside business and professional interests, and relatively indifferent to conventional political ambitions. It is possible that the composition and age structure of the House is changing in a manner which will reduce the proportion of such Members and increase the proportion of relatively young 'professional' politicians. Maybe more of these will prefer to develop the specialised skills needed to make a serious contribution to the investigation of public spending and administrative performance. If this were to happen, the problem of parliamentary resources for a further development of the accountability procedures and investigations of the House would be at least partly solved. If, however, the main preoccupation of the majority of Members remains performance on the floor of the House because this improves the chances of climbing the political ladder, then the outlook for strengthening accountability will be less rosy.

Another area where there are difficulties to be overcome is in the staffing of committees. The P.A.C. is the only committee which can be said to have a staff, and its reputedly superior performance is often attributed to the fact that it works on the basis of reports prepared by its agent, the C. & A.G. Without going into all the arguments about staff for other committees, it can be accepted that for the foreseeable future there is little prospect of equipping them with directly attached specialist staff in addition to the usual clerks of the House. Indeed, so long as the inquiries of select committees retain this highly discursive quality, with so much emphasis on explanation and general comment, the argument for professional and expert staff seconded to a particular committee must be treated with caution. (This does not, of course, rule out the practice of having temporary specialist advisers; but that is a rather different matter.)

It is, however, possible to see the staffing problem in a very different light if two points are considered. First, the comparison with the P.A.C. is misleading, because it misunderstands the relationship between the C. & A.G. and his staff, and the P.A.C. The C. & A.G. is the servant of the P.A.C., but his position (and that of his staff) is independent; he is not under instructions from the P.A.C. He submits the results of his inquiries to the P.A.C. but he and his department work as autonomous agencies in the state. This leads into the second point, namely that 'staffs' actually attached to select committees would, in the British political and administrative environment, be unlikely to strengthen the authority of their committees. They would lack discretion (unless they usurped the position of the committees) and would risk falling into conflict with the departments. In contrast the C. & A.G. and his team are accepted by public departments as an independent part of the public service, fulfilling a necessary function and at the same time serving the House of Commons' interests. The deduction to be drawn from this is that financial accountability to committees of the House can more easily be given a broader professional base if we think in terms of independent staffs, performing functions which the administration accepts as necessary, and at the same time feeding in the results to appropriate committees of the House of Commons. Given the policy limitation which seriously affects the discretion of Members of the House, all this points in the direction of a further development of efficiency audit as the area of predominantly *post facto* scrutiny in which it is possible both to solve the staffing problem and give to the House opportunities relevant to the contemporary situation. This notion will be explored further in Section 4.

It is worth concluding this section by referring to the way in which the relationship of the House to the spending agencies affects the rationale of financial accountability to Parliament. The House is always at second or third remove from the parts of the public service which actually spend: it issues no instructions to them and possesses no powers of intervention. It follows from this that arrangements for scrutinising performance, including a fully developed efficiency audit, cannot be regarded by the House as a tool of management. Yet in industry or within a department of state, this is precisely how, in the light of modern advances in management control systems, the regular analysis of performance would be regarded: as a basis for corrective action and for the readjustment of objectives. The nearer one gets to an efficiency audit concept, the more marked becomes this characteristic of audit, i.e. it is less a certificate of probity, more a tool of management.

This position presents both difficulties and opportunities

for the Commons. It points the way to a broader notion of financial accountability which will enable committees to consider problems of major importance for the performance of the public sector. It offers the prospect of means of assessing the validity of budgetary planning. Equally it has the risk of tempting Members of Parliament to see themselves in the manager's seat and to aspire to a type of executive control which they cannot hope to exercise. In the future development of financial accountability, in which efficiency considerations should play an increasing part, Members would be well advised to continue to see themselves primarily as lay assessors, charged not only with inquiring into specific spending activities and areas but also with requiring the professional auditors to justify their methods and conclusions. In this way a work of public explanation can be carried on, the importance of which the House of Commons has always recognised.

3. *Possibilities for the Further Development of Financial Accountability*

When considering how the techniques of analysing public spending activities might be further developed, and how the results of such analyses can be harnessed to improving Parliament's share in the accountability process, we must initially take account of a number of important changes which have recently affected the situation in Britain. First, the Fulton Report on the civil service has stimulated a more explicit concern in the administration with the problems of management control and the techniques by which resources may be used most effectively. The transfer of the Treasury's management functions to the new Civil Service Department has underlined the commitment to stimulating the active pursuit of improved management methods. But equally the Treasury has not been passive during this period of change in the arrangements for managing the civil service. It has pushed ahead, building on the progress already made since the Plowden Report of 1961, with working out more refined techniques both for projecting expenditure over the years to come (five-year programming) and for controlling expenditure in the departments. The Green Paper of April 1969[16] on the new presentation of public expenditure marks a further step forward from the traditional cash presentation of estimates to something nearer a functional presentation of spending proposals over five years. This will in principle facilitate a better appreciation of how priorities have been determined, what they involve in terms of resource commitments and what implications expenditure proposals have for the economy as a whole.

There is no doubt that it is developments such as these which have encouraged the House of Commons to take another look at its role in the control of public spending, control both in the traditional sense of accounting which has been discussed here, and control in the more overtly political sense of influencing or determining decisions yet to be taken. This is not the place for a full account of the September 1969 report of the Procedure Committee on the scrutiny of public expenditure and administration. But it is necessary to mention that the Committee has pressed both for more annual information from the government on spending plans, and for a new Expenditure Committee, based on the Estimates Committee, which would have a broad remit to examine public expenditure and the efficiency with which programmes are carried out. Though the report of the Procedure Committee is blurred on some aspects of the proposal, it seems reasonable to conclude that it envisages a more intense and specialised involvement of Members of Parliament in the retrospective analysis of expenditure as well as a move towards the scrutiny of spending programmes before final decisions have been taken by the government.

These suggestions raise important political issues. Depending on how they are interpreted, they could presage an important reappraisal of the view of accountability that has so far prevailed, involving the introduction of a dimension of *a priori* check and control. In this event there would very likely be serious political disagreement between the government and the House, for this development would call into question fundamental assumptions relating to the responsibilities of governments and the role of Parliament. Leaving aside these major issues (which through judicious concession may never be raised), it is worth mentioning that the Pro-

L

cedure Committee paid relatively little attention to the executive services which might be required if financial scrutiny is to be deepened in the manner proposed.

That this was so reflects the contemporary tendency to attach rather too much importance to what committees of the House of Commons can do themselves. Indeed the last few years have witnessed an altogether exaggerated faith in the benefits to be derived from unguided inquiry by Members of Parliament. What is important, and nowhere more so than in this area of financial accounting, is to consider first the means by which committees charged with primarily economic and financial scrutiny can be given a better analytic and factual basis on which to do at least part of their work. This means that we have to ask questions about the present arrangements for state audit, i.e. the Comptroller and Auditor General and his staff, and about the place and purpose of audit both in the machinery of government and in relation to Parliament's interest in financial accountability.

Some of the limitations of the current audit of expenditure and some of the weaknesses of the Exchequer and Audit Department within the structure of government have already been indicated. In carrying out his audit there is no doubt that the C. & A.G. has widened the concepts of regularity and economy so that issues bearing on efficient management can be considered. Nevertheless the emphasis does still remain more on discovering mistakes and on uncovering waste (a flexible concept anyway) than on the adaptation and improvement of organisation and management in the public services. There are many reasons for this, including the legal requirements of the Exchequer and Audit Acts, the influence of the judicial element in the C. & A.G.'s task (which is both necessary and desirable), the limitations imposed by the staffing policies of the Exchequer and Audit Department, and reluctance so far on the part of the Treasury and the Civil Service Department to see that developments towards a wide-ranging efficiency audit within the framework of the E. & A. Department might help them to solve problems to which at present they prefer to apply their own resources.

These points do not, however, present insuperable obstacles to the development of more comprehensive arrangements for a continuing efficiency audit. Nor can the need for this be seriously contested. Within the area of direct government expenditure it has long been clear that expanded permanent services are required to supplement the present type of audit, and to indicate how some of the problems uncovered even by the current audit can be overcome. (E.g. it was a tribute to the C. & A.G. that he uncovered the overpayments to Ferranti; but neither he nor any other agency could at the same time present an analysis of the area of administration involved which would indicate means of ensuring that the chances of this sort of thing happening would be reduced. In short the audit did not point to a cure: that had to be left to an *ad hoc* inquiry. And one of the diseases of British government is over-reliance on *ad hoc* investigation.) When we turn to the sector of nationalised industry the need for techniques of efficiency audit is all the more apparent, not just to assist Parliament but even more so to serve as a tool of management within the industries and to permit comparisons of performance between industries.

The immediate practical issue, therefore, is to decide how present administrative arrangements might be supplemented or changed to permit developments such as have just been outlined to take place. There are a variety of possibilities. One is to think in terms of further expanding the management services now located in the Civil Service Department, giving them something like an inspectorial function. Another is to think in terms of the departments having their own efficiency audit teams, perhaps supplemented by outside consultants, and a special department or team for scrutinising the nationalised industries (as recommended in effect by the Select Committee on Nationalised Industries). But the most promising possibility would be to develop further and in a fairly radical manner the Exchequer and Audit Department. This would mean expansion in size, and qualitative changes so that a comprehensive state audit service would emerge. The statutory basis of the Exchequer and Audit Department would have to be revised to confer an explicit duty to examine administrative efficiency. We might consider the Comptroller and Auditor General having the additional title of 'Commissioner for Administrative Efficiency'.[17] His terms of reference, at any rate in relation to efficiency audit, should at some stage be extended to embrace the public sector of industry. Perhaps in the future even local authorities might be brought in too, at any rate in relation to some of their mandatory services largely financed by Exchequer grant. Such changes would require the appointment of several Comptrollers – perhaps one for regularity and economy in government departments, one for efficiency of administration and resource management in government departments and another for efficiency in the public sector of industry. In short there would be a move to something like a collegial audit, at any rate as far as the directing posts go.

All this would entail changes in the staffing of Exchequer and Audit. These should not in principle be difficult to achieve, though they would take some years to become effective. Injections from the Treasury and Civil Service Department, selection within E. & A., recruitment of suitably qualified graduates, secondments from other departments and public industry would all play a part in creating a new kind of specialised staff to be added to the existing audit teams.

What has been outlined is a pattern of development which seems to be related rationally to the demands presented by the problem of securing the effective control of contemporary expenditure programmes. We need means of securing far more relevant information with which to correct current performance. Both government and Parliament have got to have better means of analysing what has been done in pursuance of policies authorised by them and of determining what corrective action needs to be taken to secure the best use of funds and improved performance in the public services. For these tasks the permanent instruments of financial scrutiny need to be greatly strengthened: it is unwise to rely too much on the new, fashionable device of external consultants.

At this stage we can come back to the relevance of these suggestions to parliamentary accountability. The basic problem must be seen as one of improving the state machinery: the Procedure Committee probably made the mistake, understandable in the circumstances, of approaching the issue too much in terms of how Members of Parliament should operate. But first the executive tools must be at hand, and then it will be practicable to do something about Parliament's role in the whole cycle of expenditure control. There is no reason why the House of Commons should not harness to its specific purposes such instruments of control as are developed within the framework of public administration. Indeed from the point of view of financial accountability to the House, there are marked advantages in relying on the services of a reformed public audit. New information, more critical and wider-ranging, would be made available as a basis for the analysis of performance, while the elements of judicial and impartial scrutiny on the present system could be preserved as much in the executive task of audit as in the treatment of the results by select committees.[18]

4. *Concluding Remarks on the Future of Financial Account-ability to Parliament*

If anything like the model outlined in the preceding section were to be adopted, it becomes possible to envisage a modified committee pattern in the House of Commons and a strengthening and modernisation of accountability procedures there. The reports of the new audit unit would still be presented to the House, and probably jointly to the Treasury too. They would clearly specialise both in different aspects of audit and in different areas of spending. There would still be reports similar to those now made to the Public Accounts Committee by the C. & A.G. and requiring further investigation of the kind now carried out by the P.A.C. There would be others ranging more widely over matters relevant to efficient management and administration which could be the basis for inquiries similar in many respects to those which the Estimates Committee now seeks, often without adequate supporting material, to carry out. Then there would be the results of efficiency audit in the nationalised sector: on present arrangements the Nationalised Industries Committee would be the recipient of these reports and the parliamentary investigating body. Whether three separate committees would be retained would be a matter for judgement in the light of how the system worked. Perhaps one can look forward to a time when the main committees – of accounts, of current and prospective expenditure and of the nationalised indus-tries – would collectively constitute a Control of Public Expenditure Committee, operating in three main divisions.[12]

The greater concentration on scrutinising performance and efficiency in the use of financial resources which is envisaged here need not mean that the responsible select committee (or committees) would be debarred from pursuing those more general and discursive inquiries into the condition of different parts of the government machine such as the Estimates and Nationalised Industries Committees often undertake now. There would still be a place for this. But in the light of the suggestions just made it seems doubtful whether there would be so much of a case for more experiments with committees of general administrative scrutiny such as those recently set up. Clearly it is difficult to define the functions of such committees, to introduce coherence into their work, to guarantee their permanence, and above all to give them a satisfactory basis for isolating the problems they need to investigate. Indeed, given the political restraint which the British parliamentary system inevitably imposes on select committees of the House, it is hard to decide what issues can effectively be raised which do not in some way arise out of the scrutiny of expenditure. For this reason alone this rubric offers plenty of scope.

Obviously these suggestions are no more than a sketch. Their feasibility depends on the readiness of Members of Parliament to think critically about their various controlling functions, to decide where it is worth putting the emphasis and what are the chances of doing an effective job. Just as much it depends on developments within the machinery of administration, on whether instruments can be created which will guarantee a wider species of financial accountability which the state itself needs as a tool of management, but which can equally be harnessed to the broader political requirements of the House of Commons. That these ideas remain broadly within the traditional view of accountability as concerned with judging past performance will be obvious. But to do otherwise within the pervasive framework of the conventions of the British political system is to run the risk of making no step forward at all. At any rate the development of accountability processes in the direction just outlined would offer the prospect of edging forward towards a greater capacity on the part of the House of Commons to influence current decisions on expenditure by weighing in more authoritatively with the lessons to be drawn from the analysis of past performance than is at present practicable.

Notes

1. An example of the signs of change in this approach is provided by some passages in the *First Report of the Select Committee on Procedure, 1968–69 (HC* 410), The Scrutiny of Public Expenditure and Administration. See also below for further comments.

2. The best historical survey of the P.A.C. is to be found in *The Control of Public Expenditure,* by B. Chubb (Oxford, 1952). See also *The Accountability and Audit of Governments,* by E. L. Normanton (Manchester University Press, 1966) *passim.*

3. Exchequer and Audit Acts, 1866 and 1921.

4. Memorandom by the Chairman of the P.A.C., *HC* 410 (1968–9) p. 85.

5. *Civil Appropriation Accounts 1966–67* (reports of the Comptroller and Auditor General, *HC* 51) para. 1.

6. *Second Special Report of the Public Accounts Committee, 1966–7 (HC* 290) app. 1, para. 19. (My italics.)

7. The only strict parallel is now the new Parliamentary Commissioner for Administration, who also serves a select committee.

8. It is interesting, however, that the Ferranti revelations prompted the government of the day to pre-empt the P.A.C.'s own investigations by setting up an independent inquiry. A desire to keep the P.A.C. from straying into policy issues may have played a part here.

9. For a detailed consideration of the work of the Estimates Committee after 1945, see N. Johnson, *Parliament and Administration: The Estimates Committee 1945–65* (Allen & Unwin, 1967).

10. See, for example, *Nationalised Industry and Public Ownership,* by W. A. Robinson (Allen & Unwin, 1960) and, from a different angle, *The Accountability and Audit of Governments,* by Normanton.

11. *First Report of the Nationalised Industries Committee*

1967–68 (HC 351–1), 'Ministerial Control of the Nationalised Industries'.

12. Since writing this the Committee on Agriculture has been wound up: Committees on Scottish Affairs and Overseas Aid have succeeded it.

13. See, for example, the *Report on the Nuclear Reactor Programme* 1967–68, and the *Special Report 1966–67 (HC 351)*.

14. France offers the clearest example of autonomous state accountability; Western Germany of a mixture of the state model with responsibility to Parliament. The Bundestag adds little, however, to the state audit.

15. This implication of the argument about accountable management is admitted in para. 281 of the *Fulton Report on the Civil Service*: the pill is sweetened by references to a 'purposive association' of Parliament with the civil service, whatever that may mean.

16. *Public Expenditure: A New Presentation* (Cmnd 4017).

17. An analogy may be drawn with the President of the Federal Court of Accounts in Western Germany, who has the additional title of Commissioner for Efficiency in Administration.

18. These ideas owe much to the stimulus provided by Mr Normanton's work on government audit (see n. 2 above), and Professor W. J. M. Mackenzie's introduction to that work. I gratefully acknowledge this.

19. The Select Committee on Procedure does not go this far. It envisages close links between a new Expenditure Committee on the one hand, and the P.A.C. and C. & A.G. on the other. But no eventual merging is proposed.

14 Public Accountability and Audit: A Reconnaissance

E. Leslie Normanton

To reconnoitre, says a dictionary, is to make a survey with a view to future operations. This paper accordingly aims to review the basic institutional framework of public accountability and audit as it exists in the United Kingdom, with a view to suggesting very tentatively what could be changed in the future.[1] The paper also advances a number of hypotheses about the functions of accountability and audit in government and, to borrow the technologists' phrase, 'the present state of the art'. The aspiration is to explore, rather than to prescribe. Nevertheless, the paper has, within limits, a philosophy of its own.

The Meanings of the Word 'Accountability'

The word 'accountability' is one of those terms employed in governmental studies which suffer from frequent use and imprecise or varying meaning. Our first need is to establish what is intended by it in the present study.

In its most general sense, accountability of course means a liability to reveal, to explain and to justify what one does; how one discharges responsibilities, financial or other, whose several origins may be political, constitutional, hierarchical or contractual. It is in the practical applications of this broad meaning that imprecision creeps in. In the sense that a man is accountable to his superiors in a hierarchy the word presents few problems; they are the sovereign judges of how he shall render account. The accountability of contractors to the government services whose orders they accept is a part of their contracts, and thus a subject for negotiation. But *public*

311

accountability, working outside the hierarchies and within a complex pattern of constitutional government, is very much more difficult to measure and define.

Accountability is a device as old as civilised government itself; it is indispensable to regimes of every kind. It provides the post-mortem of action, the test of obedience and judgement, the moment of truth; it can validate the power of command, or it can create favourable conditions for individual responsibility and initiative. Officials in dictatorial and absolutist states are frequently even more strictly accountable than those in Western-type states with a separation of powers.[2] But they are naturally accountable within a disciplinary structure, and ultimately to the head of state; the pattern of their accountability is essentially simple – it is that of a servant to his lord. Such hierarchical accountability usually operates in secret.

The Meaning of Public Accountability

Public accountability is a phenomenon chiefly associated with the Western-type states. It calls for openly declared facts and open debate of them by laymen and their elected representatives. It is grounded in a widely held feeling that tax-paying citizens have rights as well as duties, if not in a full doctrine of popular sovereignty over finance, such as was proclaimed during the French Revolution.

Public accountability is also a device for the support of that legislative power over taxation and the appropriation of revenues which was the historical source of parliamentary influence over policy and administration. In the nineteenth century ambitious legislatures pioneered in public accountability with a view to establishing there control over governmental activities. To a limited extent they even succeeded.

But public accountability is capable of much more: it is, actually or potentially, a rich and open source of knowledge about how government services function in actual practice, and hence of ideas about how they ought to function. It casts a spotlight upon institutions which are shy of the public's gaze, but whose qualities and imperfections have a steady cumulative impact upon our daily lives.

The question now arises: What constitutes genuine public accountability? For the power relationship between the departments and agencies who are held accountable and the legislatures to whom they account is a subtle and indirect one. There is no clear master–servant relationship; public accountability means reporting to persons other than one's own superiors who have the power to make open criticisms. Like democratic government itself, it is a tricky, if immensely worthwhile operation.

Public accountability is in fact often highly defective even in the more advanced and experienced countries, to say nothing of the others, and this paper is concerned with how and why.

Balance between Accountability and Autonomy

In the first place there is the matter of balance. The degree to which administrators of all kinds should be answerable for their actions is a matter of opinion. Each country must strike its own balance of public accountability, to provide the safeguards which contemporary thought considers necessary without impairing the fulfilment of their appointed functions by the accountable bodies. There is no natural or permanent point of balance: the factors which control the choice are constantly changing, and the choice itself should therefore be revised from time to time. If this is not done, the balance will inevitably become distorted with the years. Moreover, the point of balance will vary with the type of accountable organisation; a government contractor will not be answerable for the same things as a government department, and the position of a state enterprise is different again. It is particularly difficult to find a balance of accountability for local government authorities, which in theory have only a local allegiance. The nature, skill and operational strength of the bodies to whom account is rendered are also variable elements in the balance.

The view taken in the present paper is that in Britain the balance of accountability has in varying degrees become lost; it needs readjustment where it touches the central departments, and fundamental reassessment elsewhere. There is too much independence (which means in effect the power to work in secrecy) in the case of the nationalised industries and the local authorities, both of whom have become enormous spenders of taxation without its counterpart in public accountability. It seems possible that the reverse might be the case in the United States, at least in the case of some contractors for specialised services; this paper is not qualified to judge. But in Britain the situation is manifest: the imbalance is on the side of too little accountability rather than too much.

What It Means To Be Accountable

When public bodies are here described as accountable or non-accountable a precise meaning is implied.

It is not accountability merely to submit a certified financial account each year. To be accountable means to give reasons for and explanations of actions taken; but an account rarely provides explanations and it never gives reasons. It does not as a rule even contain much information about what has been done; it is not a sufficient record of policy and transactions. Any major financial account hides far more than it reveals. It is a protection against fraud, and the law provides that it may not conceal criminal sins; but other kinds of sins may be lost without trace within it.

Financial accounts must therefore be accompanied by explanations; but a report by the responsible officials does not by itself constitute accountability, even though that report may be the subject of discussion and questioning by a parliamentary committee. This is because the report, being the work of persons concerned to justify themselves, cannot be impartial. Anyone who has ever observed the drafting of such a document knows that a principal concern is to present matters in the best possible light, and there is no breach of trust implied by so doing. It is, moreover, impossible for even the heads to know absolutely everything about what goes on within large organisations; they may have doubts and suspicions about, for example, overstaffing or the misuse of investment funds, but it would call for costly research and perhaps cause internal tensions, to uncover and present the

314

full stories. There would seem to be very little incentive for them to make any public disclosure. The authors of annual reports may thus choose their subjects and avoid questions which have caused them difficulties and embarrassments – although it is often precisely these issues which should be the concern of public accountability.

Thus the cause and agenda of debate on an annual report may be set by its writers. It is the very essence of accountability, however, that this initiative must be held by the questioners. They therefore need an independent source of information, to ensure that no vital problem remains unmentioned or uninvestigated. Only when all the facts are thus made accessible can we hope to reach a balance of public accountability.

The Role of Audit in Public Accountability

The Key to the difference between random questioning and effective accountability for administrators is thus to be found in the existence of an independent and therefore impartial fact-finding body or bodies, with statutory power of access to administrative and financial records which are closed to private individuals. This explains the unique significance of the public auditing institutions. The details of official activity are hidden in a dense undergrowth of documentation, which the auditors alone are entitled to penetrate. Where even the public auditing bodies are excluded there is no public accountability: the difference is crucial.

If the auditors have access, however, and if their skills are sufficient, they should be able to provide facts and insights of value not only to Parliaments and governments but also to the heads of the organisations examined. This, in any event, is the only basis for an accountability which both derives its information from original sources and is impartial.

A theme of this paper must therefore be those auditing and fact-finding services which constitute the back-room strength of public accountability – the men who have been on the spot and seen for themselves. How are they organised? Do they co-operate with one another? Is their coverage sufficiently comprehensive? Is their daily work geared to modern requirements? Or are these professional critics of administration themselves open to criticism?

Before we survey the field, it may help us to understand how the duties of politicians and state auditors should dovetail if we classify accountability into *four experimental subject-categories*. We shall find that the scope for audit examinations is much wider than it used to be. These categories, which look to a specifically British situation, are:

Ministerial subjects
Administrative and financial subjects
Organisational subjects
Economic subjects.

Ministerial subjects

This category would embrace the questions within a department which, *as a matter of normal routine*, are submitted to the minister and personally decided by him; issues related to general policy are the obvious cases. It would also include the minister's external relationships, for example with other ministers, with Parliament and with public and private enterprises.

There would be plenty of room for debate about fringe matters, but it should be feasible for a department to produce at least a minimum list of subjects to be considered as the unquestioned field of the minister's own political responsibility at Westminster. It would be a notable landmark in British constitutional and administrative history if ministers were able to tell Parliament: 'I will answer any questions upon subjects within this list, because I am closely in touch with them myself. I can, of course, obtain information for you about other subjects, but I am not normally familiar with them, and there is no reason why my department should not be accountable for them otherwise than in this House – indeed it might be better so.'

Since many ministerial subjects are commonly featured by press and radio, the problem of fact-finding is not always very acute; a Member who reads the papers regularly may be able to ask searching questions without further aid.

These form the very large residue of regular departmental business after the ministerial subjects have been extracted. Such matters may be referred to ministers in exceptional cases, but in the normal run of business they are outside his personal cognisance – in large departments often far outside. The range of topics is wide and of great financial importance. It includes questions of detail consequent upon ministerial decisions.

From the point of view of accountability, the difficulty is that these are not subjects which often get into the news. The issues of importance have to be found by searching within the departmental records.

The Public Accounts Committee of the House of Commons has worked successfully in this field for a century, but the efforts of Parliament in recent decades to extend its coverage, have not, by and large, been fruitful. It could be argued that this is material which Parliament, by its nature, is ill-equipped to marshal and comprehend. The volume is too great, and most of the decisions are non-political in character. Even the Public Accounts Committee's achievement has depended upon the constant guidance of the Comptroller and Auditor General and his staff. An adequate surveillance over such a large area of activity, must, for practical reasons, be full-time and professional. It is the true domain of the state auditor.

In 1866, when the Exchequer and Audit Departments Act which created the office of the C. & A.G. was enacted, almost all government spending passed through the central departments, and the Act thus established something like a comprehensive system of accountability and audit, working through the ingenious mechanism of the P.A.C.; a balance had been struck. But since World War II the share of government spending effected through the agency of organisations outside the central departments – notably the nationalised industries and the local authorities – has grown and is growing very rapidly. The system of 1866 did not provide for such organisations, and they have no place within it. The fact that great new subjects for accountability were being created has been sensed but not acted upon. Direct accountability

317

through ministers was considered inappropriate to these bodies outside the established departments, but no new alternative to the familiar system was developed, as it might have been. There was no innovation, and, in particular, the nationalised industries were created without effective public accountability.[3]

This paper will not argue that Parliament is unfitted to act in the field of administrative and financial subjects; the case of the P.A.C. would immediately invalidate such an argument. But it does maintain that there is no *political* necessity for Parliament to be solely responsible. This is a field where more could be done in an extra-parliamentary way. And if Parliament will not, or cannot, further equip itself with outside help as it did in 1866, then it should allow others to share the responsibility. Even if Parliament did so, there is no reason why ministers should not continue to deal with Parliamentary Questions or other exceptional cases arising from administrative and financial subjects, just as they do now.[4]

Organisational and economic subjects

The third and fourth subject-categories suggested by this paper look rather to the future than to the present. They jointly comprise, together with studies of day-to-day business problems, the sphere of the 'efficiency' auditor.

His concern with organisational subjects signifies accountability for the efficient use of manpower, equipment, buildings or other assets provided out of taxation for the conduct of the public services. These are the overhead expenses of government and administration.

In Britain this subject is the responsibility of Organisation and Methods staffs within the larger ministries and the Civil Service Department, which, at least until recently, have not published reports of their findings. Indeed their internal and subordinate status would seem to render independent reporting very difficult. The student therefore finds that there is no corpus of information based upon impartial studies of the internal structure and functioning of the public services, although corresponding information is available in France, Germany and the United States.[5] There is at present no public accountability for organisational matters in Britain. In

318

1960 the former Comptroller and Auditor General implied during a lecture that he wished there were.[6]

Accountability for economic subjects implies the use of public audit to serve the requirements of economists, whose ultimate concern is the efficient use of resources as a whole, of which money is only one. This kind of accountability was pioneered in Communist countries, where for many years the auditors have verified whether state enterprises fulfilled their production norms under the general economic Plan; they have also collected information upon which future norms may be based.

In Britain there have recently been signs that economists would be glad of more information about economic decision-making, for example the pricing and investment appraisal methods of the nationalised industries.[7]

That auditors can help them may be a new discovery on the part of economists, and some time will be needed for experimentation on both sides. But this is probably something which will develop.

The Utility of Public Accountability

This paper accepts the premise that public accountability is basically a healthy thing. It obliges politicians, officials and managements to engage openly in a dialogue which calls into question what they are doing, and sometimes the assumptions upon which that activity is founded. This stands in opposition to the 'closed' tradition of administration, within which decisions are taken secretly within a small group which alone enjoys access to documents and records, and can thus select what information will be revealed and what withheld.

It may well be impossible to demonstrate with evidence whether the open or the closed system is more effective in practice; the closed system by definition permits nobody to search for evidence. The present paper is, however, persuaded that small closed groups are less and less likely to be self-sufficient and forceful in an increasingly complex modern world. It does not believe that there is any necessary connection between secrecy and efficiency. It suspects, on the contrary, that secrecy frequently blankets and even protects

319

maladministration, overcharging and inertia.

There is also an ethical factor. Public accountability can provide a kind of harmony between power and responsibility. This is not merely a matter of exposure to criticism; administration may indeed be good and merit no criticism, but it should also be publicly seen to be good.

On the practical level the objective should be to provide a mechanism which brings problems to notice and permits them to be studied comparatively. We ought perhaps to think of public accountability rather less as a critical process and increasingly as a therapeutic one. It should also provide a forum for administrative ideas.

Accountability and the Delegation of Powers

There is a further important consideration. Accountability can play a constructive role in government. This derives from the fact that if one has access to full details of the affairs of any institution one can the more safely delegate wide responsibilities to it. At a time when there are many demands for greater delegation this is a factor of real significance.

There are two ways of relating a sovereign source of power to authorities on lower levels. One is by the issue of detailed orders about everything. The other is by giving the lesser authorities wide discretion to act within the scope of their duties, and holding them accountable *a posteriori*; thus affording them the opportunity to prove themselves worthy of their responsibilities.

The two methods can be combined or used separately. The Plantagenet kings ruled almost entirely through the accountability of their provincial representatives the sheriffs, as Bishop Fitz Nigel's 'Dialogue of the Exchequer' of 1179[8] clearly shows. This can be a more flexible and less burdensome way of co-ordinating administration with government than by the issue of multifarious commands from the centre. It allows greater independence at subordinate levels, and is by way of a guarantee rather than a system of remote control. *A posteriori* accountability may indeed furnish the best solution to the problem of reconciling independence with good administration.

The principle of 'accountable management' in business and administration, as advocated for the public services by the Fulton Committee,[9] is based upon a comparable objective, the wider distribution of power to make decisions.

The application of accountability to local government and state enterprises, not merely for its own sake but as a political expedient to reconcile decentralisation with coherent government, is a subject to which we shall return.

Principles

This paper therefore takes its stand upon the principle that all kinds of public bodies which draw substantial finance from taxation should be held publicly accountable, in the sense that this means an obligation to open their books and records to qualified persons, in some way representing state and tax-payer, and this at regular intervals. The obligation should always be statutory; one does not ask sportsmen whether they will accept the presence of a referee – the need is taken for granted and built into the rules. As a practical reform, this might be achieved quite simply, by means of a new law granting to the chosen fact-finding body, or its chief officer, the power to investigate all matters related to the collection, expenditure or use of public monies.[10] This would obviate the formidable task of amending all the individual statutes of the organisations to be held accountable.

The paper also holds the view that a proper and modern public accountability should cover all or most of the subject-categories of accountability described above. These form a spectrum of interrelated activities and ideas. It is not sufficient to cover only one or two of them and leave the remaining subjects to chance.

Political Accountability

When considered on the basis of our subject-classification, the accountability of ministers to Parliament may appear to be comparatively satisfactory. When disquiet is expressed about the doctrine of ministerial responsibility, it is often because that doctrine only encompasses with great difficulty matters which are proper to subject-categories other than the ministerial. If we insist that political accountability in Parliament must comprise everything, in accordance with classical constitutional theory, matters may sometimes appear to be out of hand. But if we accept a limited category of subjects within the personal control of ministers (with the possibility of raising others in special cases), it may seem that the doctrine still applies to good effect.

The Select Committee on Nationalised Industries is proving to be a useful instrument of political accountability. The subject-matter of its reports falls largely into the ministerial category, and the impression is sometimes given that the Committee is holding the responsible ministers accountable, rather than the nationalised boards. This may indeed be an intention. It is normal that a committee of the House of Commons should concentrate upon the political relationships, and should understand them best.

The accountability of ministers is not a principal theme of this paper, which will henceforward concentrate upon the non-ministerial subject-categories. Within these, we can now identify some national needs.

Needs: (a) *The Central Departments*

The ministries and other central departments are more fully accountable for administrative and financial matters than any other spenders of public money.

But accountability for organisational subject-matters, as we have seen, scarcely yet touches the ministries with the spur of publicity. O. & M. studies remain confidential, and the Fulton Report finds that 'the work of departmental O. & M. divisions in promoting efficiency is at present often inadequate'.[11] It may therefore be suggested that at least some of the best O. & M. staffs should be placed in a position wholly independent of the executive, and thus free to publish critical reports.

The movement in favour of accountable management may gradually create widespread needs for further efficiency studies, concerned with both organisational and economic subjects, through the checking of performance against costs or other criteria. If the movement is to result in the 'hiving off' of entire activities from civil service departments to autonomous public boards or corporations,[12] it will be particularly important to find a pattern of state audit which will stimulate efficiency while ensuring that the term accountable management really means what it says. These also will be tasks suitable for specialists independent of the executive and able to publish their conclusions.

Needs: (b) The Nationalised Industries

The problem of accountability for the nationalised industries is a study in conflicting motives. The basic question still remains unresolved: namely, whether nationalised enterprises should be genuinely accountable to the public and its representatives at all. Unresolved at least in Britain; in comparable countries elsewhere the decision has long been in favour of accountability. The Select Committee appears to share these doubts to the full.

The truth is perhaps that no British government has insisted upon full public accountability because of a justifiable apprehension that published information about the corporations would be exploited to provide political arguments for and against their very existence. Secrecy thus became an element of political tactics, and paradoxically this was especially so for the parties which had always favoured nationalisation as a means of securing public accountability for powerful managements.

The nationalised boards themselves were no doubt conscious of the same political hazards. There is also a strong tradition of secrecy in private business; in the words of two students of management:

> Privacy is certainly the keynote of British business characters; any invasion of it is intensely resented and instantly attacked as injurious to the national interest.[13]

Against this background the somewhat ambivalent views of

the Select Committee on Nationalised Industries on the subject of public accountability may more easily be comprehended. The Committee said a good deal about this in its
recent report on ministerial control.

On the one hand, the Committee stressed the great size of
the interests involved. The assets of the industries were
valued at £10,500 million, and in 1966–7 their fixed investment was at the rate of some £1500 million a year, over half
of which was financed from the Exchequer. The interest of
the tax-payer was also emphasised: 'A decline of only 1 per
cent in the earning power of these industries as a whole
would mean an increase of £90 million to be provided by the
Exchequer – approximately equal to 6*d* on the standard rate
of income tax.'[14] The Committee also quoted an admission
by the Treasury that the average quality of people appointed
to boards had not been high enough.[15]

These facts alone would seem to provide a case for public
accountability, and the Committee expressed itself in agreement. It appreciated 'the importance of public accountability
and the desire for efficiency, especially when large sums of
public money are involved . . .'[16] It believed 'that as well as a
system of economic obligations and financial objectives, some
system of external efficiency studies may also be needed,
otherwise public accountability cannot be secured'.[17]

The report as a whole, however, makes it clear that in practice the Committee was thinking in terms of a special investigation into economic subjects only. For the rest, the
existing form of audit, by private professional accountants, on
the same lines as the audit of commercial firms under the
Company Acts, would have to suffice:

> Apart from the normal commercial audit, the industries
> should not be accountable in detail, and on a regular basis,
> to any body, Parliamentary, Ministerial or in some manner
> independent, for their day-to-day efficiency and their de-
> tailed managerial decisions.

Yet the Committee was 'not complacent about the standards
of efficiency of the nationalised industries', and it confided
that 'private audit comment would be a feeble restraint on
inefficiency'.[18]

324

The Committee rejected 'any form of efficiency audit that is primarily concerned with looking at the outturn of past decisions'. This despite the statement that 'Admittedly, to secure future efficiency means learning from the mistakes of the past.'[19] It must be confessed that the argumentation of the report on this particular subject is singularly unconvincing.

In Britain knowledge about how the great publicly owned enterprises actually operate thus remains very limited. This paper dissents from the Committee's apparent view that this is a desirable state of affairs.

Given the danger that political use would be made of audit findings, the expedient adopted by France in the face of a similar climate of opinion about nationalisation is of more than academic interest. The Commission de Vérification des Comptes des Entreprises Publiques, created in 1948, is an independent and non-political auditing body, closely associated with the Cour des Comptes, which places much emphasis upon questions of present and future managerial efficiency, as well as upon the outturn of past accounts. It publishes a general report, which avoids the most controversial issues; the Commission's reports upon matters which would embarrass managements or provide political ammunition if they became public are strictly confidential documents, issued only to the responsible ministers, to the Cour des Comptes, and also to the parliamentary finance commissions on request. Such security measures are realistic in the circumstances, and it may be that without them political passions over nationalisation would have prevented the establishment of any permanent machinery for state audit, as they did in the United Kingdom.

The examples of the French system and the audit of government corporations by the United States General Accounting Office were brought to the notice of the Select Committee on Nationalised Industries by Professor W. A. Robson.[20] The members considered the idea of making inquiries abroad but decided not to do so. The Committee thus did not fully examine the possibilities for state auditing of British public enterprises, and it might have done well to express an open mind on this question, which in any case was not central to its inquiries upon ministerial control.

The need which exists is expressed by Mr W. Thornhill, who advocates 'a Public Industries Audit Office, under the control of a Parliamentary Officer', which he considers to be 'a necessary complement to both the Select Committee and the professional auditors of the public corporations'.[21] This paper sympathises with this view but prefers a slightly different approach.

Needs: (c) Local Government

Beyond the nationalised industries lies the vast and almost unexplored territory of the local authorities. For reasons which now belong to history they have been treated as independent sovereign bodies for financial purposes, subject to their doing nothing illegal; the principal duty of the district auditors, appointed by the Minister of Housing and Local Government, is to disallow any expenditure not sanctioned by the law. The efficiency of local authority spending is not a subject upon which impartial audit findings are published. Whether the public receives good value for money under present arrangements is not known. The local government bodies are nominally accountable to their electorate, at least for revenues raised locally; but this accountability is liable to be construed in a narrow technical sense.

The recent tendency, moreover, has been for more and more central government spending to be delegated to local levels, at which in the 1960s expenditures have risen more than twice as fast as those of the central government.[22] Meanwhile a former Town Clerk of Bognor Regis, Paul Smith, has alleged that local authorities in general, 'lack any proper public scrutiny, overall financial, administrative or efficiency control', and are prone to very serious waste and mismanagement.[23] And yet local authorities complain of excessively close government control.

This contradiction can be explained. Local government is subject to detailed direction from several ministries in technical matters, but is exempt from public accountability except of the most formal kind. At the same time, according to Professor Birch, many local authorities are secretive about their activities, and as a result only a small minority of citizens have any knowledge of what they are doing.[24] If the books and records of local government were opened to a public efficiency audit, able to compare and report on findings from the whole country, not only would much more become known about their activities and expenditures but it might be possible for the detailed ministerial direction to be diminished.

Coming reforms of local government may be in the direction of stronger regional units and greater delegation of responsibilities from Whitehall.[25] If so the government and Parliament might in effect say to the new regional authorities: 'If you want central direction reduced to a minimum you must reassure us by accepting full public accountability. This is not to enforce decisions made in London; we are willing that you should take your own decisions, even upon expenditures, but we must have access to information about your efficiency. The tax-payers' and rate-payers' interest demands no less.'

This paper therefore directs attention to the utility of genuine public accountability for local authorities, irrespective of the sources of their separate revenues.[26] Their value-for-money problems could be assessed and tackled on an adequate scale, and a relaxation of central direction would be less of a hazardous adventure. Accountability is one of the forces which will enable local administrative independence to assert itself without destroying all unity in the state.

Having surveyed the needs we can now review the institutional resources to meet them.

The Established Auditing Bodies

The Exchequer and Audit Departments Act of 1866 created the office of Comptroller and Auditor General and charged him to certify and report upon the public accounts and to ensure that expenditures were authorised by Parliament and supported by the Treasury. This role was regulatory in conception, but in recent years it has, with the encouragement of the Public Accounts Committee, but without any reform of statute, been broadened into a search for cases of waste and extravagance. The reports of the C. & A.G. and the P.A.C.

are by far the best regular source we have for the assessment and study of waste.

However, a large and increasing proportion of public spending now escapes from direct Treasury control, and with it the scrutiny of the C. & A.G. (the two have normally been applied together, but no doubt they could also work separately). After a prolonged campaign by the P.A.C., the C. & A.G. has gained access to the books and records of the universities. But he appears to be losing control of the Post Office to the Select Committee on Nationalised Industries.[27]

The C. & A.G.'s staff in the Exchequer and Audit Department comprises some 500 persons, of whom the auditing personnel are of civil service executive class status.

The district auditors are officials employed by the central government, who trace their origins back to the Poor Law Amendment Act of 1834. They had in 1967 an audit and supporting staff of 587 for England and Wales. The auditors are equal in official status to those of the E. & A. Department. We are told that their advisory functions are increasingly important to local authorities, but they are not a constitutional source of information about the broad problems of local government spending. It must also be noted that only 11 out of 82 county boroughs and 105 out of 270 non-county boroughs make use of their services at all.[28]

The 'Organisation and Methods' staffs of the Civil Service Department (formerly of the Treasury) and of the larger ministries, whose status is similar to those of the E. & A. Department and the District Audit, represent the legacy of a pioneering attempt, beginning during World War II, to tackle the problem of efficient utilisation of manpower. Much enthusiasm has been lavished upon O. & M., but from the point of view of public accountability it has the crucial defect of being an internal service of the executive, and thus responsible to the same department heads as the staffs whose structure and operations they have to criticise. The Fulton Committee finds that the staff employed upon O. & M. work lack expertise and 'have not the rank or authority to operate at higher levels'.[29]

Finally, some public expenditures are audited by private auditors, notably those of the nationalised corporations and of a number of boroughs and county boroughs. The private auditors aim to prevent fraud and ensure accounting correctness, as they are required to do in the case of commercial firms by the Company Acts. They also advise their clients when asked to do so. But they cannot contribute to public accountability, because they are not independent; subject to due fulfilment of their normal statutory duty, they are anxious to maintain the best possible relations with the bodies which pay their fees. Where public spending is subject only to this kind of audit, we obtain no published information about waste, nor indeed about anything, unless the auditing firm feels obliged to qualify its report, which happens very seldom.

Recent Government Inquiries into Finance and Administration

In the last few years there has been an exceptionally keen search for knowledge about British administrative institutions, reminiscent of the epoch of the Benthamite reformers. In addition to the royal and other commissions entrusted with major special inquiries (which are not our direct concern here), governments and others have appointed a variety of investigators to report on financial and administrative matters of the moment. The following are some examples.

In 1963, the Minister of Aviation commissioned a private professional accountant, Mr Corbett, to inquire into the financial affairs of B.O.A.C., whose management was then under a cloud. The well-known American management consultancy firm, McKinsey & Co., has been engaged to investigate the Post Office, British Railways and the Bank of England. All these are now within the sphere of the Select Committee on Nationalised Industries; so also is the Independent Television Authority. In a parliamentary share-out of public bodies in 1967, responsibility for examining the B.B.C. and the Industrial Reorganisation Corporation fell to the Estimates Committee. The new Select Committee on Science and Technology reported in November 1967 on the controversial nuclear power generating programme.

In the summer of 1968 the government announced the appointment of a panel of businessmen and industrialists,

329

headed by a former Lord Mayor of London, Sir Robert Bellinger, to search for possible manpower savings in the civil service. At the same time a chartered accountant, John Mallabar, chairman of Harland & Wolff, was invited to examine the efficiency of government industrial establishments, which are mainly the royal dockyards and ordnance factories. A newly created division within the Management Services Group of the Civil Service Department is to undertake a major study of management services throughout the civil service, and a working party in the same department is considering the scope for 'hiving off' work from the ministries to outside agencies.[30]

Above all, the last three years have witnessed the energetic and well-publicised activities of that strange prodigy, the National Board for Prices and Incomes. This is not, of course, a public auditing body as the term is normally understood, but a product of crisis in the national economy, intended, as its Chairman says, 'to intercede on behalf of the consumer at the wage-bargaining table and in the boardroom where prices are fixed'. Yet it has played a fact-finding role at some otherwise inaccessible points in both the private sector and the nationalised industries, helping to alleviate what Mr Aubrey Jones called 'the poverty of our knowledge of what is actually going on in our economy'.[31]

If we take the view that the national economy stands or falls as a single unit, there is no reason why the private sector should not be to some extent accountable as well as the public sector (the average performance of private enterprise since 1945 has scarcely been such as to prove any assertion of inherent superiority). There is a new national thirst for hidden economic facts; the Bow Group has even advocated public accountability for the royal family.

Nevertheless, the essential function of the N.B.P.I. is political rather than administrative, and a government heavily committed to free-market doctrines might well put an end to it (Mr Powell has said he would do so, and Mr Macleod later agreed). The Board nevertheless hopes to survive. The intention of the Labour-government is to combine it with the Monopolies Commission. It has been able to attract a staff of specialists, including accountants, statisticians, industrial consultants and economists (the total complement had risen by

1968 to some 220), and it also uses outside consultants.

A variety of organisations, established and *ad hoc*, is now associated with the business of public accountability; some, like the Exchequer and Audit Department, by deliberate intention embodied in the law; and some, like the N.B.P.I., more or less by accident. With the exception of the C. & A.G.'s work with the P.A.C., they all operate in relative isolation: there is no common store of information and experience. Each is attached to its own duties and procedures, and the sum of their efforts still leaves large gaps in the national pattern of accountability; as we have noted, very extensive areas of our public finances remain uncharted. The overall picture is of a patchwork, unplanned since 1866. Replanning would be a principal task for a Royal Commission on Public Accountability.

Parliamentary Committees

Could replanning be founded upon the expedient, which has some influential advocates, of creating more parliamentary committees?

To some extent the answer depends upon their methods of inquiry. There are two means of access to information. One is by questioning the heads of the public bodies concerned. This is the method of the newer parliamentary committees. The other is on-the-spot investigation by qualified auditors, basing themselves upon the original records, financial and other, and supplementing the written sources by discussion at all levels – not only with the heads.

Unless it obtains inside information by employing its own investigating staff (in which respect the P.A.C. remains unique) a parliamentary committee is at a disadvantage. It can be a centre for debate about known problems, but not a source of disclosure about unknown ones. Persons held accountable should never be in a position to dictate which aspects of their business will be examined, but a select committee without an investigating staff is not equipped to hold the initiative in this respect.

Moreover, whereas state audit is a frequent control, the occasional committee inquiry into the affairs of a nationalised corporation or other public body is usually followed by immunity from investigation for many years.

It must in fact be doubted whether an extension of the committee system would solve our problem. This is not merely because the committees lack inside information, but because in some ways they are not ideal bodies for the task. Professor Nevil Johnson found from his experience of the Estimates Committee that most M.P.s were reluctant to specialise and to brief themselves in detail. He attributed this to British overestimation of the capacity of the lay critic, 'especially when he is faced with the complexities of contemporary government'.[32] To this observation may be added the point made by Mr Tam Dalyell, in reply to the idea that Parliament should, as he put it, 'go American' and set up more committees, namely that many M.P.s are not really in a position to be uninhibited critics:

> Unlike Congress, the House of Commons is not only a legislature with power to criticise the Executive ... it is also the pool of talent from which 90 per cent of the Executives are drawn. No aspiring British politician in his senses would dream of treating his own party Minister with the fruitful irreverence that is commonplace in Congress.[33]

And, in addition to these drawbacks, an innovator in the parliamentary committee field may be faced with back-bench manpower shortages. The example of the Select Committee on Nationalised Industries suggests that if all these difficulties are overcome and a new committee is founded, the membership will show a flair principally for the sort of subjects which we have classified as ministerial. Without a C. & A.G. to guide them, the headway which they will make within the other subject-categories may be modest.

Perhaps Parliament still has the capacity to do a little more than it already does, and one of the most practical things which it might do would be to establish a Committee on Regional and Local Government, able to inquire about the enormous public expenditures incurred locally. But the consensus of experienced Westminsterologists seems to be that in present conditions Parliament is unlikely to do very much more. In the short term, therefore, the objective should be to equip the existing committees with fact-finding resources adequate for the modern job of investigation which confronts them.

A Rationalisation of the Auditing Forces

The emphasis of change in the field of public accountability must accordingly be upon the audit.

It is necessary to keep an open mind on the question of how to effect this; partly because it is not clear how far existing organisations would be willing and able to fit into a new scheme. Partly also because there are unsolved technical problems: for example, how much effort should be devoted to 'efficiency' or 'management' audits, and how much to the more familiar checks of 'regularity'?[34] Should an efficiency audit be based upon the annual accounts or given a free-ranging mission? What sorts of staff should be employed, and how, from the highest level downwards, should they be chosen? Should the basic approach be that of professional accountants (as in the United States), of lawyers (as in Germany), of elite generalist officials (as in France), or should it derive from some new blend of disciplines and outlook? Should an audit operate with teams and task forces, or, like the Exchequer and Audit Department, through groups permanently attached to the accountable bodies? These sort of options bring one back to the need for a royal commission; those whose careers are involved would in any case be likely to demand a hearing.

Upon a few points, however, a measure of certitude is permissible. Firstly, in the field of public audit, as in so many others, unity is strength. Dispersal of effort among many separate auditing and investigating bodies means also a dispersal of knowledge and skills. The comparison of institutions and procedures is essential to progressive thinking about administration, but it must be a comparison over a sufficiently wide range. An audit department confined to the examination of a small sector, composed of official or commercial units all more or less alike, would be bound to suffer the atrophy of its comparative faculty. There is a strong advantage in having as comprehensive an audit service as possible, accumulating a unified stock of ability and experience, and using it in accordance with a coherent working plan. A unified audit with a planned and co-ordinated programme would also give a better return in terms of its own operating costs; fragmentation is wasteful of money as well as effort.

Constitutional Relationships

It is even more important that the audit should be independent. For the state auditor independence is a tool of work.

This implies, first and foremost, independence of the executive. The suggestions which are sometimes made that efficiency auditing should be confided solely to the personnel of ministries and departments do not seem to take account of administrative realities. An internal auditor is a most useful functionary, but if he tries to go beyond a circumscribed role and raises fundamental questions of principle he may well find that his superiors and colleagues resent his intervention without adopting his suggestions. An external state auditor is in a far stronger position; he has no divided loyalties and no fear of career influences, and he may be able to exert some pressure through publicity, in order to secure attention to his observations. Accountability of the executive to a unit of the executive would in any case be a contradiction in terms. All this does not mean that state audit cannot perform services for the executive – on the contrary, there is wide scope for it to do so, although on a basis of co-operation rather than subordination. What such services might be is discussed in the concluding section of this paper.

Relations with the legislature offer a freer choice. An audit body can, like the Exchequer and Audit Department, serve a single parliamentary committee; it can, like the U.S. General Accounting Office, be officially 'a part of the legislative branch of the government', with allegiance to the whole of the Congress rather than to any particular element within it. Or it can, like the French Cour des Comptes, operate in the no-man's-land between the executive and the legislature, belonging to neither and claiming responsibility only to 'the Nation'.

Each of these choices is instructive. The century-old

alliance between the C. & A.G. and the P.A.C. (indeed the presence of the Treasury entitles us to speak of a triple alliance) has been a classic of administrative precision. It has rendered great service to the executive, as well as to Parliament. On the other hand, the fact that so successful an idea has not been copied, even by other committees of the same House of Commons, is significant; nobody has been sure that Gladstonian financial discipline would be suitable for new institutions.

The French Cour des Comptes has had to get into the habit of working in total constitutional independence; counting from the foundation of the Cour in 1807, France is now living under its ninth different constitution. Neither governments nor parliaments have enjoyed stability and continuity, and the Cour has preferred to steer a course between them. This isolation may be splendid, but it is scarcely an ideal situation from which to give effect to audit findings. The reports of the Cour des Comptes receive a good coverage in the press, but nobody is officially charged to give the recommendations which they contain a hearing and to feed them into the machinery of state. So they often go unheeded – or so the Cour itself complains.[35]

The General Accounting Office, on the other hand, is in very close association with the American legislature. It serves both Houses of Congress and all congressional committees and individual Members who seek its help. This service is something quite beyond European experience. In 1968 the G.A.O. not only issued 157 reports to the Congress and 231 to committees and individual Members but it supplied 120 staff members to assist the committees. On 33 occasions G.A.O. representatives testified before committees, and 356 reports on pending legislation were furnished at the request of the chairmen. In 1967 the G.A.O. recommended new legislation in 31 cases; where appropriate, it submitted its own drafts of bills to Congress. It maintains an Office of Legislative Liaison, in continuous contact with staff of the committees, and 'available at any time to give personal attention to the requests of Members'. The G.A.O. evidently takes its legislative role very seriously, and it enjoys budgetary independence from the executive, drawing its operating funds directly from Congress.

For its part, the legislature also takes the G.A.O. more and more seriously, and has begun to embody specific instructions to it in legislation. Amendments to the Economic Opportunity Act in 1967 charged the G.A.O. to inquire into the efficiency of the programmes of the Office of Economic Opportunity, which was set up to administer the so-called War on Poverty. There have been many allegations of errors and abuses, and the General Accounting Office is currently issuing a series of reports which aim to establish the cold facts.

Despite its legislative affiliation, the G.A.O. co-operates with agencies of the executive in various ways: it advises upon financial management, accounting systems, automatic data processing, internal auditing and, since 1967, the so-called planning-programming-budgeting (P.P.B.) system. In the fiscal year 1968, it issued 765 audit reports to departments and agencies, in addition to the 388 sent to Congress and its committees. The reports to Congress are, however, the most important, and the emphasis of the G.A.O.'s audit work is very much upon service to the legislature.

In 1946 the G.A.O. employed no less than 14,904 persons, who were said to have 'simple clerical skills and a familiarity with regulations'. At that time the Office was just beginning to audit U.S. federal enterprises under the terms of the Government Corporation Control Act of 1945, and this made a new recruitment policy essential. By 30 June 1968 the staff had fallen to 4310, but these included 2593 professional employees, the great majority of whom had specialised in accounting; the policy is now to recruit 'recently qualified students of very high quality'. The disadvantages of over-specialisation have begun to be realised: in the year ended on 30 June 1968, in addition to the usual contingent of accountancy students, the G.A.O. also recruited three 'management interns', eleven management analysts, one engineer, nine mathematicians, six economists and two statisticians.[36]

We can bear some of these facts in mind while imagining an institutional solution for Britain. It cannot be one of subordination to the executive. It would avoid the isolation of the Cour des Comptes. It could not have the close legislative involvement of the G.A.O., because Parliament shows no signs of wishing it. Between these constitutional extremes we must try to visualise something appropriate to the national

336

needs: we shall find that a middle road has real practical advantages.

An Idealised Solution

Let us then suppose the creation of a collegiate Council for Administrative Efficiency, under the chairmanship of the Comptroller and Auditor General, bringing together at the Council table state audit findings concerning the central departments (and their hived-off agencies), the nationalised industries and the local authorities, together with O. & M.-type reports from an efficiency auditing service external to the executive.[37] This considerable flow of information would be examined and edited by the Council, for transmission by the C. & A.G. to four parliamentary committees, three of which already exist. The P.A.C. would continue to be the principal of these addressees. The C. & A.G. would also report to the ministers responsible for the nationalised industries and for local government. Everything possible would be published, but the French view that much concerning the nationalised industries must remain confidential could be accepted.

The executive, including the Prime Minister's Office, would have its own representatives at the Council table to select whatever they needed from the information available, and to ask for other matters to be taken up by the auditors as required. Similarly, ministers, M.P.s, parliamentary committees and the House of Commons itself would be free to invite the C. & A.G. to initiate special audit studies through the Council.

The debating strength of the Council would be reinforced by the presence of consultants on the subjects under discussion, such as management specialists, economists, scientists or lawyers. The Council would have a permanent member representing a Research Unit for Public Expenditure Studies, to whom very difficult problems brought to notice by the auditors could be referred for consideration in depth by the Unit: such matters might, for example, be the application of new budgeting and accounting techniques, problems of profitability in state enterprises, contract pricing questions or the control of capital investments.[38]

The Council would have no powers of direction, except over its auditors 'in the field'; its functions would be to investigate, to inform, to criticise and to recommend. Its situation is expressly designed to bring together in the closest contact the suppliers and the users of information about public expenditures and revenue, and about the efficiency or otherwise of management in the official and commercial agencies of the state and the regions. The Council would be an Intelligence Staff for the public services. It would combine independence of status and debate with a strategic position in the communications system of government: that position would be the basis and the guarantee of an active and constructive role. The guiding principle throughout is that public accountability should not only provide administrative safeguards but should, by improving the flow and the quality of information, make an important contribution to the efficient conduct of government. Accountability can and should be *useful*.

The Council would draw strength from the fact that it was largely created out of existing institutions and familiar relationships, and conceived to meet specific needs; it would not be an alien graft upon the constitutional tree. It would aim to inform Parliament comprehensively and expeditiously, and to provide at least some of the special facilities which the G.A.O. makes available to Members of Congress. The C. & A.G. would, as now, personally maintain the contacts between the audit on the one hand and political powers and persons on the other, but over a much wider range of subjects. All reports to Parliament and its membership, including reports to ministers, would be presented by him, and he would receive their requests for information or investigations. Parliamentary committees might, when confronted with difficult questions, invite the C. & A.G. to detach specialist staff to assist them. In all this, the apprehensions of M.P.s about changes in the machinery of public accountability, which have been expressed in the paper by David Howell have been borne in mind.

The Council would also aim to provide services for the executive, in its role as the directing and managing branch of the constitution. The most massive service would be the general one of gathering together and presenting, in the presence of the representatives of the executive at the Council's table, information about administrative efficiency which is not at present available: from studies of an O. & M. type, from the nationalised industries, from local authorities and from hived-off agencies. Some sort of overall impression of the actual working – or malfunctioning – of the entire machine of the public services might eventually be obtainable.

In addition, the Council would perform individual tasks of investigation at the request of its members from the executive) – although only by consent of the whole Council. It would refuse any request which it considered either impracticable or improper to its constitutional role. It would also have full control of its own working methods, its operating budget and its staffing and recruitment policies.

Subject to these guarantees of independence, the Council could undertake a wide variety of *ad hoc* inquiries and efficiency auditing missions for the information of the executive. It could, for example, give an opinion upon departmental estimates or requests for increases of personnel. It could examine costs or overheads wherever anomalies should appear. It could report on overspending of estimates for scientific research, building programmes and other costly activities. It might comment upon pricing policies, accounting procedures or the employment of grants to local authorities. A Prime Minister interested in administrative reform could make use of the Council to investigate the management implications of his proposals.

The special value to the executive of such services would be that which anyone hopes to obtain when he seeks the views of a consultant: namely an expert opinion, but above all an impartial one, detached from the influences of responsibility and consequence which those directly involved cannot overlook. The independent assessment may also be valued as a corrective to the views of the participant. If Britain is ever to have a central efficiency audit of the highest quality, it must be independent if it is to report its findings freely; but it would be wasteful of both money and skill to create such a service and then deny the executive all contact with it. This paper believes rather that the contacts should become accepted as a matter of normal routine, and the permanent representation of the executive on the Council is proposed with this in mind. Fortunately there is an old tradition of service to the executive by British state auditors: the Exchequer and Audit Department has for many years carried out control functions on behalf of the Treasury, even though functions of a very different kind from those envisaged above.

From the point of view of those held accountable, the Council would not represent an additional form of centralised direction. Indeed, it might for many authorities largely replace that. The audit would no longer place stress upon the enforcement of central decisions and regulations, since many public bodies might have begun to make their own. Its inquiries would be empirical, and criticism might be reserved for activities so wasteful or so inefficient as to damage the interests of the community. The efficiency auditors could advise managements as well as question them.

It is at least possible that these changes could be effected with no greater number of state auditors than the total at present employed in the various separate auditing and investigating bodies. They might be self-supporting in terms of savings effected, even without equalling the General Accounting Office, which lists specific cash recoveries and 'measurable savings' exceeding a billion dollars during the five years which ended on 30 June 1968, compared with operating costs of $238 million. But most of the benefits which could accrue from an organisation such as this paper has imagined would be indirect and incapable of any cash assessment.

The basic idea behind public accountability as it was developed in the nineteenth century was probably that of keeping officials in their place, by means of a meticulous financial discipline – and thereby limiting the powers of government and keeping down taxation. It was, in truth, an essentially negative intention.

The need of the present derives from the vastly increased complexity and cost of modern government. It might be described as a positive form of public accountability, aiming to assess and improve the working of the manifold organisations which now depend upon national and local revenues, and thus help to tone up the administrative machine as a whole and reduce wasteful expenditure.

To adapt the constitutional arrangements and the institutions of the nineteenth century in response to the needs of the late twentieth, to accept a new purpose without entirely abandoning the old one: these are operations of undoubted difficulty. While admiring the efforts which several countries have made in recent decades, this paper is not convinced that any one of them has yet fully succeeded. It has not, therefore, chosen one single country as its exemplar, but has rather borrowed selectively from each and attempted to advance a little further than any.

Notes

1. Although the fundamental problems of accountability in government are universal (*how* shall holders of political and administrative office be held accountable, and *to what extent*?), this paper is compelled by its declared objective to discuss them in the context of British institutions and usages, which may not always be entirely meaningful to the non-British reader.

2. This paper does not always differentiate between 'parliamentary' and 'presidential' systems, provided that each includes a legislative body able to criticise the executive. It takes this fact to mean that there is *some* separation of powers; the fact that the separation is wider in some countries than others is not, in the immediate context, very important.

3. This is not the official view. In 1963, a statement was made in the House of Commons on behalf of the Chancellor of the Exchequer to the effect that the government were satisfied that existing arrangements provided sufficient accountability for the nationalised industries (*Hansard*, 2 April 1963. 'Oral Answers', col. 234). In 1969 a statement by the Labour government contained a similar declaration (note by Prof. W. A. Robson in the *Political Quarterly*, Oct.–Dec. 1969). This paper derives no comfort from these assurances, believing them to be at variance with the observable facts. The British corporations are unique in escaping any kind of constitutional control through audit.

4. In accepting the appointment of a Parliamentary Commissioner for Administration (Ombudsman) Parliament has

in fact already delegated some of its responsibility. The objective, however, is equity rather than efficiency in administration, and is not directly related to the subject-matter of this paper.

5. The U.S. General Accounting Office evidently regards organisational questions as within the scope of its normal auditing functions. The annual reports of the Comptroller General of the United States frequently mention them. In France and Germany special efficiency auditing units are responsible.

6. Sir Edmund Compton's actual words were, 'I realise that I may be asking for the impossible, but it is a pity that the spending Departments, or the Treasury on their behalf, cannot find some way of regularly reporting the year's operations in the field of O. & M. and staff control, with positive indications, where these can be measured, of the year's gains in economy and efficiency' (lecture to the Institute of Municipal Treasurers and Accountants on 'Control of Public Expenditure', 15 June 1960). An O. & M. report on the civil service has in fact recently been published (*The Times*, 26 Aug. 1969).

7. See the *First Report of the Select Committee on Nationalised Industries, 1967–68,* 'Ministerial Control of the Nationalised Industries', vol. 1 (*HC* 371–I), which places great emphasis upon such questions, and upon ensuring that the managements use the latest assessment techniques (for example, paras 157, 192 and 726). See also the criticism of the Committee's approach by Professor W. A. Robson in *Political Quarterly*, Jan–Mar 1969.

8. Dialogus de Scaccario, ed. Charles Johnson (Nelson, London, 1950).

9. *Report of the Fulton Committee, 1966–68* (Cmnd 3638), 'The Civil Service', vol. 1, ch. 5.

10. A similar result was achieved in France by the Law of 4 April 1941, which declared that all public *comptables* (receiving and paying officers for public funds) were subject to the jurisdiction of the Cour des Comptes, which in consequence claims the role of 'common-law judge of public funds'. An exception of any kind must be established by legislation.

11. *Report of the Fulton Committee, 1966–68,* para. 164.

12. Ibid., paras 188–91.

13. Roy Lewis and Rosemary Stewart, *The Managers* (Mentor Books, New York, 1961) p. 29.

14. *HC* 371–I, paras 6 and 7.

15. Ibid., para. 292.

16. Ibid., para. 789.

17. Ibid., para. 156.

18. Ibid., paras 782–3.

19. Ibid., paras 785 and 787.

20. Ibid., vol. 2, pp. 535–6.

21. W. Thornhill, *The Nationalised Industries: An Introduction* (Nelson, London, 1968) p. 188.

22. According to the report of the Royal Commission on Local Government in England (the Maud Report, Cmnd 4039), local authorities' expenditure has recently been growing three times as fast as the whole income of the country. Over half of their spending is of grants from the central government, and the proportion is rising. This tendency, says the report, 'is not a healthy one ... they are spending money which they do not raise and do not have to account for to their electors'.

23. *The Times Business News*, 17 Jan. 1968.

24. A. H. Birch, *The British System of Government* (Allen & Unwin, London, 1967) p. 242.

25. The Maud Report recommends that England be divided into sixty-one local government areas, grouped into eight provinces, each with a provincial council. See also J. P. Mackintosh, *The Devolution of Power* (Penguin Books, London, 1968).

26. A need for improved accountability for federal grants-in-aid to state and local governments is currently being felt in the United States. (Elmer B. Staats, 'The Growing Importance of the Accountant to Better Management of Public Affairs in the United States', pp. 23–4).

27. The new Post Office Corporation will no doubt be in the same situation as the older nationalised industries. The minister with general responsibility for the Corporation will 'appoint the auditors', i.e. presumably private professional auditors (Thornhill, *The Nationalised Industries*, pp. 165–74). The C. & A.G.'s reports on the Post Office have sometimes contained very interesting information about the price-fixing

practices of certain major suppliers of P.O. equipment. Such activities will presumably henceforward escape from publicity.

The Chairman of the Post Office Corporation, Lord Hall, has been quoted as saying, 'I regard the corporation as a large business of which every citizen is a shareholder. The shareholders' committee is a highly critical Parliament which will study our reports each year. Therefore we must make each report as clear and frank as we can...' (*The Times*, 3 Oct. 1969). This is a laudable intention, but this paper reiterates that self-criticism is never wholly impartial and cannot on its own form the basis of proper accountability.

28. David Regan, 'Auditing Local Government', in *New Society*, 7 Dec. 1967. Also J. A. G. Griffith, *Central Departments and Local Authorities* (Allen & Unwin, London, 1966) pp. 58–9.

29. Cmnd 3638, vol. 1, para. 164.

30. *The Times*, 25 Feb. and 23 May 1969.

31. Rt. Hon. Aubrey Jones, 'The National Board for Prices and Incomes', in *Political Quarterly*, April–June 1968.

32. Nevil Johnson, *Parliament and Administration: The Estimates Committee, 1945–65* (Allen & Unwin, London, 1966) p. 169.

33. Tam Dalyell, M.P., 'Making Parliament Work', in *New Statesman*, 23 Aug. 1968.

34. The Comptroller General of the United States states: 'Along with the growth of internal auditing staffs in the operating agencies ... there has been an accompanying decline in the more traditional financial audit by the G.A.O. This type of audit now represents a relatively small portion of our activity... we have placed more and more emphasis upon what is usually described as management audits...' (Staats, 'The Growing Importance of the Accountant to Better Management of Public Affairs in the United States', p. 11.)

35. The Cour des Comptes is far from being alone in making such a complaint. How to make the maximum use of state audit findings is one of the most difficult problems in public accountability – a reflection which has much influenced the concluding suggestions in this paper.

36. Comptroller General of the United States, Annual Reports, 1967 and 1968, *passim*.

37. A membership and operating plan of the suggested Council forms the Annex to this paper (see following pages). The title of the Council is suggested because it implies a broad general function. Similarly the title of Audit Counsellor for the permanent members of the Council on the audit side is suggested in order to denote an advisory duty, based upon practical experience of state auditing problems, in addition to one of liaison. (Consideration might be given to the award of irremovable status to these senior representatives of the auditing force, in order to reinforce their personal independence: such status is granted in both France and Germany.)

38. For the concept of a Public Expenditures Research Unit, see E. L. Normanton, 'In Search of Value for Public Money', in *Political Quarterly*, April–June 1968.

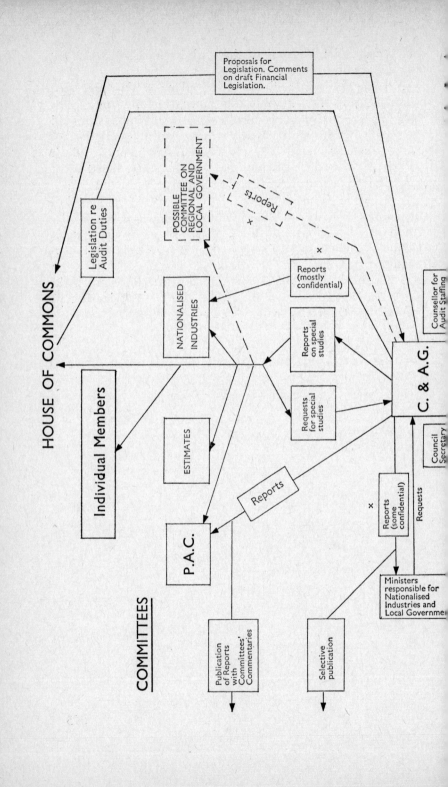

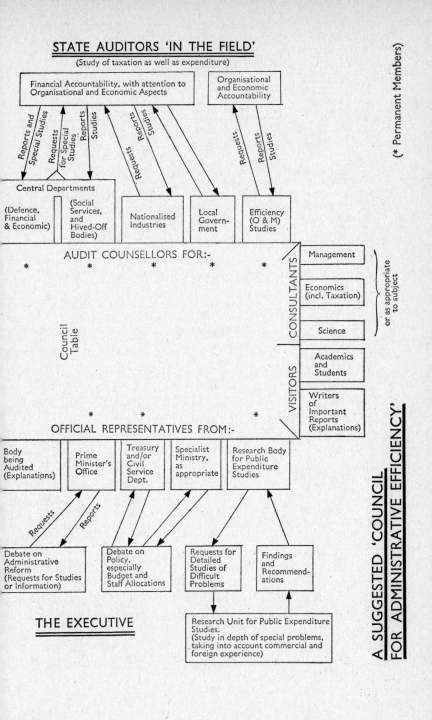

STATE AUDITORS 'IN THE FIELD'

(Study of taxation as well as expenditure)

Financial Accountability, with attention to Organisational and Economic Aspects

Organisational and Economic Accountability

(* Permanent Members)

Reports and Special Studies

Requests for Special Studies

Reports

Studies

Requests

Reports

Studies

Requests

Reports

Studies

Central Departments

(Defence, Financial & Economic)

(Social Services, and Hived-Off Bodies)

Nationalised Industries

Local Government

Efficiency (O & M) Studies

AUDIT COUNSELLORS FOR:-

*   *   *   *   *

CONSULTANTS

Management

Economics (incl. Taxation)

Science

or as appropriate to subject

Council Table

VISITORS

Academics and Students

Writers of Important Reports (Explanations)

*   *   *

OFFICIAL REPRESENTATIVES FROM:-

Body being Audited (Explanations)

Prime Minister's Office

Treasury and/or Civil Service Dept.

Specialist Ministry, as appropriate

Research Body for Public Expenditure Studies

Requests

Reports

Debate on Administrative Reform (Requests for Studies or Information)

Debate on Policy, especially Budget and Staff Allocations

Requests for Detailed Studies of Difficult Problems

Findings and Recommendations

THE EXECUTIVE

Research Unit for Public Expenditure Studies. (Study in depth of special problems, taking into account commercial and foreign experience)

A SUGGESTED 'COUNCIL FOR ADMINISTRATIVE EFFICIENCY'

15 Exchange of Letters

Don K. Price, Elmer B. Staats

Editors' Introduction

In April 1962 the President of the United States transmitted to the Congress a report entitled 'Government Contracting for Research and Development'. The report contained recommendations on a number of issues relating to the use of outside contractors by government departments – for example, the use of the 'fee' or management allowance provided to non-profit contractors, the ownership of physical facilities acquired under government contract, and the proposed creation of a new class of Government Institutes which would have some of the attributes of the independent contractor while presumably being more directly accountable to the government. These ideas have remained the subject of continuing controversy. In early 1969, the General Accounting Office issued a report to the Congress calling for improved guidelines in contracting for research with government-sponsored non-profit contractors. The exchange of letters reprinted here concerned the 1969 report of the General Accounting Office. We include this thoughtful exchange with the kind permission of the writers, both participants in the Carnegie accountability project, because the letters explore a critical dimension in the relationship between government and the contractor: the nature of the administrative independence required for the contractor to make a creative contribution to the public end sought. Don K. Price, Dean of the John F. Kennedy School of Government, Harvard University, argues forcefully that the principal value of independent organisations is their independence. It seems inconsistent for the government to seek the services of an independent organisation, and then to find something improper in the contractual relationships that make the degree of independence possible. Comptroller General Elmer B.

346

Staats rejoins that the 'fee' or management allowance has not in fact been used for the purposes originally intended, and that the conditions which initially justified the fee no longer obtain. Clearer guidelines on the rationale and the use of the management fee, in his view, are in order. Both men agree that a thorough review of the subject would be highly useful.

Letter from Don K. Price to Elmer B. Staats

26 February 1969

Dear Elmer

Many thanks for your thoughtfulness in sending me a copy of your report to the Congress on government-sponsored non-profit contractors.

I am glad to give you my reactions for whatever they are worth.

In case you may wish to let some of your associates read this letter, I will start by stating what you already know: I am a trustee of the Rand Corporation. I note this point not mainly because I think it puts me in any conflict of interest, but because it may explain my rather special point of view on this problem. I do not think my attitude about these organisations is any different now from what it was when, as a staff member of the Ford Foundation, and of its original study group that planned its basic programme, I had something to do with the Foundation's grants to help both Rand and the Institute for Defence Analyses get their programmes under way. If I have a bias it is caused by my desire to see institutions succeed that I once had a hand in putting money into, rather than from any benefit that I may be getting personally from my present association. That, of course, I freely acknowledge, may be the most dangerous kind of bias, as I am always warning students who have semi-Marxist theoretical inclinations.

I have no question about the main purpose of your report: I think that systematic study of this whole range of institutions would be very desirable.

On the other hand, I hope that such a study will not accept what seem to me the clear assumptions of this particular report.

347

The first such assumption is that all these animals are essentially alike, and ought to be treated alike. The term 'government-sponsored non-profit contractors' covers a tremendous variety of institutional purposes. I think that variety in the terms of the contracts should be taken as *ipso facto* desirable, rather than the contrary.

Second, I see no reason to single out not-for-profit corporations, by contrast with profit-making corporations, for special treatment. If the government can get a particular type of job done without paying fees, with equally good results, I do not think it should pay fees at all. On the other hand if the payment of fees will contribute to the accomplishment of the purpose, I see no reason why a not-for-profit corporation should not receive the fee just because its directors are willing to work for a public purpose without benefit of profits and stock options. Quite obviously the great bulk of government contracting is going to go to profit-making corporations, and they do not want much competition from not-for-profits. I not only concede but would affirm the wisdom of not pushing the creation of too many not-for-profit corporations, but I would not for a moment agree with the principle that it is in some sense immoral for a corporation which is undertaking to accomplish a public purpose to earn a fee, and have the right to treat it as private property, just because it chooses not to pay dividends to stockholders. The contrary assumption seems to me to amount to a belief that our national defence and our military power exist for the purpose of making profits for stockholders, a belief which I hear expressed all too often these days and do not wish to share.

Third, if it is in the interest of the government, for certain specific purposes, to turn over what is normally a government function to a not-for-profit corporation, for the principal reason that this arrangement makes it easier to permit a degree of independence that is not easy to attain in normal government operations, it seems to me the height of absurdity to turn around and say that the specific contractual arrangements which make that degree of independence possible are improper. If the independence is not needed, the government should not make use of the contracting device at all; if it is needed, it seems to me quite wrong to chip away, out of motives of book-keeping uniformity, at the contractual provisions which give a measure of reality to the concept of independence.

If there is to be an inquiry with respect to the contracting device, which would seem to me highly desirable, I think it would be a great mistake to study it from the point of view of the contracting officer's seeking to reduce fees, rather than from an overall administrative – indeed, almost constitutional – point of view, seeking to find out what types of modern functions that are essential to the purposes of government ought to be carried out under what types of contracting arrangements. My own view is that the Air Force for very special reasons may have overdone this type of arrangement. But I would be more inclined to look critically at, for example, a contract with a major airline to administer a missile base (a contract on which I assume full profit-making fees are paid) than to worry about the fees paid to a research organisation. We have been so worried about government moving bureaucracy into the realms of private enterprise that we have not paid any attention to the dangers caused by government taking governmental functions like national defence and turning over important pieces of them to private institutions. On the whole I think this has been a desirable development; I have devoted major parts of a couple of books to defending it. But it is in detail certainly open to reconsideration.

But I do not think that reconsideration ought to be based on an approach which treats all functions alike, or which discriminates between profit-making and non-profit contractors, or which assumes that uniformity in contractual provisions is desirable. I think that such consideration should be in the hands of people who start from a concern for the nature of the function, and the nature of our constitutional, political and economic system, and not from the point of view of a contracting officer or an accountant – I do not underrate, I trust, the functions and importance of both types of officers, but I do think that their professional skills are not precisely relevant to the problem.

Finally, a word about the notion of the government research institutes, the idea which Harold Seidman put into the Bell Report. I think this idea a very useful one because it helps to bring out the nature of the problem. The problem is that for certain types of purposes our normal system of administrative organisation and procedures presents a great handicap to the successful conduct of the business. The government-sponsored non-profit contractors were all created, I suppose, to help make up for these deficiencies. If instead of setting them up as private corporations they could have been set up as government agencies, and then given by special legislative enactment, administrative delegation and settled tradition the same degree of independence and the same types of privileges that have been conceded to the corporations, of course they would have been just as good. But the notion that it would be possible to do the job this way seems to me to be politically unrealistic – and to be getting more unrealistic every day. The experience over the years of the government corporations, which were set up with the purpose of giving them special types of operating independence and which generally found themselves reduced to status not very different from the regular bureaus, seems to me a case in point. The existence of the state university shows that it is not absolutely impossible to create, within the framework of government, institutions with quite separate types of administrative tenure and operating privileges, but that example shows too how hard it is, how dependent on the existence of a private institution of comparable function to provide a procedural standard for imitation, and how fragile it is under political pressure.

Many thanks again for sending me a copy of the report; you can judge my interest in the subject by the length and contentiousness of this letter.

With all best wishes,

Yours ever
[signed] Don K. Price

Letter from Elmer B. Staats to Don K. Price
8 March 1969

Dear Don
I do indeed appreciate your thoughtful letter of 26 February, in connection with our report on non-profit organisations. I hope that you will be at the Ditchley Park Conference, which will give us a chance to talk about it further.

But, in case we do not have that opportunity, let me make three or four points which I believe might clarify my thinking at least on the subject and why we undertook the study.

First, let me emphasise that I believe you and the Ford Foundation rendered a real service in getting organisations such as Rand and IDA off the ground. They filled a real void at that time, and I believe that the Defence Department certainly has benefited from having an able and prestigious organisation to focus on key issues.

Incidentally, I should say that I did not initiate the 1962 study, although I had the primary responsibility for conducting it. It grew out of the widespread unhappiness and feeling in the executive branch that conditions had changed since the time when these organisations had been created, that their relationships to the government were unclear, and that they tended to draw off financial support and personnel from the executive branch agencies. This was particularly true in the field of physical and natural science although by no means limited to that field.

I hope that we made a contribution in the 1962 report, although I must say that we did not really have the time or the staff to do the kind of job that we should have, given the importance of the subject. And we decided – I think wisely at the time – to operate on a consensus basis rather than issuing the usual Bureau of the Budget type report.

Second, I would certainly agree that there are great variations and differences among the government-sponsored not-for-profit organisations just as there are among the non-government-sponsored not-for-profit organisations. Incidentally, we use the word 'government-sponsored' to differentiate these organisations from the not-for-profit organisations which operate without the direct tie which these organisations have. It is the same terminology which we followed in the 1962 report.

Third, you seem to feel that we have some reservation about paying a fee. I thought we had made our point clear in the report, but apparently we did not. A fee is usually paid, however, in the commercial market to compensate for the element of risk and competition involved. It is also a return on capital. This obtains for not-for-profit organisations as well as profit-making organisations.

We were making essentially two points in connection with the subject of fees: the first and the simplest one is that the guidelines established in the 1962 report have not been applied, and someone should either see that they are applied or should change them. The second and more important point is that the fee was justified primarily in the 1962 study as the vital point to assure the independence about which you speak in your letter. The facts are that the fee has not been used in any substantial way for this purpose and indeed there is evidence that some government in-house organisations may have at least equal if not more freedom than the government-sponsored non-profit organisations. I recognise that this is a subjective point in part, but I believe that you would get a lot of testimony from people both in and out of government to support this point. I certainly want to dispel any notion that we are interested in a 'book-keeping uniformity' and would agree with you that the study which we suggest should be at least as broad as the 1962 review and I would hope done better than we were able to do at that time.

The whole subject of government–non-government relationships is a highly complex and confused one, to say the least. As a current example, we have been tossed the thorny issue of cost-sharing and overhead allowances on research grants and contracts growing out of Senator Mansfield's efforts to put in a statutory limitation last year. Some agencies have been using the grant device; other agencies have been using the contract device. Obviously there should not be cost-sharing on government contracts, but where is the line to be drawn between the two? Lincoln Gordon is chairing an *ad hoc* committee of the American Council on Education on the subject, and we have been discussing with him whether it might be feasible to develop some general criteria as to when the contract device should be used as against the grant device.

Conceptually there can be a very great difference in the event that Congress wants to establish a policy on cost-sharing, as it appears to be in the mood to do. (Incidentally, Richard Leahy of Harvard University is on the Gordon Committee.) Personally, I have serious reservations on any blanket policy on cost-sharing, a principle which was born in part from policy established by private foundations and in part from the fact that there has been great competition among universities for limited research dollars.

To sum up what I have been trying to say, we need a lot of clarification in many phases of government relationships with non-government organisations in carrying out government-financed programmes. The increasing complexity of research and development, together with the increasing size of private institutions, underscores this point. Nearly 90 per cent of all defence procurement last year was negotiated, and more than 50 per cent was with single source suppliers. This whole subject of relationships has given rise to the proposal of Congressman Chet Holifield to establish a Hoover-type commission on government procurement. This would be a long-range study which would look at the whole range of government programmes in procuring goods and services for its use – patent policy included.

I really haven't tried to outdo you on the length of our letters, but I do believe that there has been very radical change over the past ten to fifteen years in the capability of the private sector – profit and non-profit (including universities) – as contrasted with the situation existing when most of the sponsored organisations were established. And I think likewise there has been drastic improvement in the capability of the government to perform certain of these services in-house – budgets have improved, salaries are higher, etc. What I am really pleading for is that we ought to recognise that times do change and we ought not to accept existing arrangements simply because they were established in response to an earlier need. I know from our many conversations on this subject that you share in this basic idea.

Best wishes.

Sincerely
[signed] Elmer B. Staats

Letter from Don K. Price to Elmer B. Staats

11 March 1969

Dear Elmer

Many thanks for your letter of 8 March. I feel much less guilty about having written you such a long letter now that you evened the score.

Obviously we have no fundamental disagreement. I strongly support your view that we need to clarify the whole picture of government relations with non-government organisations – here I would think it even more important to include the profit-making as well as the non-profit institutions.

I wish I could be at the Ditchley meeting but the dates for it were set, by bad luck, to coincide with the Godkin Lectures here for which I have the primary responsibility.

I hope we have another chance to chat about problems like this some time soon.

Yours ever
[signed] Don K. Price

15 Accountability, Independence and Management Science

D. C. Hague

The current fashion in the United Kingdom is to stress the benefits which organisations of all kinds can obtain from applying modern management thinking and the techniques associated with it. In this paper, I shall use the term 'management science' to cover all examples of the application of logical thinking to managerial problems, both economic and organisational. However, I shall use my expertise as an economist as an excuse for spending most of my time on economic issues. The aim of the paper is to discover whether recent developments in management science – which have been impressive – have made the problems of how to combine accountability with independence in quasi-non-governmental organisations easier to solve over recent years. Do the recent advances in management science mean that we are now in a better position to solve the problems of accountability – which of themselves become more complex with bigger organisations and with rapidly advancing technology? Or are we simply struggling still with the age-old, frustrating and never-ending problem of how to ensure that those to whom activities are devolved in a democratic society are able to operate responsibly and to accomplish difficult tasks well? This paper tries to give a tentative answer to these questions by looking at problems of accountability and independence in two kinds of institution. Both of these are in the public sector of the British economy, namely, the nationalised industries and the universities.

1. *Some General Problems of Accountability*

I should like to begin by emphasising the similarities between problems of accountability and independence in public and in private organisations. It seems to me that these problems arise in all relationships between employer and employee, superior and subordinate, in all organisations. Anyone who performs any activity for any organisation meets them. How can the organisation ensure that the job done is the job required? That is the problem of accountability. How can the person doing the job be given sufficient discretion to feel that his job is worth while? That is the problem of independence.

To be sure, there will be cases where there is little independence. A manual worker doing a routine job will rarely be able to decide how to do the job or even (say, on an assembly line) how fast to do it. With other jobs – even manual ones – there will be more room for choice of the method and/or pace of work. If proof of this were needed, it exists in the enormous literature on how to devise wage payment systems that, put in our terms, will induce the employee to use his freedom of choice to work at the speed the employer wants. Independence is given only to be partly taken away again. With managerial jobs, greater independence is given. This is partly because the manager is more likely to want it than the worker, but also because the nature of the job is such that he will work better if more independence is given.

The size of the organisation comes in too. Provided he is prepared to risk the consequences of denying independence to his subordinates, anyone running a small organisation can make them directly accountable to him and tell them in detail what they are to do. Once the organisation grows, this is no longer possible. Those in charge of parts of the organisation must be given tasks to perform and be held accountable for the way they are carried out. The need to make subordinates accountable therefore arises in any large organisation – large either in terms of numbers of employees or of geographically dispersed activities. A complex product is likely to cause very similar problems, particularly if people with certain skills have to be trusted to use their professional expertise efficiently in carrying out particular operations. The large organisation, or the organisation making a complex product, can operate efficiently only if its chief executive delegates most of its activities to managers who are then made accountable to him. The need to have a system of account-ability is the price a firm pays for the benefits of operating on a large scale.

The problem of devising a good system for ensuring accountability is especially great where no money value can be attributed to a product – because it is not sold on the market. However, even where products do have money values, the biggest problem of accountability within the firm is still that of finding an acceptable measure of performance. A measure which allows a department to maximise its con-tribution to profit is clearly preferable to one requiring it to minimise costs, since those in the department will then feel they have some autonomy. They are not simply instructed to produce a given output at minimum cost. However, even if a department is producing a commodity or service with a market price, it is not often easy to divide that price between it and the other departments that contribute to making the product. Yet only thus can one calculate the 'contribution' each of them is making to the firm's total profit. With func-tional departments like finance, market research or per-sonnel, such a calculation is usually impossible, because one cannot 'price' the activities of such departments.

It follows that the cost–benefit problems that arise in the public sector because products and services often do not have a market value differ less from the problems of private in-dustry than is frequently supposed. It may well be easier for a city to calculate the benefit given to the community by a 'free' road than for a private firm to calculate the benefit that it derives from one, or indeed all, of its specialist depart-ments. Nor may it be easy for individual production depart-ments to calculate their 'contribution' to the firm's profit. It is true that the firm should not have much difficulty in calculating its overall profitability or productivity, but that does not help it in evaluating the performance of individual managers or departments. I do not deny that the problems of calculating the benefits given by products that have no market value are met with more frequently in the public than in the private sector. It is probably true, also, that there is more conflict and controversy, and more need to balance conflicting values, in public-sector organisations. But, at the very least, the fact that they do face similar problems means

357

that both public and private organisations have a great deal to learn from each other about the way in which problems of accountability and independence can be solved.

The other factor which makes accountability difficult in both public and private institutions is, of course, that management is often taking decisions whose success or failure does not become evident for months or years. All of these decisions are in effect investment decisions, whether they are concerned with expenditure on fixed capital, on research and development or on marketing. To judge decisions soon after they are taken would be impossible, whether it is expected profit or expected benefit which would have to be calculated. To wait until a decision can be fairly judged may mean that those who took that decision are no longer in the same department – or even the same organisation. It may also mean that a series of bad decisions cannot be broken at an early stage by removing those who make them.

This discussion is intended not so much to show the difficulties of providing accountability. The aim is to emphasise that similar problems of accountability arise in both commercial and non-profit organisations, in both the public and private sectors. Indeed, whether one is concerned with the public or private sector, we have seen that accountability is easier to arrange if one is dealing with a firm which sells its output on the open market, and where it is the performance of the firm as a whole which is being judged. These conditions are fulfilled when one is evaluating the performance of a British nationalised industry.

2. Accountability in the Nationalised Industries

I therefore turn now to the problem of accountability in the nationalised industries. Like all who are interested in this subject, my task has been greatly eased by a recent publication of the Select Committee on Nationalised Industries.[1] I should like to express my debt to the Committee.

There are widely differing views about the way in which British nationalised industries should operate. At one extreme, what the Select Committee calls 'the more "Commercial" view'[2] emphasises the need for each industry to

358

pursue commercial objectives, to make profits or to keep down losses. At the other extreme, there are those who would argue that some, at least, of the nationalised industries should be considered as public services with, for example, public transport provided free to commuters in an effort to reduce the number of cars going into big towns. Between these extremes, one finds a variety of differing views, each advocating a different combination of commercial and public-service objectives.

There is a similarly wide range of views on the extent to which ministers should intervene in the detailed operation of individual industries. Those who hold the 'commercial view' argue that the minister should concern himself with few policy questions, and that each nationalised industry should be left to pursue certain 'commercial' objectives. The whole point of giving the nationalised industries commercial objectives to pursue is seen as being that they should then be freed to operate as independently as possible. At the other extreme, there are those who would like to see ministers concern themselves in great detail (as indeed some have) with the running of nationalised industries. The 'middle view' here was expressed by Lord Morrison of Lambeth, who argued that the attraction of the public corporation was that 'we can combine progressive modern business management with a proper degree of public accountability'.[3]

That we should be meeting at all is sufficient indication of the difficulty of ensuring 'a proper degree of public accountability'. In British nationalised industries, the inevitable and universal problems of accountability have been supplemented by others. Certainly, until 1961, when the Treasury clarified their financial obligations in the White Paper discussed below, the nationalised industries lacked clear criteria by which their managements were to be judged and there was an unwillingness or inability to leave what arrangements for control there were unchanged for sufficiently long to prove themselves. There was rarely, if ever, time for outsiders to judge the efficiency of management in nationalised industries or for managements themselves to settle down to manage. It is true that one can go too far on this. A business school teacher is always in danger of preferring clean, tidy, uncluttered administration to the disorder engendered even by

359

healthy political controversy. Even so, my own feeling is that British nationalised industries in the 1950s were faced by too much, not too little, change in the objectives they were asked to pursue and the administrative structures within which they worked.

One of the most important measures of efficiency in a nationalised industry must be its financial objective. At present, this is the rate of return it earns on capital employed. The Select Committee tells the story of how financial objectives have been used. The statutes which set up British nationalised industries simply required them at least to meet all revenue expenditures, including depreciation, interest, redemption of capital and the provision of reserves. They were simply expected to 'pay their way' and not to seek to make large and regular surpluses.[4] With no statutory definition of what were appropriate amounts for depreciation or transfers to reserves, and with no guidance on other aspects of economic policy, it is hardly surprising that doubts should have arisen over the financial performance that was required of the nationalised industries.

In 1961, the Treasury took the responsibility for setting such standards. In a White Paper,[5] it gave clear definitions of the correct levels for depreciation charges and for transfers to reserves, clarified the arrangements for reviews of investment programmes and for ministerial control, and indeed defined more clearly the whole range of economic and financial obligations of these industries. The White Paper also set a precise financial objective for each industry. This showed how much the industry would be expected to earn, in a five-year period, beyond paying its way. However, it did not go into the question of exactly how social objectives should be allowed for apart from accepting, for the first time, that industries should be compensated if the government asked them to undertake unprofitable activities.

The arrangements set out in the White Paper thus had the merit of giving a single, simple criterion by which the performance of any industry could be judged. The fact that the financial surpluses earned by nationalised industries increased after 1961 is prima facie evidence that the system worked. Certainly, if only one criterion is to be used, that of the rate of return on capital is the best there is. However, since 1961, criticism has concentrated more and more on the fact that a simple financial objective like this fails to give guidance on pricing and investment policy. As the Select Committee points out, 'experience has shown, particularly in monopolistic situations, that it is in these fields that Ministers have most felt the need to be involved, and hence it is here that most guidance, in the public interest, is probably required'.[6] One problem has been that industries could reach their financial targets by raising prices rather than by cutting costs. Another problem was that there was no strong incentive to link the prices of particular products or services to the identifiable costs of producing them.

With investment, an important criticism was that settling an overall rate of return on an industry's existing assets gave it no guidance on the return which it ought to be trying to obtain from new assets or on the cut-off rate of return below which no investment ought to be justified on commercial grounds. A further criticism was that the financial targets merely looked at the return obtained from the industry's investments during the five-year period for which a given financial objective had been set. An industry might therefore fail to invest in a worth-while project because this would contribute little to achieving the financial objective during a given five-year period. Or it might invest in a project which was not worth while over its whole life, simply because it would give a good return during these five years.

More generally, the problem of using the return to be earned from the overall assets of an industry during a five-year period as an indicator of efficiency is that this return is slow to reflect the results of new investment. Investment undertaken in any one year adds a relatively small proportion to the total assets of the industry. Even if the rate of return on the additional assets created during any year is too low, it may be several years before this has a clearly discernible effect on the financial performance of the industry.

In 1967, a new White Paper[7] concentrated on setting out the correct criteria for pricing and investment decisions and took the view that if these led to good pricing and investment policies, then the right economic results would be achieved and the desired financial objective would follow from them. 'Financial results should be an expression of economic

N

policies and not an end in themselves.'[8] It is too early to know what results this new policy will have. Indeed, the outside observer finds it hard to know how far the 1967 policy is being followed at all. Even so, some conclusions may be hazarded. First, the idea of setting down a number of criteria for nationalised industries to follow in taking investment and pricing decisions is attractive. If an effective method is to be developed for ensuring efficient operation of the nationalised industries, it will have to be based on more than the pursuit of a single, financial objective. Indeed, one doubts whether the 1967 White Paper itself goes far enough. One would like to see more explicit objectives set for, say, cost reduction, productivity increases and, especially in gas and electricity, a narrowing of the gap between the rate of growth of peak demand and that of total demand.

However, there is a problem already even if we consider only the objectives for pricing, investment and the financial surplus. Since these are interrelated, then even in the most favourable circumstances not more than two of them can be set in isolation. If criteria are established for pricing and investment, then the financial result will flow from these, and so on. Ideally, one would like to see an annual calculation of what rate of return would follow in each of the next five years from pursuing a given price and investment policy. In consultation with whoever was responsible for their efficient operation, the financial target and the criteria to be followed in the pricing and investment policies could then be adjusted to each other.

One hopes that it would not be necessary to alter pricing and investment policies to fit in with what would presumably be the rather short-term need for a bigger or smaller surplus. If it were, then at least it would be possible (but would it happen?) to look at the three criteria together and decide which should have priority. As the Select Committee points out, the Treasury's evidence to it revealed 'a conflict between the earlier and the new economic thinking. Indeed the Treasury appear loath to accept some of the consequences of their own thinking.'[9] It is perhaps worth suggesting that the Treasury has added to genuine difficulties here by a lack of clarity and crispness in both of the White Papers. One suspects that this springs at least as much from committee authorship as from the civil servant's unwillingness to commit himself. No doubt all this shows the difficulty of reconciling conflicting objectives; but that is what management is about! Only if such conflicts are brought into the open can those who operate nationalised industries be given clear criteria by which their performance may be judged.

My own suggestion that a larger number of criteria should be used in judging the performance of the nationalised industries would obviously mean even greater problems in reconciling these criteria. I believe that the attempt should be made. It would force the managements of nationalised industries to look more closely at their objectives, and I believe this would be all to the good. Complete consistency might be hard to achieve. Only by accident is it likely that any nationalised industry would be able to predict what financial return given pricing and investment criteria would allow it to earn. Even if complete consistency could not be achieved, this would probably not matter too much. One of the new orthodoxies in business school thinking stems from the work of men like Simon, Cyert and March at Carnegie Tech. It is now accepted that firms pursue multiple objectives, some at least of which may well not be completely consistent with each other. It is further accepted that firms are able to organise themselves so that they operate satisfactorily despite this lack of consistency between objectives. In particular, firms can do this because they consider different objectives sequentially rather than simultaneously, and because there is a good deal of 'organisational slack' which can be taken up if particular objectives fail to be met. There is no reason to suppose that British nationalised industries are exceptions to these rules.

In the world as we know it, and as far into the future as we can see, most (if not all) firms will inevitably operate as Cyert and March suggest they do. Procedures for making organisations accountable will not be unsatisfactory simply because there is not complete consistency between all the firm's objectives. But, as we shall suggest later, it is much better that objectives should be agreed with the boards of nationalised industries rather than imposed on them. There will be many cases where a minister requires an industry to operate in a particular way because of its social responsibilities. Then there will usually have to be an instruction (and a subsidy) from above. In all other cases, the industry would improve its performance far more willingly if its objectives were set by agreement. Nevertheless, I believe that it will be right to concentrate on more than one, but still a limited number, of economic and financial objectives in any system for making nationalised industries accountable. In a sentence, I do not believe that this kind of accountability for nationalised industries has failed in Britain: it has simply not yet been tried.

Underlying all of this, there are two fundamental prerequisites for an efficient industry. First, the industry must want, or be forced by competition, to be efficient; second, it must know *how* to be efficient. This is as true of private as of nationalised industry. One can see the problem in an extreme form in Lancashire textiles, where there have been enormous competitive pressures in a rapidly declining industry, over fifty years. Despite their keenness, these competitive pressures have not forced the general run of firms to become better managed and, above all, better marketers. The main reason has been that most managers in Lancashire textiles simply did not know how to manage well enough.

In nationalised industries, competitive pressures are rarely as keen as this, while capital is easy (perhaps too easy) to obtain. Indeed, a major problem may be that survival calls for too little effort and that the stimulus to commercial excellence is too small. For example, over the last decade, the gas industry has certainly transformed both its image and its morale in selling first 'high-speed' and then natural gas. This transformation seems to have owed more to the ability and enthusiasm of individuals than to competitive pressures on the industry. Even so, one wonders whether the desire for technological advance in the gas industry has been matched by equal enthusiasm for taking good marketing and investment decisions. While not impossible, it seems dangerous for the nationalised industries to base their hopes of increased efficiency on a self-generated desire to have good management for its own sake. Nor is there a case for relying on competition to generate enough pressure to make efficient management essential, given the relatively unexposed position of nationalised industries.

We have seen that even this is only half the story, though perhaps it is the most difficult half. However much they may be spurred on by enthusiasm or by competition, the managements of nationalised industries cannot display a greater degree of professionalism than they possess. My impression is that, like much of the rest of British industry, the nationalised industries are stronger in technical than in financial and commercial expertise. Indeed, the two may oppose rather than supplement each other. The scientist or engineer finds it hard to understand why a course of action which is clearly the best on technical grounds is turned down because it does not provide an adequate rate of return. He may well come to regard the financial criteria by which the success of his industry is judged as positively harmful to technological advance.

In one way or another the managements of nationalised industries, at all levels, must learn to use much more rigorous and logical approaches to commercial problems. This need not come wholly from formal education, though electricity and the railways are leaders in this, and one would like to see even more management education at all levels in nationalised industry, including top management.

All this means that there must be some machinery for making nationalised industries accountable. Arrangements for making them responsible to a sponsoring ministry seem to be ruled out, if only because of the close and continuing consultation that goes on between the nationalised industries and their sponsoring departments. This makes the latter far from independent judges on most of the important issues. The sponsoring ministry is supposed to question nationalised industry on its progress. It seems clear that, up to now, the questions asked have often not been pointed enough. Indeed, this raises one of the big issues. The main difficulty faced by anyone who challenges proposals put forward by managements of nationalised industries (or indeed by any other specialists) is that it is those who put the proposals forward who have all the facts. As if this were not already sufficient of an advantage, the proposals will often raise technical issues on which only someone with scientific or engineering training can judge. (I do not believe that this means more than that any audit body must contain the right technical and economic skills, but it is clearly an important issue and I may well be over-optimistic.)

The Electricity Council clearly takes this view. In evidence to the Select Committee it dealt with the idea of establishing an efficiency audit system for the nationalised industries. Emphasising the difficulty which outsiders would have in carrying out audits, it doubted 'whether there are any consultants available whose insight into, say, the system of grid control could be such as to justify their making expert comment on the way this function is discharged, and the way it has been developed over the years'.[10] I am clearly in no position to dispute this statement, but it is important to realise that to accept such a view would mean that in large parts of the public sector one would have to rely entirely on the ability and willingness of those directly concerned to run nationalised enterprises efficiently. This would be so, however much one might doubt their economic as distinct from their technical expertise. The Gas Council, in its evidence to the Select Committee, seems to go even farther. It believes that 'apart from the financial objectives agreed with H.M. Government, there are few, if any, criteria by which the performance of nationalised industries can be assessed'.[11] Put so baldly, this is simply not true, however much the Gas Council might like to believe it. Private industry finds such criteria; so do European audit bodies.

What we need is a more 'open' system of government generally.[12] The best way of improving the accountability of nationalised industries must be through a more active legislature, a more vigorous press, more criticism from the intelligent lay public, and so on. Ways should be devised of ensuring both that broad policy issues are discussed before decisions are taken and that enough information is provided for the performance of nationalised industries to be judged, in retrospect, by outsiders. There should be programme and process accountability as well as fiscal accountability – which indeed the normal accountancy annual audit of the nationalised industries' accounts already largely provides.

A situation where everybody – parliament, public, universities, etc. – feels free to have a hand in all major policy decisions would alarm both civil servants and ministers. Yet the present system is often worse. Is it more or less desirable that nationalised industries, and perhaps even ministries, should be accountable to everyone than that they should be accountable to no one? The latter is what we often have now.

Indeed, one might go farther. Paradoxical though it may seem, one could advocate the granting of greater independence to nationalised industries simply *in order* to get greater accountability. The present arrangements for running the nationalised industries probably mean more blurring of lines of authority than if they were more independent. They certainly mean that issues are often settled within Whitehall without Parliament, press or public knowing what those issues were. Or the issues are discovered too late to influence decisions.

It is perhaps worth reminding ourselves at this point that one way of reducing the burden on auditing procedures would be to allow some finance for nationalised industries to come directly from the private capital market and not through loans from the government. Especially if there were some equity capital, this would mean that the expertise of investment analysts and others in the City would be at work on behalf of shareholders in evaluating the performance of the nationalised industries. This might well be worth trying. If one takes the view, as one surely should, that introducing private capital into nationalised industries would increase their independence, this is a case where greater independence could lead to greater accountability. It would certainly be useful to have the expertise of the City at work, studying nationalised industries. It would have the advantage that there would be a greater incentive to efficiency in the nationalised industries; there would also be a greater demand for information from the City.

It might well be argued that a group of government auditors with access to information on a continuing basis could do better. However, as we shall see later, the danger is that this would simply keep information within Whitehall. It would be valuable to have a second opinion, and investment analysts working on behalf of shareholders probably provide the best there is. It must be remembered, however, that private shareholdings are probably not possible in all nationalised industries – coal and transport are two examples of industries that private capital would be reluctant to re-enter.

The alternative view, taken by Mr Normanton and others, is that neither accountability to ministries nor accountability to the community at large is acceptable. The former leaves too much possibility that there will be open or tacit agreement to leave difficult problems undiscussed; the latter looks too much like bedlam. The solution advocated is therefore to establish an audit body which would be independent both of nationalised industries and of ministries, but which would report to the Cabinet or to the Prime Minister. The problem with this idea is that it shows too much faith in the expert and that it also keeps the whole audit process cosily within Whitehall.[13] Criticism could be hushed up (and probably would be); the audit body would simply become part of the civil service 'establishment'.

This is not to rule out the possibility that there is a role for an audit body. There are two main ways in which it might help. First, it is important that there should be a greater emphasis on programme accountability. Nationalised industries must be encouraged to set out their objectives at intervals, in some detail. In doing so, the attempt should be to encourage a genuine desire for improved efficiency in management, not grudging compliance or, worse still, outright hostility to the idea of auditing. To be sure the omens are not good. However, we should not give up too easily.

Nationalised industries should then be judged by how far they achieve these objectives. This type of programme accountability could be arranged by sponsoring ministries, but it would be better to accumulate the necessary expertise in an audit body. What matters is that the expertise should be developed – and used.

The second need is to devise some way of overcoming the refusal of nationalised industries to admit that any outsider can judge them on purely technical issues. Part of the answer, of course, must be that they rarely are *purely* technical issues. Most issues are both technical and economic. Another part of the answer must be that we shall have to develop individuals with both technical and economic skills that do enable them to judge in this way. It may well be that an audit body would provide the most satisfactory working environment for such people.

However, the most important issue is that of publicity. If

an audit body were to be established, it could be effective only if its reports were made public. This alone would ensure that the scrutiny of the operations in the nationalised industries was tough enough.

We return to the broader question of how to raise the standard of commercial thinking in the nationalised industries. No one should suppose that this will be a quick process. It is not only a question of nationalised industries increasing their use of what are now referred to as modern management techniques. A whole way of thinking, almost a new philosophy, lies behind these, and this must be learned. An attempt to apply a number of new, and perhaps unrelated, techniques will do little good. One essential thing is for managers (and indeed civil servants) to learn to think marginally. This is not always easy, as the Prices and Incomes Board shows in describing how marginal costs behave in the gas industry.[14] It is something which managers in private as well as nationalised firms find hard to do. The convention of thinking in terms of pence per therm or pounds per ton dies hard. The habit of thinking in terms of those increments of cost and of revenue which are relevant to each decision seems to be surprisingly difficult to learn. But this is what is needed. Until they think marginally almost as a reflex action, nationalised industries will find the 1967 White Paper proposals for setting prices on the basis of marginal cost, and using D.C.F. in taking investment decisions, something of a nightmare.

It is clear from this discussion that there are likely to be problems in persuading nationalised industries to accept a more 'open' system. For example, the Electricity Council mentions the possibility that even an efficiency audit may give 'the impression of a witch hunt'[15] while the Gas Council believes that 'an efficiency audit ... with independent status and unlimited scope, could hinder rather than promote the efficiency of nationalised industries'.[16]

There does, however, seem to be room for some kind of compromise to be worked out. The Electricity Council in its comments on the French system of auditing in nationalised industries notes that this 'falls a long way short of being an efficiency audit in depth'[17] because it concentrates mainly on financial criteria. Yet if the arguments in this paper are correct, this is a large part of what an effective auditing procedure should require. Provided the financial, and perhaps other, criteria can be chosen correctly, there is no need for anything remotely resembling a witch hunt. But there is still a need for the more 'open' system.

3. *Accountability and University Research*

This discussion of the nationalised industries shows how difficult it has been to establish satisfactory arrangements for ensuring accountability. Yet, in a sense, the problem considered has been too easy. The nationalised industries do at least sell their output on the open market and we have been considering the firm as a unit.

The kind of accountability problem met where the unit generates benefit and not revenue is the one faced in any attempt to evaluate the performance of universities either as teaching or as research institutions. A university economist interested in establishing the principle of accountability in the public sector of the United Kingdom economy is in something of a dilemma. As a university teacher, he is inclined to argue, as his colleagues do, that no outsider can judge his technical competence as a teacher, just as we have seen that the Electricity Council argued that it alone could judge the efficiency of schemes for grid control. As an economist, he feels that it cannot be beyond the wit of man to devise ways of judging the efficiency of universities, even though he knows that success would put weapons into the hands of M.P.s and others who would be only too delighted to use them to interfere in detail with the way universities are run. His colleagues may thus judge him as harshly as civilisation judges those war-time scientists who developed the atomic bomb. Yet there is no reason why universities should be allowed to consider themselves any more unique than, say, the electricity grid. Although I wrote this paragraph before the Prices and Incomes Board reported on university salaries,[18] the university reaction to that report strengthens my argument.

In looking at universities as an example of how to combine independence and accountability, I shall consider some aspects of the problem of evaluating the effectiveness of university research, though hastening to add that teaching presents very similar issues. There appear to be two problems. First, those who finance research, whether from public or private funds, need some criterion to use in deciding which projects to support. How can they decide which projects will yield useful results? This is a matter of programmes. To ensure that the research will produce useful findings, the donors must discover what will be the most successful combination of research topic and researcher – in a situation where there must be enormous uncertainty over what the results of particular research projects will be. Discovering afterwards whether funds provided for a given project have been effectively used is a problem of programme accountability. It will not be an easy one. Even if the research is judged to be a success in an absolute sense, it may not have been as successful as it could have been, while an alternative project which was turned down might have produced better results.

It is hard to see that much can be done to improve matters, although research now being carried out in various places to find the best ways of selecting research and development projects may provide some suggestions. There are, however, one or two things to be said. First, either human beings can choose rationally between research projects or they cannot. If not, then one should simply choose projects at random. Few people would accept this suggestion. While I agree with them, and cannot rid myself of the feeling that rational choice must be better than random choice, the idea of choosing at random is not altogether ludicrous in all contexts. I have often suggested, for example, that universities should not go through the lengthy interviewing procedures that they use in selecting undergraduate students. They should simply select all applicants with at least some minimum level of qualification and pick out the required number from these at random. The interview method is so unsatisfactory that random choice would probably be better.

However, if a rational process is to be used in selecting research projects, two things should be done. First, applications for research funds should be considered by panels from the same discipline as the applicant – if necessary with comments from specialists who are not members of the panel but who are experts in the area of research. This already happens with the British medical, science and social science research

371

councils. However, it would be useful (again if this is not already done) to add one or two perceptive and sceptical people from other disciplines. It would also be worth, at intervals, taking a small number of projects at random and carrying out an audit after they had been completed to try to discover how successful they were. The aim would be to see whether there were any clues to how one might discover in advance whether any decision to grant research funds was likely to be good or bad, so that future decisions of the same kind could be made more effectively.

The other major issue in evaluating university research is that of process accountability. Given that a particular project *has* been chosen, has there been an acceptable balance between the amount of money spent and the results achieved? I believe that in most British universities a major problem in deciding how much an individual research project will cost is this. If the researchers are academics, it is usually difficult to appoint anyone to work on a particular research project except from October to October. This, I believe, is the most important practical problem of the economics of research in British universities. Even where research is carried out by quite junior staff, they cannot easily accept research contracts (from whatever source) except for multiples of a year. The pattern of hiring in teaching (usually for the academic year) largely sets the pattern of hiring for research as well, whether or not a year turns out to be the correct basic time unit for any particular piece of research. There seems to be only one solution. One has to accept that there is a minimum economic size of research unit. It should have a staff of at least five or six, with several projects being carried out simultaneously. When one project ends, staff can then be moved to others. This will not always be possible with small research units. Larger research units should, in any case, be encouraged because bigger research teams are likely to be more lively.

This leads me to the question of how one can predict the length of time any research project will take. It seems to me that we can learn a good deal from the kind of ideas which have been formalised in the notion of Management by Objectives. One of the difficulties in this field is that general ideas of the kind taught in business schools can be put into a 'package' and 'sold' to organisations in the public and private sectors. There is then a danger both that the novelty of the package will be exaggerated and that its relationship to the basic ideas of management science will not be understood. Management by Objectives is one of these packages. However, with this cautionary word, I shall use the phrase to cover the relevant parts of Management Science. Management by Objectives asks that, having made, or been given, strategic and tactical plans by his bosses, each manager's superior should determine with him what he is expected to achieve in the next time period by analysing his 'key tasks' and setting standards of performance. An essential part of the idea is for managers to be personally involved in setting these standards and to be motivated, trained and developed to perform better.[19] Returning to the problem of evaluating university research, Management by Objectives would therefore suggest that there should be consultations with those in charge of each piece of research. These consultations would determine how long a period seemed to be necessary for it and would set precise objectives to be achieved in that period. It is true that if a particular piece of research takes longer than was expected good reasons for this can always be found. Nevertheless, it is my own experience over a decade that significant increases in the 'productivity' of research expenditure can be achieved by a judicious, but gentle, mixture of bullying and prodding of this kind. In the Centre for Business Research of Manchester University an important function of the Centre's Director is to agree research timetables with those engaged on research projects in this way. He then does what he can to ensure that each stage of each project is completed on time. It may be that I am maligning my colleagues in other British universities, but I believe that what is done in the C.B.R. in Manchester is unusual, if not unique. The C.B.R. is unusual in being a collective venture financed by business and with pressure for a 'businesslike' approach to its activities from the businessmen on its board of management. British university professors are not usually willing to be hustled in this way: the normal reply to such suggestions is that academic activities are not amenable to work study. Precisely what those who say this (usually Arts professors) mean by work study is not clear, except that the

373

term is intended to be pejorative. I presume they believe that university research will not be carried out successfully if researchers are under continuous pressure to use time and money as effectively as possible.

Yet it is clear that research can often be carried out more quickly if there *is* pressure to do so. Apart from institutional, and in a sense artificial, pressures of the kind we use in the C.B.R., the fear that other researchers might solve the problem first can also be a powerful spur. *The Double Helix* shows this clearly in the case of D.N.A.[20]

As with the resources of nationalised industries, obtaining the most efficient use of research resources in universities requires a desire to do so on the one hand and a knowledge of what is possible on the other. With university research, the latter problem is usually much less severe than it is in managing a nationalised industry. Nothing very sophisticated is needed, though an understanding of how to apply the kinds of ideas underlying Management by Objectives would help. What is needed is a change of attitudes – a willingness to accept that university researchers have as much of a duty to use the resources they command economically as does anyone else, and a willingness to see that they are so used. One can think of a whole series of questions, most of which are regarded as taboo in most universities. How far do we consider the balance between the salary we pay to each researcher and the quality of work done? How far do we strike an optimal balance between the two? How far can one use shorter appointments to give one a sanction to ensure efficiency? For example, can one appoint researchers on a temporary basis until they have proved themselves? (Indeed, why does one not do this more often in teaching jobs?) I believe that considerable gains could be made by concentrating research in larger units where questions like these were asked.

As I have admitted earlier, however, a major difficulty is that if such ideas were used by outside auditors to increase university efficiency, this outside intervention could easily extend to more precious and more important freedoms. It may be necessary to give nationalised industries more independence in order to make them more accountable. No one at present wishes to give *more* independence to universities. Indeed, it may now be too late for the universities (encouraged by those providing research funds) to forestall the imposition of control procedures from outside by themselves moving on quickly to use them in an enlightened way. But should we not try?

As I have mentioned, the reaction to the Prices and Incomes Board report has been instructive. What was justified was the academics' refusal to accept, as a proposition unsupported by adequate evidence, that universities should do less research and more teaching. It is its research effort, after all, which distinguishes a university from a technical college. Perhaps the balance *is* wrong, but one would need more evidence before being sure that it is.

What was not justified, in my view, was the rejection by most of the academics who wrote letters to the press of the idea that increased 'productivity' should be an objective in universities as well as in the rest of the economy. However deeply academics may believe in the case against making the universities accountable to an outside body, I do not see any hope that the community will accept this case unless the universities show that they are making a real effort to improve their own efficiency. Rightly or wrongly, the community will not be prepared to allow the large sums of money spent on university education to be subject to different criteria of efficiency from other public, or private, spending. I believe that universities should already be making each individual department and faculty 'accountable' by the kind of measures I have described in this paper. It is perhaps not widely recognised that universities try to maintain standards in examinations by appointing external examiners from other universities. I believe a good deal could be gained if external examiners were used more in course design during the whole year, and not simply during the examination period itself.

I have already explained that I think it would be beneficial for nationalised industries to be more precise about their objectives; it would be even more beneficial for universities, and one objective ought surely to be to do a progressively better job as time passes. There has been far too little thinking in universities about how students learn, and indeed how far learning is the same as teaching. University teachers often behave as though the printing press had never been invented.

Whether or not it may be the case that universities should research less and teach more, it is certainly the case that they should do all they can to raise standards of both teaching *and* research. And they should do this whatever the ratio between the two they think is the correct one.

Because competition is unlikely to be keen enough to force the nationalised industries to increase efficiency it seems that some kind of audit procedure will be needed. The universities are stoutly resisting the notion that they might be made accountable in the same way. If they are to avoid it, then I argue that their only hope is to begin to apply such measures themselves on an adequate scale. I find it hard to believe that they will.

4. *Conclusions*

The aim of this paper was to discover whether developments in Management Science had made the problems of combining accountability with independence in quasi-non-governmental organisations easier to solve in recent years. The answer, I think, can be only a qualified 'yes'.

I have defined Management Science as covering all examples of the application of logical thinking to management problems. As I think my discussion of developments in the British nationalised industries shows, we are now much more logical in the way we make these accountable. Management Science has had some impact here, though the universities either resist it or resent it, or both.

However, I must now make my qualifications. First, as I have explained, the new ways of thinking embodied in Management Science do not yet come easily to managers. I have no doubt that Management Science could have had a greater impact than it has on all quasi-non-governmental organisations. It has not been fully used, and has therefore not been adequately tested. In nationalised industries it has had some effect, but not as much as one would have liked. In universities, and I suppose in most other quasi-non-governmental organisations, it has had scarcely any impact at all — though again it could have had.

Second, the growing complexity of quasi-non-governmental

376

organisations has made their problems more difficult to solve, even while the techniques for solving them have become more powerful. On balance, I think that the advances in techniques have been greater than the increase in the complexity of organisations. However, the previous paragraph has shown that this is not the point. The real question is how far we are using the techniques we have; not how many more we have developed. There is great scope for using Management Science more than we do.

A third qualification is this. While the development of Management Science puts new weapons into the hands of those in the United Kingdom who have to tackle problems of accountability in quasi-non-governmental organisations, the system used to provide accountability is often what requires changing. Above all, there is a need for the more 'open' system I have advocated: though there are moves in this direction, they are as yet too slow. There must be more informed discussion of all the issues by politicians, press, radio, television and the lay public.

In short, I am saying that the development of new management techniques, and, more important, the fact that we have not yet applied older ones widely enough, means that we can use all of them to obtain greater accountability and to give greater independence in quasi-non-governmental organisations. However, the progress still needed if this is to happen is so great that we also need the more 'open' civil service, Parliament and administrative system generally. This alone will ensure that there is enough pressure on government, civil service and quasi-non-governmental organisations to ensure that problems of accountability and independence are treated as important matters of general public concern.

Notes

1. *First Report of the Select Committee on Nationalised Industries* (H.M.S.O., London, July 1968). To save space, this is referred to henceforth as the *Report*.
2. *Report*, vol. 1, para. 54.
3. Ibid., para. 53.
4. Ibid., para. 165.

5. *The Financial and Economic Obligations of Nationalised Industries* (Cmnd 1337, H.M.S.O., London, 1961).

6. *Report*, vol. 1, para. 185.

7. *Economic and Financial Objectives of Nationalised Industries* (Cmnd 3437, H.M.S.O., London, 1967).

8. *Report*, vol. 1, para. 192.

9. Ibid., para. 223.

10. *Report*, vol. 3, para. 215.

11. Ibid., para. 218.

12. The validity of this remark is emphasised by the fact that I am revising this paper on the day when Jeremy Bray has resigned from the British government. He has done so because it is not thought proper for a minister to publish a book analysing the process of economic decision-taking in his own government.

13. As Mr Normanton says in his paper, 'Everything possible would be published, but the French view that much concerning the nationalised industries must remain confidential could be accepted.'

14. *National Board for Prices and Incomes Report No. 102* (Cmnd 3924, H.M.S.O., London, 1969) app. D.

15. *Report*, vol. 3, para. 215.

16. Ibid., para. 219.

17. Ibid., para. 216.

18. *National Board for Prices and Incomes Report No. 98* (Cmnd 3866, H.M.S.O., London, 1968).

19. See, for example, *Improving Business Results*, by J. W. Humble (Management Centre Europe, Brussels, 1967).

20. *The Double Helix*, by J. D. Watson (London, 1968).

Index

Britain, 190–201: accountability to ministries, 191–7; accountability to Parliament, 197–203; and D/C organisations, 207–10; choice of reactors, 190–6, 200–1; commitment to gas–graphite line, 194–5; disagreements with C.E.G.B., 193–4; R. & D. and design work by consortia, 203–5

Atomic Energy Commission (U.S.A.), viii, 120, 182

Audit agencies: and policy evaluation, 44; modern role, 43–5, 66; possibility of more independence, 45; possible alterations, 43; traditional role, 42–3, 45

Audit and public accountability, 311–45

Audit system in Britain, limitations of, 304–5

Autonomy and accountability, balance between, 313–14

Avco and D.O.D. contracts, 136

Ballistic Missile Defence System, 127

Bank of England: and Select Committee on Nationalised Industries, 240; investigation by McKinsey & Co., 329

Bannerman, Graeme C., 140

B.B.C., 18, 329

Beck, Bertram M., xiii, 17, 60: 'Governmental Contracts with Non-Profit Social Welfare Corporations', 213–29

Bell, David, and Bell Committee and Report, 34, 65, 138, 349

Bellinger, Sir Robert, and inquiry on manpower savings in civil service, 330

BEV accelerator, 41

Beveridge Report, 7

Birch, Professor A. H., 326

Bloc grants, see Institutional grants

Blue Steel contract, 156, 158, 159

B.O.A.C., inquiry into financial affairs of, 329

Boeing, and D.O.D. contracts, 136

Bow Group, and accountability for royal family, 330

Brademas, Hon. John, 89, 93

Bristol Siddeley contract (1965), 148–68, 288: company's requirements, 154; 'fair and reasonable profit',
149, 154–5, 162; fixed-price contract, 150–1, 154–5; investigation by special committee, 149–50; knowledge of overcharging, 152–3; lack of trust between contracting parties, 162; over-estimate of costs, 151; straightforward nature of contract, 148–50; total profit to company, 149; withholding of information, 152–3

British administration, 6–9: impulse towards greater accountability, 7; position of public sector, 7–8; traditional concepts, 6

British Council, 18

British Parliament, 46–7, 90–2: and financial accountability, 283–310; and public expenditure, 90; contrasted with Congress, 46–7; future role of public accountability, 242–5; increase in committee activity, 46; possible expansion of committee system, 243–6, 331–3; response to changing structure of government, 238–42; select committee procedure, 242–3

British Petroleum, 159

British Railways, investigated by McKinsey & Co., 329

Bureau of the Budget, 188, 351

Bureaucracy: and the 'inner check', 52–3; conventional view of its evils, 23–5; tendency to run down in efficiency, 52

Bush, Vannevar, 263

Calder Hall reactors, 194, 195

California: Department of Education, 132; information system, 133

California Institute of Technology, Jet Propulsion Laboratory, 119, 120

California, University of, Livermore and Los Alamos Laboratories, 119

Canadian Royal Commission on Government Reorganisation (Glassco Report), 249

Carey, William, 30

Carnegie Corporation, vii, 3

Carnegie Foundation, 173

Categorical grants, 259–61, 268–9

Catholic Church, and use of public funds, 216

Central Electricity Authority, 196

Central Electricity Generating Board

hundred contractors, 135–7; 'total package procurement' for weapons systems, 33

Department of Health, Education and Welfare (H.E.W.), viii, 21–2, 188: Audit Agency, 271; regional educational laboratories, 32

Department of Housing and Urban Development (H.U.D.), 11, 22

Department of Justice, 21

Department of Transportation, 22, 130

Design and construction (D/C) organisations in British nuclear industry, 207–10

Development contracts, 156–7

'Dialogue of the Exchequer' (1179), 320, 342

Diamond, John, 162

Diffusion of sovereignty, 6, 27–8

Dispersion in place of delegation, 91–2

District auditors, 328

Ditchley Conference (March 1969), viii, 7, 18, 19, 22, 23, 28–31, 41, 42, 48–50, 53, 56, 62, 63, 350, 354: 'A British View', 70–99; list of participants, xi–xii

Double Helix, The (Watson), 374, 378

Drucker, Peter F., 23, 24, 57

Dugdale, Sir Thomas, 58, 288–9

Dungeness reactor, 197

Dunnett, Sir James, 90, 91

Eastman Kodak, and D.O.D. contracts, 136

Economic Opportunity Act (1964), 171, 222, 261: amendments (1967), 336

Economic subjects, 319

Edmonds, Martin, xiii: 'Government Contracting in Industry', 148–68

Education task force, 182

Educational Associate, Inc. (E.A.I.), *see* Institute for Services to Education

Educational laboratories, 182–6, 188–9

Eisenhower, President Dwight D., 56

Electricity Council, 366, 369, 370

Elementary and Secondary Education Act, 12, 182, 184

Erlenborn, Congressman John N., 23

Estimates Committee, 241, 247–50, 285, 288, 291–5, 297, 307, 308, 329, 332: and characteristics of efficiency audit, 292–3; debates on its reports, 292; investigation of A.E.A., 198; staffing problems, 293; subcommittees, 244, 247, 249

Exchequer and Audit Acts, 304, 309, 317, 327

Exchequer and Audit Department, 284, 286, 288–9, 294, 328, 331, 333, 334, 340: limitations, 304; possibility of development, 304–6; professional staff, 288–9

Farmers Home Administration, 262

Fast Breeder Reactors (F.B.R.), 190–1, 195

Federal Contract Research Centres (F.C.R.C.s), 119–20

Federal Property and Administrative Services Act (1949), 10

Federalism and 'federalism by contract', 259–64: bloc or consolidated grant arrangements, 260; categorical or special-purpose grants, 259–61; revenue sharing, 260; statutory advisory councils, 263–4; use of private organisations, 262–3

Ferranti contract (1964), 148–68, 288, 290, 305, 309: company's arguments, 154; 'fair and reasonable profit', 149, 154–5, 162; fixed-price contract, 150–1, 154–5; investigation by special committee, 149–50, 309; knowledge of overcharging, 152–3; lack of trust between contracting parties, 162; overstatement of costs, 151; straightforward nature of contract, 148–50; total profit to company, 149; withholding of information, 152–3

Financial accountability to Parliament, 283–310: Comptroller and Auditor-General, 286–90; current patterns, 285–97; Estimates Committee, 291–4; Exchequer and Audit Department, 288–9; government departments' accounting branches, 289; limitations of current audit system, 304–5; new select committees, 296–7; possibilities for further development, 302–7; proposal for Control of Public Expenditure

Committee, 307–8; Public Accounts Committee, 286–90; Select Committee on Nationalised Industries, 294–6; staffing of committees, 288–9, 293, 300–1; views and requirements of Members of Parliament, 298–300

Financial subjects, 317–18

Firestone Iron and Rubber, and D.O.D. contracts, 136

Fiscal accountability, 29, 30, 43, 76, 80, 111–13, 366

Fitzhugh, Gilbert, 56

Fitz Nigel, Bishop, 320

Fixed-price contracts, 150–1, 154–5, 160

Flight, 161

Flowers, Professor Sir Brian, 76, 77

Ford, and D.O.D. contracts, 136

Ford Foundation, 174, 347, 351

Formula-type grants, 255, 260

France: and autonomous state accountability, 310; Cour des Comptes, 325, 334–6, 342, 344; information on organisation in public services, 318; system of audit, 325, 333

Frost, Richard T., xiii–xiv, 29: 'Project Upward Bound', 169–80

Fulton Report on the civil service, 34, 65, 233–7, 239, 302, 310, 321, 322, 328, 342

Gardner, John W.: and the Urban Coalition, 50; chairman of education task force, 182

Gas Council, 366, 369

Gaus, John M., 69: and the 'inner check', 52

General Accounting Office (G.A.O.), 43, 66, 88, 90, 179, 289, 325, 334–6, 338, 340, 342, 344: and legislation, 335–6; and mismanagement in university research, 108; co-operation with executive agencies, 336; Office of Legislative Liaison, 335; on government contracting for research, 346–54; reports, 335, 336; staff, 336

General Dynamics Corporation, 132: and D.O.D. contracts, 136

General Electric Company, 133

General Motors, and D.O.D. contracts, 136

General Post Office, Britain, 328, 343–4; investigated by McKinsey & Co., 329; turned into 'commercial' undertaking, 70

General research support (G.R.S.) grants, 256, 258

General Services Administration (G.S.A.), 17, 20–1

Gilliland Report, 279

Gladstone, W. E., and Gladstonian finance, 283, 285, 335

Glassco Report, 249

Goldberg, Delphis C., xiv, 60: 'Independence and Accountability in Government Support of Academic Science', 251–82

Gordon, Lincoln, and Gordon Committee, 352

Government contracting in industry: establishment of Review Board, 163–5; Ferranti and Bristol Siddeley contracts, 148–68; government working party (1966), 162; need for accurate record and publication of costs and profits, 161; responsibility for efficient execution, 159–61; trust between contracting parties, 162

Government contracts for R. & D. in education, 181–9: auguries of success, 186, 188; constraints on freedom of action, 185; difficulties, 185; educational laboratories, 182–6, 188–9; obstacles to independence and accountability, 186–8; possibilities of improvement, 189; qualities of leadership, 188–9; salient features of educational R. & D., 183–4; university centres, 183–6, 188–9

Government Contracts Review Board, 163–5: and post-costing, 164, 165; constitution, 163; functions, 163; gaps in terms of reference, 165

Government Corporation Control Act (1945), 336

Government industrial establishments, 330

Government-oriented corporations, 129–47: adverse side effects, 137–43; application to civilian public sector activities, 145–6; communications systems, 132–3; cost-plus contracting, 141–2; development of

Mitchell, Mrs Fanny, list of quasi-non-governmental organisations in Britain, 71, 99
Mitre Corporation, 119
Mobilisation for Youth (M.F.Y.), 12, 222, 226–7
Model Cities programme, 12, 95
Models for problems of accountability, 81–4
Monopolies Commission, 73, 330
Moos, Malcolm, 56
Morningside Citizens' Coalition, Inc., 68
Morrill Acts: (1862), 254, (1890), 254–5
Morrison of Lambeth, Lord, 359
Mutual accountability, 97–8

National Academy of Sciences: Committee on Science and Public Policy, 265; survey of support of doctorate recipients, 267
National Aeronautics and Space Administration (NASA), viii, 22, 121, 130, 182; and Saturn rocket booster, 145; influence on contractors, 137, 138, 140; top hundred contractors, 135
National Board for Prices and Incomes (N.B.P.I.), 330–1: and marginal costs in gas industry, 369, 378; political function, 330; report on university salaries, 370, 375, 378
National Coal Board (N.C.B.), and nuclear power programme, 201
National Defence Education Act, 251
'National emphasis' programmes, 171
National Institute of Mental Health (N.I.M.H.), 263, 264, 268, 280
National Institutes of Health (N.I.H.), 182, 251, 252, 256–9, 265, 268, 269, 271, 277: general research support (G.R.S.) grants, 256, 258; statutory advisory councils, 263–4
National Programme of Educational Laboratories, 183–4
National Science Foundation (N.S.F.), 106–8, 177, 251, 252, 256, 268: and educational development, 182; institutional grant programmes, 256, 258–9; 'total effort reporting' for academic scientists, 33

National Science Foundation Bill, vetoed by President Truman, 263, 279
Nationalised industries in Britain, 58, 85–6: accountability, 295–6, 358–70, 376–8; competitive pressures, 364; criteria for performance, 360–4; differing views on performance and ministerial intervention, 358–9; financial objectives, 360–4; machinery for accountability, 365–7; need for more 'open' system, 366, 369; needs, 323–6; possibility of audit body, 366–9; pricing and investment decisions, 361–3; raising standard of commercial thinking, 365, 369; Treasury White Papers (1961 and 1967), 359–62, 369, 378
Neighbourhood Councils, 226, 227
Nelson, Bryce, 280
New York City: child welfare, 217; day care, 217; Henry Street Settlement, 226–8; maladministration of poverty programme, 42; Mobilisation for Youth programme, 222, 226–7; private institutions seeking to exercise public functions, 68; problems of urban living, 92; public hospital system, 59; Social Welfare Law, 218
Newport News Shipbuilding, and D.O.D. contracts, 136
Nixon, President Richard M., and Nixon Administration, 56, 62
Non-profit social welfare corporations, governmental contracts with, 213–29: anti-poverty programme and organisations, 220–2; child welfare, 214, 217; day care, 217; lump-sum subsidies, 214–15; neighbourhood councils, 226, 227; private citizens on boards of directors, 218; quasi-non-governmental agencies, 219–21, 223–4, 226, 227; sectarian agencies, 216–18; study of expenditures in urban centres (1960), 214; true voluntary associations, 218–19, 221, 223–6
Normanton, E. Leslie, xv, 45, 59, 60, 62, 66, 309, 310, 368, 378: 'Public Accountability and Audit: A Reconnaissance', 311–45
North American Rockwell, and D.O.D. contracts, 136

386

Northrop Corporation, 132: and D.O.D. contracts, 136

Nuclear energy programme in Britain, and the problem of accountability, 190–212: accountability of consortia and private firms, 191, 203–10; commercial programmes, 196–7; design and construction (D/C) organisations, 207–10; Parliamentary accountability, 197–203; proposal for Atomic Energy Board, 208, 210; public accountability of A.E.A. and G.E.G.B., 191–203; reactor systems, 190–1, 193–6, 200–1; reorganisation, 207

Off-campus laboratories, 119–28: and classified work, 120; financial arrangements, 121; hierarchical management structure, 120; size, 120; support from federal agencies, 120–1

Office of Economic Opportunity (O.E.O.), viii, 5, 22, 61, 221–2, 336: and Project Upward Bound, 169–80; Community Action programmes, 12, 16, 93–5, 169, 171, 173, 221–2, 261, 278

Office of Education (U.S.O.E.), 11, 177, 179–80, 186, 188, 251: Division of Educational Laboratories, 183, 188; 'Talent Search' idea, 173, 179

Office of Naval Research, 40

Ombudsman devices, 45, 243

Organisation and Methods (O. & M.): report on civil service, 342; staffs in ministries, 318, 322, 328

Organisational subjects, 318–19: absence of information and accountability in Britain, 318

Parliamentary Commissioner for Administration, 243, 309, 341: restricted scope of his powers, 249. *See also* Ombudsman

Parole Board, 62

Participation, 92–9: as technique or objective, 92–3, 221; Community Action programmes, 93–5; doubts about its value, 95–6

Participatory contracts, 12–13, 38

Party system and accountability, 245–8: chairmen of parliamentary committees, 245–6; professional staffing of committees, 247

Peace Corps, the, 171, 172

Peer judgement and peer groups, 40–1, 257

Pennsylvania: criminal justice information system, 132; lump-sum subsidies to voluntary agencies, 215; water system, 132

Philadelphia Plan, 63, 66

Pifer, Alan, vii–ix, 7, 58, 65, 70, 74, 75, 94, 183, 218, 219, 221

Planning-programming-budget (P.P.B.) system, 41, 88, 237, 336

Plowden Reports: (1961), 302; on aircraft industry (1965), 159

'Policy' different use of term in Britain and U.S.A., 57–8

Political accountability, 341–2

Poor Law Amendment Act (1834), and district auditors, 328

Post-costing, 164, 165

Post Office Corporation, 343–4

Post Office, U.S.A., 21, 59

Poverty programme in United States, 94, 95, 169, 220–2, 261, 336

Powell, Representative Adam, 171

Powell, Enoch, 330

President's Science Advisory Committee, 279

Price, Don K., xv, 59–62, 65, 277: correspondence with Elmer B. Staats, 346–54

Private institutions and private sector, 3–4, 6, 27–8: and participatory contracts, 38; aspects of independence, 37–8; degrees of independence, 36; grants, 15–16, 21; marshalling of voluntary energies, 50–2; need for government confidence in management, 36; quality of management, 36–9

Private service agencies, 219, 225–6

Process accountability, 29, 30, 76, 109–10, 179, 366

Progress payments, 139

Project grants, 11, 17, 255–6, 260, 267–9: use for non-research purposes, 267–8

Project management and managers, 157–8

Project Upward Bound, *see* Upward Bound

Public accountability: trends and Parliamentary implications, 233–50: accountability and the party

logically advanced profits, 156–7; expenditure escaping its control, 22; Green Paper on *Public Expenditure*, 299, 302, 310; transfer of management functions to Civil Service Department, 302; White Papers on nationalised industries (1961 and 1967), 359–62, 369, 378

Treasury Department, U.S.A., 21, 139

Truman, President Harry S., vetoes National Science Foundation Bill, 263, 279

TSR 2, 156, 158–60

Turtle Mountain Bearing Plant, 142

Uniroyal, and D.O.D. contracts, 136

United Aircraft Corporation and reverse osmosis, 142

United States administrative practice, 5–6, 8–26, 91: characteristics of contracting effort, 14–19; contracting-for-participation, 12–13; early use of contract device, 9; magnitude of use of contracts, 19–26; negotiation of contracts, 10

United States Air Force, viii, 349: analysis of procurement expenditure, 137; and MIRV contract, 14–15

United States civil service, 34–5

United States Congress, 46–8, 88–92, 94, 95, 254, 283, 291: and examination of programmes, 89–90: and G.A.O., 334–6; and support for academic science, 272–5; Appropriations Committees, 255; bills for institutional science grants, 257; committees and committee structure, 46, 47, 112, 272–4, 332; contrasted with British Parliament, 46–7; legislature–executive relations, 47–8; oversight of modern public sector, 48. *See also* Library of Congress

United States Navy, 106

Universal accountability, doctrine of, 28

University Corporation for Atmospheric Research, 119

University Grants Committee, 11, 24

University-managed laboratories, 118–28: basic and undirected research, 123; benefit to universities, 124–5; consortia for creating and sponsoring special institutions, 118–19; Federal Contract Research Centres, 119–20; flexibility and its limits, 127–8; government university laboratory triangle, 124–8; internal accountability, 127; off-campus laboratories, 119–28; universities and public service, 118–20, 125–6; variations in nature of accountability, 122–4

University research and accountability, 370–6: estimate of time for projects, 372–3; evaluation of effectiveness, 370–2, 374–5; maintenance of standards, 375–6; Management by Objectives, 372–4; Prices and Incomes Board report on university salaries, 370, 375, 378; process accountability, 372; research and teaching, 375–6; selection of projects, 371–2

Upward Bound, Project, 29, 37, 61, 62, 169–80: and academic interest groups, 174, 176, 178; attacks on Project, 178–9; contract, 169, 175–7; extent of achievement, 177–8; idea of Head Start for engineers, 172–3; national emphasis programmes, 171; origins of contract, 174–5; traditionalist objectives, 170; transferred to U.S.O.E., 179–80

Urban Coalition, the, 50, 51

Urban Renewal programme, 12

'Value received' principle, 39–40

Vocational Education Act (1963), 183

Voluntary agencies, 213–19: true voluntary associations, 218–19, 221, 223–6

Warner, John C., 174–6

Water systems, development of, 132

Webb, M. E., 202

Weidenbaum, Murray L., xvi, 10, 19, 56, 60, 63–5: 'The Government-Oriented Corporation', 129–47

West Virginia, information system, 133

Western Germany: and responsibility to legislature, 310; auditing staffs, 333; information on organisation in public services, 318

Westinghouse Electric Corporation, and Pennsylvania water system, 142